The first edition of this guide was researched and written by **John Curtin** (left) who lives at the foot of the North Downs Way in Abinger Hammer, Surrey.

The second and third editions were rewalked and updated by **Henry Stedman**, who was born in Chatham, Kent, and went to school in Rochester, just a mile or so from the North Downs Way. Henry has been writing guidebooks for over a quarter of a century and is the author of: *Kilimanjaro*, *Coast to Coast Path*, *Hadrian's Wall Path*, *Cleveland Way*, *London LOOP*, *Dales Way* and all three books in the *South-West Coast Path* series. He's also updated *Offa's Dyke*, *Pembrokeshire Coast Path*, *Cotswold Way*, *South Downs Way* and *The Ridgeway*. With him on this trek, as with every walk he does in the UK, was **Daisy** (below), his (mostly) faithful dog. An experienced long-distance walker, Daisy has already completed all the trails above with Henry and her ambition is to walk all 16 National Trails.

Authors

North Downs Way

First edition: 2006; this third edition: 2025

Publisher: Trailblazer Publications
The Old Manse, Tower Rd, Hindhead, Surrey GU26 6SU, UK
trailblazer-guides.com

British Library Cataloguing in Publication Data
A catalogue record for this book is available from the British Library

ISBN 978-1-912716-50-0

Series editor: Anna Jacomb-Hood
Editor: Nicky Slade **Cartography**: Nick Hill
Layout: Nicky Slade **Index and proof-reading**: Anna Jacomb-Hood
Photographs (flora): © Bryn Thomas unless otherwise indicated
All other photographs: © Henry Stedman unless otherwise indicated

The maps in this guide were prepared from out-of-Crown-copyright Ordnance Survey maps amended and updated by Trailblazer.

Acknowledgements

From Henry: Firstly, thank you to John Curtin for writing the first edition of this guide. Thanks also to Daisy for accompanying me every step of the way on the second and third editions – what a dog! – and to Zoe for enabling me to complete the trail, and for making each return home such a pleasant one; and to Henry Jr, of course, for being brilliant. A big thank you to all the readers who sent in suggestions for this new edition, in particular Richard Alcock, Shirley Alexander, George Moberly, Jeremy Servian, Colin Tompson, Steve Unsworth and Keith Wartnaby. At Trailblazer, thanks to Nicky Slade for her usual forensic approach to editing the text, Nick Hill for the maps, Anna Jacomb-Hood for the index and proofreading and to Bryn Thomas, as always, for keeping me busy.

A request

The authors and publisher have tried to ensure that this guide is as accurate as possible. Nevertheless things change even on these well-worn routes. If you notice any changes or omissions please write to Trailblazer (address as above) or email us at 🖳 info@trailblazer-guides.com. A free copy of the next edition will be sent to persons making a significant contribution.

Warning: long-distance walking can be dangerous

Please read the notes on when to go (pp13-15) and health and safety (pp51-3). Every effort has been made by the author and publisher to ensure that the information contained herein is as accurate and up to date as possible. However, they are unable to accept responsibility for any inconvenience, loss or injury sustained by anyone as a result of the advice and information given in this guide.

Photos – Cover: Newlands Corner (©BT) **This page**: Daisy and companion pause to admire the scenery from the viewpoint (see p144), before Hollingbourne.

Updated information will be available on: 🖳 **trailblazer-guides.com**

Printed in China; print production by D'Print (☎ +65-6581 3832), Singapore

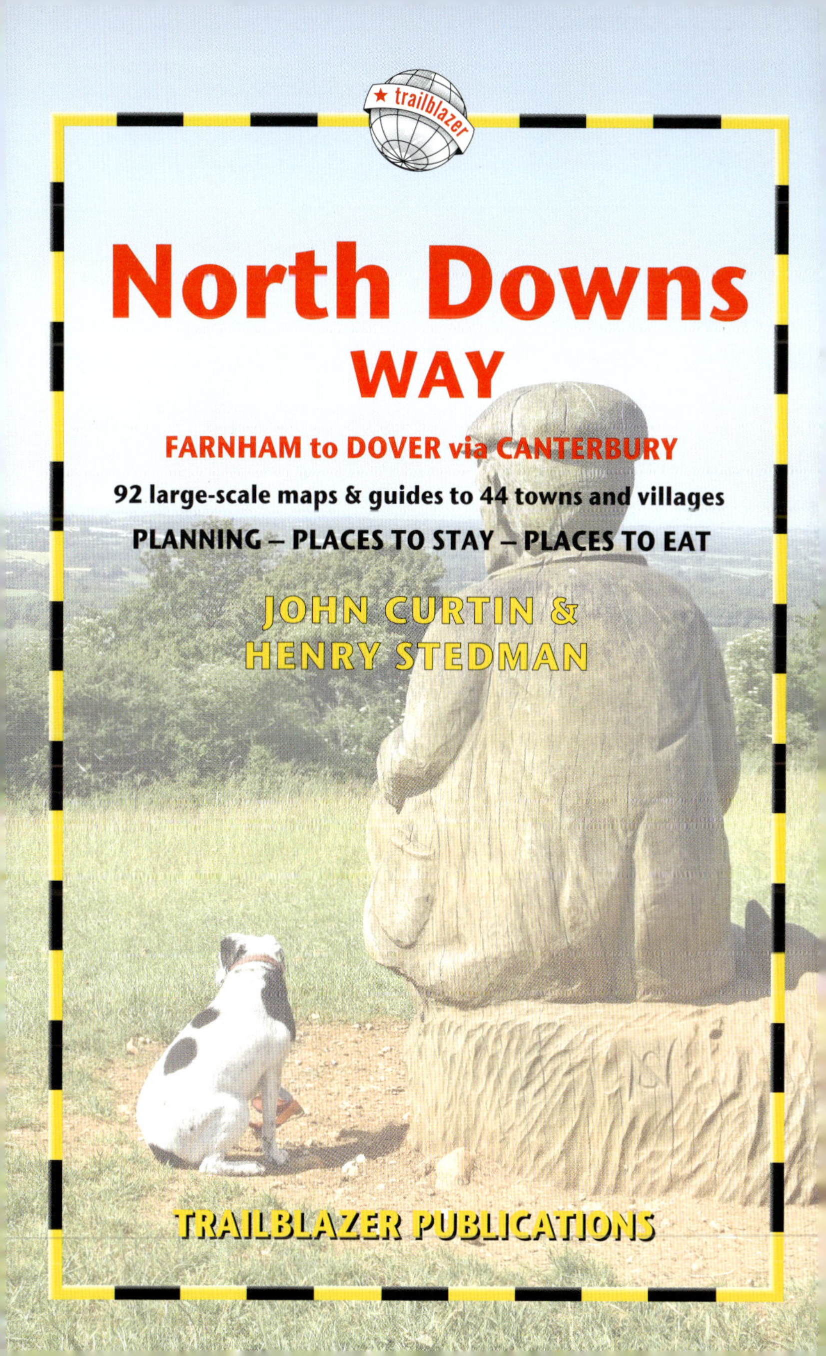

★ trailblazer

North Downs WAY

FARNHAM to DOVER via CANTERBURY

92 large-scale maps & guides to 44 towns and villages

PLANNING – PLACES TO STAY – PLACES TO EAT

JOHN CURTIN &
HENRY STEDMAN

TRAILBLAZER PUBLICATIONS

Contents

Contents

PART 4: ROUTE GUIDE AND MAPS

ABOUT THIS BOOK

This guidebook contains all the information you need. The hard work has been done for you so you can plan your trip without having to consult numerous websites and other books and maps.

When you're packed and ready to go, there's comprehensive public transport information to get you to and from the trail and detailed maps (1:20,000) and town plans to help you find your way along it.

- Where to stay: from campsites to luxurious hotels
- Details of walking companies if you'd prefer an organised holiday and luggage-transfer services if you just want your luggage carried
- Itineraries for all levels of walkers
- Answers to all your questions: when to go, how challenging it is, what to pack and the approximate cost of the whole walking holiday.
- Walking times and GPS waypoints
- Cafés, pubs, teashops, takeaways and restaurants as well as shops and supermarkets for supplies
- Rail, bus and taxi information for all places along the path
- Street plans of the main towns and villages
- Historical, cultural and geographical background information

❑ MINIMUM IMPACT FOR MAXIMUM INSIGHT

Nature's peace will flow into you as the sunshine flows into trees. The winds will blow their freshness into you and storms their energy, while cares will drop off like autumn leaves. **John Muir** (one of the world's earliest and most influential environmentalists, born in 1838)

It is no surprise that, since the time of John Muir, walkers and adventurers have been concerned about the natural environment; this book seeks to continue that tradition. By developing a deeper ecological awareness through a better understanding of nature and by supporting rural economies, local businesses, sensitive forms of transport and low-impact methods of farming and land-use we can all do our bit for a brighter future.

As we work harder and live our lives at an ever faster pace a walking holiday is a chance to escape from the daily grind and the natural pace gives us time to think and relax. This can have a positive impact not only on our own well-being but also on that of the area we pass through. There can be few activities as 'environmentally friendly' as walking.

INTRODUCTION

'I can assure those townsfolk who send forth a cry that wild nature and scenery are becoming difficult to find, that any amount of both still exists, within a short railway ride from London.' **Denham Jordan**, author of *On Surrey Hills*.

Every day tens of thousands of people wend their dreary way along three of the major transport arteries of South-East England – the M25, M26 & M20. Doubtless many of these same people from time to time turn their gaze from the tarmac to look wistfully up at the gentle grassy slopes that line one side of the motorways and wonder to themselves exactly what lies atop those hills.

It's probably just as well that they don't know, or else they may be tempted to swerve rashly onto the hard shoulder, screech to a halt and run straight up those same verdant slopes – which, if everyone did so, would have dire consequences for the smooth running of UK transport network's south-eastern division. For hidden amidst the trees that crown the downs is the North Downs Way stretching all the way from Farnham, in Surrey, to Dover, in Kent. Extending for 131.6 miles (211.6km) if taking the northern route via Canterbury – or 124.2 miles (200km) for the shorter southern finish – it's no coincidence that the North Downs Way is shadowed for much of its length by these major thoroughfares; because for several millennia

At the top of St Martha's Hill, St Martha's Church (see p80), also known as the Pilgrims' Church, is one of the landmarks of the North Downs Way.

Above: Kit's Coty (see p138), a 5000-year-old burial site, lies just a few yards off the trail in a beautiful flower-filled meadow.

the North Downs Way was the major transport route between Dover on England's eastern shore and the major trading and population centres of Canterbury, the Medway towns and on into Surrey. Indeed, **Stone Age burial sites** and other monoliths in Northern Kent testify to how long the Downs have been inhabited. Given that the trail follows a ridge of chalk hills running across Surrey and Kent, it doesn't take much imagination to see how even Britain's first inhabitants would have followed this trail. By following the line of this natural geological phenomenon they would have found it easy to orientate themselves and avoid getting lost – something that walkers still appreciate today!

For several millennia the North Downs Way was the major transport route between Dover, Canterbury, the Medway towns and Surrey

If you want to get an idea of just how important this route was, just look at the buildings that you can see along the way. No fewer than **eight castles** and **three cathedrals** lie on or just off the trail, not to mention several **archbishops' palaces** (now, sadly, all in ruins), an assortment of WWII defences and one folly. It is the cathedrals – and, in particular, Canterbury Cathedral, arguably the most important Christian building in England and certainly one of the oldest – that did much to popularise the trail that we now call the North Downs Way, as pilgrims flocked to the cathedral to pray at the tomb of St Thomas à Becket. Indeed, for much of its western half the North Downs Way follows the so-called 'Old Road', also known as the **Pilgrims' Way** that worshippers followed from Winchester to Canterbury. It wasn't only pilgrims and traders who took advantage of this ancient trackway, however. The list of **authors** who found inspiration on the Downs reads like a veritable *Who's Who*. Writers such as Geoffrey Chaucer (who wrote about people on the Pilgrims' Way, of course), John Bunyan, Lewis Carroll, Jonathan Swift, William Cobbett, Charles Dickens, Jane Austen, Rudyard Kipling, JM Barrie, Henry James, Max Beerbohm, George Meredith, Edmund Spenser, John

Above: Among the abandoned WWII (and earlier) defences you'll pass on the south coast is this intriguing 'Listening Ear Mirror' (see p199).

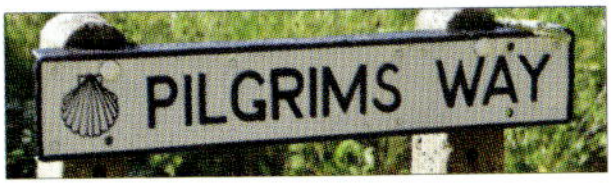

Keats, Alfred Lord Tennyson and Wilfrid Blunt all found inspiration from both the North Downs and the trail that runs along its length. And throughout this book we have, on occasion, quoted some of them directly.

Science has also benefitted from the Downs, with the home of **Charles Darwin** lying to the north of the trail. Darwin lived with his family for over forty years at the appropriately named Down House and it was here that he would take daily walks around the gardens in order to work on his theories; ideas that would eventually coalesce into *On the Origin of the Species*, the book that not only made his name (while simultaneously scandalising Victorian society with its decidedly secular viewpoint) but which also completely changed the course of science.

Above: Pilgrim sculpture outside the gates of Chilham Castle (see p160), one of several such statues along the Way. **Below**: Many of the buildings in the attractive old centre of Canterbury date back several hundred years.

Above: National Trail milestones, such as this one in the woods above the White Horse Stone outside Aylesford, crop up regularly along the path. **Below**: You can see all the way down to the English Channel from the Millennium Stone above Wye Crown (see p188).

It's not difficult to see what inspired them. The North Downs is a refuge for nature in what was, even in their day, the most populated and developed corner of the British Isles. The trail itself spends most of its time on the top of the chalky ridge, an area of short grazed grass and thick woodland, stooping only to cross five rivers that bisect the Downs at various points. It's a path that is a veritable haven for wildflowers, as well as several mammals and insects which have been eradicated from much of the rest of the south-east.

But has this natural beauty of the North Downs Way been compromised by the proximity of the motorways? Not to any great degree, in this author's opinion at least. For one thing, the path actually takes you through two sizeable National Landscapes (formerly known as Areas of Outstanding Natural Beauty) – the Surrey Hills and the Kent Downs. Furthermore, the roads, where they are visible, are usually

far enough away to render the noise of the traffic to a barely audible hum – a hum that serves to emphasise rather than detract from the sense of tranquillity at the top of the Downs. Plus, of course, the proximity of such major roads means that transport along the way is, by the standards of the sixteen National Trails of England and Wales, fairly plentiful – allowing you a lot of flexibility when planning your trail.

So there you have it: a splendid two week jaunt along the course of a spectacular geological feature, following a trail that's replete with history, ancient buildings and beautiful scenery – and all within a short train ride from London.

History

The North Downs Way was officially opened as a national trail in 1978 by the then Archbishop of Canterbury, Dr Donald Coggan. The route follows the chalk ridge that forms the North Downs between Farnham and Dover. It also follows, in parts, the Pilgrims' Way, reputedly taken by pilgrims to the shrine of St Thomas à Becket at Canterbury Cathedral, though its existence on maps only appeared from the late 19th century. In all likelihood prehistoric man used trackways along the North Downs which were also later used by drovers and traders keen to avoid toll roads. It is a natural route east to the Continent.

How difficult is the path?

The length of the North Downs Way is 131.6-miles (211.6km) for the northern finish via Canterbury, or 124.2 miles (200km) if completing the southern route ending along the coast; and it's 155.9 miles (250.9km) if you manage somehow to complete both end sections without missing or repeating any part of either trail. Not only is it well signposted throughout its length, but it is also one of the less taxing trails, as you walk over generally level and firm ground with very few steep ascents or descents. You do not need previous experience of long-distance path walking. What you do need, however, is suitable clothing, money, time, a half-decent pair of leg muscles and a realistic assessment of your fitness. Remember you don't have to do it all in one go and because transport options are so good you can tackle it in bite-sized stages. The main thing is not to push yourself beyond your ability.

If you want to skip the less interesting parts where motorways intrude, there are excellent transport links to most parts of the North Downs Way from London and the south making day and weekend trips easy (see Highlights box pp32-3).

How long do you need?

Whilst it's achievable in a week if you are fit and determined to crack off the miles day after day, that really feels like a race against time. You can have an invigorating holiday easily completing the walk in 10 days, or 14 if you prefer a more relaxed pace. Bear in mind that if you are camping, carrying a heavier pack will slow you down and many of the official campsites are well off the

Marbled White (*Melanargia galathea*)

Large Skipper (*Ochlodes sylvanus*

trail. You may also want to take a day off. Canterbury is the obvious choice, of course, though both Guildford and Rochester are worth at least half a day each which will add to the time needed. See pp31-2 for some suggested itineraries based on different walking speeds. Alternatively, cherry-pick the best **day** and **weekend walks** (pp32-3) which benefit from easy access and excellent transport links.

You can have an invigorating holiday easily completing the walk in 10 days, or 14 if you prefer a more relaxed pace.

When to go

SEASONS

The old joke is Britain doesn't have a climate; it has weather and if you don't like it just wait five minutes. Walking the North Downs Way can be enjoyed year-round as long as you dress suitably and take it for granted that even in summer parts of the trail may be muddy. However, severe conditions of heat, cold or rain seldom last for long.

You may get wet on the North Downs but you're unlikely to perish. Temperatures seldom dip below 0°C in winter or above 32°C in summer and the south-east tends to have the highest temperatures and the greatest number of sunshine hours in Britain. In summer it tends to be slightly cooler by the coast because the sea takes longer to heat up. Conversely in winter it takes longer for the sea to cool so it's milder by the coast because of the warming effect of the sea.

Spring

This is a great time of year for stands of bluebells and spring wild flowers along the Surrey sections of the North Downs Way. With the first leaf growth coming on there is a tapestry of green before the views become obscured later in the

Below: Butterfly-filled meadows such as here, near Titsey Plantation, are a feature of the Downs.

❏ FESTIVALS & ANNUAL EVENTS

There are numerous village fêtes and events during the summer months and it's fun to go along if you happen to be there on the day. There are also annual events to be aware of because they may make finding accommodation difficult.

May

- **Surrey Hills International Music Festival** (🖳 shimf.co.uk) is a fortnight-long classical music festival held in various locations including Guildford and the RHS Garden Wisley.
- **Chatham Maritime Food and Drink Festival** (🖳 cmtrust.co.uk/play/food-and-drink-festival) takes place over the last bank holiday weekend in May, and celebrates locally-produced foods, beer, wine and cider.

July

- **Kent County Agricultural Show** (🖳 https://kcas.org.uk) Agricultural show (and much more) that celebrated its centenary in 2023, held over three days in early July at the showground near Detling.
- Rochester, quite the party place, has regular **concerts** at the castle (🖳 www.rochestercastlelive.com, **fb**).

September and October

- **Guildford Book Festival** (🖳 guildfordbookfestival.co.uk) is in early Oct.
- **Canterbury Festival** (🖳 canterburyfestival.co.uk) celebrates the arts in the city and around Kent in autumn/winter.

year. It's difficult to predict the weather from year to year but there's often a settled period of fine weather around mid May. The trail is generally quiet but gets busier around the Easter and May holidays. Days are getting longer and temperatures are rising, pubs open beer gardens and a few brave/foolhardy souls turn their minds to BBQs.

Summer

June can start unsettled and blustery but later in the season it can get very hot on the Downs. Fortunately much of the Surrey section is wooded so while you may miss the views the worst of the heat is taken by the trees. The open fields of Kent can be like outdoor ovens so bring plenty of water with you. Expect the trail to be busier and you'll be competing for accommodation with other holidaymakers and those on their way across the Channel. With early dawns and long days there's little need to rush on the trail though you may find it dusty across the Kent arable fields as the farmers gather in the harvest.

Autumn

The weather is generally settled early in the season and everything seems to slow down after the August Bank Holiday. Children are back at school, holidays are over and it's easier to find accommodation. September is a wonderful time to walk. There can be crisp bright days with a slight chill in the air and later the vivid autumn colours emerge as the leaves begin to change and the nights start to draw in. Farmers will be ploughing so you can expect some tough going over recently ploughed fields, especially if it's been raining.

Winter

There is nothing like a bright, clear, frosty day to admire the views from the North Downs' ridgeline and we often get a spell of weather like that early in the New Year. But wet, relatively mild, damp days tend to be the norm. With good waterproofs there is nothing to hold you back from walking the North Downs even if it's a bit dispiriting. Without the leaves on the trees the views on a clear day are uninterrupted. Most pubs and B&Bs remain open as their business here is year-round so it will be easier to find accommodation but do make sure you get an early start each day as the nights draw in quickly.

Above: Dover and the end in sight. The approach to the town and busy harbour viewed from high on the cliffs on the Southern Route.

TEMPERATURE

Generally, temperatures are comfortable year-round. In winter, warmer clothes will be needed as the temperature drops towards and, on occasion, just below freezing. Summer is usually pleasantly warm with temperatures around 16°C to 23°C but temperatures as high as the 30s Celsius do occur on at least a few days during July or August.

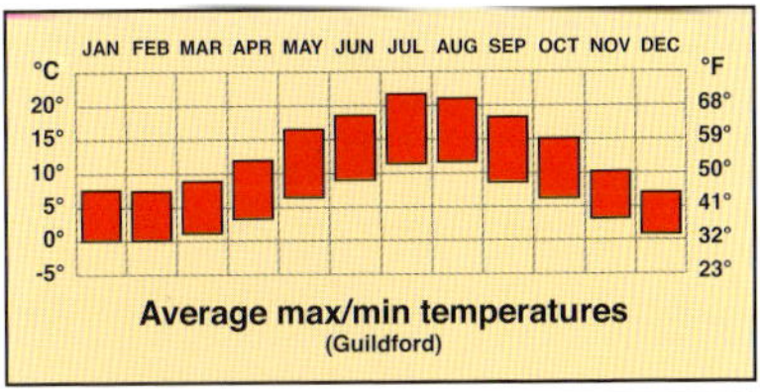

RAINFALL

The weather in England is affected mostly by the weather systems that come from the south-west. These are usually low-pressure systems that contain a lot of rain. Rain can and does fall in any month of the year but dry weather is usually more likely in the early summer.

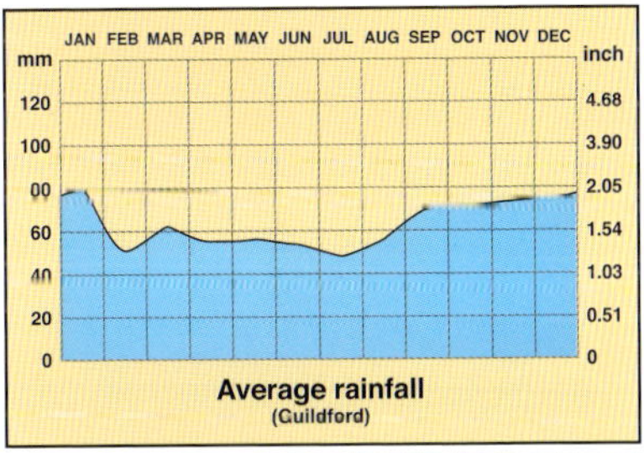

DAYLIGHT HOURS

If walking in autumn, winter and early spring, you must take account of how far you can walk in the available light. Also bear in mind that, depending on the weather, you may get a further 30-45 minutes of usable light before sunrise and after sunset.

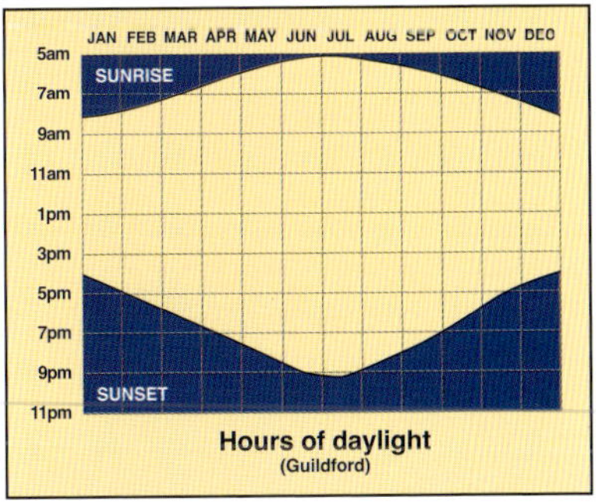

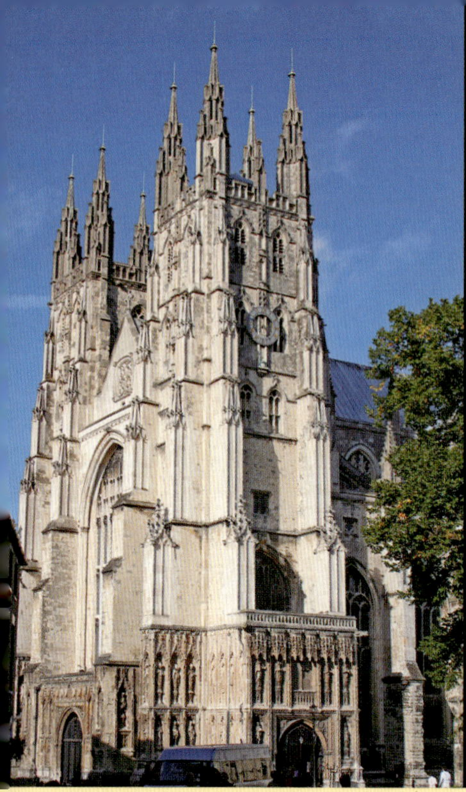

Above: A highlight of this walk, **Canterbury Cathedral** (see p167) was founded in 597. After the murder of Archbishop Thomas à Becket in 1170 the cathedral became one of the most important pilgrimage centres in the medieval world. Following the Pilgrims' Way from London, people came to make offerings at his tomb. The impressive Perpendicular nave was completed in 1405. (Photos © Bryn Thomas). **Below**: Poppies provide a colourful border to many of the fields en route, such as here just outside Detling.

PLANNING YOUR WALK

1

Practical information for the walker

ROUTE FINDING

There is little chance of becoming lost for long on the trail. Not only are you following the top of a natural – and obvious – chalk ridge but you're following in the footsteps of tens of thousands of people who have walked this way before you, from neolithic settlers to pilgrims and trekkers, so it's fair to say the path is pretty well established. There's also plenty of signage with signposts and waymark posts positioned at very frequent intervals. Indeed, such is their regularity that you actually start to doubt you're on the right path if, after a few hundred metres, you don't see one; and if you haven't seen a North Downs Way sign or waymark for 15 minutes or more, it's pretty safe to say that you really have come off the trail. But if and when the signage does fail you, the aim of this book is to keep you on the correct path with detailed instructions on the maps at key points.

Any slightly tricky directions not immediately obvious on the ground are noted on the appropriate trail guide maps in Part 4 of this book. In most cases the path is obvious and well trodden and certainly on weekends, in particular, there are bound to be other walkers about to point you in the right direction. A compass is not necessary

Do remember that summer foliage may obscure signs or they may go missing so it's best to read ahead in the trail guide and refer to the maps occasionally to confirm your location.

ELECTRONIC NAVIGATION AIDS AND MAPPING APPS

I never carried a compass, preferring to rely on a good sense of direction ... I never bothered to understand how a compass works or what it is supposed to do ... To me a compass is a gadget, and I don't get on well with gadgets of any sort.

Alfred Wainwright

While Wainwright's acolytes may scoff, most walkers will accept GPS technology as a well-established and incredibly useful navigational aid. With a clear view of the sky, a **GPS receiver** will establish your position as well as elevation in a variety of formats, including the British OS grid system, anywhere on earth to an accuracy of within a few metres. Most **smartphones** have a GPS receiver built in and can receive a GPS satellite signal from space as well as estimate its position often as accurately using mobile data signals from hilltop masts. Unless you happen to already own one with a decent-sized colour screen and decent maps installed, there's little benefit in buying a **handheld GPS** device just for walking the North Downs Way.

Accessing an online map with mobile data (internet via your phone signal, not wi-fi), your position can be pinpointed with great accuracy. But with no mobile signal – as is the case in Britain's remoter regions – your phone will have to rely on maps covering the route downloaded in advance via a smartphone mapping app.

Perhaps the most popular free map app is **Maps.me**, which offers 10 free map downloads that include simple contour lines, distance-measuring software and the ability to mark waypoints.

Other apps such as **Ordnance Survey** (via the OS Survey app) charge an annual subscription; OS charges £6.99 for one month or £34.99 for a year's access to their 1:25,000 scale maps, although you can also buy individual maps and load them onto your phone.

Memory Map (memory-map.com) sell OS Explorer 1:25,000 and Landranger 1:50,000 mapping covering the whole of Britain through their app, with prices from £22.50 (1:25k) for a one-year subscription. **Anquet** (anquet.com) offers similar coverage from £28 per annual subscription.

Other subscription-based mapping apps to test out include **TopoGPS**, **Gaia GPS**, **OutDoors GPS**, **Outdooractive** and **Hiiker**; the last two offer the range of Harvey maps. To buy Harvey's digital *North Downs Way* map ($14.99) you need to use the US Avenza maps app (store.avenza.com/collections/harvey-maps).

Tracklogs

A **tracklog** is a continuous winding line marking the walk from end to end, displayed on your screen. Whatever app you use be sure to download and install a North Downs Way tracklog into the app and your on-screen location dot will be pulsing right on that track as you walk along. National Trails have a free tracklog at nationaltrail.co.uk/en_GB/trails – look for 'GPX downloads'.

Alternatively, if the map in the mapping app you install already has the National Trails on it (eg on OS maps, where National Trails are shown as a line of green diamonds) you wouldn't need to also install a separate tracklog.

Waypoints and what3words

Besides those navigation options, this book offers an additional one. The maps in the book all feature at least one numbered **waypoint**, marked directly onto the map. Where a tracklog is a continuous line, waypoints are single points like cairns. These waypoints correlate to the list on pp201-3 which gives the grid reference and description. For these waypoints we've now also listed the three-word geocode used by **what3words** (what3words.com, p52 and pp201-3) which could be useful in an emergency.

You can either manually key the nearest presumed waypoint from the list at the back of this book into your phone/GPS (a process prone to user errors), or just download the list for free at trailblazer-guides.com/gps-waypoints.

To install these Trailblazer waypoints onto Maps.me you'll first need to convert the .gpx format file to .kml format before loading it into maps.me. Use an online website such as 💻 gpx2kml.com to do this then email the kml file to your phone and open it in maps.me.

Note that using mapping apps drains your battery quickly, so you will need to use them sparingly or carry a spare battery pack to recharge your phone towards the end of the day. You can extend your phone's battery life by turning on airplane mode. For these reasons it's important to understand that **treating GPS as a complete replacement for maps, a compass and common sense is a mistake**. Every electronic device is susceptible to battery failure or some electronic malfunction that might leave you in the dark.

ACCOMMODATION

The route guide (Part 4) lists a comprehensive selection of places to stay along the full length of the trail and often in each town or village there are several options though these may require a detour off the route. In the ever-more populated and prosperous south-east, low-cost accommodation is increasingly hard to find and should always be booked well in advance. Proximity to London, soaring property values and a healthy demand for rooms from business travellers drives prices up.

Camping

Official campsites are few and far between on the North Downs Way. Of those sites that could be described as serving the North Downs Way, many are a fair distance from the actual trail. They also vary widely in what they offer: some sites have no facilities, others have coin-operated showers and laundry facilities, whilst others are swish holiday parks with some tent spaces.

Given the paucity of 'official campsites', one option is to look at the web site 💻 campspace.com, where homeowners advertise the possibility of pitching a tent on their property in return for a small fee. All of which is useful, of course, but they're not cheap – around £14-30 per night for a spot in someone's back garden seems to be the going rate – and there still aren't really enough to make camping every night a viable option unless you illegally wild camp (see below).

It's a rare trekker who would want to camp every night anyway, particularly as there is always the temptation to have a hot bath in a cosy B&B and rest your head on a feather pillow. If you're camping you'll be carrying a heavier pack which can slow you down and could add an extra day and additional costs to your walk.

Wild camping Camping on land that is not a recognised campsite is possible along the route – though do note that it's also, officially, illegal. You must try to obtain the landowner's permission first but this is often impossible as you won't know who the landowner is, or even if you do you may not be able to find the relevant person. The amount of cultivated arable land in Kent reduces the number of potential sites and Surrey is very wooded; the most versatile set up is a bivvy bag or lightweight tarp.

Wild camping is not permitted on National Trust (NT) land. Expect wardens to be particularly alert to campers in Surrey where there have been problems with raves in the past. Elsewhere, wild camping is not for the fainthearted and you'll be carrying extra gear but it does add a sense of freedom and adventure. See also p51.

Bunkhouses and hostels

There is only one **bunkhouse** along the North Downs Way, at Puttenham (see p68), just a few miles from the start of the walk at Farnham. This provides comfortable accommodation on foam-lined wooden sleeping platforms and has a basic kitchen facility. Both a sleeping bag and booking in advance are essential.

With the sad closure of two of the three Youth Hostel Association (YHA; ☎ 0800 0191 700 or ☎ 01629 592700, 💻 yha.org.uk) **hostels** on this trail, the only one left that is of interest to North Downs walkers is at Canterbury (see p110). Note that dogs are not allowed in a YHA hostel though they can stay in cabins.

Bed and breakfast (B&B)

The B&B is a British institution. Although normally a reserved nation, you're welcomed into people's homes as a guest, provided with a comfortable bed (usually) and sent on your way the next morning with breakfast.

Some B&Bs are charming, some luxurious, others are modest. Rates (based on two sharing) vary from about £35 per person (pp), though £40pp or above is more common. Often the solo walker will pay a supplement to occupy a double or twin room when a single isn't available; this may mean paying most or all of the full room rate at peak times.

The listings in this book concentrate on establishments close to the trail but you should be prepared to walk for up to a mile, sometimes more, descending off the North Downs ridge to the villages and towns below at the end of the day.

❑ BOOKING ACCOMMODATION IN ADVANCE

Always book your accommodation and I suggest doing so several weeks before departure. Because the trail is close to London and major business arteries, a busy port, as well as two of the country's busiest airports and top tourist attractions it means that demand for rooms is always high. Furthermore there has been quite a serious decline in B&Bs and pubs offering accommodation over the past decade or so. It doesn't take long for all beds to go if one of the major motorways is forced to close, either. The M25 shut down twice in the course of researching the first edition of this book and within hours there was no room in any manger.

Booking in advance means you risk losing your deposit and tie yourself to a schedule, but you'll be assured of a bed and have an idea of what to expect and know the price. If you do have to cancel a booking let the owners know as soon as possible so they can re-let the room.

While many B&Bs offer **en suite facilities**; these are often squeezed into the corner of an already tight room. It can take Houdini-like contortions to shower in a tiny cubicle fighting back a clinging shower curtain, so don't turn your nose up at separate, **private facilities** with a bath for a restorative post-hike soak.

Owners may offer to collect walkers from the trail but do check when booking. It's an added service, so if no fee is specified an offer to pay the petrol money will be appreciated. Your offer may be refused but it's a courtesy that doesn't cost much.

Pubs/inns

Many walkers write off pubs as noisy and perhaps not offering the best in the way of B&B. That hasn't been my experience. True they're sometimes less personal, but no worse for that and often a great deal less precious about muddy boots. I must confess the Devil's at my elbow and it's difficult to resist the sybaritic pleasure of bed, bath, booze and board under one roof at the end of a long day's walk. Prices start at £35pp. If you want to get an early start the next day, do check that this is possible as landlords tend to keep later hours, though if you are booked into a Wetherspoon hotel, breakfast (additional cost) is served from 8am.

Hotels

Hotels along the North Downs Way fall into two very different categories. The first are what we consider to be the 'traditional' hotel. Often (but not always) independently run, they are the most upmarket accommodation you can find along the trail and, while more used to seeing businessmen than hikers, they are great if you want a touch of luxury at the end of the day. Several are very characterful and are amongst the most historic buildings in town. Often relying on business travellers for their custom during the week, you may find some discounted rates at the weekend at several hotels on the trail.

The second category is the budget hotel as provided by two main nationwide companies: **Travelodge** and **Premier Inn**. While people are often sniffy about them, with only one hostel and one bunkhouse on the North Downs Way, it is these brands that provide the nearest thing to budget accommodation along the path, there being twelve in total covering seven of the major towns and cities. And with prices occasionally dropping to £35 per room per night if booked far enough in advance, you can't fault the value. True, you won't find much in the way of 'frills' in your room and even breakfast is extra. But you do get a clean en suite room, usually with a shower over a bath, with TV and facilities for making a hot drink.

As to the main difference between the two, Travelodges are generally cheaper and allow dogs (£20 per stay), though you have to pay extra for wi-fi. Premier Inns tend to be a little more expensive and dogs aren't allowed but the wi-fi is free.

Airbnb
The rise and rise of Airbnb (🖳 airbnb.co.uk) has seen private homes and apartments opened up to overnight travellers on an informal basis. While accommodation is primarily based in cities, the concept is spreading to tourist hotspots in more rural areas, but do check thoroughly what you are getting and the precise location. While the first couple of options listed may be in the area you're after, others may be far too far afield for walkers. Be aware that these places are not registered B&Bs, so standards may vary, yet prices may not necessarily be any lower. Note that we do not review Airbnb accommodation in this guide, as they tend to 'come and go'.

FOOD AND DRINK

Breakfast and lunch
If staying in a B&B, guesthouse or hotel you may be served an enormous **full English breakfast** – often bacon, sausages, eggs, sometimes baked beans, maybe black pudding, all fried and washed down with lashings of tea or coffee and of course accompanied by buttered toast and marmalade. It's great but two weeks of this and you're ready for the cardiac unit.

However, some places offer a lighter **continental breakfast** which you may prefer first thing in the morning and some also are happy to provide vegetarian/vegan breakfasts with prior warning. If requested in advance, and for an additional cost (or instead of breakfast, if you are planning an early start), many places can also provide you with a **packed lunch**.

Alternatively, breakfast and packed lunches can be bought along the Way from one of the many great cafés and bakeries, or made yourself from supermarket or village store ingredients. Remember that certain stretches of the walk

❑ BEER AND WINE
Farnham had five breweries and Guildford had nine during the heyday of brewing in the 19th century. But now most pubs and brewers are owned by one of the international conglomerates although there are still some independent ones.

The **Hogs Back Brewery** (🖳 hogsback.co.uk) survives as a small independent brewery and has a thriving mail-order service for its bottle-conditioned ales. A particular favourites is the classic Tongham TEA (Traditional English Ale) at 4.2%.

Beer is also produced by **Surrey Hills Brewery** (🖳 surreyhills.co.uk), who are based on the Denbies Wine Estate (see p90), the largest vineyard in Britain. Their winery tour and tasting is highly recommended. Their Surrey Gold is a delicate 11.5% white aperitif wine, perfect on a summer evening.

Located on the Surrey/Kent border at the highest point of the North Downs Way is more recent arrival **Titsey Brewing Co** (🖳 titseybrewingco.com), established in 2017.

Finally, in Kent the granddaddy of them all is **Shepherd Neame** (🖳 shepherdneame.co.uk), with beers from Britain's oldest brewer and still a family company.

are devoid of places to eat so check the information in Part 4 to ensure you don't go hungry.

Evening meals

There is nothing like a pint at the end of a day's walking and many of the pubs on the North Downs Way can trace their origins back to the 15th and 16th centuries. Most are now owned by one or other of the drinks conglomerates but by and large retain their individual character thanks to a resident landlord. Some have à la carte restaurants as well as a bar menu, which is usually cheaper, and some have become 'gastropubs' serving restaurant quality food in a pub environment, but often at near restaurant prices.

There is a wide choice of restaurants and takeaways in the larger villages and towns from Italian to Indian, burger joints to modern British, Asian fusion to fast food. Of course the Great British culinary institution, the fish 'n' chip shop, can also be found along the route.

Finally, some B&Bs offer a evening meal, though often you need to book this in advance and there will be an additional charge.

Camping supplies

There are plenty of shops along the North Downs Way for you to buy food and there are outdoor shops in Farnham, Guildford, Shere, Dorking, Redhill and Canterbury where you can get gas and other essential camping supplies.

Drinking water

There are next to no drinking-water taps along the North Downs Way – the only one we found was at Box Hill by the toilets there – so take plenty of water with you each day. There are five rivers on this walk and drinking water from those is not recommended. Even if you do purify the water using a filter or iodine tables you will not succeed in removing heavy metals or pesticides present from run-off from roads and agricultural use.

Luckily there are many tea shops, pubs and refreshment kiosks within easy access of the North Downs Way so buying bottles of water should not be a problem, or ask if they'd mind filling up your water bottle from the tap. The website and app 💻 refill.org.uk has a map showing where you can top up your water bottle for free.

MONEY

Since the pandemic, cash is less acceptable than it once was and many establishments, even small and seasonal businesses, now prefer you to pay by **card**. Nevertheless, it is worth having some **cash** for those that may not, such as some B&Bs and campsites.

High street banks are a rarity in most small towns these days so your best option for an **ATM/cashpoint** is to head to a supermarket or convenience store.

Several banks in Britain have an agreement with the **Post Office** allowing customers with a debit card and PIN to make cash withdrawals at post office counters (see 💻 www.postoffice.co.uk/branch-finder).

OTHER SERVICES

Many villages and all the towns have at least one **food shop** or **supermarket** and a **post office**. Post offices can be useful for sending unnecessary equipment home which may be weighing you down.

In Part 4 mention is given to services that may be of use to the walker such

❑ INFORMATION FOR FOREIGN VISITORS

• **Currency** The British pound (£) comes in notes of £50, £20, £10 and £5, and coins of £2 and £1. The pound is divided into 100 pence (usually referred to as 'p', pronounced 'pee') which come in silver coins of 50p, 20p, 10p and 5p, and copper coins of 2p and 1p.

A guide to currency **exchange rates** can be found on 💻 xe.com/currencyconverter; however, the actual rate used by post offices, banks and travel agents varies.

• **Business hours** If we assume that the whole COVID pandemic is behind us by the time you read this, you'll find most **shops and supermarkets** are open Monday to Saturday 7/8am-8pm (sometimes up to 15 hours a day) and on Sunday from about 9am to 5 or 6pm, though main branches of supermarkets generally open on Sunday 10am-4pm or 11am-5pm. Occasionally, especially in rural areas, you'll come across a local shop that closes at lunchtime on one day during the week, usually a Wednesday or Thursday; this is a throwback to the days when all towns and villages had an 'early closing day'.

Main **post offices** are open at least from Monday to Friday 9am-5pm and Saturday 9am-12.30pm; branches in village stores are often now open the same hours as the store. **Banks** typically open at 9.30am Monday to Friday and close at 3.30pm or 4pm though in some places they may open only two or three days a week and/or in the morning only; **ATMs (cash machines)** though are open all the time as long as they are outside; any inside a shop or pub will only be accessible when that place is open. Note that ATMs that charge (see p22), such as Link machines, may not accept foreign-issued cards.

Pub hours are less predictable although many open daily 11am-11pm; often in rural areas opening hours are Monday to Saturday 11am-3pm & 5 or 6-11pm, Sunday 11am/noon-3pm & 6 or 7-10.30pm. Last entry to most **museums and galleries** is half an hour, or an hour, before the official closing time.

• **National (bank) holidays** Most businesses are shut on 1 January, Good Friday (March/April), Easter Monday (March/April), first and last Monday in May, last Monday in August, 25 December and 26 December.

• **School holidays** State-school holidays in England are generally as follows: a one-week break late October, two weeks over Christmas and the New Year, a week mid February, two weeks around Easter, one week at the end of May/early June (to coincide with the bank holiday at the end of May) and five to six weeks from late July to early September. Private-school holidays fall at the same time, but tend to be slightly longer.

• **Electronic Travel Authorisation (ETA)** Since 2024 – though for European citizens this is scheduled to start in March 2025 – non-UK citizens who didn't need a visa to enter the UK (eg the USA, EU countries, Australia, Canada) need to apply and pay for Electronic Travel Authorisation (💻 www.gov.uk/guidance/apply-for-an-electronic-travel-authorisation-visa) online before arriving in the UK.

as banks, ATMs, outdoor equipment shops, pharmacies/chemists, tourist information centres and public toilets.

WALKING COMPANIES

If you want to carry just a day pack, consider one of the following companies

• **Travel/medical insurance** Even though the UK left the European Union in 2020, the European Health Insurance Card (EHIC) entitled EU nationals (on production of a valid card) to necessary medical treatment under the UK's National Health Service (NHS) while on a temporary visit here. However, this is not likely to be the case for EU nationals once their EHIC card has expired; check on 🖳 nhs.uk/nhs-services (click on: 'Visiting-or-moving-to-England') before you come to the UK.

Also, this is not a substitute for proper medical cover on your travel insurance for unforeseen bills and for getting you home should that be necessary.

Also consider cover for loss or theft of personal belongings, especially if you're camping or staying in bunkhouses, as there may be times when you'll have to leave your luggage unattended.

• **Weights and measures** In Britain, milk can be sold in pints (1 pint = 568ml), as can beer in pubs, though most other **liquids** including petrol (gasoline) and diesel are sold in litres. Distances on road and path signs are given in miles (1 mile = 1.6km) rather than kilometres, and yards (1yd = 0.9m) rather than metres.

The population remains divided between those who still use inches (1 inch = 2.5cm), feet (1ft = 0.3m) and yards for **distances** and those who are happy with millimetres, centimetres and metres; you'll often be told that 'it's only a hundred yards or so' to somewhere, rather than a hundred metres or so.

Most food is sold in metric weights (g and kg) but the imperial weights of pounds (lb: 1lb = 453g) and ounces (oz: 1oz = 28g) are frequently displayed too. The **weather** – a frequent topic of conversation – is also an issue: while most forecasts predict temperatures in Celsius (C), some older people continue to think in terms of Fahrenheit (F; see the temperature chart on p15 for conversions).

• **Smoking & vaping** The ban on smoking in public places relates not only to pubs and restaurants, but also to B&Bs, hostels and hotels. These latter have the right to designate one or more bedrooms where the occupants can smoke, but the ban is in force in all enclosed areas open to the public – even in a private home such as a B&B. Should you be foolhardy enough to light up in a no-smoking area, which includes pretty well any indoor public place, you could be fined £50, but it's the owners of the premises who suffer most if they fail to stop you, with a potential fine of £2500.

Although the ban does not apply to vaping, premises can and do impose their own restrictions on the use of e-cigarettes indoors.

• **Time** During the winter, the whole of Britain is on Greenwich Meantime (GMT). The clocks move one hour forward on the last Sunday in March, remaining on British Summer Time (BST) until the last Sunday in October.

• **Telephone** The international country access code for Britain is ☎ 44 followed by the area code minus the first 0, and then the number you require. Within Britain, to call a landline number with the same code as the landline phone you are calling from, the code can be omitted: dial the number only. If you're using a mobile phone that is registered overseas, consider buying a local SIM card to keep costs down.

• **Emergency services** For police, ambulance, fire or coastguard dial ☎ 999 or ☎ 112.

as they'll transport your bags, book your accommodation and provide **guided** or **self-guided** itineraries to suit your needs.

• **Boots on Adventures** (☎ 07730-095759), 💻 bootsonadventures.co.uk; Faversham) North Downs Way specialists offering self-guided and guided walks along the whole of the North Downs Way and in parts.
• **British & Irish Walks** (☎ 01242-254353, 💻 britishandirishwalks.com; Cheltenham) Itineraries from Rochester to Canterbury in 5 nights, and also offer the complete North Downs Way.
• **Contours Walking Holidays** (☎ 01629-821900, 💻 contours.co.uk; Derbyshire) Offers self-guided 11-, 12- and 13-night itineraries on both the Canterbury and Folkestone routes, including luggage transfer (one suitcase per person). They also have 7- and 8-night itineraries from Farnham to Rochester and 5- to 6-night sections from Rochester to Dover via either Folkestone or Canterbury for those who want to do it in two stages, as well as a 3-night 'taster' from Canterbury to Dover.
• **Embark Walking Holidays** (☎ 01873-379100, 💻 embarkwalkingholidays.com; Monmouthshire) will shortly be offering walks on the North Downs Way.
• **Freedom Walking Holidays** (☎ 07733-885390, 💻 freedomwalkingholidays.co.uk; Goring-on-Thames) Offer the whole North Downs Way.
• **Let's Go Walking** (☎ 01837-880075, 💻 letsgowalking.com; Devon) Offer the whole North Downs Way and The Pilgrims' Way.
• **Responsible Travel** (☎ 01273-823700, 💻 responsibletravel.com; Brighton) Offer both the North Downs Way and The Pilgrims' Way.
• **Walk Awhile** (☎ 01227-752762, 💻 walkawhile.co.uk; Kent) Offer a 5-night itinerary on The Pilgrims' Way from Rochester to Canterbury, either guided or self-guided, as well as a 14-night itinerary covering the whole trail.
• **Wild with Wheels** (☎ 07787-181550. 💻 wildwithwheels.com; Dover). Free, supported and accessible walks for all including wheelchair and mobility scooter users on the North Downs Way between Canterbury and Dover, along with Kent's Coastal paths.

PLANNING YOUR WALK

❑ DISABLED ACCESS

Unfortunately most of the North Downs Way is inaccessible to disabled people but there are some areas where roads provide access to good views and stretches of the trail that can be followed, particularly at Newlands Corner (see p82) and Blue Bell Hill picnic site (see p137).

Disabled Ramblers (💻 disabledramblers.co.uk) is a national charity of like-minded disabled people who enjoy being in the countryside and get about using a variety of mobility aids. They have a busy calendar of events including rambles along the North Downs near Guildford. Resisting being ghettoised and confined to areas catering to every conceivable need, their rambles take them nationwide. See also Wild with Wheels, above.

TAKING DOGS ALONG THE NORTH DOWNS WAY

The North Downs Way is dog-friendly but owners must behave in a responsible way; see pp203-5. The first thing to decide is whether you think your dog will actually enjoy the walk. Dogs should always be kept under close control to avoid disturbing wildlife, livestock and other walkers. Man's best friend is not everyone's best friend and your pet may be uneasy and unwelcome in the presence of working farm dogs.

Budgeting

England is not a cheap place to go travelling at the best of times and the North Downs Way, with its proximity to London, is in one of the most affluent areas in the UK. Add to this the demand from other tourists and business travellers and it is easy to understand why prices are high. Budget accommodation is scarce and camping opportunities are at a minimum. After you've allowed for accommodation and food and the cost of getting to and from the start of the trail you'll have to allow for incidentals and unexpected expenditure: beer, snacks, bus and taxi fares, admission tickets and so on. It all adds up.

CAMPING AND BUDGET ACCOMMODATION

With some campsites costing more than £20 per person and the cost of food and the effort involved in carrying all the gear, camping might not be the attractive option it is elsewhere. It's also unlikely you'll be able to **camp** all the way so you'll have to budget for some nights in a **hostel**, **bunkhouse** or **budget hotel**. In all, reckon on needing a minimum of £30-40 per person (pp) per day.

The only YHA hostel on the route, at Canterbury, costs from £30pp, while you'll get a bunk at Puttenham camping barn for £23pp. Budget hotels (Premier Inn and Travelodge) are much more readily available and can be as little as £29 per room but that varies wildly depending on the time of year and how far in advance you book. With any of these options you'll also have to buy breakfast, lunch and dinner and just getting by will set you back a minimum of £35pp a day but probably £50-75pp is more realistic.

B&Bs, PUBS AND HOTELS

The cheapest B&B on this walk charges around £35pp (based on two sharing) and breakfast isn't included though you have the use of the kitchen; most cost around £40-50pp but expect to pay more for single occupancy of a room. Add on the cost of lunch, dinner and a couple of pints in the evening and you should reckon on about £80pp minimum per day.

VILLAGE & TOWN FACILITIES & DISTANCES

Walking EAST from Farnham to Dover

PLACE & DISTANCE APPROX MILES / *KM* FROM PLACE ABOVE	ATM (BANK)	POST OFFICE	INFO	EATING PLACE	FOOD SHOP	CAMP-SITE	HOSTEL	B&B HOTEL
WALKING TO DOVER								
Farnham	✓	✓		✓✓✓	✓			✓✓
t/o (Seale) **4.1** / ***6.7*** (+0.3/*0.5*)				✓		✓(0)		
Puttenham 2.5 / ***4***				✓✓			B	
Compton (Watts Gallery) 1.7 / ***2.7***				✓✓				✓
t/o (Guildford) **2.5** / ***4*** (+1.2/2)	✓	✓	TIC	✓✓✓	✓			✓✓✓
& (Shalford) (+1.2/2)	✓	✓		✓✓✓	✓			
t/o (Chilworth) **2** / ***3.1*** (+1.2/2)				✓				✓
t/o (Albury) **1** / ***1.6*** (+1.2/2)		✓		✓	✓			✓
Newlands Corner 1 / ***1.6***				✓✓				✓
t/o (Shere) **2.1** / ***3.4*** (+0.75/*1.2*)		✓		✓✓✓	✓			✓
Ranmore Common 5.3 / ***8.5***								
Denbies Wine Estate 1.8 / ***3***				✓✓✓				✓✓
t/o (Dorking) **0.4** / ***0.7*** (+2/*3*)	✓	✓		✓✓✓	✓			✓✓✓
Box Hill 1.2 / ***2***				✓✓				
t/o (Box Hill village) **1.5** / ***2.4*** (+0.5/*0.8*)		✓			✓			
Reigate Hill 5.2 / ***8.5***				✓✓				✓
t/o (Redhill) **0.3** / ***0.5*** (+1.8/*3*)	✓	✓		✓✓✓	✓			✓✓
Merstham 2 / ***3.3***	✓			✓	✓			
t/o (Oxted) **8.6** / ***13.8*** (+1/*1.6*)	✓	✓		✓✓✓	✓			✓
t/o (Westerham) **4.3** / ***7*** (+1.5/*2.4*)	✓	✓		✓✓✓	✓			✓✓
t/o (Knockholt Pound) **4** / ***6.5*** (+0.3/*0.5*)				✓✓				
Dunton Green 2 / ***3.3***				✓✓✓	✓			✓
Otford 1.8 / ***3***	✓	✓		✓✓✓	✓			
t/o (Kemsing) **2** / ***3.3*** (+0.5/*0.8*)				✓✓	✓			✓
Wrotham 4 / ***6.6***	✓			✓✓	✓	✓(2)		✓
t/o (Ryarsh) **4.1** / ***6.7***				✓				
Cuxton 5.2 / ***8.4***				✓✓	✓			✓
t/o (Rochester) **2.5** / ***4*** (+1.8/*3*)	✓	✓		✓✓✓	✓			✓✓✓
t/o (Aylesford) **5** / ***8*** (+1.5/*2.5*)				✓✓✓	✓	✓(½)		✓✓
Detling 4.6 / ***7.4***		✓		✓✓				
Thurnham 1.4 / ***2.2***				✓				✓
Hollingbourne 4 / ***6.6***				✓✓				✓
t/o (Harrietsham) **2.2** / ***3.7*** (+1/*1.6*)		✓		✓✓	✓			
t/o (Lenham) **1.6** / ***2.5*** (+0.6/*1*)	✓	✓		✓✓✓	✓			✓
t/o (Charing) **4.2** / ***6.8*** (+0.9/*1.4*)				✓	✓			
Westwell 2.6 / ***4.2***						✓(0)		
Eastwell 1.6 / ***2.7***				✓				✓
Boughton Lees 0.6 / ***1***				✓		✓(¼)		✓

cont'd on p30

NOTES PLACE & DISTANCE Places in **bold** are on the path; places in brackets and not in bold – eg (Seale) – are a short walk off the path. DISTANCE is given from the place above. Distances are between **places on the route** or to the **main turnoff (t/o)** to places in brackets. For example the distance from Farnham to the **turnoff** for Seale is 4.1 miles/*6.7km*. Bracketed distances eg (+1) show the additional distance off the route – eg Seale is +0.3 miles/*0.5km* off the Way.

VILLAGE & TOWN FACILITIES & DISTANCES

Walking WEST from Dover to Farnham

PLACE & DISTANCE APPROX MILES / *KM* FROM PLACE ABOVE	ATM (BANK)	POST OFFICE	INFO	EATING PLACE	FOOD SHOP	CAMP- SITE	HOSTEL	B&B HOTEL
WALKING TO FARNHAM								
NORTHERN ROUTE								
Dover	✓	✓	TIC	✓✓✓	✓	✓(4)*		✓✓✓
Shepherdswell 9.1/*14.7*	✓			✓✓	✓			
t/o (Bridge) **7.3/*11.8*** (+0.8/*1.2*)	✓	(✓)		✓✓	✓			
Canterbury 3.5/*5.7*	✓	✓	TIC	✓✓✓	✓	✓(1)	YHA	✓✓✓
Chartham Hatch/(Chartham) **4/*6.6*** (+0.9/*1.4*)				✓				
Chilham 3.3/*5.3*		✓		✓✓✓	✓			✓✓✓
Boughton Lees 6/*9.6*				✓		✓(¼)		✓
SOUTHERN ROUTE								
Dover	✓	✓	TIC	✓✓✓	✓	✓(4)*		✓✓✓
Capel-le-Ferne 6.3/*10.2*				✓✓✓				
Etchinghill 6/*9.7*				✓				✓
Stowting 4.7/*7.7*				✓				
t/o (Brabourne) **1.6/*2.6*** (+0.5/*0.8*)				✓				✓
Wye 5/*8*		✓		✓✓✓	✓			
Boughton Lees 2.3/*3.7*				✓		✓(¼)		✓
MAIN ROUTE (after Broughton Lees)								
Eastwell 0.6/*1*				✓				✓
Westwell 1.6/*2.7*						✓(0)		
t/o (Charing) **2.6/*4.2*** (+0.9/*1.4*)				✓	✓			
t/o (Lenham) **4.2/*6.8*** (+0.6/*1*)	✓	✓		✓✓✓	✓			✓
t/o (Harrietsham) **1.6/*2.5*** (+1/*1.6*)		✓		✓✓	✓			
Hollingbourne 2.2/*3.7*				✓✓				✓
Thurnham 4/*6.6*				✓				✓
Detling 1.4/*2.*		✓		✓✓				
t/o (Aylesford) **4.6/*7.4*** (+1.5/*2.5*)				✓✓✓	✓	✓(½)		✓✓
t/o (Rochester) **5/*8***(+1.8/*3*)	✓	✓		✓✓✓	✓			✓✓✓
Cuxton 2.5/*4*				✓✓	✓			✓
t/o (Ryarsh) **5.2/*8.4***				✓				
Wrotham 4.1/*6.7*	✓			✓✓	✓	✓(2)		✓
t/o (Kemsing) **4/*6.6*** (+0.5/*0.8*)				✓✓	✓			✓
Otford 2/*3.3*	✓	✓		✓✓✓	✓			
Dunton Green 1.8/*3*				✓✓✓	✓			✓
t/o (Knockholt Pound) **2/*3.3*** (+0.3/*0.5*)				✓✓				
t/o (Westerham) **4/*6.5*** (+1.5/*2.4*)	✓	✓		✓✓✓	✓			✓✓
t/o (Oxted) **4.3/*7*** (+1/*1.6*)	✓	✓		✓✓✓	✓			✓
Merstham 8.6/*13.8*	✓			✓	✓			
t/o (Redhill) **2/*3.3*** (+1.8/*3*)	✓	✓		✓✓✓	✓			✓✓

cont'd on p31

B&B/HOTEL/CAMPSITE/EATING PLACE ✓ = one place ✓✓ = two ✓✓✓ = three or more
HOSTEL YHA = YHA hostel B = bunkhouse
CAMPSITE Bracketed distance eg (¼) shows mileage from North Downs Way
* Nearest campsite is 4 miles away at Hawthorn Farm, 400m from Martin Mill Railway Station
POST OFFICE (✓) = limited hours **INFO** TIC = Tourist Information Centre

PLANNING YOUR WALK

(cont'd from p28)

VILLAGE & TOWN FACILITIES & DISTANCES

Walking EAST from Farnham to Dover

PLACE & DISTANCE APPROX MILES / *KM* FROM PLACE ABOVE	ATM (BANK)	POST OFFICE	INFO	EATING PLACE	FOOD SHOP	CAMP-SITE	HOSTEL	B&B HOTEL
WALKING TO DOVER								
NORTHERN ROUTE (after Broughton Lees)								
Chilham 6 / *9.6*		✓		✓✓✓	✓			✓✓✓
Chartham Hatch/(Chartham) **3.3 / *5.3*** (+0.9/*1.4*)				✓				
Canterbury 4 / *6.6*	✓	✓	TIC	✓✓✓	✓	✓(1)	YHA	✓✓✓
t/o (Bridge) **3.5 / *5.7*** (+0.8/*1.2*)	✓	(✓)		✓✓	✓			
Shepherdswell 7.3 / *11.8*	✓			✓✓	✓			
Dover 9.1 / *14.7*	✓	✓	TIC	✓✓✓	✓	✓(4)*		✓✓✓
SOUTHERN ROUTE (after Broughton Lees)								
Wye 2.3 / *3.7*		✓		✓✓✓	✓			
t/o (Brabourne) **5 / *8*** (+0.5/*0.8*)				✓				✓
Stowting 1.6 / *2.6*				✓				
Etchinghill 4.7 / *7.7*				✓				✓
Capel-le-Ferne 6 / *9.7*				✓✓✓				
Dover 6.3 / *10.2*	✓	✓	TIC	✓✓✓	✓	✓(4)*		✓✓✓

*Nearest campsite is 4 miles away at Hawthorn Farm, 400m from Martin Mill Railway Station

(for key and other notes see previous page)

SOME SUGGESTED ITINERARIES – WALKING TO DOVER

Night	Relaxed: Place	Approx Distance miles	*km*	Medium/Fast: Place	Approx Distance miles	*km*	Fast: Place	Approx Distance miles	*km*
0	Farnham			Farnham			Farnham		
1	Guildford	10.8	*17.4*	Newlands Cnr	15.4	*24.8*	Shere	17.5	*28.2*
2	Dorking	13.6	*21.9*	Reigate Hill	17.3	*27.8*	Oxted	25.6	*41.2*
3	Reigate Hill	7.9	*12.7*	Dunton Green	20.3	*32.7*	Cuxton	26.8	*43.0*
4	Westerham	15.2	*24.4*	Rochester	19.5	*31.3*	Harrietsham	19.7	*31.7*
5	Wrotham	13.8	*22.2*	Lenham	18.6	*29.9*	Chilham **NR**	16.2	*26.7*
6	Rochester	11.8	*18.9*	Canterbury **NR**	21.1	*34.0*	Dover **NR**	25.8	*41.5*
7	Hollingbourne	15.0	*24.1*	Dover **NR**	19.4	*31.2*	Boughton L **SR**	30.3	*48.7*
8	Boughton Lees	12.8	*20.6*	Brabourne **SR**	16.3	*26.2*	Dover **SR**	25.9	*41.7*
	Northern Route (NR)			Dover **SR**	18.6	*29.9*			
9	Canterbury	13.3	*21.4*						
10	Shepherdswell*	10.8	*17.4*						
11	Dover	9.1	*14.6*						
	Southern Route (SR)								
9	Etchinghill	13.6	*21.9*						
10	Dover	12.3	*19.8*						

Note that distances in these itineraries given are to nearest point on the trail to the village or town. Please refer to the Village & Town Facilities tables (above) for the additional distance, usually about a mile, you may have to walk.

* No accommodation here so take train to Canterbury or Dover from Shepherdswell

(cont'd from p29)

VILLAGE & TOWN FACILITIES & DISTANCES

Walking WEST from Dover to Farnham

PLACE & DISTANCE approx miles / *km* from place above	ATM (BANK)	POST OFFICE	INFO	EATING PLACE	FOOD SHOP	CAMP-SITE	HOSTEL	B&B HOTEL
WALKING TO FARNHAM								
Reigate Hill 0.3 /*0.5*				✔✔				✔
t/o (Box Hill village) **5.2 /*8.5*** (+0.5/*0.8*)		✔			✔			
Box Hill 1.5 /*2.4*				✔✔				
t/o (Dorking) **1.2 /*2*** (+2/*3*)	✔	✔		✔✔✔	✔			✔✔✔
Denbies Wine Estate 0.4 /*0.7*				✔✔✔				✔✔
Ranmore Common 1.8 /*3*								
t/o (Shere) **5.3 /*8.5*** (+0.75/*1.2*)		✔		✔✔✔	✔			✔
Newlands Corner 2.1 /*3.4*				✔✔				✔
t/o (Albury) **1 /*1.6*** (+1.2/*2*)		✔		✔	✔			✔
t/o (Chilworth) **1 /*1.6*** (+1.2/*2*)				✔				✔
t/o (Guildford) **2 /*3.1*** (+1.2/*2*)	✔	✔	TIC	✔✔✔	✔			✔✔✔
& (Shalford) (+1.2/*2*)	✔	✔		✔✔✔	✔			
Compton (Watts Gallery) 2.5 /*4*				✔✔				✔
Puttenham 1.7 /*2.7*				✔✔			B	
t/o (Seale) **2.5 /*4*** (+400m)				✔		✔(0)		
Farnham 4.1 /*6.7*	✔	✔		✔✔✔	✔			✔✔

SOME SUGGESTED ITINERARIES – WALKING TO FARNHAM

Night	Relaxed – Place	Approx Distance miles	*km*	Medium/Fast – Place	Approx Distance miles	*km*	Fast – Place	Approx Distance miles	*km*
Southern Route (SR)									
0	Dover **SR**			Dover **SR**			Dover **SR**		
1	Etchinghill **SR**	12.3	*19.8*	Brabourne **SR**	18.6	*29.9*	Boughton Lees	25.9	*41.7*
2	Boughton Lees	13.6	*21.9*	Lenham	16.3	*26.2*	Cuxton	30.3	*48.7*
Northern Route (NR)									
0	Dover			Dover **NR**			Dover **NR**		
1	Shepherdswell*	9.1	*14.6*	Canterbury **NR**	19.4	*31.2*	Chilham **NR**	25.8	*41.5*
2	Canterbury	10.8	*17.4*	Lenham	21.1	*34.0*	Harrietsham	16.2	*26.7*
3	Boughton Lees	13.3	*21.4*	Rochester	18.6	*29.9*	Cuxton	19.7	*31.7*
4	Hollingbourne	12.8	*20.6*	Dunton Green	19.5	*31.3*	Oxted	26.8	*43.0*
5	Rochester	15.0	*24.1*	Reigate Hill	20.3	*32.7*	Shere	25.6	*41.2*
6	Wrotham	11.8	*18.9*	Newlands Cnr	17.3	*27.8*	Farnham	17.5	*28.2*
7	Westerham	13.8	*22.2*	Farnham	15.4	*24.8*			
8	Reigate Hill	15.2	*24.4*						
9	Dorking	7.9	*12.7*						
10	Guildford	13.6	*21.9*						
11	Farnham	10.8	*17.4*						

Note that distances in these itineraries given are to nearest point on the trail to the village or town. Please refer to the Village & Town Facilities tables (above) for the additional distance, usually about a mile.

* No accommodation here so take train to Canterbury or Dover from Shepherdswell

❑ HIGHLIGHTS – DAY WALKS AND WEEKEND WALKS

There is nothing like walking the entire length of a long-distance path in one go but some people don't have the time and others want to experience only the best of what the trail has to offer. For details of public transport to and from the start and finish of each walk see pp42-7. The weekend walks can be split in two to suit day walkers, or combined and completed in a day by those who want a challenge. That would, however, leave little time for sightseeing which is a pity on this culturally rich route.

Day walks

• **Farnham to Guildford** 12 miles/19.3km (see pp68-77) Walk through farmland, woodland and along sandy bridleways to Guildford where there is plenty of sightseeing. Visit the ancient burial tumulus at Puttenham Heath, itself geologically unusual in this area of chalk, and stop at the excellent Watts Gallery and the Cemetery Chapel, Compton (see p72), where you can rest up awhile at the café.

• **Guildford to Shere** 5½ miles/8.9km (see pp80-6) A relaxed pace crossing the River Wey, the path climbs through woods (bluebell-filled in spring) to the top of St Martha's Hill and Newlands Corner from where there are great views on a clear day. You can then detour to Shere, Surrey's prettiest village.

• **Otford to Rochester** 17¾ miles/28.6km (see pp120-35) Not the prettiest or quietest of sections and one of the longest but it passes through Kemsing Downs, a significant chalk grassland habitat, the woods of Trosley Country Park, with a short detour to see one of Kent's best-known megaliths, Coldrum Barrow. Much of the walk is in woodland and surprisingly isolated from the industrial Medway valley towns. It emerges by pretty Upper Bush into Cuxton before crossing the M2 and Channel Tunnel Rail link. Rochester is 35-40 minutes off the trail from where there are fast train connections to London, Canterbury and Dover. Consider an overnight stay there – the Norman Castle, England's second oldest cathedral, and Restoration House are well worth visiting.

Chilham, the prettiest village on the North Downs Way, makes the perfect start or end to a day's walk.

• **Charing to Chilham** 10½ miles/16.9km (see pp150-61) A stroll through a quintessential Kentish landscape, with oast-houses and orchards abounding, and finishing at the prettiest village on the trail. Great fun.

• **Chilham to Canterbury** 6½ miles/10.3km (see pp160-9) Starting at the loveliest little settlement on the trail and finishing at the most important city, this tranquil stroll is untaxing but filled with some lovely walking, including a visit to No Man's Orchard and some lengthy sections through even more of Kent's idyllic agrarian landscape.

• **Folkestone outskirts to Dover** 5 miles/8km (see pp194-200) You'll need to hike a couple of miles (3km) uphill from Folkestone's Central Station to join this, the ultimate section of the North Downs Way's Southern Route (see pp186-200). Once on the trail, however, you can enjoy some fantastic cliff-top walking, with the Battle of Britain Memorial, Norman encampments, Napoleonic forts, sonar mirrors and WW2 pillboxes en route and the sound of the sea a constant accompaniment.

Weekend (two-day) walks

• **Farnham to Dorking** 24¾ miles/40km (see pp68-92) This is easy walking through farmland, heath and woodland to overnight in Guildford (12 miles/19.3km).

After a climb to St Martha's – the Pilgrims' Church – with wonderful views and a further climb across Albury Downs the path gains the ridgeline at Newlands Corner, and follows a mostly wooded drove road to descend through England's largest vineyard, Denbies Wine Estate, with views to Box Hill on the outskirts of Dorking. Two castles, one cathedral, a gallery to eminent Victorian artist, George Frederic Watts, a Gilbert Scott church, WWII fortifications, good wine, and views that stretch for miles on a clear day – not bad for two days' walking.

• **Charing to Canterbury** 16¾ miles/27.2km (see pp150-69) Follow in the footsteps of pilgrims passing the ruined archbishop's palace in Charing to follow the Pilgrims' Way emerging from dense woodland into the tranquil landscape of Eastwell. Climb to Soakham Downs with extensive views over the Stour valley and emerge from the King's Wood to overnight in Chilham with its remarkably preserved medieval square (10½ miles/16.9km).

The following day's walk is through Kent's orchard country before arriving at Canterbury, worth at least a day's exploration (6½ miles/10.3km).

Itineraries

To help you plan your walk there is a planning map (see map inside back cover) and the table of village/town facilities (pp28-31); the latter gives a snapshot of the essential information you will need regarding accommodation possibilities and services. Alternatively, you could follow or adapt the suggested itineraries (pp30-1). There is also a list of recommended linear day and weekend walks (above) which cover the best of the North Downs Way, all of which are well served by public transport. The public transport map and tables are on pp42-7.

Some accommodation and public transport options may be a considerable distance off the trail and where this is the case it is noted in Part 4 and on the maps where appropriate. Be sure to add travelling time before and after the walk. This is especially important in winter when there are fewer hours of daylight.

If you find it hard to get accommodation at a stop to suit the length of your day's walk it may be worth considering staying in a place for two nights and getting a taxi to and from where you left off the night before.

WHICH DIRECTION?

Most people tackle the North Downs Way west to east and Part 4 has been written that way. It's perfectly possible to walk it in the opposite direction (the waymarking is in place and the reverse timings are on our maps) but there are advantages in doing it west to east. The prevailing wind tends to be at your back as is the sun if you get a later start. As most others are going this direction, if you are walking alone but want some company you can fall in step with them. Also it's worth having a destination to look forward to and Canterbury, though not at the end, is a worthy penultimate goal. And like a river on its journey it seems natural to follow the route to the sea. Certainly, the seafront at Dover is a far more fitting and dramatic end to your odyssey than the side of the A31 in Farnham.

SIDE TRIPS

The North Downs Way is plenty long enough to satisfy energetic walkers. Yet the path cuts through a part of Britain that's packed with castles, grand country houses and sites of great antiquity. A glance at the Ordnance Survey map will give you some idea for side trips and possible walking trails to them as well as other long-distance paths such as the Greensand Way (Haslemere, Surrey, to Hamstreet, near Ashford in Kent) and Weald Way (Gravesend in Kent to Eastbourne in East Sussex). A detailed description is beyond the scope of this book but you can find information online.

Those inspired to try more Downs walking may want to tackle the South Downs Way for which there is a Trailblazer guide (see p208). The Downs Link, a 32-mile bridleway utilising a disused railway line links the North Downs Way at St Martha's (see Map 7, p81) with the South Downs Way, near Steyning (and on for another five miles to Shoreham and the seaside).

What to take

What you take depends on personal preference and experience. For those new to long-distance walking the suggestions below are a guide. What you must ensure is that you have all the equipment necessary to make the trip safe and comfortable.

KEEP YOUR LUGGAGE LIGHT

There are a few ways to do this. Buy the lightest equipment you can afford. Choose the smaller of pack sizes so you don't overpack (see below). Before packing lay out only what you deem essential. With the exception of the first-aid kit (see p37) ask whether or not you will use the item every day. If not, consider very carefully whether or not to pack it. Remember on the North Downs Way you are not so far away from a town or village that you can't get something you've forgotten even if it does mean interrupting your walk. If you have booked a self-guided holiday (see p26) your main luggage is likely to be transferred to your next accommodation stop and you can instead head off onto the trail with just the essentials you need for the day.

HOW TO CARRY IT

The size and type of backpack you carry will depend on how you plan to walk the North Downs Way. If you are day hiking, or have booked a self-guided holiday, at a minimum you should have a small daypack filled with those items that you will need during the day: water bottle, this book, a map, sun screen, hat, gloves, wet-weather gear, some food, camera, money, first-aid kit and so on.

If you are hiking the route end to end with no baggage service you will have to consider carefully the type of backpack you use. Its size will depend largely on where you plan to stay but do try to err on the smaller of sizes as it's so easy to overpack – and thus overburden yourself.

With all backpacks make sure it is adjustable so you can fit it to your back length and body shape, with chest and hip belts to distribute the weight and improve stability. Some shops allow you to take a pack home to try out (check by filling it with what you intend to take) and return it if it isn't right for you.

Campers bringing a tent, cooking equipment and food will probably need a 65- to 75-litre pack while if you plan on staying at B&B-style accommodation you should need no more than a 30- to 40-litre pack. A small daypack is useful so you can carry essentials on a day off around town or when leaving the main pack at your lodgings. Don't rely on manufacturers' claims to water resistance – it doesn't take a long shower to soak through most packs. Pack everything inside in waterproof liners or canoe bags or save weight and money by using strong plastic bags or bin liners.

FOOTWEAR

Boots

Quality is remembered long after the price is forgotten; invest in a pair of suitable boots. The North Downs Way has few sustained ascents or descents, is on a generally firm track with little rough or stony ground but it can be muddy. Look for boots that are waterproof (Gore-Tex lined), provide sufficient ankle support but retain residual flexibility for comfort and don't require much breaking in. If you are camping you may need to consider a boot with greater ankle support to cope with carrying a heavier pack; it is money well spent. When you go to try boots do so later in the day when your feet have swelled a little so you get a proper fit and also try on several brands.

Some people like to bring a change of shoes for the evening. If you are carrying all your own gear consider something lightweight such as flip flops or sports sandals – or just make do with the one pair.

Socks

Modern hi-tech socks are very comfortable if you spend a bit more on a high-quality pair designed for walking. Many swear by a liner sock under a thicker wool sock – each to their own but modern fibres dry quicker. Two pairs are fine, three are ample. You can wash socks each evening leaving them to dry overnight.

CLOTHES

British weather is notoriously changeable and you should bring clothes that can cope with the sun, rain and cold. But you needn't bankrupt yourself. Wear clothes that are lightweight, durable, quick drying and that can keep you warm, cool and dry depending on the weather conditions. While you can get away with hiking in ordinary cotton-based clothes, provided you have a waterproof outer layer, you will feel more comfortable in specialised outdoor clothes. The number of retailers also means they have to work hard to keep prices keen.

On this trail you will encounter cyclists and horse riders and in the short sections which are by-ways you may encounter off-road vehicles so you may want to opt for bright colours or reflective strips to ensure you are easily seen, especially in low light levels.

Modern hi-tech outdoor clothes still follow the basic two- or three-layer principle, with an inner **base layer** to transport sweat away from your skin, a **mid-layer** for warmth and an **outer layer** to protect you from the wind and rain. A thin lightweight **thermal top** of a synthetic material is ideal as the base layer as it draws sweat away from your body keeping you cool in hot weather and warm when worn under other clothes in cold weather. A light- to mid-weight polyester **fleece** over this will help keep you warm in cold weather. Fleeces are ideal trekking gear being light, fairly water-resistant, quick drying, remain warm when wet and pack down small in backpacks. A **waterproof jacket**, preferably with Gore-Tex, is essential and 'breathable' jackets help to cut down the build up of condensation. In dry weather this layer can be worn to keep the wind out.

Leg wear

Most modern **trekking trousers** are light, durable and quick-drying, making them a good investment. Never walk in denim jeans which are heavy and cling uncomfortably to your legs when wet. Trekking trousers with zip-off legs to convert to shorts are practical and a good compromise, weight-wise. Thermal longjohns are useful if camping and could come in handy in winter.

On wet or particularly cold days you may want to bring a pair of **waterproof trousers**. A less bulky and lighter solution, at least for the lower half of the leg, is **gaiters**. They provide extra protection when walking through muddy ground and when the vegetation around the trail is dripping wet after bad weather or early morning dew. They also help keep you looking presentable when you pitch up at the pub.

Underwear

Three changes of underwear are plenty and you may want to invest in the kind made from modern wickable fabrics that can be washed and dried overnight. Because backpacks can cause bra straps to dig painfully into the shoulders, women may find a sports bra more comfortable.

Other clothes

In winter don't leave home without a warm **hat** as you never know when you might need one (a **sun hat** is useful in summer). Many people bring **gloves**, too, in the winter.

TOILETRIES

Once again, take the minimum. **Soap**, a small microfibre **towel**, a **toothbrush** and **toothpaste** are pretty much essential (although those staying in B&Bs will find that most provide soap and towels anyway). Some **toilet paper** could also prove vital on the trail, particularly if using public toilets (which occasionally run out of it). If defecating outdoors you will also need **bags** to pack out the used paper and a plastic trowel to bury the evidence (see p50 for further tips). Other items to consider taking are: **razor**; **deodorant**; **tampons/sanitary towels**. **lip balm** and a high-factor **sun-screen**.

FIRST-AID KIT

Medical facilities in Britain are excellent so you need only take a small kit to cover common problems and emergencies. A basic kit will contain a pack of **aspirin** or **paracetamol** for treating mild to moderate pain and fever; **plasters/ Band Aids** for minor cuts; **blister patches** such as 'moleskin', 'Compeed' or 'Second skin'; a **bandage** for holding dressings, splints or limbs in place and for supporting a sprained ankle; an **elastic knee support** for a weak knee; a small selection of different-sized **sterile dressings** for wounds; **porous adhesive tape**; **antiseptic wipes**; **antiseptic cream**; **safety pins** (also useful for attaching wet clothes to your backpack so they can dry as you walk); **tweezers** and a small pair of **scissors**. Pack the kit in a waterproof container.

GENERAL ITEMS

Essentials

Many people find a **smartphone** pretty much essential these days, providing camera, GPS, torch, notepad, clock and alarm as well as enabling you to look up bus timetables, accommodation details or the nearest town (and how to get to it). You can also use it as a phone(!), confirming accommodation bookings or letting them know what time you're hoping to arrive. There is reception throughout most of the North Downs Way. Just as essential as the phone itself is its **charger** and a **battery pack** for when it dies on the trail (as they always do). It could prove to be a lifesaver.

Always carry at least a one-litre **water bottle** or **pouch** and some emergency **food** such as dried fruit, nuts or chocolate which will give an instant energy boost (see p52). Most people like to carry a separate **torch** too (I find a headtorch more useful, so you can keep both hands free) and spare **batteries**, as well as a **penknife** and a **plastic bag** for your litter. **Walking poles** will take the strain off your knees, especially on descents. **Sunglasses** are also recommended.

Hopefully you'll never need it, but in an emergency you'll be glad you brought a **whistle** (see p52 for details of the international distress signal), which carries further than any amount of shouting to attract attention.

Useful

Consider bringing a **notebook** (don't forget a **pen**) to record your impressions rather than taking endless photos on your phone. A **map** (see pp38-9) is useful if you are planning to explore off the North Downs Way.

With **binoculars** you'll get a closer look at wildlife but these would also add extra weight.

CAMPING GEAR

Campers and those intending to stay in the bunkhouse at Puttenham will need a **sleeping bag**. A two- to three-season bag should suffice for summer. In addition, campers will need: a decent **bivvy bag** or tarp, if travelling light, or a **tent**; and a **sleeping mat**. If you intend doing any cooking you will also need: **fuel** and **stove**; **pans**; **cutlery**; a **cup**; and a **scrubber** for washing up.

MONEY

Since the pandemic, accepting payment by debit/credit card has become much more widespread, even for small and seasonal businesses. Nevertheless, it's always a good idea to have a little cash with you, just in case. **ATMs** (cash machines) are common along the North Downs Way; many post offices and shops (particularly supermarkets) along the trail have them. There are also still some banks with ATMs in the larger towns. See also p23.

MAPS [for digital mapping see p18]

The hand-drawn maps in this book cover the trail at a scale of 1:20,000, better than any other scale currently available for the whole route; notes, tips and com-

❑ SOURCES OF FURTHER INFORMATION

Trail information The latest trail information including any diversions to the route can be found on 🖳 nationaltrail.co.uk/north-downs-way.

Tourist information centres (TICs) Tourist information centres provide all manner of locally specific information for visitors. The TICs along or near the North Downs Way are at Guildford (see p77), Canterbury (p167) and Dover (p184). Several other towns have websites with useful tourist information (see Part 4 for details).

Tourism South East (🖳 visitsoutheastengland.com) There is a whole host of information on its website about accommodation, things to do and see, and upcoming festivals and events. Surrey (🖳 visitsurrey.com) and Kent (🖳 visitkent.co.uk) also have lots of information on their respective websites.

Organisations for walkers

- **The Long Distance Walkers' Association** (🖳 ldwa.org.uk) An association for people with the common interest of long-distance walking in rural, mountainous and moorland areas. Membership includes a journal, *Strider*, three times per year giving details of challenge events and local group walks as well as articles on the subject. Membership costs £18 per year.
- **Ramblers** (🖳 ramblers.org.uk) Looks after the interests of walkers, providing group walks, routes on an app and publishing lots of useful information including their quarterly Walk magazine. Individual/joint membership costs £41/55.
- **The Backpackers' Club** (🖳 backpackersclub.co.uk) A club aimed at people who are involved or interested in lightweight camping through walking and other outdoor activities. They produce a quarterly magazine, provide members with a comprehensive advisory and information service on all aspects of backpacking, organise weekend trips and also publish a farm-pitch directory. Membership costs £20 per year.

ments are written on the maps so you should not need any others if you are walking just the North Downs Way. But if you want to explore further afield it is a good idea to have Ordnance Survey (🖳 ordnancesurvey.co.uk) maps. The OS Landranger series (1:50,000) for this area are 186 (Aldershot & Guildford); 187 (Dorking & Reigate); 188 (Maidstone & Royal Tunbridge Wells); 178 (The Thames Estuary); 189 (Ashford & Romney Marsh); 179 (Canterbury & East Kent). The larger-scale OS Explorer series (1:25,000) are Nos 145 (Guildford & Farnham); 146 (Dorking, Box Hill & Reigate); 147 (Sevenoaks & Tonbridge); 148 (Maidstone & the Medway Towns); 149 (Sittingbourne & Faversham); 150 (Canterbury & the Isle of Thanet); 137 (Ashford); 138 (Dover, Folkestone & Hythe). Note that OS also have an app for smartphones with a monthly subscription, which may well prove cheaper than buying the whole set; though many public libraries in Britain have maps that members can borrow.

Cheaper and lighter than buying the whole set of maps, Harveys (🖳 harveymaps.co.uk) produce strip maps (1:40,000) covering the whole of the North Downs Way as well as an app for smartphones covering the entire route.

For more on digital versions of these maps and other apps, see p18.

RECOMMENDED READING

Some of the following books can be found in the tourist information centres and they may also have books about the towns and villages en route, usually printed by small, local publishers.

For a thematic treatment of the North Downs through the eyes of painters, poets and novelists Kent County Council produced a richly illustrated guide, *North Downs Way: An Inspirational Journey* by Gillian Duff (out of print but still available second-hand online).

The *North Downs Way* by Belinda Knox (published by Kneading; out of print but available second-hand online) is a photographic guide to the Way.

The Pilgrims' Way: Fact and Fiction of an Ancient Trackway (2011) by Derek Bright is about the various origins of The Pilgrims' Way and provides a great background resource for anyone walking this path.

Flora and fauna field guides

Collins Bird Guide with its beautiful illustrations of British and European birds continues to be the favourite field guide of both ornithologists and laymen alike. For a guide to the flora you'll encounter on the North Downs Way, *The Wild Flower Key* (Warne) by Francis Rose and Clare O'Reilly, is arranged to make it easy to identify unfamiliar flowers. Another in the Collins Gem series, *Wild Flowers*, is more pocket-sized and thus more suitable for walkers.

There are also several useful field guide apps for phones. For identifying birds by their song as well as by their appearance try *Merlin Bird ID* (free), *Smart Bird ID* (free) or *Collins British Bird Guide* (£6.99). For flower identification there's *Flora incognita* (free) or *Picture This Plant Identifier* (free) while for butterflies try *Butterfly ID UK Field Guide* (£3.99). Newer iPhones have built-in plant identification – just take a photo then click on the leaf icon below it.

Getting to and from the North Downs Way

Surrey and Kent have excellent transport services and with its proximity to London the North Downs Way is easily accessible by public transport.

NATIONAL TRANSPORT

Train

You are only ever an hour or two from London on the North Downs Way with convenient and frequent train services to many places on or near the path. You can expect at least one train an hour and from some mainline stations up to four an hour. Trains to stations on or close to the North Downs Way depart from London Waterloo, London Victoria, London Charing Cross, London Bridge and, less frequently, St Pancras & St Pancras International.

All timetable and fare information can be found at **National Rail Enquiries** (🖳 nationalrail.co.uk), or through the relevant operator (see box pp42-3).

Tickets can be bought online through the relevant operator, or at 🖳 thetrainline.com. For the cheapest fares book well in advance.

Train tickets are available that include bus travel at your destination: see the Plusbus website (🖳 plusbus.info). If you think you'll want a taxi when you arrive look at 🖳 traintaxi.co.uk or consult the town guides in this book, many of which have taxi numbers in their transport sections.

Coach

National Express (🖳 nationalexpress.com) is the principal coach (long-distance bus) operator in Britain. Coach travel is generally cheaper but takes longer than travel by train.

Whilst there are excellent services between London, Dover and Canterbury (London to Dover/Deal via Canterbury NX007; London to Ramsgate via Canterbury NX022) there are none to Farnham but the NX030 calls at Guildford (London to Fareham via Portsmouth).

Car

The south-east of England is criss-crossed by roads and motorways and the North Downs Way itself crosses the M25, M20, M23 and M2 on its journey east to Dover. Whilst driving might seem an easy option, long-term parking will be more of an issue. With such an abundance of public transport in this region, it's usually best to leave the car at home.

LOCAL TRANSPORT

The number of railway stations and bus services on or close to the route opens up the possibility of linear walks throughout the length of the North Downs Way lasting several hours or days without needing a car. The map on pp46-7 gives an overview of the principal direct routes of use to walkers and an indication of the frequency of services in both directions and who you should contact for further information.

❑ GETTING TO BRITAIN

Air

There are plenty of cheap flights to London's airports. The most convenient for the trail are **Heathrow** (💻 heathrow.com) – from where you can take the RailAir RA2 (💻 www.railair.com/timetables/RA2) coach service from Terminal 3, 2 or 5 to Woking (2/hr) or to Guildford (1/hr), or the London Underground to Waterloo and onwards to Farnham – and **Gatwick Airport** (💻 gatwickairport.com), with train and bus services to Redhill. **London City Airport** (💻 londoncityairport.com) has good transport links on the Docklands Light Railway to Bank station on the London Underground with easy connections to London Waterloo and onwards to Farnham.

Far less convenient is **Luton** (💻 london-luton.co.uk); there is the Luton Dart shuttle (💻 london-luton.co.uk/luton-dart; 24hrs/day; £4.90) from the airport to Luton Airport Parkway railway station and from there trains (Thameslink see box p43 and East Midland Railway 💻 eastmidlandsrailway.co.uk; both daily 2/hr) run to London St Pancras International, from where you can take the London Underground to Waterloo. Thameslink (see box p43) also stops at Redhill from where there are rail connections to stations on the North Downs Way. Easybus (💻 easybus.com), National Express (💻 nationalexpress.com), Megabus (💻 uk.megabus.com) and Greenline (💻 arrivabus.co.uk/greenline) coaches go to London Victoria from Luton.

The quickest way from **Stansted** (💻 stanstedairport.com) is to take the Stansted Express rail service to London Liverpool Street and then London Underground to Waterloo and onwards to the start of the trail.

From Europe by train

Eurostar (💻 eurostar.com), the high speed rail link, travels between Paris, Brussels and Amsterdam to London's St Pancras International, from where there are connections to the London Underground to reach all other main railway stations in London. For more information about rail services to the UK contact Railteam (💻 railteam.eu).

From Europe by coach (bus)

Flixbus (💻 flixbus.com) have taken over where Eurolines left off, with a huge network of long-distance coach (bus) services connecting mainland Europe to London.

From Europe by ferry and car

The shortest sea crossing from Europe is Calais–Dover and regular services are run by **DFDS Seaways** (💻 dfds.com) and **P&O Ferries** (💻 poferries.com); the journey takes about 90 minutes. There are also ferry services from Bilbao and Santander and ports in western France to Portsmouth, as well as Santander and Roscoff to Plymouth, and Cherbourg to Poole. Look at 💻 ferrysavers.com or 💻 directferries.com for a full list of companies and services.

LeShuttle (💻 leshuttle.com), formerly Eurotunnel, is the train service for vehicles via the Channel Tunnel between Calais and Folkestone.

For general information about bus links, for this edition we found the website with the most up-to-date, comprehensive (as it includes all stops) and accurate information was 🖳 bustimes.org. Alternatively see the relevant operator's website (see box pp44-5 for contact details), or the information service traveline (🖳 traveline.info), which has public transport information for the whole of the UK. Check the services you might use before you plan to travel as bus services, in particular, may be cancelled. Note that on many bus routes there is no Sunday

❑ RAIL SERVICES

Note: not all stops are listed. Places in **bold** *are on or very near the North Downs Way.*

South Western Railway (🖳 southwesternrailway.com)

- London Waterloo to Alton via Clapham Junction, Woking, Aldershot & **Farnham**, Mon-Sat 2/hr, Sun 1/hr
- London Waterloo to **Guildford** via Clapham Junction, Epsom & Leatherhead, daily 1/hr
- London Waterloo to **Guildford** via Woking, daily 2/hr, Sun services call at Clapham Junction
- London Waterloo to Portsmouth Harbour via Woking & **Guildford**, daily 2/hr
- London Waterloo to **Guildford** via Clapham Junction & Effingham Junction, Mon-Sat 3/hr, Sun 2/hr
- London Waterloo to Dorking via Clapham Junction, Epsom, Leatherhead & **Box Hill & Westhumble**, daily 1/hr
- Ascot to **Guildford** via Aldershot, Mon-Sat 2/hr, Sun 1/hr
- **Guildford** to **Farnham** via Aldershot, Mon-Sat 2/hr

Southern Railway (🖳 southernrailway.com)

Note: Monday to Friday some services are operated by Thameslink

- London Victoria to Horsham via Clapham Junction, Sutton, Epsom, Leatherhead, **Box Hill & Westhumble** & **Dorking**, Mon-Sat 1/hr
- London Victoria to East Grinstead via Clapham Junction, East Croydon, **Oxted** & Hurst Green, daily 1-2/hr
- London Victoria to Reigate via Clapham Junction & **Redhill**, Mon-Sat 2/hr, Sun 1hr
- London Bridge to Uckfield via East Croydon, **Oxted**, Hurst Green, Edenbridge Town & Crowborough, Mon-Sat 1/hr, East Croydon to Uckfield Sun 1/hr
- Eastbourn to Ashford International via Hastings, daily 1/hr

GWR (🖳 gwr.com)

- Gatwick Airport to Reading via **Redhill**, Reigate, Betchworth (Mon-Sat 10-13/day, Sun 9/day), Dorking Deepdene, **Dorking West** (Mon-Sat 10-13/day, Sun 8/day), **Chilworth** (Mon-Sat 10-12/day, Sun 9/day), **Shalford** & **Guildford**, Mon-Sat 1-2/hr unless specified

South Eastern Railway (🖳 southeasternrailway.co.uk)

- London Charing Cross to **Dover Priory** via Waterloo East, London Bridge, Tonbridge, Ashford International & Folkestone (West & Central), daily 1/hr service, or a limited one. Train services are better, Kemsing (South Eastern Railway) being the only station not to have any trains on a Sunday.

At the time of writing single bus fares are capped at £3 until the end of 2025. Services are sometimes infrequent so you may find it cheaper and more convenient to take a taxi for short hops, especially if there are two or more of you. Taxi fares generally cost a few pounds minimum charge with a per-mile charge thereafter.

Also note that owing to the government's planned renationalisation of the railways, the companies below may eventually be rebranded 'GBR'.

South Eastern Railway [*cont'd*]

- London Charing Cross to Ramsgate via Waterloo East, London Bridge, Tonbridge, Ashford International, **Wye**, **Chilham**, Chartham & **Canterbury West**, daily 1/hr
- London Charing Cross to Maidstone East via London Bridge, **Otford** & **Borough Green & Wrotham**, Mon-Sat 1/hr
- London Charing Cross to Sevenoaks via Waterloo East, London Bridge, Orpington, **Knockholt** & **Dunton Green**, daily 1-2/hr
- London Victoria to Ashford International via Bromley South, Swanley, **Otford**, **Kemsing** (Mon-Sat only), **Borough Green & Wrotham**, Maidstone East, Bearsted (for Leeds Castle), **Hollingbourne**, **Harrietsham**, **Lenham** & Charing, Mon-Fri 1-2/hr, Sat & Sun 1/hr
- London Victoria to Ramsgate via Bromley South, **Rochester**, Chatham, Gillingham & Faversham, Mon-Sat 2/hr, Sun 1/hr
- London Victoria to Gillingham via Bromley South, Sole Street, **Rochester** & Chatham, Mon-Fri 2/hr, Sat 1/hr
- London Victoria to Dover Priory via Bromley South, **Rochester**, Chatham, Gillingham, Sittingbourne, Faversham, **Canterbury East**, **Bekesbourne** & **Shepherds Well**, daily 1/hr
- St Pancras International to Ramsgate via **Rochester**, Chatham, Gillingham, Sittingbourne & Faversham, daily 1/hr
- St Pancras International to Ramsgate via Ebbsfleet International, Ashford International, Folkestone West, **Dover Priory** & Sandwich, daily 1/hr
- Strood to Paddock Wood via **Cuxton**, **Aylesford** & Maidstone West, Mon-Sat 2/hr, Sun 1/hr (change at Paddock Wood for Tonbridge)

Thameslink Railway (💻 thameslinkrailway.com)

- West Hampstead Thameslink to Sevenoaks via St Pancras International, London Blackfriars, Bromley South, Swanley & **Otford**, Mon-Fri peak times from St Pancras, rest of day from Blackfriars; Sat & Sun 2/hr from Blackfriars only
- Bedford to Rainham (Kent) via Luton Airport Parkway, St Pancras International, Strood & **Rochester**, Mon-Sat 2/hr, Sun from St Pancras only 2/hr
- St Pancras to Three Bridges via London Bridge, **Redhill** & Gatwick Airport, Mon-Sat 1/hr, Sun 1/hr from London Bridge only 1/hr (see also Southern)
- St Pancras to Rainham via London Bridge, Dartford, Gravesend, Strood, **Rochester**, Chatham & Gillingham, daily 1/hr
- St Pancras International to Horsham via London Bridge, East Croydon, **Merstham**, **Redhill** & Gatwick Airport, Mon-Sat 2/hr, Sun 1/hr

❑ LOCAL BUS SERVICES

[see maps p46-7]

Note: not all stops are listed for all routes.

No	Operator	Route and frequency details
1A	Stagecoach	Chartham to **Canterbury**, Mon-Fri 8/day, Sat 6/day
1X	Stagecoach	Ashford to **Canterbury** via **Chilham** & Chartham, Mon-Fri 9/day, Sat 8/day
3	Stagecoach	Faversham to **Canterbury**, daily 1/hr
X3	Stagecoach	**Canterbury** to Maidstone via Faversham (1/day via **Detling**), Mon-Sat 1/hr
4/5	Stagecoach	Aldershot to **Farnham**, Mon-Sat 2/hr, Sun 1/hr (routes vary so check in advance)
10X	Stagecoach	Maidstone to Ashford via **Hollingbourne**, **Harrietsham**, **Lenham** & **Charing**, Mon-Fri 13/day, Sat 11/day
13/14	Nu-Venture	**Hollingbourne** to Maidstone via Leeds Castle, Mon-Fri 5-6/day
14	Stagecoach	Ashford to **Wye**, Mon-Fri 4/day
15	Stagecoach	**Canterbury** to **Dover**, Mon-Sat 3/hr, Sun 13/day
16	Stagecoach	**Canterbury** to Folkestone, Mon-Sat 3/hr, Sun 2/hr
17	Stagecoach	**Canterbury** to Folkestone via **Bridge**, Mon-Sat approx 1/hr, Sun 4/day
18	Stagecoach	**Canterbury** to Hythe via **Postling**, Mon-Sat 4/day
19	Stagecoach	Aldershot to Haslemere via **Farnham**, Mon-Sat 1/hr
20	Stagecoach	Aldershot to **Guildford**, daily 3/hr
21	Metrobus	Crawley to Epsom via **Dorking**, Box Hill & Leatherhead, Mon-Sat 5/day plus 1/day to Leatherhead
22	Metrobus	Crawley to Holmbury St Mary via Gatwick Airport, **Dorking**, Westcott, **Shere** (1/day term-time only), Abinger Hammer & Abinger Common, Mon-Fri 4/day plus 1/day from Gatwick Airport
24	Compass	Cranleigh to **Guildford** via **Shalford**, Mon-Fri 6/day, Sat 5/day
25	Compass	Cranleigh to **Guildford** via **Shere** & **Newlands Corner**, Mon-Fri 4/day
32	Compass	**Guildford** to **Redhill** via **Shalford**, **Chilworth**, **Albury**, **Shere**, Gomshall, Abinger Hammer, Westcott, **Dorking**, Betchworth & **Reigate**, Mon-Sat 9/day (Sun/bank hol 4/day operated by Metrobus)
46	Stagecoach	**Farnham** to **Guildford** via Elstead, Godalming & **Compton**, Mon-Sat 11/day
53	Stagecoach	Ewhurst to **Guildford** via Cranleigh & **Shalford**, daily 1/hr
63	Stagecoach	Horsham to **Guildford** via Cranleigh & **Shalford**, Mon-Sat 1/hr
65	Stagecoach	Alton to **Guildford** via **Farnham** & Puttenham, daily 1/hr
142	Nu-Venture	Chatham circular route via **Rochester**, **Kit's Coty** & **Blue Bell Hill**, Mon-Sat 2-3/day

151	Nu-Venture	Chatham to West Malling via **Rochester**, Strood & **Cuxton**, Mon-Fri 11/day, Sat 7/day, Sun 5/day
155	Arriva	Chatham to Borstal via **Rochester**, daily 8-10/day
172	Nu-Venture	Chatham to Wainscott via **Rochester** & Strood, Mon-Fri 3/day
173/197	Nu-Venture	Chatham to Strood via **Rochester**, Mon-Sat 5-7/day
222	Autocar	Tonbridge to **Borough Green**, Mon-Fri 5/day, 1-2/day continue to/start from **Wrotham**
236	Metrobus	East Grinstead to **Oxted** via Lingfield & **Westerham**, Mon-Fri 4/day
246	TfL	Bromley to **Westerham** via Hayes & Biggin Hill, Mon-Sat 2/hr, Sun 1/hr
306	Red Route	Gravesend to **Trosley Country Park** (Vigo Village), Mon-Sat 2/day
308	Red Route	Gravesend to Sevenoaks via **Trosley Country Park** (Vigo Village), Mon-Sat 5-6/day
400	Metrobus	East Grinstead to Caterham via Crawley, Gatwick Airport & **Redhill**, Mon-Sat approx 1/hr, Sun 9/day
405	TfL	**Redhill** to Croydon via **Merstham** & Purley, Mon-Sat 3-4/hr, Sun 2/hr
410	Metrobus	**Redhill** to Hurst Green via **Oxted**, Mon-Sat 2/hr, Sun 8/day
420	Metrobus	Crawley to Sutton via Gatwick Airport, **Redhill** & **Reigate**, Mon-Fri 10/day, Sat 13/day, Sun 5/day
430/435	Metrobus	**Merstham** circular route via **Redhill** & **Reigate**, Mon-Sat 2/hr, Sun 1/hr
460	Metrobus	Crawley to Epsom via Gatwick Airport, **Redhill** & **Reigate**, Mon-Sat approx 1/hr, Sun 6/day
465	TfL	Kingston-upon-Thames to Dorking via **Denbies Wine Estate**, Mon-Sat 2/hr, Sun 1/hr
594/595	Metrobus	**Oxted** to **Westerham**, Mon-Fri 12/day, Sat 9/day
666	Stagecoach	Ashford to Faversham via **Boughton Lees** & **Canterbury**, Mon-Fri 10/day, Sat 6/day

Operator contact details

- **Arriva Kent & Surrey** (🖳 arrivabus.co.uk/kent-and-surrey)
- **Autocar Bus & Coach Services** (☎ 01892-833830)
- **Compass Travel** (🖳 compass-travel.co.uk)
- **Go Bus** (🖳 go-coach.co.uk)
- **Metrobus** (☎ 01273 886200, 🖳 metrobus.co.uk)
- **Nu-Venture** (☎ 01622-882288, 🖳 nu-venture.online)
- **Red Route Buses** (🖳 redroutebuses.co.uk)
- **Stagecoach** (🖳 stagecoachbus.com/timetables)
- **TfL** (🖳 tfl.gov.uk)

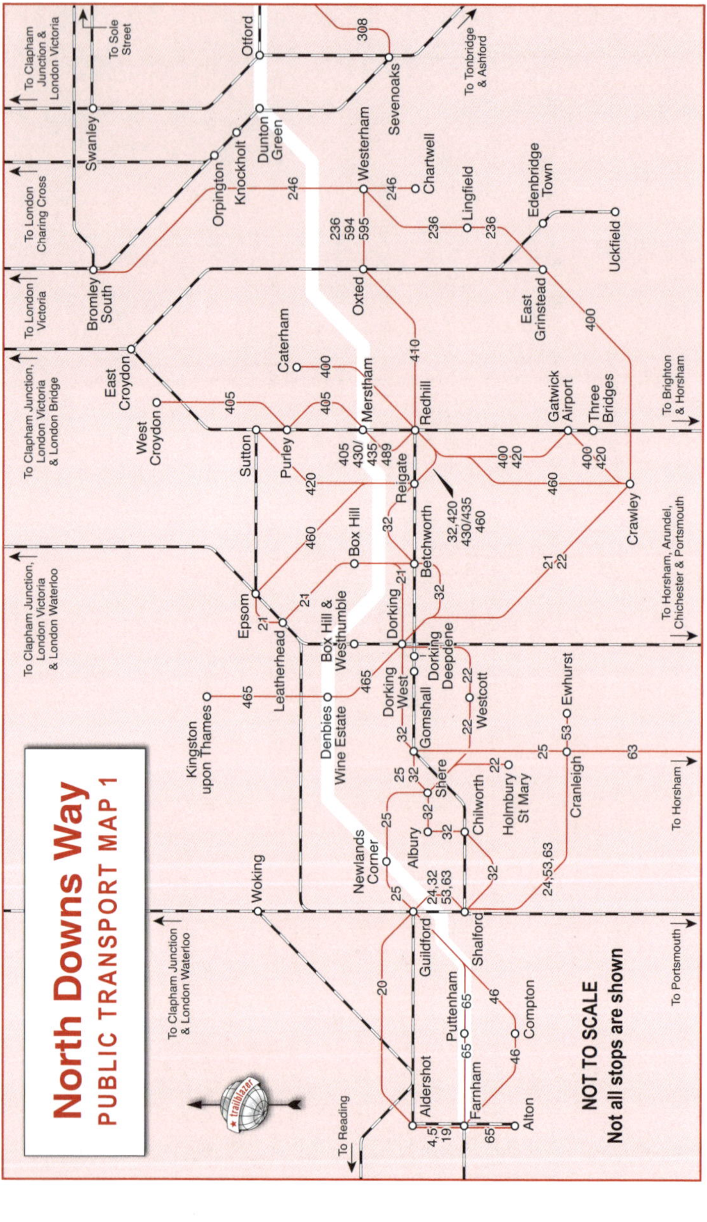
North Downs Way
PUBLIC TRANSPORT MAP 1
NOT TO SCALE
Not all stops are shown
trailblazer
To Clapham Junction & London Victoria
To Sole Street
To London Charing Cross
To London Victoria
To Clapham Junction, London Victoria & London Bridge
To Clapham Junction, London Victoria & London Waterloo
To Clapham Junction & London Waterloo
To Reading
To Tonbridge & Ashford
To Brighton & Horsham
To Horsham, Arundel, Chichester & Portsmouth
To Horsham
To Portsmouth
Swanley
Otford
Dunton Green
Knockholt
Orpington
Sevenoaks
Westerham
Chartwell
Lingfield
Edenbridge Town
Uckfield
Bromley South
Oxted
East Grinstead
East Croydon
West Croydon
Caterham
Sutton
Purley
Merstham
Redhill
Gatwick Airport
Three Bridges
Reigate
Crawley
Box Hill
Betchworth
Epsom
Leatherhead
Box Hill & Westhumble
Dorking
Dorking Deepdene
Dorking West
Kingston upon Thames
Denbies Wine Estate
Gomshall
Westcott
Ewhurst
Shere
Holmbury St Mary
Cranleigh
Chilworth
Albury
Newlands Corner
Woking
Guildford
Shalford
Puttenham
Compton
Aldershot
Farnham
Alton
308
246
236 594 595
236
400
410
405
420
405/ 430/ 435 489
400 420
460
32,420 430/435 460
32
21
21 22
465
22
53
25
63
24,32 53,63
24,53,63
20
65
46
4,5 19

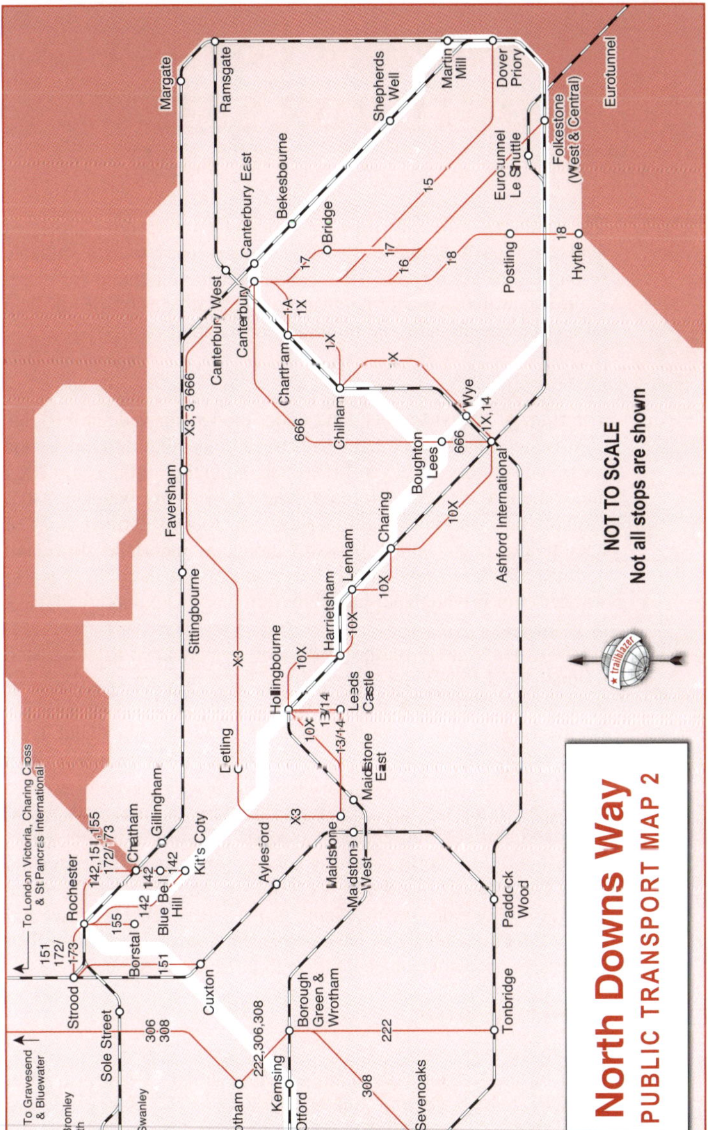
North Downs Way
PUBLIC TRANSPORT MAP 2
NOT TO SCALE
Not all stops are shown
To London Victoria, Charing Cross & St Pancras International
To Gravesend & Bluewater
To Bromley South
To Swanley
Strood
Rochester
Chatham
Gillingham
Borstal
Blue Bell Hill
Kit's Coty
Cuxton
Sole Street
Wrotham
Kemsing
Otford
Sevenoaks
Borough Green & Wrotham
Aylesford
Maidstone West
Maidstone East
Tonbridge
Paddock Wood
Detling
Hollingbourne
Leeds Castle
Harrietsham
Lenham
Charing
Ashford International
Boughton Lees
Wye
Chilham
Chartham
Canterbury
Canterbury West
Canterbury East
Bridge
Bekesbourne
Shepherds Well
Martin Mill
Dover Priory
Postling
Hythe
Eurotunnel Le Shuttle
Folkestone (West & Central)
Eurotunnel
Faversham
Sittingbourne
Margate
Ramsgate
X3, 3, 666
666
10X
13/14
1A
1X
1X, 14
15
16
17
18
142
151
155
172/173
222
222,306,308
306
308
X3

2 MINIMUM IMPACT & OUTDOOR SAFETY

The south-east of England is a congested place and having protected landscapes such as the North Downs to get away to is a valuable resource. The countryside is becoming ever more popular for recreation and walkers should be aware of their responsibilities to help protect the countryside and minimise their impact on it.

ACCESS

The right of access to open land under the Countryside and Rights of Way Act 2000 (CRoW), dubbed 'freedom or right to roam' by the press and walkers alike, was first rolled out in the south-east in 2004 and came into effect in full throughout England and Wales in 2005. Walkers have the legal right to access on foot to defined areas of uncultivated open country, basically mountain, moorland, downland and heathland. However, the act does **not** give walkers the right to wander over private land, including farmland, woodland, paddocks or gardens.

So when you are on the North Downs Way keep to designated footpaths and follow the 'acorn' signs. There are, however, areas of open access land adjacent to the trail, notably land managed by the National Trust, the Forestry Commission and the Woodland Trust and areas of registered common land such as St Martha's Hill (Map 7, p81) and Newlands Corner (Map 8, p83).

Rights of access have also been created over areas such as the open land north of Hollingbourne (see Map 42, p145). But the effect of the Act on the North Downs is not so significant when compared to the large tracts of land now accessible in the Peak District, or the opening up of land on the South Downs between Poynings and Upper Beeding which now have permanent access rights rather than permissive access which could be withdrawn at any time.

ECONOMIC IMPACT

Buy local

Rural businesses and communities in Britain have been hit hard in recent years by a seemingly endless series of crises. Most people are aware of the Countryside Code – not dropping litter and closing the gate behind you are still as pertinent as ever – but in light of the economic pressures that local countryside businesses are under, there is something else you can do: buy local. Look and ask for local produce to buy and eat. Not only does this cut down on the amount of pollution and congestion that the transportation of food creates – so-called 'food miles' – but also ensures that you are supporting local farmers and producers, the very people who have moulded the countryside you have come to see and who are in the best position to protect it.

Money spent at local level perhaps in a market, or at the greengrocer, or in an independent pub – has a far greater impact for good in that community than the equivalent spent in a branch of a national chain store or restaurant. It would be going too far to advocate that walkers boycott the larger supermarkets, which after all do provide local employment, but it's worth remembering that smaller businesses in rural communities rely heavily on visitors for their very existence. If we want to keep these local shops and post offices, we must use them.

> ❑ **THE COUNTRYSIDE CODE**
>
> **Respect other people**
> - Be considerate to those living and working in the countryside
> - Leave gates & property as you find them
> - Do not block access to gateways or driveways when parking
> - Follow local signs and keep to marked paths, even if they're muddy
>
> **Protect the environment**
> - Take all your litter home
> - Do not light fires
> - Always keep dogs under control and in sight.
> - Dog poo – bag it and bin it in any public waste bin
> - Care for nature – do not cause damage or disturbance
>
> **Enjoy the outdoors**
> - Check your route and local conditions
> - Plan your adventure – know what to expect and what you can do

ENVIRONMENTAL IMPACT

By choosing a walking holiday you are taking a positive step towards minimising your impact on the environment. The following are some ideas on how you can go a few steps further while walking the North Downs Way.

Use public transport whenever possible

Public transport to and along the North Downs Way is generally excellent with just about everywhere served by at least one bus or train; see pp42-7 for more details. Public transport is always preferable to using private cars as it benefits everyone: visitors, locals and the environment.

Never leave litter

Leaving litter shows disrespect for the natural world and others coming after you. As well as being unsightly litter pollutes the environment and can be dangerous to farm animals. Please carry a plastic bag so you can dispose of your rubbish in a bin in the next village. It would be very helpful if you could pick up litter left by other people too.

- **Is it OK if it's biodegradable?** No. Would you like to see litter at your picnic spot? When was the last time you saw a citrus grove on the North Downs Way? It spoils the natural beauty of the trail. Apple cores, banana skins, orange peel and the like are unsightly, encourage flies, ants and wasps and ruin a picnic spot.

• **The lasting impact of litter** A piece of orange peel left on the ground takes six months to decompose; silver foil 18 months; a plastic bag 10 years and an aluminium can 85 years. As for clothing, while natural fibres will decompose within 5 years, synthetics are non-biodegradable and can take 200 years or more.

Erosion

• **Stay on the main trail** The effect of your footsteps may seem minuscule but when they are multiplied by several thousand walkers each year they become rather more significant.

Avoid taking shortcuts, widening the trail or taking more than one path; your boots will be followed by many others. This is particularly true on the North Downs Way which is heavily used by local day walkers.

• **Consider walking out of season** It's possible to walk the North Downs Way at any time of year but it's particularly popular in spring and summer. Consider walking at less busy times – autumn and mid-winter can be just as enjoyable and sometimes afford better views. And it may be a more relaxing experience with fewer people on the path and less competition for accommodation.

• **Respect all wildlife** Care for all wildlife you come across along the path; it has as much right to be there as you. Leave wild flowers so the next people who pass can enjoy them too. If you want to identify them photograph them and use an app (see p39). Don't break branches off or damage trees in any way.

If you come across wildlife keep your distance and don't watch for too long. Your presence can cause considerable stress, particularly if the adults are with young, or in winter when the weather is harsh and food is scarce.

Young birds and animals aren't usually abandoned – just leave them alone and their mothers will return.

The code of the outdoor loo

You're never far from a proper toilet on the North Downs Way, be it in a village or at a café or refreshment kiosk, but the chances are you will need to 'go' outdoors at some point.

• **Where to go** Wherever possible use a toilet. Where there are public toilets on the trail they are marked on the trail maps in this guide and you will also find facilities in pubs, cafés and campsites along the North Downs Way.

If you do have to go outdoors choose a site at least 30 metres away from running water and 200 metres away from the trail. Use a trowel or stick to dig a small hole about 15cm (6 inches) deep to bury your excrement in. It decomposes quicker when in contact with the top layer of soil or leaf mould. Do not squash it under rocks as this slows down the composting process.

• **Toilet paper and sanitary towels** These take a long time to decompose whether buried or not and may be dug up by animals and then blow into water sources or onto the path. To avoid this pack them out: put the used items in a paper bag which you then place inside a plastic bag (or two). Then simply empty the contents of the paper bag at the next toilet you come across and throw the bag away.

Wild camping

There is no general right to camp on land in England. You must first obtain the permission of the landowner and in the absence of this you may be trespassing. Camping outside official sites on National Trust land is against its bye-laws. Much of the North Downs Way is heavily wooded. Most open land is private farmland and much of this is arable cropland. The opportunities for wild camping are therefore limited. But wild camping provides the walker with a uniquely fulfilling experience of living in a simple and sustainable way in which the habitual activities of cooking, eating, washing and sleeping take on greater importance. Follow these suggestions:

- **Be discreet** Camp alone or in small groups, spend only one night in each place and pitch your tent, tarp or bivvy late and move off early.
- **Never light a fire** The deep burn caused by camp fires, no matter how small, damages the turf which can take years to recover. Cook on a camp stove instead.
- **Don't use soap or detergent** There's no need to use soap; even biodegradable soaps and detergents pollute streams. You won't be away from a shower for more than a day or so. Wash up without detergent; use a plastic or metal scourer, or failing that, a handful of fine pebbles or some bracken or grass.
- **Leave no trace** Learn the skill of moving on without leaving any sign of having been there: no moved rocks, ripped up vegetation or dug drainage ditches. Make a final check of your campsite before departing; pick up any litter that you or anyone else has left, so leaving the place in a better state than you found it.

Outdoor safety

AVOIDANCE OF HAZARDS

The North Downs Way is not a difficult or dangerous walk and with common sense as well as good planning and preparation most hazards can be avoided. This information is just as important for those out on a day walk as for those walking the entire trail. To ensure a safe and stress-free trip **follow the Countryside Code** (see box p49) and:

- Before going out **get information** about where and when you can go;
- Check **weather forecasts** on your phone and by visiting one of the online forecasts such as 💻 bbc.co.uk/weather or 💻 metoffice.gov.uk;
- Make sure that **somebody knows your plans** for every day you are on the trail. This could be a friend or relative whom you have promised to call every night, or the owners of the B&Bs that you plan to stay in at the end of each day's walk. That way, if you fail to turn up or call that evening, they can raise the alarm;
- **Stick to the path** and avoid old quarries or taking shortcuts on steep sections of the escarpment;
- **Check your location** regularly on the map; it's unlikely that you'll lose your way on the Downs but it'll save you missing a turning to a village and the frus-

tration of retracing your steps at the end of a long day;
- Always fill your **water** bottles/pouches at every available opportunity and drink regularly;
- Make sure you have some **high-energy snacks** – fruit, nuts, or chocolate – to keep you going on the last few miles of a long day or in an emergency;
- Always carry a **torch** and **whistle** (the international distress signal is six blasts on the whistle or six flashes on a torch); a compass is not vital on this trail;
- Wear strong **boots** with good ankle support and a good grip, not trainers, and have **suitable clothes** including wet-weather gear (see pp35-6).
- Be extra vigilant with **children** and dogs (see pp203-5);
- Take a **first-aid kit** (see p37). If there is a casualty use basic first aid to treat the injury to the best of your ability. Work out exactly where you are. The What3Words **app** (💻 what3words.com) can pinpoint your location to a 3 sq m area – familiarise yourself with it before you go walking. If possible leave someone with the casualty while others go to get help if you are not able to summon help via a mobile. If there are only two people, you have a dilemma. If you decide to get help leave all spare clothing and food with the casualty. On this trail you are never far from a road, village or house where you can get help;
- In an emergency dial ☎ 999.

BLISTERS

It is important to break in new boots before embarking on a long trek. Make sure the boots are comfortable and try to avoid getting them wet on the inside. Air your feet at lunchtime, keep them clean and change your socks regularly. If you feel any hot spots stop immediately and apply Compeed or Second Skin before the blister develops. Applied at the right time it's magic stuff. If you've left it too late, do not burst the blister as this can lead to infection; dress it with any blister kit to protect it from abrasion. If the skin is broken keep the area clean with antiseptic and cover with a non-adhesive dressing material held in place with tape.

SUNBURN, HYPERTHERMIA & HEATSTROKE

Owing to climate change, summers in the UK are becoming increasingly warm, so **sunburn** can be a risk, even on overcast days. The only surefire way to avoid it is to stay wrapped up but that's not always an option. You should always wear a hat, preferably a wide-brimmed one, and use plenty of high-factor sunscreen, reapplied regularly throughout the day. Don't forget your lips, nose, the back of your neck and under your chin to protect against rays reflected from the ground.

Hyperthermia occurs when the body generates too much heat, eg heat exhaustion and heatstroke. Symptoms of **heat exhaustion** include thirst, fatigue, giddiness, a rapid pulse, raised body temperature, low urine output and, if not treated, delirium and finally a coma. The best cure is to drink plenty of water. **Heatstroke** is another matter altogether, and even more serious. A high body temperature and an absence of sweating are early indications, followed by symptoms similar to hypothermia (see above and opposite) such as a lack of co-ordination and convulsions. Coma and death will follow if treatment is not given instantly. Sponge the victim down, wrap them in wet towels, fan them, and get help immediately.

HYPOTHERMIA

Hypothermia, also known as exposure, occurs when the body can't generate enough heat to maintain its normal temperature, usually as a result of being wet, cold, unprotected from the wind, tired and hungry. The risk of hypothermia while walking on the Downs is low. However, it is worth being aware of the dangers. Hypothermia is easily avoided by wearing suitable clothing, carrying and eating enough food and drink, being aware of the weather conditions and checking the morale of your companions.

Early signs to watch for are feeling cold and tired with involuntary shivering. Find some shelter as soon as possible and warm the victim up with a hot drink and some chocolate or other high-energy food. If possible give them another warm layer of clothing and allow them to rest until feeling better.

If untreated, strange behaviour, slurring of speech and poor co-ordination will become apparent and the victim can quickly progress into unconsciousness, followed by coma and death. In the unlikely event of a severe case of hypothermia, quickly get the victim out of wind and rain, improvising a shelter if necessary. Rapid restoration of bodily warmth is essential and best achieved by bare-skin contact: someone should get into the same sleeping bag as the patient, both having stripped to their underwear with any spare clothing under or over them to build up heat. Send urgently for help.

PERSONAL SAFETY

This is an issue usually raised by women walking or travelling alone. The North Downs Way is much safer than any city and you are more likely to twist an ankle and have to hobble painfully to the nearest village than become a crime victim. However, if you do walk on your own it's all the more important to make sure someone knows your plans for the day (see p51), and take all the usual precautions such as keeping an eye on your belongings at all times.

OTHER USERS

Just under 20% of the North Downs Way is bridleway, almost the same amount is metalled road, and about 14% is classed as a byway. So you may encounter off-road vehicles. Most of the byways are in Kent. The petrolheads I've encountered (luckily not many) have stopped their engines and let me pass. Whatever you think about them in the countryside, and I don't like it, those I've met have been courteous and they were riding where they were allowed. When it comes to horses I've had many encounters with riders who are clearly over-mounted as they grimly try to control the equine equivalent of an F1 racing car. Give them a wide berth. Mountain-bikers are allowed to use bridleways and you just have to keep an eye out for the fast youthful types. Most cyclists, though, are a decent bunch. Hot spots include Newlands Corner through to Dorking.

3 THE ENVIRONMENT & NATURE

Conserving the North Downs Way

Britain is an overcrowded island, and England is the most densely populated part of it. The south-east has suffered a great deal of pressure from both over-population and competition for land use. The landscape of the North Downs in Surrey and Kent is the embankment holding back London's sprawl.

Thankfully there are several bodies at local and national level whose job it is to protect and conserve that landscape for future generations.

NATURAL ENGLAND

The official responsibilities of Natural England (🖳 gov.uk/government/organisations/natural-england) are to 'enhance biodiversity and our landscapes and wildlife in rural, urban, coastal and marine areas; promote access, recreation and public well-being, and contribute to the way natural resources are managed, so they can be enjoyed now and for future generations'. Essentially this organisation gives advice and information, designates Sites of Special Scientific Interest, National Parks, National Landscapes, manages some of the National Nature Reserves and enforces existing regulations. Natural England also manages England's National Trails.

There are 34 **National Landscapes**, previously known as Areas of Outstanding Natural Beauty (AONBs), in England, covering some 15% of the country. Their primary objective is conservation of the natural beauty of a landscape and responsibility for this falls to the local authority within whose boundary they fall. The North Downs Way passes through two: **Surrey Hills** (🖳 surreyhills.org) and **Kent Downs** (🖳 kentdowns.org.uk).

Of the 219 **national nature reserves** (NNRs) in England, only Wye Downs, at the eastern end on the southern route, is actually on the Way. **Local nature reserves** (LNRs) are designated and managed by local councils. The main wildlife sites/local nature reserves along the North Downs Way are: Colekitchen Down (off Map 10, p87), Ranmore Common, White Downs and Denbies Hillside (Map 11, p88 and Map 12, p89), Box Hill (Map 13, p91), Kemsing Downs

(Map 28, p122), Shoulder of Mutton Wood (Map 36, p133) and Blue Bell Hill (Map 38, p139) plus Wye Downs which is on the southern route.

The route also passes through other areas of protected land designated as **Sites of Special Scientific Interest** (SSSI); see for example Box Hill (p96) and Oxted Downs (Map 21, p107). There are over 4100 SSSIs in England (including 62 in Surrey and 98 in Kent), ranging in size from little pockets protecting wild-flower meadows, important nesting sites or special geological features, to vast swathes of upland, moorland and wetland. SSSIs are managed by Natural England in cooperation with their owners who are prevented from doing any work that is likely to damage the special features of the site. Many SSSIs are also either a NNR or a LNR.

Special Areas of Conservation (SAC) is an international designation which came into being as a result of the 1992 Earth Summit in Rio de Janeiro, Brazil. This European-wide network of sites is designed to promote the conservation of habitats, wild animals and plants, both on land and at sea. At the time of writing 242 land sites in England had been designated as SACs. Almost all UK SACs are based on SSSIs (although SSSIs cannot extend beyond low tide whereas SACs can).

The **Environmental Stewardship Scheme** provides financial incentives to farmers to adopt low-impact agricultural practices. Particular priority is given to applications by farmers which will help conserve and restore chalk grassland along the scarp of the North Downs Way (NDW) and between the NDW and the so-called Pilgrims' Way. Farmers are also encouraged (financially) to establish grass margins, protect historic field boundaries and create and enhance bird habitats with the assistance of the RSPB (see box p56).

There is no doubt that these designations play a vital role in safeguarding the land they cover for future generations. However, the very fact that we rely on these labels for protecting limited areas begs the question: what are we doing to the vast majority of land that remains relatively unprotected? Surely we should be aiming to protect the natural environment outside protected areas just as much as within them?

Natural England also oversees the **National Trails** (🖳 nationaltrail.co.uk) staff who are responsible for the day-to-day management and running of the North Downs Way. They employ wardens and conservation officers – many of them volunteers – to maintain the trail and they also organise guided events and publish information about the North Downs Way for the public. Natural England provides most of the funding and resources for path maintenance.

General maintenance of the trail includes such things as surface repairs, signpost and waymark installation and replacement, converting stiles to gates and installing water taps and troughs. They are also responsible for the protection of endemic species and habitats, as well as geological features, along the North Downs Way. If necessary this may involve access restrictions, especially for motorised vehicles. However, promoting public access and the appreciation of the North Downs Way's natural heritage is also of importance, as is educating locals and visitors about the significance of the environment.

Fauna and flora

MAMMALS

Mammals in Britain tend to stay well hidden, emerging to feed at dawn, twilight or night so you may only see evidence of their existence from their tracks or scat. Nevertheless, it would be very strange not to see a **rabbit** (*Oryctolagus cuniculus*) especially as the trail crosses several warrens. You may see a **hare** (*Lepus europaeus*) which is bigger, has erect black-tipped ears, and is capable of running at speeds of up to 40mph/64km to escape its predator the **fox** (*Vulpes vulpes*), one of the more adaptable of Britain's native species. Although generally nocturnal, you do occasionally see foxes during the day. They are also

❑ CAMPAIGNING/CONSERVATION ORGANISATIONS AND CHARITIES

A number of voluntary organisations started the conservation movement in the mid 19th century. They rely on public support and can concentrate their resources either on acquiring land, which can then be managed purely for conservation purposes, or on influencing political decision-makers by lobbying and campaigning.

- **National Trust** (nationaltrust.org.uk) Europe's largest conservation charity, boasting over five million members, which aims to protect, through ownership, threatened coastline, countryside, historic houses, castles and gardens, and archaeological remains for everybody to enjoy. Box Hill (see p96) is managed by the National Trust as is much of the land through which the NDW passes from Brockham to Reigate Hill (Maps 14-16).
- **Royal Society for the Protection of Birds** (RSPB; rspb.org.uk) The largest nature conservation body in Europe, with 200 reserves and over a million members.
- The umbrella organisation for the 46 wildlife trusts in the UK is **The Wildlife Trusts** (wildlifetrusts.org); two relevant to the North Downs Way are: **Surrey Wildlife Trust** (surreywildlifetrust.org), and **Kent Wildlife Trust** (kentwildlifetrust.org.uk).
- **The Countryside Charity** (formerly Campaign to Protect Rural England; CPRE; cpre.org.uk) A charity which exists to promote the beauty and diversity of rural England by encouraging the sustainable use of land and other natural resources in town and country and whose members care about the countryside and campaign for it to be protected and enhanced.
- **Woodland Trust** (www.woodlandtrust.org.uk) The trust aims to conserve, restore and re-establish native woodlands throughout the UK.
- **The Conservation Volunteers** (TCV; tcv.org.uk) Encourages people to value their environment and take practical action to improve it.
- **Common Ground** (commonground.org.uk) Organises arts and environmental events believing that celebrations are the starting point for actions to improve localities.
- **World Wide Fund for Nature** (WWF; wwf.org.uk) One of the world's largest conservation organisations, protecting endangered species and threatened habitats.
- **Friends of the Earth** (friendsoftheearth.uk) Campaigns for a better environment worldwide.

common in urban areas, of course, feeding well on our leftovers and scraps.

The **badger** (*Meles meles*), with its distinctive black and white markings, is fairly common judging by the numbers killed crossing roads on their habitual routes called runs. They live in underground setts, often dug next to a tree in the side of a bank. The **hedgehog** (*Erinaceus europaeus*), alas, is fast disappearing from the British countryside and if you do see one, it will most commonly be as roadkill.

Of the 18 species of **bat** (see 💻 bats.org.uk) in the UK, 17 actually breed here too (the 18th, the greater mouse-eared bat, is so rare it is no longer officially counted as a resident species). The tiny **pipistrelle** (*Pipistrellus pipistrellus*) is the most common and easy to spot flitting at speed over water and hedgerows picking off insects just after dusk.

There are signs that the **otter** (*Lutra lutra*) is making something of a comeback in Surrey and this is a good indication of a healthy environment. Now even Kent, the last county to see the otter reappear within its borders, has reported otters building holts on the rivers Medway and Eden.

The North American **grey squirrel** (*Sciurus carolinensis*) is constantly rustling about in the woodlands along the trail but sadly the smaller **red squirrel** (*Sciurus vulgaris*) has lost its habitat to the grey squirrel and you won't see it on the North Downs Way. There are also some species of mice, voles and shrew.

With all the woodland along the trail there's a good chance of seeing **roe deer** (*Capreolus capreolus*), a small native species that likes to inhabit woodland and may be seen grazing in fields. Early mornings are your best chance of a sighting.

BIRDS

The landscape of the North Downs is ideal for a variety of birds – the woodlands are an obvious habitat but there are also species at home on the open downs.

In woodland areas on the trail, look out for **treecreepers** (*Certhia familiaris*), **tits** (family *Paridae*, including blue, great, coal and long tailed), **nuthatches** (*Sitta europaea*) and **goldcrests** (*Regulus regulus*). These are tiny and you'll probably hear their high pitched 'see see' call in the conifers, a habitat also popular with **siskins** (*Carduelis spinus*). They'll be joined by **spotted flycatchers** (*Muscicapa striata*) in summer and **chiffchaffs** (*Phylloscopus collybita*).

You'll see a lot of **pheasant** (*Phasianus colchicus*), many of which are bred by gamekeepers for shooting; you may come across the feeding hoppers or bins deep in the woods. This encourages the bird to stay in an area and during the season (Oct-early Feb) the birds are driven from the woods by 'beaters' to fly over guns. The plumage of the male is beautiful, with distinctive red head-sides and often a glossy green-black head. The female is a dull brown.

The **woodcock** (*Scolopax rusticola*) with its long straight beak and plump body frequents damp woodland where it can lie hidden thanks to its leafy brown plumage. It is most easily sighted in the spring at dusk and dawn. This is when the males perform their courtship flight known as 'roding' which involves two distinct calls, one a low grunting noise, the other a sharp 'k-wik k-wik' call.

The most frequently seen birds of prey are the **kestrel** (*Falco tinnunculus*) and the **sparrowhawk** (*Accipter nisus*), small and agile, well able to pursue prey through forests. If you hear a loud hooting and a sharp 'ke-wick' after dark the **tawny owl** (*Strix aluco*) is responsible and you may see a **barn owl** (*Tyto alba*) with its pale plumage, white breast and heart-shaped face, glide silently by as it hunts open country along the woodland edge.

The sight and sound of a **skylark** (*Alauda arvensis*) is a joy, with its warbling song pouring out, getting higher pitched the further it spirals upwards specking out against a blue sky. A good place to see and hear skylarks is crossing Reigate Hill Golf Club (see Map 17, p102) but they are common along the open land of the North Downs Way.

Although it's more common on the downland of the South Downs Way you may catch sight of the **stonechat** (*Saxicola torquata*), a colourful little bird with a deep orange breast and a black head. They are easily identified by their habit of flitting from the top of one bush to another, only pausing to call out across the fields. The call sounds much like the sound of two stones being struck together, hence the name.

One of the most attractive birds the Downs walker might spot, usually seen feeding on open arable farmland, is the **lapwing** (*Vanellus vanellus*), which is also known as the peewit after its characteristic call. It has long legs, a short bill and a distinctive long head crest. Sadly, this attractive bird is declining in numbers. The name comes from its lilting flight, frequently changing direction with its large rounded wings. It is also identified by a white belly, black and white head, black throat patch and distinctive dark green wings that look black from a distance.

The **yellowhammer** (*Emberiza citrinella*), also known as the yellow bunting, can sometimes be seen perched on the top of gorse bushes. Most field guides to birds along with most old romantic country folk will claim that the distinctive song of the yellowhammer sounds like it's saying 'a little bit of bread and no cheese'. At a push they are right but the yellowhammer is certainly no talking parrot.

If you see a **kingfisher** (*Alcedo atthis*) you are in for a treat. Likely places are along the river Wey and the Mole but don't blink – these vivid blue birds with a long spiked beak streak past just above the water when disturbed.

The **green woodpecker** (*Picus viridis*) is not all green, sporting a bright red and black head. Green woodpeckers are sometimes spotted clinging to a vertical tree trunk or feeding on the ground in open fields. The most common view, however, is as the bird flies away when disturbed. The undulating flight pattern of the woodpecker is characterised by rapid wing beats as the bird rises followed by a pause when the bird slowly drops. This is accompanied by a loud laughing call that has earned the bird its old English name of 'yaffle'.

REPTILES

Reptiles have had a bad rap ever since slithering into the Garden of Eden. Britain's only poisonous snake, the **adder** (*Vipera berus*) is recognised by its zig-zag body pattern. They pose very little risk to walkers but dogs can get bitten when snakes come out of hibernation to warm themselves, often on a sunny path. They only bite when provoked, preferring to hide instead, and the venom is designed to kill small mammals such as mice, voles and shrews, so deaths in humans are very rare (14 attributed to adder bites since 1876) but a bite can be extremely unpleasant and occasionally dangerous for children or the elderly. Adders are a measure of the health of an environment and Kent Reptile & Amphibian Group (kentarg.org) has projects in Kent recording their distribution. The **common lizard** (*Lacerta vivipara*) may sometimes be seen basking in the sun and is harmless.

BUTTERFLIES

Two species that are dependant on the chalk grassland for their survival are the **Adonis blue** (*Polyommatus bellargus*) and the **chalk hill blue** (*Polyommatus coridon*). Both feed on horseshoe vetch and August is a good time to spot them. The best butterfly spotting is on Box Hill where over two-thirds of the British butterfly species have been recorded.

Two species you may see are the **brimstone** (*Gonepteryx rhamni*) and the less common **white admiral** (*Limenitis camilla*) which is in fact predominantly black with white banded wings. Look for it on woodland edges and in brambles where it feeds on honeysuckle. The male brimstone is easy to identify – it's bright yellow. The name butterfly may have come from this and it's said the brighter the brimstone the better the summer will be. Expect to see it along Albury Downs (see Map 8, p83).

Chances are you'll see, at some point on the walk, the familiar orange-winged **small tortoiseshell** (*Aglais urticae*) common in many gardens and urban parks.

TREES

The number of trees and the amount of woodland along the North Downs Way are a striking feature of this walk. Surrey is England's most wooded county but since 1600 much of its ancient woodland has been felled for fuel and building material or cleared for agriculture.

Since the mid 20th century, 88% of coppiced woodland has disappeared. But coppicing and old woodland skills are making a comeback and the northern slopes of the North Downs Way remain heavily wooded.

Much of the woodland is mixed deciduous, historically made up largely of **oak** (*Quercus petraea*) and **ash** (*Fraxinus excelsior*), although that is changing with the inexorable spread of the fungal disease 'ash dieback' which has been killing ash trees in the UK since 2012.

The **beech** (*Fagus sylvatica*) with its thick, silvery trunk is one of the most attractive native trees. It can grow to a height of forty metres with the high canopies blocking out much of the light. As a result the floors of beech woodlands tend to be fairly bare of vegetation. They favour well-drained soil, hence their liking for the steep scarp slope. In autumn the colours of the turning leaves can be quite spectacular.

Other trees that flourish include **silver birch** *(Betula pendula*) and **hazel** (*Corylus avellana*) which has traditionally been used for coppicing. There is frequent coppicing carried out in King's Wood (see Map 51, p159). The trees are cut off at ground level every few years yielding many slender, straight and pliable branches used for making charcoal, fences, hurdles, bean poles, barrels and by some as dowsing rods for water divining.

The **alder** (*Alnus glutinosa*) is a tree which thrives near reliable sources of water and thus is often found along riverbanks. The River Mole is known for its picturesque stands of alders. The **whitebeam** (*Sorbus aria*), though not a common tree, can be seen in parts of Surrey along the trail. It gets its name from the white mealy down which covers the undersides of the leaves; beam is Saxon for 'tree'.

Famous for its life expectancy, lasting for well over 1000 years in some cases, the **common yew** (*Taxus baccata*) is abundant in churchyards but there are also natural stands among beech woodland. The dark glossy needles are quite distinctive as is the flaky red bark of the often gnarled and twisted old trunks and branches. The bright red berries are poisonous if eaten, though the taxine they contain has been used to make a drug for cancer treatment.

Hawthorn (Crataegus monogyna) is common in hedgerows and a valuable supply of berries for birds as is **holly** (*Ilex aquifolium*). Solitary hawthorn trees are also associated with spirits and fairies.

At Box Hill there are fine stands of **box** (*Buxus sempervirens*) after which it is named. This is one of the few places in Britain where the box grows wild: until the advent of box blight it was more often seen neatly clipped in gardens. Box is the hardest and heaviest of all European woods, the only one which does not float in water.

Many of the woods are owned and cared for by the National Trust, the most significant being Denbies Hillside (see Map 12, p89) and Box Hill (Map 13, p91). Kemsing Parish Council owns Kemsing Down Nature Reserve where in addition to woodland there are important chalk grassland and scrub habitats.

FLOWERS

Woodland and hedgerows

Spring is the time to come and see the rich displays of colour on the North Downs Way. From March to May **bluebells** (*Hyacinthoides non-scripta*) proliferate on the woodland floor along the North Downs Way forming large carpets of bright blue, bell-shaped flowers.

❏ UNUSUAL INSECTS

Perhaps the most unusual insect on the North Downs Way is the **glow worm** (*Lampyris noctiluca*). It's not actually a worm but a beetle and related to the firefly. The best time to see these creatures is at night (10pm to midnight), between mid June and mid July, when the female uses her vivid glow to attract males. The light glows like a luminous watch dial and is caused by a chemical reaction on the underside of the adult female. Unlike fireflies the glow can't be switched on and off instantly but takes several minutes to turn on and off. A good place to see them is Box Hill (Map 13, p91); visit 🖳 glowworms.org.uk for lots more information.

Other common spring woodland flowers are the pink-tinged **wood anemone** (*Anemone nemorosa*) and the yellow clump-forming **primrose** (*Primula vulgaris*). The feathery **Travellers' Joy** (*Clematis vitalba*) has pale-cream fluffy blooms in autumn – hence its other name **old man's beard** – and twists through hedgerow and trees. Another climber is the **honeysuckle** (*Lonicera periclymemum*), a valuable butterfly food plant. A member of the carrot family, but not edible, is Queen Anne's Lace or **cow parsley**, with its white flowers covering banks and verges from early summer. **Red campion** (*Silene dioica*) is a decorative, vivid pink flower with five petals and is common on the path edge between March and October. The pretty pink geranium **herb robert** flowers through to September.

At the woodland edge and in scrubland you will also find **bramble** (*Rubus fruticosus*), a common vigorous shrub; edible blackberry fruits ripen from late summer into autumn. They can be quite tart and very pippy with a free-running and staining purple juice. Fairly common in scrubland and on woodland edges is the **dog rose** (*Rosa canina*) which has a large pink flower, the fruits or 'hips' of which are rich in Vitamin C and can be used to make the delicious rose-hip syrup.

Other flowering plants to look for in wooded areas and in hedgerows include the tall **foxglove** (*Digitalis purpurea*) with its trumpet-like flowers and **forget-me-not** (*Myosotis arvensis*) with tiny, delicate blue flowers.

Perhaps the most aromatic plant is **wild garlic** (*Allium ursinum*) whose broad pointed leaves release an onion bouquet when crushed. This plant carpets the verge of War Coppice Rd (see Map 19, p104) and is abundant in Marden Park and Church Woods (see Map 20, p105). Its early summer white, star-like flowers, held high on a stem, add a splash of colour to the woodland floor.

The chalk grassland

The flowers of the chalk grassland are a hardy group. A farmer tells me that to grow anything well there you'd need rain every day and a dose of manure on Sundays. Battered by wind and grazed by sheep and rabbits, they eke out an existence in a poor, thin chalk soil. The best way to look at them is up close and personal so drop to your knees at the top of Box Hill (see Map 13, p91) or on

Oxted Downs (see Map 21, p107). They've all adapted to the poor soil and a relatively harsh environment. The dominant grass, **sheep's fescue** (*Festuca ovina*), has folded leaves to protect its delicate stomata, openings that allow carbon dioxide and light to pass through for photosynthesis, and the leaf is narrow to reduce loss of water.

The best defence against sheep and rabbits is to grow low to the ground and form a mat. So rosette leaves are common like those on the **cowslip** (*Primula veris*) anchoring the plant to the ground. Only the yellow flowers are held upright so the bees can pollinate. Tea made from the drooping flowers is said to cure insomnia. **Horseshoe vetch** (*Hippocrepis comosa*), an important butterfly food plant, bears its small pea-flower-shaped yellow flowers on a dense close-fitting mat. Other strategies are to put out roots wherever a stem touches the soil or to interweave a network of stems just below the surface as **birdsfoot trefoil** (*Lotus corniculatus*) does.

The tiny yellow flower of **tormentil** (*Potentilla tormentilla*) can be seen hugging the ground in short grassland. It gets its name from an age when it was used as a medicinal remedy for diarrhoea and haemorrhoids: the taste is so foul that it tormented whoever took it.

Another tiny flower that can also be found close to the ground is the **scarlet pimpernel** (*Anagallis arvensis*), a member of the primrose family. The flowers are tiny at just 5mm in diameter but stand out from their grassy background thanks to their light red colour.

There are many **orchids** on the Downs and some are relatively common including the **early purple orchid** (*Orchis mascula*), as its name suggests, the first of the British orchids to flower from April onwards, and the widespread **bee orchid** (*Ophrys apifera*) which gets its name from the bee-shaped flowers produced in early summer. The National Nature Reserve at Wye is said to boast no fewer than 21 different species of orchid.

The showiest plant is probably the **common poppy** (*Papaver rhoeas*), which splashes colour, with its deep-red petals, on the open fields of the Kent landscape in late summer.

Heath

Puttenham Heath, close to the path, is an isolated area of heath where acid-loving plants thrive on the greensand soil. The most common is **heather** (*Calluna vulgaris*), a versatile plant used for thatching, basket work, brooms and fuel for fires. You will also find a collection of acid-loving species about Hackhurst Downs (Map 10, p87).

Thorny **gorse** (*Ulex europaeus*) bushes brighten up the summer with their small yellow flowers that burst open from February until June.

ROUTE GUIDE & MAPS 4

Using this guide

This trail guide has been described from west to east and divided into stages. There are seven stages to the point at which the northern and southern routes diverge, then a further four for the northern route or two for the southern route. Each stage is approximately a day's walk in length though that doesn't mean you have to divide the trail up this way; with such good transport links and plenty of accommodation, you can of course divide the trail up however you wish. Much will depend on the speed you walk at, your interests and where you stay.

There is excellent access by public transport if you're doing the walk in day stages or from a fixed base. See p30 for some suggested itineraries.

To enable you to plan your own itinerary **practical information** is presented clearly on the trail maps. This includes walking times for both directions, places to stay, camp and eat, as well as shops where you can buy supplies. Further service **details** are given in the text under the entry for each place. For an overview of this information see the village and town facilities table on pp28-31.

For **map profiles** see the colour pages at the end of the book.

TRAIL MAPS [for key map see inside back cover; for map symbols key see inside front cover]

Scale and walking times

The trail maps are to a scale of 1:20,000 (1cm = 200m; 3 1/8 inches = one mile). Walking times are given along the side of each map and the arrow shows the direction to which the time refers. Black triangles indicate the points between which the times have been taken. **See box below for note on walking times.** The times on the maps are there as an aid to planning your walk not to judge your ability. There are many variables which will affect your speed including weather,

❑ **IMPORTANT NOTE – WALKING TIMES**

Unless otherwise specified, **all times in this book refer only to the time spent walking**. You will need to add 20-30% to allow for rests, photography, checking the map, drinking water etc, not to mention time to simply stand and stare. When planning the day's hike count on 5-7 hours' actual walking.

> **DIRECTION INDICATORS ON MAP SIDE BARS**
>
> TO DOVER — Walking in an easterly direction from Farnham to Dover
>
> 5 — Route to Dover continues on Map 5
>
> TO FARNM — Walking in a westerly direction from Dover to Farnham
>
> 8 — Route to Farnham continues on Map 8

ground conditions, whether you are walking alone or with company and how many photos you take along the way.

Up or down?

Other than when on a track or bridleway the trail is shown as a dotted line. An arrow across the trail indicates the slope; two arrows show that it is steep. Note that the arrow points towards the higher part of the trail. If, for example, you are walking from A (at 80m) to B (at 200m) and the trail between the two is short and steep, it would be shown thus: A – – – >> – – – – B. Reversed arrow heads indicate a downward gradient.

Accommodation

The accommodation shown on the maps is either on the trail or within easy reach of it. Some hosts are prepared to collect walkers from points on the trail where the accommodation is a mile or two off the path and it is worth asking if this is possible when booking. There may be a fee for this service, but if not, an offer to pay petrol money will generally be appreciated.

Details of each place are given in the accompanying text. The number and type of rooms is given for each one: **S** = single bed, **T** = twin beds, **D** = double bed or twin beds put together, **Tr/Qd** = triple/quad ie rooms that can sleep up to three/four people, but note that this often means two people sharing a double bed and the other(s) in bunk beds; these rooms can also be used as doubles or twins.

Rates given are **per person (pp)** based on two people sharing a room for a one-night stay – rates are almost always discounted for a longer stay. Where a single room (**sgl**) is available the rate for that is quoted if different from the per person rate. The rate for single occupancy (**sgl occ**) of a double/twin is generally higher, and the rate for three or more sharing a room may be lower. Unless specified, rates are for **bed and breakfast** (B&B). At some places the only option is a **room rate**; this will be the same whether one or two people share. Don't bank on negotiating a discount in the off-season; year-round demand from business travellers, holidaymakers and weekenders for accommodation along and near the North Downs Way keeps prices high. But some of the larger establishments catering to business travellers may offer a lower weekend rate; it's worth checking when you book. See p27 for more details on prices.

Almost all places to stay and/or eat offer free **wi-fi** nowadays so this is only specified where that isn't the case. The text also mentions whether the premises have a **bath** (🛁) available in, or for, at least one room; if packed lunches (Ⓛ) can be provided (usually subject to preorder and an additional cost); and whether **dogs** (🐕) are welcome. Most places will not take more than one dog in a room, subject to prior arrangement. Many make an additional charge (usually per night but occasionally per stay), while others may require a deposit which is refundable if the dog doesn't make a mess. See also pp203-5.

Above: The Battle of Britain Memorial (see p194) above the White Cliffs of Dover on the Southern Route. **Below, left**: Dating back to the 11th century, Dover Castle stands high above the town. **Right**: Following the clifftop path towards Dover on the Southern Route (pp186-200).

C2 Some common flora

Early Purple Orchid
Orchis mascula

Common Spotted-Orchid
Dactylorhiza fuchsii

Rosebay Willowherb
Epilobium angustifolium

Foxglove
Digitalis purpurea

Bee Orchid
Ophrys apifera
© Tim Muddle

Pyramidal Orchid
Anacamptis pyramidalis

Red Campion
Silene dioica

Common Dog Violet
Viola riviniana

Forget-me-not
Myosotis arvensis

Old Man's Beard
Clematis vitalba

Scarlet Pimpernel
Anagallis arvensis

Tormentil
Potentilla erecta

Rowan (tree)
Sorbus aucuparia

Ramsons (Wild Garlic)
Allium ursinum

Common Hawthorn
Crataegus monogyna

Common Centaury
Centaurium erythraea

Common Ragwort
Senecio jacobaea

Cowslip
Primula veris

Yarrow
Achillea millefolium

Gorse
Ulex europaeus

Bird's-foot trefoil
Lotus corniculatus

Meadow Buttercup
Ranunculus acris

Marsh Marigold
(Kingcup)
Caltha palustris

Herb-Robert
Geranium robertianum

Primrose
Primula vulgaris

St John's Wort
Hypericum perforatum

Dog Rose
Rosa canina

Honeysuckle
Lonicera periclymemum

Bluebell
Hyacinthoides non-scripta

Common Knapweed
Centaurea nigra

Red Admiral butterfly (*Vanessa atalanta*) on Hemp Agrimony (*Eupatorium cannabinum)*

Above, **left**: The Guildhall (p77) with its impressive 17th-century clock is at the top of Guildford's cobbled High St. **Right**: The stunning gesso murals in the terracotta-tiled Watts Cemetery Chapel (p72) were completed in 1904. **Below**: The attractive hamlet of Seale (p68), with St Laurence Church at its centre, lies only five minutes from the trail (if you're in need of a coffee).

The route guide

FARNHAM [MAP 1a, p67]

Roughly halfway between Winchester and London, Farnham made its money from trade in wool, then corn, and in the 19th century its wealth came from brewing. Now it services well-off commuters but it also has a vibrant arts scene, a wonderful museum housed in a Grade 1 listed building and a fine medieval street pattern with a well-preserved Georgian streetscape in Castle St, West St and The Borough.

This is the reputed birthplace of William Cobbett, the 18th-century politician and author of *Rural Rides*, in which he writes glowingly of the area covered in the first stage of the North Downs Way, His former home is now a pub, ***The William Cobbett*** (see Where to eat & drink) just outside the centre in Bridge Square.

What to see and do

If you have the time, follow the comprehensive **Farnham Heritage Trail**; download a free leaflet from 🖳 farnham.gov.uk.

Overlooking the town is **Farnham Castle Keep** (☎ 0370 333 1181, 🖳 english-heritage.co.uk; Mon-Fri 9am-5pm, Sat & Sun 10am-4pm, free). Construction began in 1138 under Henry de Blois and the castle accommodated the bishops of Winchester until 1955. Mary Tudor stayed here on her way to marry Philip of Spain in Winchester and Elizabeth I visited several times.

Also worth a visit is the **Museum of Farnham** (☎ 01252-715094, 🖳 farnhammaltings.com/museum; Wed-Sat 10am-4pm; free); it's located in Wilmer House, 38 West St, a graciously proportioned Grade 1 listed building dating from 1718.

There is a monthly market at **Farnham Maltings**, Bridge Square (☎ 01252-745444, 🖳 farnhammaltings.com; first Sat of month 9am-4.30pm; £1), which is also the focus of a thriving music and arts scene, and a **Farmers' Market** fourth Sun of month except Dec; 10am-1.30pm), in the Central Car Park, off Victoria Rd.

Services

Tourist information is available online (🖳 farnham.gov.uk).

There are **ATMs** on The Borough and in WH Smith's there's the main **post office** (Mon-Sat 9am-5.30pm). Sainsbury's **supermarket** (Mon-Thur & Sat 7am-8pm, Fri to 9pm, Sun 10am-4pm) is on South St and Boots **pharmacy** (Mon-Sat 8.30am-6pm, Sun 10.30am-4pm) is on The Borough.

Transport

The **railway** station is on Station Hill, about five minutes from the start/end of the Way. South Western Railway operate services (see box pp42-3) direct to Guildford and London Waterloo.

Several **bus** services call here: Nos 4 & 5 (to Aldershot); No 19 (Aldershot to Haslemere); No 46 (to Guildford); and No

The accident of the Surrey Hills made all men who wished to get to the south-western ports from the Thames Valley and the east pass through Farnham. Travellers going west and north from the Weald were equally compelled, if they would avoid the ridge, to pass through Farnham. The former had to come down north of the Hog's Back, the latter from the south of it, and it was ever at Farnham they met… and after Farnham the western tracks, now all in one, proceed to the Straits of Dover.

Hilaire Belloc, *The Old Road*

65 (Alton to Guildford; only stops on The Borough). See pp44-7 for details.

For a **taxi** try Farnham Station Taxis (☎ 01252-735735, 💻 farnhamstationtaxis.co.uk) or VGT Taxis (☎ 01252-737475, 💻 vgtravel.co.uk/taxis-farnham/).

Where to stay

The location of the ***Premier Inn*** (☎ 0333-2346490, 💻 premierinn.com; 62 rooms, all en suite; ☕), on Guildford Rd near the roundabout on the A31, may not be the most attractive, but you can't argue with the price, with rooms starting at around £35.

If location, not price, is your mantra try the 17th-century former coaching inn, ***Bush Hotel*** (☎ 01252-234800, 💻 farnhambush.com; 94D or T, all en suite; ☕; 🐕) on The Borough (though the entrance is round the corner on South St). Rates vary depending on demand, though start at around the £50pp mark (sgl occ room rate); breakfast costs £18.50pp.

Where to eat and drink

For a **coffee**, there are the usual nationwide chain outlets such as ***Caffè Nero*** (Mon-Fri 6.30am-6pm, Sat 7am-6pm, Sun 7.30am-5.30pm), at the bottom of Castle St, and ***Costa*** (Mon-Fri 7.30am-6pm, Sat to 5.30pm, Sun 8am-5pm) on West St.

For something more independent, ***The Spire Café*** (Mon-Fri 10am-2pm, to noon on Sat) is in a Methodist church on South St and offers decent, warm coffee served by decent, warm people, as well as some great-value light meals (Mon-Fri only). There's also an outlet of local coffee chain ***Harris & Hoole*** (💻 harrisandhoole.co.uk; Mon-Sat 7am-6pm, Sun 8am-5pm) on West St,

Castle St is the best place to head for breakfasts. At the upmarket eatery ***Bill's*** (💻 bills-website.co.uk; Mon-Wed 8am-10pm, Thur-Sat to 11pm, Sun 9am-10pm; 🐕) they charge £10.95 for their Full English; they also have some delicious lunchtime options (£14.50).

Right by Caffè Nero, ***Gail's*** (☎ 01252-722955, 💻 gails.com; Mon-Fri 7am-6pm, Sat to 5.30pm, Sun & Bank Hols to 5pm) is a branch of an 'artisan bakery' chain, with a fine line in breakfasts.

On Lion & Lamb Way, Italian café restaurant ***Via Leone*** (☎ 01252-597010, 💻 vialeone.co.uk; Mon 9am-3pm, Tue-Fri 9am-3pm & 5-10pm, Sat 9am-10pm, Sun 9am-4pm) serves breakfast (full English £11.95), lunch (panini from £6.95) and smart evening meals from pasta and risotto to the likes of *saltinbocca* (£17.95).

Back on Castle St, ***Giggling Squid*** (☎ 01252-727552, 💻 gigglingsquid.com; daily noon-10.30pm) is a Thai chain renowned for its salt & pepper squid (£8.80).

Nearby ***Zizzi*** (☎ 01483-808328, 💻 zizzi.co.uk; Mon-Fri 11.30am-10pm, Fri & Sat to 11pm) is a lively Italian joint with pizzas from £14.50. On the subject of pizza, there's a branch of the takeaway ***Domino's*** (☎ 01252-717000, 💻 dominos.co.uk/farnham; Mon-Thur 11am-11pm, Fri & Sat to 11.30pm, Sun to 10.30pm) on East St.

Indian food is at its best in Farnham at ***Farnham Tandoori*** (☎ 01252-716853, 💻 farnhamtandoori.co.uk; Mon-Sat 5.30-11pm, Sun to 10.30pm), 47 West St, with mains starting at around a tenner.

As a former brewery town, you'd expect to find a number of **pubs**, including several that serve food too. ***The Mulberry*** (☎ 01252-726673, 💻 mulberryfarnham.co.uk; pizza only Tue 6-9.30pm; pub menu Wed & Thur noon-2.30pm & 6-9.30pm, Fri & Sat noon-10pm, Sun noon-8pm; 🐕 bar area only), opposite the station, does a nice line in tasty burgers including a vegan 'Greta Thunburger' (£15). The bar is open from noon every day.

The Wheatsheaf (☎ 01252-717135, 💻 thewheatsheaffarnham.co.uk; 🐕; food Tue-Thur noon-4pm & 5-9pm, Fri & Sat noon-9pm, Sun noon-4pm) is popular, particularly on a Sunday when they offer a selection of expensive but tasty roasts (£21.95-25.95).

The Nelson Arms (☎ 01252-727222, 💻 thenelsonarmsfarnham.co.uk; food Tue-Sat noon-2.30pm & 6-9pm, Sun noon-7pm), on Castle St, is a low-beamed gastropub dating back to the 16th century (so pre-Nelson) with mains such as honey and mustard roast ham, eggs and chips (£14).

The ***Slug & Lettuce*** (☎ 01252-722011, 💻 slugandlettuce.co.uk/farnham; daily

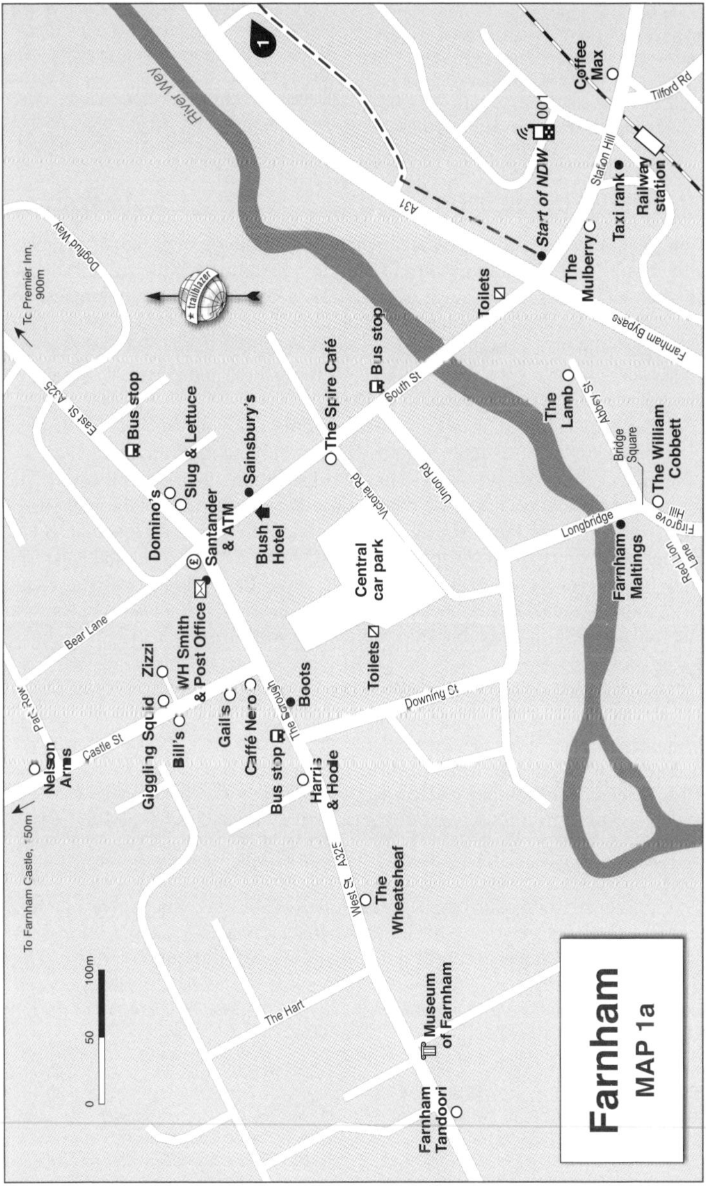
Farnham
MAP 1a
River Wey
To Premier Inn, 900m
Dogflud Way
East St A325
Bus stop
Slug & Lettuce
Domino's
Sainsbury's
Santander & ATM
Bush Hotel
The Spire Café
Bus stop
South St
Toilets
A31
Start of NDW
001
Coffee Max
Tilford Rd
Station Hill
Taxi rank
Railway station
The Mulberry
Farnham Bypass
The Lamb
Abbey St
Bridge Square
The William Cobbett
Firgrove Hill
Red Lion Lane
Longbridge
Farnham Maltings
Union Rd
Victoria Rd
Central car park
Toilets
Bear Lane
WH Smith & Post Office
Zizzi
Giggling Squid
Bill's
Gail's
Caffé Nero
Boots
The Borough
Downing St
Bus stop
Harris & Hoole
Castle St
Nelson Arms
Park Row
To Farnham Castle, 150m
West St A325
The Wheatsheaf
The Hart
Museum of Farnham
Farnham Tandoori
0
50
100m

noon-9pm; 🐕), on the A325 (East St), is a huge place, part of a chain and not to everyone's taste. Nevertheless, they serve very good-value food (mains from £11.50, and even the steak and chips is only £16.95).

South of the river are a couple of drinks-only pubs. On Bridge Square is the lively and historic ***William Cobbett*** (**fb**; Sun-Thur 3-11pm, Fri & Sat noon to midnight), while nearby on Abbey St, ***The Lamb*** (☎ 01252-714133, 💻 lambfarnham.co.uk; Mon-Thur noon-11pm, Fri & Sat noon-midnight, Sun to 10pm) serves lovely Spitfire ale from Shepherd Neame.

FARNHAM TO GUILDFORD [MAPS 1-6b]

Not too strenuous, very pretty and punctuated by plenty of points of interest – this first **12-mile/19.3km (3¾hrs to 5hrs** to a reunion with the River Wey and the turn-off to Guildford) stage of the NDW is, in many ways, a microcosm of the whole trail. True, for some this may all be a bit tame – but fear not, for it does get wilder in subsequent stages. So do up those laces and strap on that backpack – you've got a long way to go between here and Dover. We've talked the talk: now it's time to walk the chalk.

The start of the trail is fairly unspectacular. Having freed yourself from Farnham's civilised clutches (though if you've forgotten anything there's a small 24-hr M&S Simply Food at the petrol station by the side of the trail), the first place of note occurs just a couple of miles into the trek as the trail passes the drive of **Moor Park House** (Map 1), one-time home of Jonathan Swift, author of *Gulliver's Travels*. It's your own travels – and travails – that are probably of more interest to you now however, and if the trail is already proving a little tough sustenance can be sought at **Seale** (Map 3), just a few minutes from the trail and the first possible stopover on the North Downs Way.

SEALE [MAP 3, p71]

A five-minute detour will bring you to this hamlet with its attractive church, **St Laurence**, and the fair-value ***Manor Farm Tea Room*** (☎ 01252-783661; **fb**; Tue-Sun 10am-4pm; 🐕). Set in a converted milking parlour with a wood-burning stove, a hot drink and a cheese scone will cost about a £6 and will set you up nicely for the climb before Puttenham. Back on the trail itself, ***Waggoner's Campsite*** (☎ 07385 812842, 💻 waggonerscampsite.co.uk; 🐕; from £16pp) describes itself as an 'off-grid eco-campsite' with composting toilets and unheated showers. Other facilities include wash huts and barbecue pits. Note they are open Thursday to Saturday only.

Don't tarry too long over your teacake in Seale, however, for you've still got a fair way to go before you reach Guildford. In fact, you've got several 'fairways' to go as the trail traces a course through a couple of golf courses; this is, after all, wealthy Surrey, where for some people golf is a way of life. How appropriate, therefore, that the village which precedes the second golf course of the day should be called Puttenham…

PUTTENHAM [MAP 4, p73]

Walkers will benefit from ***Puttenham Barn Bunkhouse*** (☎ 01483-811001, 💻 puttenhambarn.uk; 5pm-10am Easter to end Oct; 11 spaces, booking essential) which provides budget accommodation (from £23pp) in bunk beds or a wooden platform designed

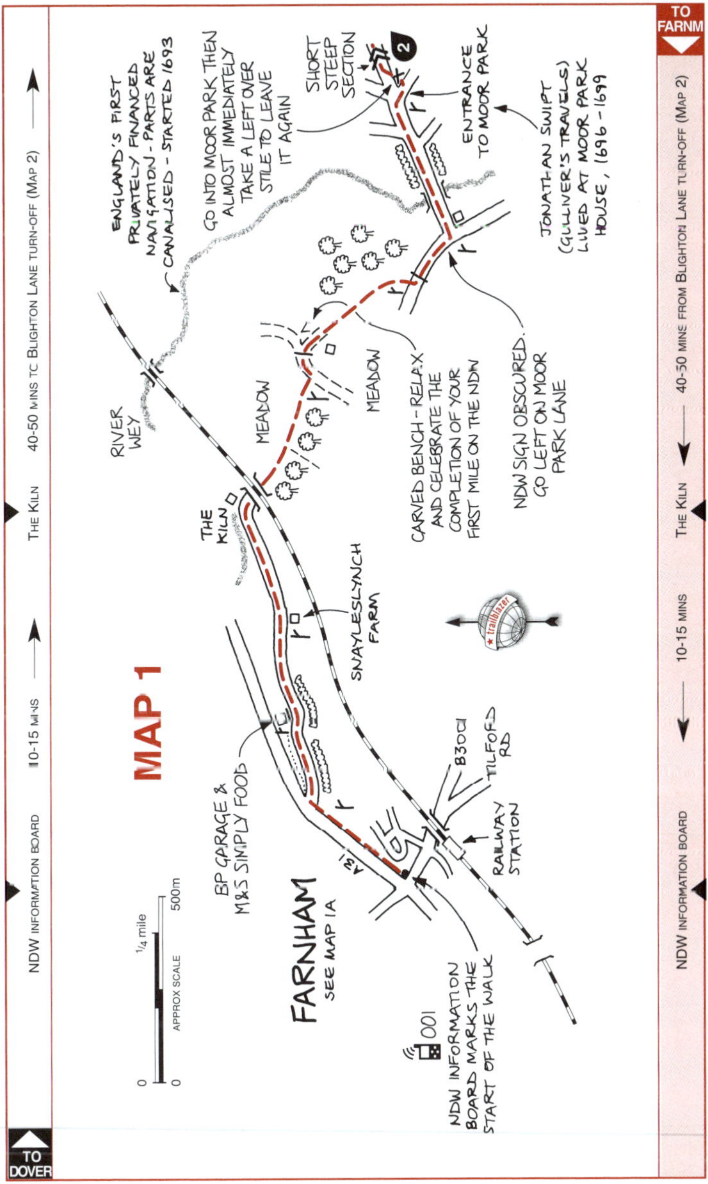
MAP 1
NDW INFORMATION BOARD
10-15 MINS
THE KILN
40-50 MINS TO BLIGHTON LANE TURN-OFF (MAP 2)
40-50 MINS FROM BLIGHTON LANE TURN-OFF (MAP 2)
THE KILN
10-15 MINS
NDW INFORMATION BOARD
TO DOVER
TO FARNM
0
1/4 mile
APPROX SCALE
0
500m
FARNHAM
SEE MAP 1A
BP GARAGE & M&S SIMPLY FOOD
001
NDW INFORMATION BOARD MARKS THE START OF THE WALK
RAILWAY STATION
B3001
TILFORD RD
SNAYLESLYNCH FARM
THE KILN
RIVER WEY
MEADOW
MEADOW
CARVED BENCH - RELAX AND CELEBRATE THE COMPLETION OF YOUR FIRST MILE ON THE NDW
NDW SIGN OBSCURED. GO LEFT ON MOOR PARK LANE
ENGLAND'S FIRST PRIVATELY FINANCED NAVIGATION - PARTS ARE CANALISED - STARTED 1693
GO INTO MOOR PARK THEN ALMOST IMMEDIATELY TAKE A LEFT OVER STILE TO LEAVE IT AGAIN
SHORT STEEP SECTION
2
ENTRANCE TO MOOR PARK
JONATHAN SWIFT (GULLIVER'S TRAVELS) LIVED AT MOOR PARK HOUSE, 1696 - 1699
trailblazer

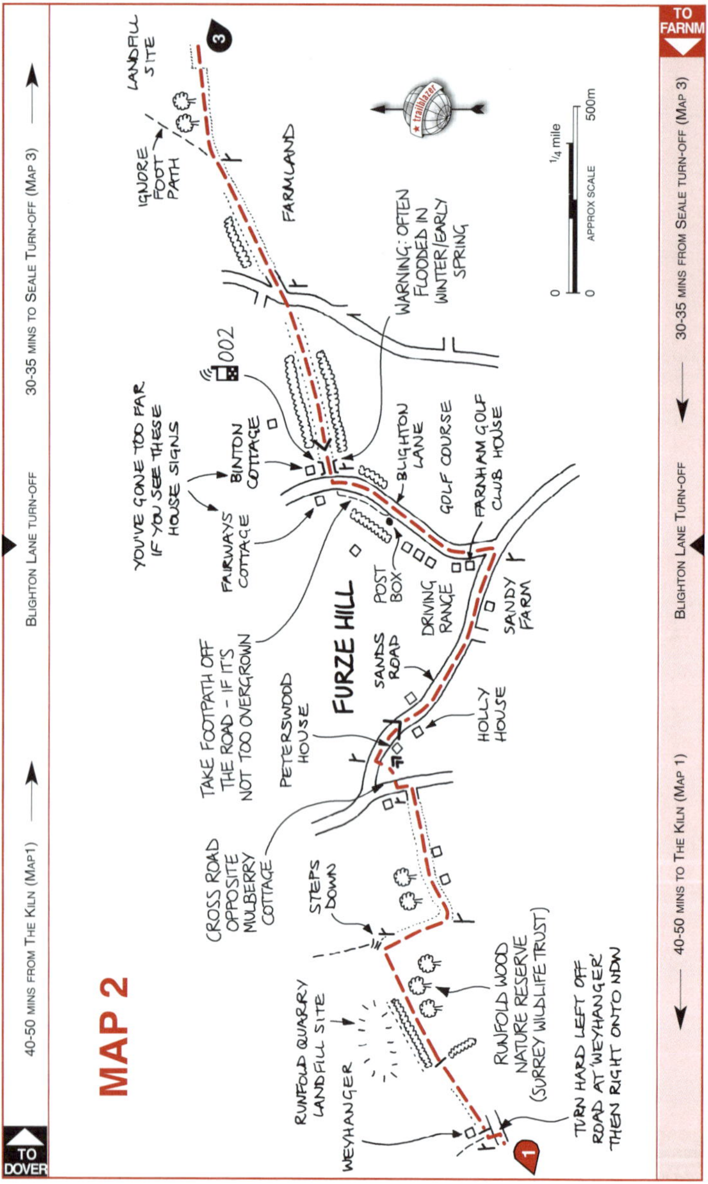
MAP 2
TO DOVER
TO FARNM
40-50 MINS FROM THE KILN (MAP1) →
BLIGHTON LANE TURN-OFF
30-35 MINS TO SEALE TURN-OFF (MAP 3) →
← 30-35 MINS FROM SEALE TURN-OFF (MAP 3)
BLIGHTON LANE TURN-OFF
← 40-50 MINS TO THE KILN (MAP 1)
WEYHANGER
RUNFOLD QUARRY LANDFILL SITE
RUNFOLD WOOD NATURE RESERVE (SURREY WILDLIFE TRUST)
TURN HARD LEFT OFF ROAD AT 'WEYHANGER' THEN RIGHT ONTO NDW
STEPS DOWN
CROSS ROAD OPPOSITE MULBERRY COTTAGE
TAKE FOOTPATH OFF THE ROAD – IF IT'S NOT TOO OVERGROWN
PETERSWOOD HOUSE
FURZE HILL
HOLLY HOUSE
SANDS ROAD
DRIVING RANGE
SANDY FARM
POST BOX
YOU'VE GONE TOO FAR IF YOU SEE THESE HOUSE SIGNS
FAIRWAYS COTTAGE
BINTON COTTAGE
BLIGHTON LANE
GOLF COURSE
FARNHAM GOLF CLUB HOUSE
002
WARNING: OFTEN FLOODED IN WINTER/EARLY SPRING
FARMLAND
IGNORE FOOT PATH
LANDFILL SITE
trailblazer
0
¼ mile
0
APPROX SCALE
500m

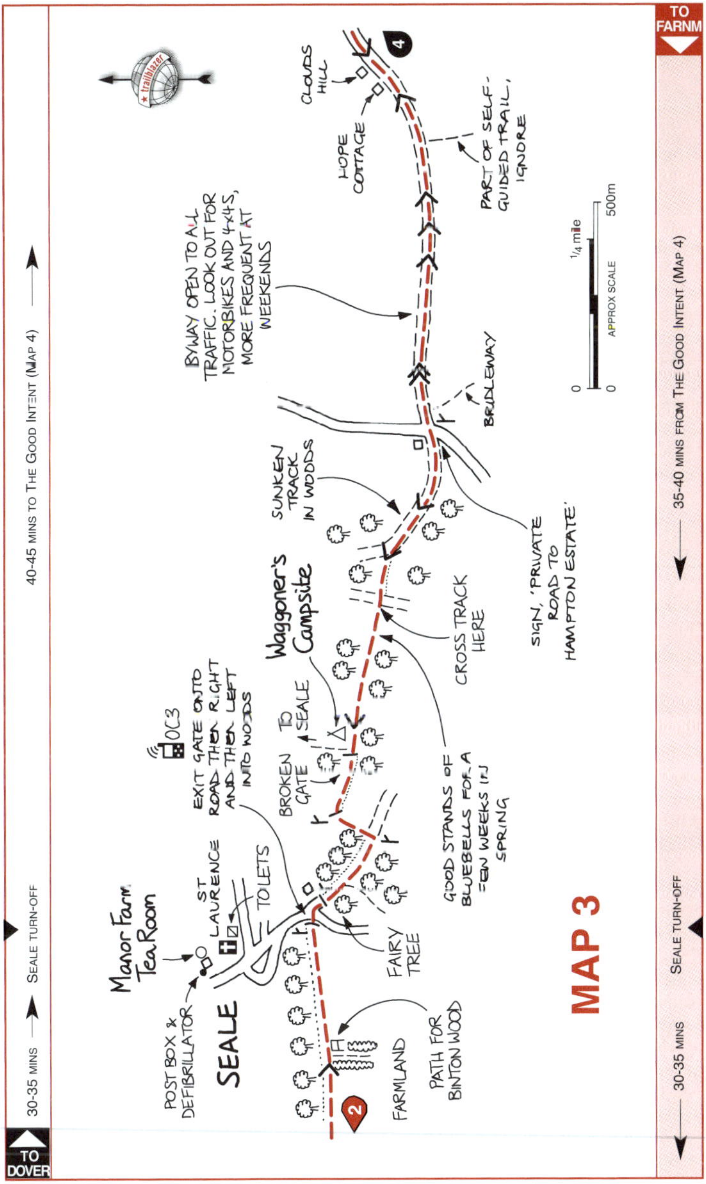
30-35 MINS → SEALE TURN-OFF → 40-45 MINS TO THE GOOD INTENT (MAP 4) →
TO DOVER
TO FARNM
MAP 3
SEALE
POST BOX & DEFIBRILLATOR
Manor Farm Tea Room
ST LAURENCE
TOILETS
FARMLAND
PATH FOR BINTON WOOD
FAIRY TREE
EXIT GATE ONTO ROAD THEN RIGHT AND THEN LEFT INTO WOODS
OC3
BROKEN GATE
TO SEALE
Waggoner's Campsite
GOOD STANDS OF BLUEBELLS FOR A FEW WEEKS IN SPRING
CROSS TRACK HERE
SUNKEN TRACK IN WOODS
SIGN, 'PRIVATE ROAD TO HAMPTON ESTATE'
BRIDLEWAY
BYWAY OPEN TO ALL TRAFFIC. LOOK OUT FOR MOTORBIKES AND 4x4S, MORE FREQUENT AT WEEKENDS
HOPE COTTAGE
CLOUDS HILL
PART OF SELF-GUIDED TRAIL, IGNORE
0 1/4 mile
0 500m
APPROX SCALE
← 35-40 MINS FROM THE GOOD INTENT (MAP 4) ← SEALE TURN-OFF ← 30-35 MINS
2
4

❏ BRAVE NEW PUTTENHAM?

'*Puttenham was a modest little village nine stories high, with silos, a poultry farm, and a small vitamin-D factory.*'

Thus did **Aldous Huxley** imagine the future of Puttenham (Map 4) in his 1932 work, *Brave New World*. His vision may still come to pass, of course, though if it does, this long village, lined with pretty brick, stone, timber and tile-hung cottages, would have to undergo a complete transformation.

for three. The barn is a listed building restored using sustainable materials and solar energy. A sleeping bag is essential but can be hired (£5). Kitchen, toilet and shower facilities are available.

For a meal there's ***The Good Intent*** (☎ 01483-923434, 🖳 goodintentputtenham.co.uk; food Mon noon-2.30pm, Tue-Sat noon-2.30pm & 6.9pm, Sun noon-6pm; 🐕), a popular low-beamed pub with inglenook fireplace which does a good line in standard pub food (sandwiches £6.95-10.95).

Note that ***The Little Coffee Pantry*** (**fb**; Thur-Sun 9am-2pm), advertised on the trail, is almost 1½ miles away in the Upper Car Park on Suffield Lane, a significant detour for walkers; you're better off in the pub or continuing along the trail to the tea shop at **Compton** (Map 5).

Stagecoach's **bus** No 65 (Alton to Guildford; see pp44-7) stops by The Good Intent.

In our experience, most walkers prefer the words 'cream' and 'tea' to 'green' and 'tee', so having departed Puttenham from opposite **The Pickled Pig** (closed for refurbishment at the time of writing), and after marching briskly past golf course and woodland bordering Puttenham Heath – geologically unusual in this area of chalk – it is with some relief to find yourself emerging onto the outskirts of **Compton** and its fine tea shop.

COMPTON [MAP 5, p74]

The trail brings you out just below **Watts Gallery** (☎ 01483-810235, 🖳 wattsgallery.org.uk; daily 10.30am-4pm; £15, an intimate space exhibiting works of Victorian artist and sculptor George Frederic Watts, which is well worth a visit.

Also on Down Lane is the red-brick **Watts Cemetery Chapel** (daily 10am-5pm; free), built by Watts's wife. His remains are interred in the cloister nearby. The floral forms, tendrils and crosses on the exterior reveal the Art Nouveau, Celtic, Romanesque and Egyptian influences. Don't miss the incredible interior, with every available surface decorated with red, silver and gold images and angels.

Continuing south to the village, the 11th century **parish church of St Nicholas** is worth a visit, particularly to see the two-storey sanctuary with a magnificent vault and nine-arch balustrade above it.

Next door to the Watts Gallery, in the former pottery workshop of Compton Potters Guild, is ***Compton Tea Shop*** (☎ 01483-813590; daily 10am-5pm), just the place for gooey Welsh rarebit (from £8.95).

Upmarket eatery ***The Withies Inn*** (off Map 5; ☎ 01483-421158, 🖳 thewithiesinn.com; Mon-Thur 7-9.30am, noon-5pm & 6-9pm, Fri-Sat 8-10am, noon-5pm & 6-9pm, Sun 8-10am and noon-3pm; advance booking only for breakfast) lies outside the village; evening mains start at £18.50 for a vegetarian mushroom stroganoff with rice. They also have smart **B&B** rooms (7D en suite) that start at £70-85pp (sgl occ full room rate).

There's a **bus** stop outside the gallery, with Stagecoach's No 46 (see pp44-7) calling here.

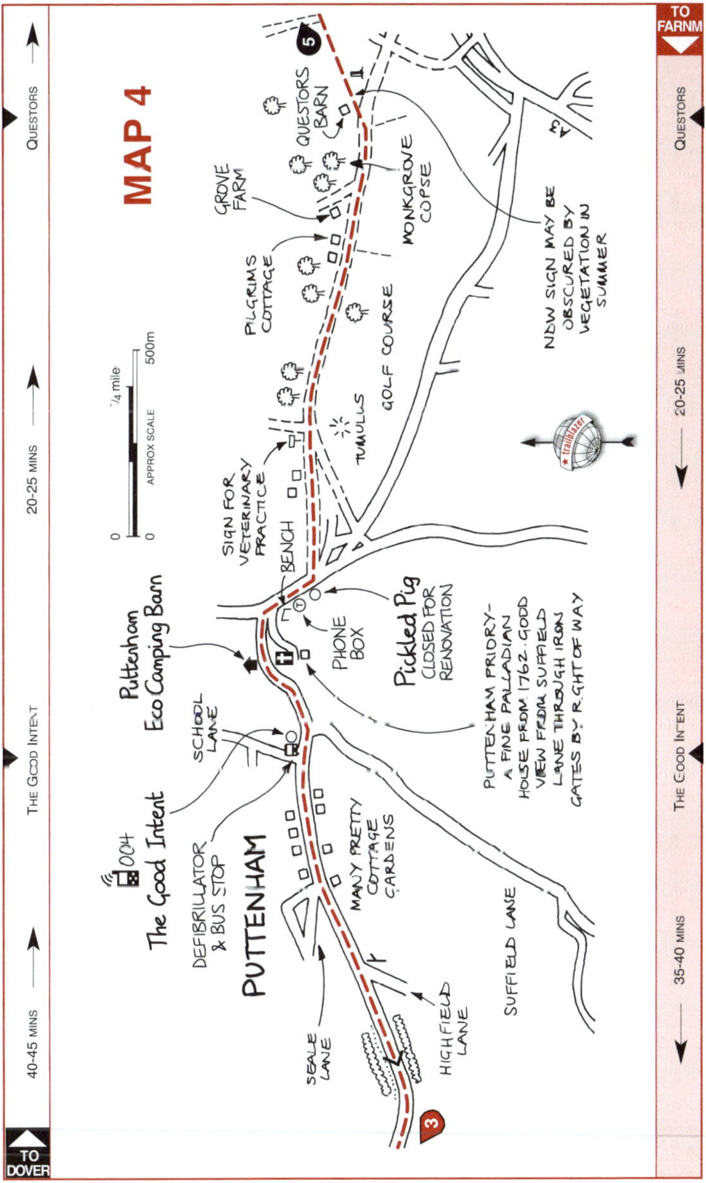
MAP 4
0
0
APPROX SCALE
¼ mile
500m
TO DOVER
40-45 MINS
The Good Intent
20-25 MINS
Questors
TO FARNM
Questors
20-25 MINS
The Good Intent
35-40 MINS
The Good Intent
004
DEFIBRILLATOR & BUS STOP
PUTTENHAM
SCHOOL LANE
Puttenham Eco Camping Barn
PHONE BOX
Pickled Pig
CLOSED FOR RENOVATION
BENCH
SIGN FOR VETERINARY PRACTICE
TUMULUS
GOLF COURSE
PILGRIMS COTTAGE
GROVE FARM
MONKGROVE COPSE
QUESTORS BARN
NEW SIGN MAY BE OBSCURED BY VEGETATION IN SUMMER
A3
PUTTENHAM PRIORY - A FINE PALLADIAN HOUSE FROM 1762. GOOD VIEW FROM SUFFIELD LANE THROUGH IRON GATES BY RIGHT OF WAY
MANY PRETTY COTTAGE GARDENS
SUFFIELD LANE
SEALE LANE
HIGHFIELD LANE
trailblazer
3
5

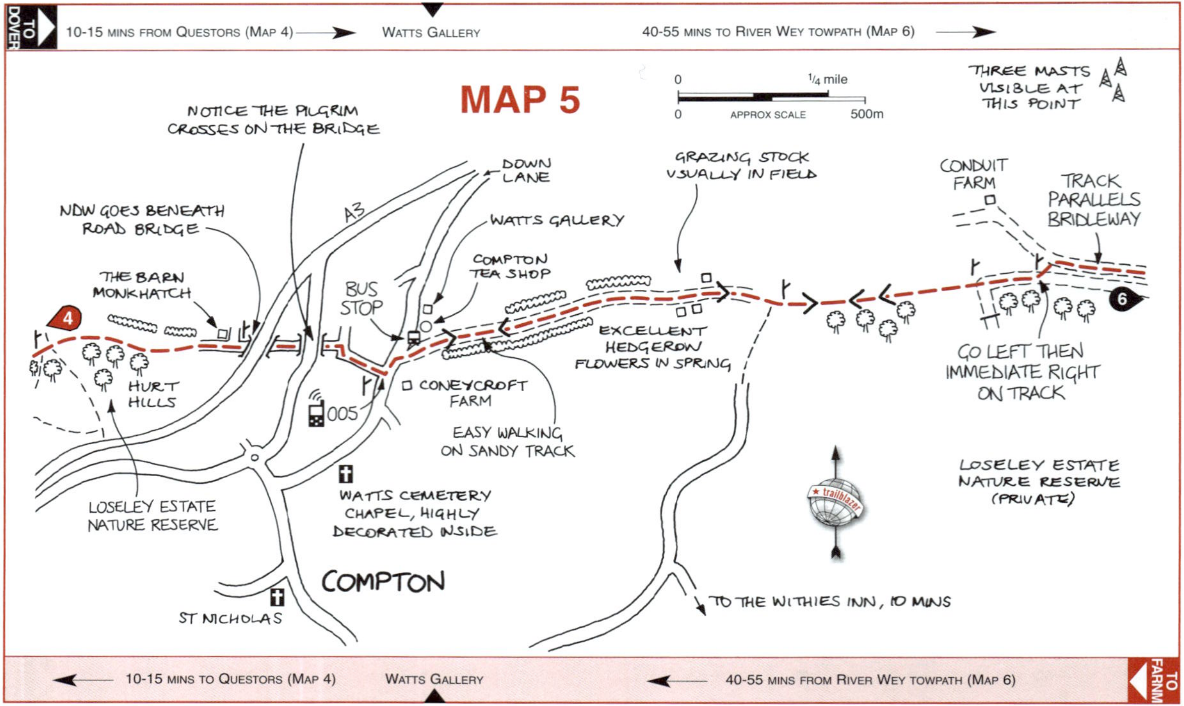
TO DOVER
10-15 MINS FROM QUESTORS (MAP 4)
WATTS GALLERY
40-55 MINS TO RIVER WEY TOWPATH (MAP 6)
MAP 5
0 1/4 mile
0 APPROX SCALE 500m
THREE MASTS VISIBLE AT THIS POINT
NOTICE THE PILGRIM CROSSES ON THE BRIDGE
DOWN LANE
A3
NDW GOES BENEATH ROAD BRIDGE
WATTS GALLERY
COMPTON TEA SHOP
THE BARN MONKHATCH
BUS STOP
4
HURT HILLS
005
CONEYCROFT FARM
EASY WALKING ON SANDY TRACK
GRAZING STOCK USUALLY IN FIELD
EXCELLENT HEDGEROW FLOWERS IN SPRING
CONDUIT FARM
TRACK PARALLELS BRIDLEWAY
6
GO LEFT THEN IMMEDIATE RIGHT ON TRACK
LOSELEY ESTATE NATURE RESERVE
WATTS CEMETERY CHAPEL, HIGHLY DECORATED INSIDE
COMPTON
ST NICHOLAS
TO THE WITHIES INN, 10 MINS
LOSELEY ESTATE NATURE RESERVE (PRIVATE)
trailblazer
10-15 MINS TO QUESTORS (MAP 4)
WATTS GALLERY
40-55 MINS FROM RIVER WEY TOWPATH (MAP 6)
TO FARNM

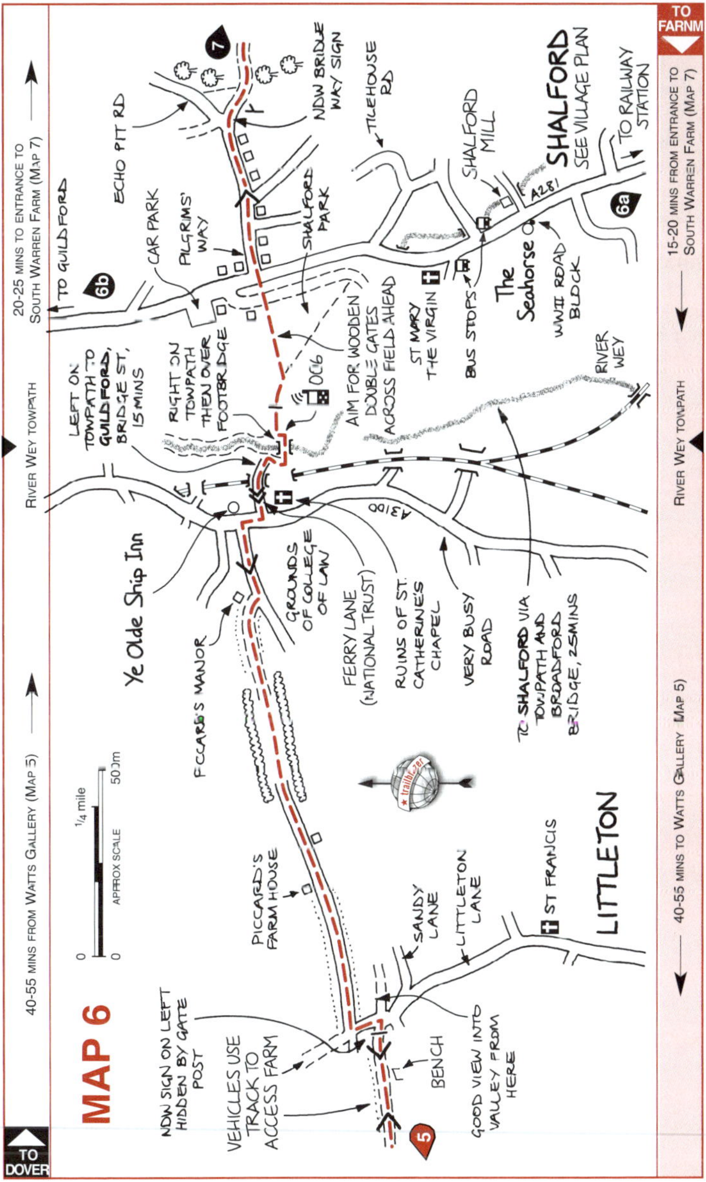
MAP 6
TO DOVER
TO FARNM
20-25 MINS TO ENTRANCE TO SOUTH WARREN FARM (MAP 7)
40-55 MINS FROM WATTS GALLERY (MAP 5)
RIVER WEY TOWPATH
15-20 MINS FROM ENTRANCE TO SOUTH WARREN FARM (MAP 7)
RIVER WEY TOWPATH
40-55 MINS TO WATTS GALLERY (MAP 5)
0
1/4 mile
APPROX SCALE
0
500m
TO GUILDFORD
6b
ECHO PIT RD
CAR PARK
PILGRIMS' WAY
7
NDW BRIDLE WAY SIGN
TILEHOUSE RD
SHALFORD PARK
SHALFORD MILL
SHALFORD
SEE VILLAGE PLAN
A281
TO RAILWAY STATION
6a
The Seahorse
WWII ROAD BLOCK
BUS STOPS
ST MARY THE VIRGIN
AIM FOR WOODEN DOUBLE GATES ACROSS FIELD AHEAD
006
RIGHT ON TOWPATH THEN OVER FOOTBRIDGE
LEFT ON TOWPATH TO GUILDFORD, BRIDGE ST, 15 MINS
RIVER WEY
A3100
Ye Olde Ship Inn
PICCARD'S MANOR
GROUNDS OF COLLEGE OF LAW
FERRY LANE (NATIONAL TRUST)
RUINS OF ST. CATHERINE'S CHAPEL
VERY BUSY ROAD
TO SHALFORD VIA TOWPATH AND BROADFORD BRIDGE, 25MINS
PICCARD'S FARM HOUSE
SANDY LANE
LITTLETON LANE
ST FRANCIS
LITTLETON
NDW SIGN ON LEFT HIDDEN BY GATE POST
VEHICLES USE TRACK TO ACCESS FARM
BENCH
GOOD VIEW INTO VALLEY FROM HERE
5

From Compton the path meanders somewhat as it makes its way through yet more land belonging to the Loseley Estate.

Passing above **Littleton** (Map 6), you soon emerge at the dog-friendly ***Ye Olde Ship Inn*** (☎ 01483-575731, 💻 yeoldeshipinn.pub; food Tue-Thur noon-3pm & 5-9pm, Fri-Sat noon-9pm, Sun noon-7pm; 🐕) on the outskirts of Guildford, with pizzas from £15. From here, steep Ferry Lane takes you down to the River Wey where you have a choice: turn right and south to **Shalford** (Map 6a) for a meal or to catch a train; or left and north to **Guildford** (Map 6b) along the towpath to stay the night – or continue straight on along the trail.

SHALFORD [MAP 6a]

Shalford has an attractive village green complete with cricketers most of the summer but, unfortunately, there are currently no places to stay.

Temporarily closed for conservation works, the timber-framed **Shalford Mill** (☎ 01483-561389, 💻 nationaltrust.org.uk) was given to the National Trust in 1932 by anonymous benefactors calling themselves Ferguson's Gang.

Hanging in the parish **Church of St Mary the Virgin is** a large embroidery by the WI depicting **John Bunyan's** *Pilgrim's Progress*, an allegory of Christian life where the main character, Christian, travels from the city of Destruction to the Celestial City encountering countless temptations on the road to Salvation. Bunyan allegedly came to the Surrey Hills when his preaching got him into trouble. Some claim that the boggy ground on Shalford Common inspired the phrase 'the Slough of Despond'.

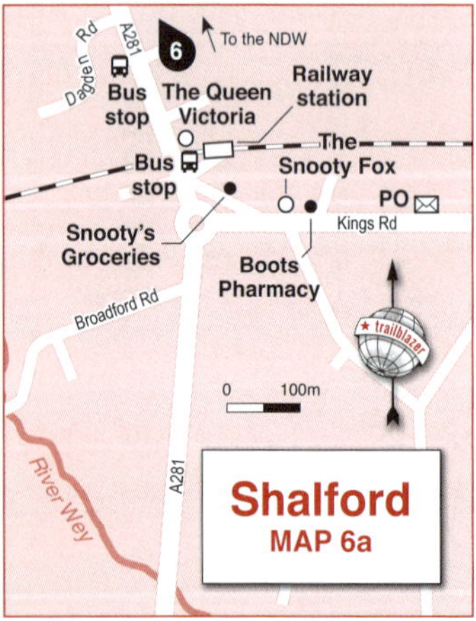

At the eastern end of the village is the **post office** (Mon-Fri 8am-10pm, Sat 8am-8pm, Sun 8am-6pm). Before it, at 8 Kings Rd, is **Boots Pharmacy** (Mon-Fri 9am-6pm, Sat to 5pm) at 8 Kings Rd.

Near the station, ***The Snooty Fox Store & Café*** (☎ 01483-303038, 💻 thesnootyfox.uk) comprises both **grocery store** (Mon-Fri 6.30am-8.30pm, Sat from 7am, Sun 8am-6pm) for essential provisions (and an **ATM**) and ***café*** (Mon-Fri 7am-4.30pm, Sat & Sun 8am-4.30pm) with a great reputation. It's nearly always busy and the food is good too. Sandwiches start at £4.50.

Two **pubs** also serve food. ***The Seahorse*** (Map 6; ☎ 01483-514351, 💻 theseahorseguildford.co.uk; food Mon-Sat noon-9.30pm, Sun to 8.30pm; 🐕 bar area only) boasts an extensive menu with mains from £13.75 for the panzanella salad. On the wall of the pub is a plaque marking the location of a **WWII road block** (Map 6), the last-ditch defence against an expected German invasion in 1940.

Community run, ***The Queen Victoria*** (☎ 01483-893030, 💻 thequeenvic.pub; food Wed-Sat noon-3pm & 6-9pm, Sun noon-4pm) serves traditional pub meals (ham, egg & chips £11.95) in a relaxed, unfussy setting.

Shalford is a stop on GWR's **rail service** between Gatwick Airport/Redhill and Reading; see box pp42-3.

Several bus services call at Shalford en route to/from Guildford, including the Nos 24 & 53 (to Cranleigh), 32 (Redhill) and 63 (Horsham). They all stop at the railway station; see pp44-7 for details.

GUILDFORD [MAP 6b, p79]

Guildford is the lively county town of Surrey and an ideal access point to the North Downs Way with good public transport links, plenty of accommodation, a wide range of restaurants and lots to see and do. The River Wey that runs through it cuts through the North Downs, so down the centuries Guildford emerged in importance as a 'gap town' for those heading north to London or south towards the coast.

Charles Dickens described Guildford High St as 'the most beautiful in the kingdom' and there is still much to recommend it, with many significant historic buildings including the Guildhall with its projecting town clock, the one surviving coaching inn, The Angel Posting House (now Angel Hotel, see Where to stay), and the almshouses of Abbot's Hospital. Indeed the whole car-free cobbled High St, criss-crossed by alleys and lanes, is one of the more handsome on the trail. Much of the town is given over to shopping and nightlife these days, but whether wandering through The Shambles, a maze of narrow alleys, around the castle, or along Tunsgate take time to look up and admire the façades and get a sense of the town's medieval, Jacobean and Regency market town past.

What to see and do

It's easy to go from medieval to modern so rich is Guildford's architectural history despite the best efforts of 1960s' planners and busy roads scything close to the High St.

The **Guildhall** (🖳 guildford.gov.uk/guildhall; May-Sep Tue 10am 2pm; free) was built in the 16th century and its bracket clock, jutting over the High St and dating from 1683, is the town's symbol.

Further east is **Abbot's Hospital** (🖳 abbotshospital.org; main gates open Mon-Sat 9am-4pm; guided tours Easter-Oct Thur, Fri & 1st Tue of month at 11am for £5), an almshouse that is still providing accommodation for the elderly poor. Do peer into the courtyard and admire the fine Jacobean brickwork.

Guildford Castle (☎ 01483-444751, 🖳 guildford.gov.uk/castle; Keep open Easter-Oct Wed-Sat noon-4.30pm; 🐕 on lead; £4.50) dates from the 13th century. There are spectacular displays of bedding plants in the grounds (free) in summer.

Guildford Cathedral (☎ 01483-547860, 🖳 guildford-cathedral.org; Mon & Wed-Sat 8.30am-4.30pm, Tue from 7.30am, Sun 11am-4.30pm) overlooks the town from its commanding position to the west on Stag Hill. Movie buffs will recognise it from the 1976 classic *The Omen*. Italian marble floors and Somerset sandstone grace the pale interior of the first post-Reformation cathedral to be built on a new site.

Accessible from the town centre via a towpath or Woodbridge Rd, the National Trust's **Dapdune Wharf** (☎ 01483-561389, 🖳 nationaltrust.org.uk; Easter/Apr-end Oct Mon & Thur-Sun 11am-4pm, daily in summer hols; boat trip £8.90) tells the story of England's first privately financed navigation – the River Wey.

If you want to rest your legs you might to like to see a show at the Yvonne Arnaud **theatre** (☎ 01483-440000, 🖳 yvonne-arnaud.co.uk), where many productions are pre West End, or a **film** at the Odeon cinema (🖳 odeon.co.uk). The theatre also has a **café** (see Where to eat).

Services

The **tourist information centre** (TIC; ☎ 01483-444333, 🖳 visitsurrey.com/guildford; Tue-Sat 10am-4.30pm) is at 155 High St.

For kit requirements, there are several **trekking stores**, including Cotswold (Mon-Sat 9am-6pm, Sun 11am-5pm), on Friary Passage, and a Decathlon (Mon-Sat 9am-6pm, Sun 11am-5pm) and Trespass (Mon-Sat 9am-6pm, Sun 10.30am-4.30pm) opposite each other on North St. Timpson's **shoe repairers** (Mon-Sat 8.30am-5.30pm, Sun 10am-4pm) is on North St.

The **post office** (Mon-Sat 8.30am-6pm, Sun 11am-3pm) is in WH Smith's towards the bottom of the hill. **Sainsbury's** supermarket (Mon-Sat 7am-9pm, Sun 11am-5pm) is on the High St, as is a Boots **chemist** (Mon-Sat 8.30am-6pm, Sun 11am-5pm). There is a **farmers' market** on the High St on the first Tuesday of each month.

Transport

The Friary **bus station** is by the eponymous shopping centre. The Nos 24, 25, 32, 46, 53, 63 & 65 services call here; see pp44-7 for details.

National Express **coaches** NX030 service (see p40) between London and Portsmouth stop by the large Tesco superstore on Egerton Rd, way out from the town centre to the west; to get there turn off Farnham Rd at Guildford Park Rd.

The **railway station** is a stop on several of South Western Railway's (SWR) services. GWR's services between Gatwick Airport/Redhill and Reading also call here. See box pp42-3.

For a **taxi** call Surrey Cars (☎ 01483-449999, 🖳 surreycarsguildford.com) or A3 Cars (☎ 01483-606060, 🖳 a3cars.com).

Where to stay

Both main budget hotel chains (see also p21) have branches in Guildford. ***Travelodge*** (☎ 08719 846295, 🖳 travelodge.co.uk; 152 rooms; ☕; 🐕; from £31 per room) lies about 1½ miles north of the High St on Woodbridge Meadows; ***Premier Inn*** (☎ 0333-0031689, 🖳 premierinn.com; 114 rooms; ☕; from £35 per room) is slightly further away on The Parkway, on the banks of the Wey, near the A25/A3 interchange.

For a B&B, at No 73 Farnham Rd is ***Asperion Hotel*** (☎ 01483-579299, 🖳 asperionhotels.com/asperion; 3S/11D all en suite, 1S private bathroom) with singles starting at £70 and doubles for £50-65pp (sgl occ room rate).

If you feel you are carrying too much weight ***Angel Hotel*** (see p77; ☎ 01483-564555, 🖳 angelpostinghouse.com; 11D/10D or T, all en suite; ☕; 🐕), at 91 High St, will lighten your wallet with rack rates in the range of £55-90pp (room only; sgl occ room rate). It's a characterful place, parts of which date back to the 1300s, such as the vaulted undercroft or basement, where banquets are sometimes held, and the remains of a spiral staircase.

Where to eat and drink

Guildford has some good independent **coffee shops**. They include ***Coffee Culture*** (☎ 01483-564200, 🖳 mycoffeeculture.co.uk; Wed-Fri 8am-5pm, Sat to 6pm, Sun 9am-5pm) down an alleyway called Angel Gate; and ***Harris & Hoole*** (☎ 01483-561035, 🖳 harrisandhoole.co.uk; Mon-Fri 7.30am-6.30pm, Sat 8am-6.30pm, Sun 8.30am-6pm; 🐕) on North St – which is actually something of a small chain itself now, with 40 branches in London and the South-East.

Of the big chains, ***Starbucks*** (Mon-Sat 7am-6pm, Sat from 8am, Sun 9am-5pm) is on the High St opposite Quarry St, and ***Caffè Nero*** (Mon-Sat 7am-7pm, Sun 8am-6pm) is at 69 High St, both offering lunches and snacks as well as excellent coffee. For a bite on the go try the Guildford branch of ***Greggs*** (Mon-Sat 7am-7pm, Sun 8am-5pm) at 42 North St.

At the Yvonne Arnaud Theatre (see What to see & do) ***The Riverbank Kitchen*** (Tue-Sat 10am-3.30pm) serves coffee, cakes and sandwiches in a lovely setting.

For food in the evening there are two main centres for **restaurants**, each different in character. The first is Friary St, where the restaurants are shiny, glass-fronted affairs with international chains including: the Japanese-style ***Wagamama*** (☎ 01483-457779, 🖳 wagamama.com; Sun-Thur 11am-10pm, Fri & Sat to 11pm); the chicken specialists ***Nando's*** (☎ 01483-568083, 🖳 nandos.co.uk; daily 11.30am-10pm); the fun and lively burger-joint ***Five Guys*** (☎ 01483-570580, 🖳 fiveguys.co.uk; Sun-Thur 11am-10pm, Fri & Sat 11am-11pm); and ***Tortilla*** (☎ 01483-375947, 🖳 tortilla.co.uk; daily 11am-9.30pm) for Tex-Mex.

Alternatively head to Chapel St, where you'll find more independent options. They include ***La Casita*** (☎ 01483-455155, 🖳 lacasitaguildford.com; Mon-Thur noon-3pm & 5-10pm, Fri, Sat & bank hol noon-10pm, Sun noon-9pm), a Mediterranean restaurant serving tapas (bowls from £3.50) as well as mains (from £17.50 for the baked fish casserole with cod, mussels, prawns, squid rings & potatoes, served in a rich tomato, garlic & chilli sauce).

Nearby at the bottom of Castle St is ***Olivo*** (☎ 01483-303535, 🖳 olivo.co.uk; Mon-Sat noon-10.30pm, Sun & bank hols noon-9.30pm). Housed in an old Tudor

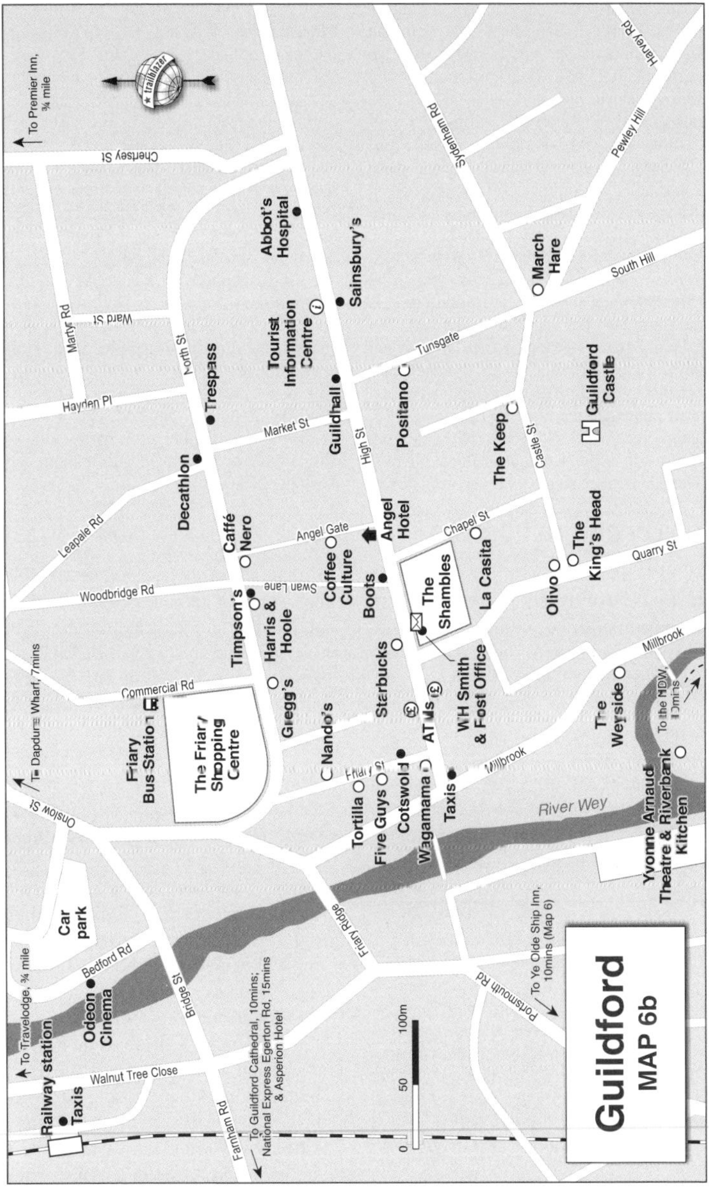
Guildford
MAP 6b
To Premier Inn, ¾ mile
Chertsey St
Abbot's Hospital
Sainsbury's
Tourist Information Centre
Sydenham Rd
Pewley Hill
Harvey Rd
March Hare
South Hill
Tunsgate
Ward St
Martyr Rd
North St
Hayden Pl
Trespass
Guildhall
Positano
Market St
High St
The Keep
Castle St
Guildford Castle
Decathlon
Leapale Rd
Caffé Nero
Angel Gate
Angel Hotel
Chapel St
Coffee Culture
Boots
The Shambles
La Casita
Olivo
The King's Head
Quarry St
Woodbridge Rd
Swan Lane
Timpson's
Harris & Hoole
WH Smith & Post Office
Starbucks
ATMs
Millbrook
Commercial Rd
Friary Bus Station
The Friary Shopping Centre
Gregg's
Nando's
The Weyside
To the NDW, 10mins
Friary St
Tortilla
Five Guys
Cotswold
Wagamama
Taxis
River Wey
Yvonne Arnaud Theatre & Riverbank Kitchen
Onslow St
Car park
Bedford Rd
Odeon Cinema
Bridge St
Friary Ridge
Portsmouth Rd
To Ye Olde Ship Inn, 10mins (Map 6)
To Travelodge, ¾ mile
Railway station
Taxis
Walnut Tree Close
Farnham Rd
To Guildford Cathedral, 10mins; National Express Egerton Rd, 15mins & Asperion Hotel
0
50
100m

beamed house this cosy Italian restaurant serves classy Italian dishes; if you can stretch to it, try the *buridda* (Genoese fish casserole, £22.95). There is another fine Italian, ***Positano*** (☎ 01483-563277, 💻 positano-restaurant.co.uk; Mon-Fri noon-2.45pm & 5.30-10.15pm, Sat noon-10.15pm, Sun noon-9.15pm), housed in an Elizabethan building just off the High St on Tunsgate, with a large menu and a good line in risotto (from £15.95).

For **pub food**, ***The Weyside*** (☎ 01483-568024, 💻 theweyside.co.uk; 🐕; food Mon-Sat noon-9.30pm, Sun noon-9pm) is the first place you reach from the path. It's a lovely place to stop, particularly if you have a dog, with dog towels, blankets and biscuits available. The (short) menu is good with mains from £17 for burger and fries. The terrace overlooking the river is a great spot to sit in the sun and air those blisters. There are also some great choices down Castle St. Opposite the top of Tunsgate, ***March Hare*** (☎ 01483-401530, 💻 marchhareguildford.com; food Mon-Sat noon-9.45pm, Sun noon-9pm; 🐕 bar area only) is a pub and brasserie with mains such as Toulouse sausages (£15.25) or classic beef and ale pie (£18.95).

A little further down Castle St, ***The Keep*** (☎ 01483-450600, 💻 thekeepguildford.com; food Wed-Fri from 5pm, Sat noon-6pm; 🐕) is more traditional with decent no-nonsense pub grub.

At the bottom of Castle St and the junction with Quarry St is Guildford's oldest pub, ***The King's Head*** (☎ 01483-575004, 💻 thekingsheadpub.co.uk; food Mon-Thur noon-3pm & 5-9pm, Fri noon-3pm & 5-8pm, Sat noon-8pm, Sun noon-5pm; 🐕), reputedly haunted, with a pretty fast-food (pizzas, burgers) menu though with a few pub classics including ham, egg & chips, £16).

GUILDFORD TO DORKING [MAPS 6-13a]

Whilst the names 'Guildford' and 'Dorking' may not in themselves be enough to arouse excitement in those walkers seeking isolation and an escape from the modern world, nor conjure up images of untainted wilderness and nature at its most untrammelled, there is actually much to enjoy on this **12.9-mile/20.7km** stage (**4¼hrs-5¼hrs**). The trail certainly does its utmost to show off the best that Surrey has to offer, including two very fine churches, the county's prettiest village and the country's largest vineyard. There are also large tracts of walking in mature and beautiful woodland on this stage – a feature of the North Downs Way that is as surprising as it is welcome. But it's the views that walkers are afforded throughout the day that are this stage's real highlight. Those good folk whose job it is to maintain and enhance the North Downs Way clearly recognise this fact, for throughout the day there are benches aplenty to entice you to slow down, put your feet up and just drink in the scenery; thus ensuring that this stage, which could be done in **4¼hrs-5¼hrs** without breaks, usually takes a whole day to complete at a more relaxed pace.

> *'It has been very fine to-day. Yesterday morning there was snow on Reigate Hill, enough to look white from where we were in the valley. We set off about half-past one o'clock, and came all down the valley, through Buckland, Betchworth, Dorking, Sheer and Aldbury, to this place. Very few prettier rides in England, and the weather beautifully fine.'*
>
> **William Cobbett**, ***Rural Rides***

The first of these stretches of woodland walking – and the first breathtaking views – occur early on this stage with a climb through **Chantry Wood** (Map 7) and up the slopes of **St Martha's Hill** to the

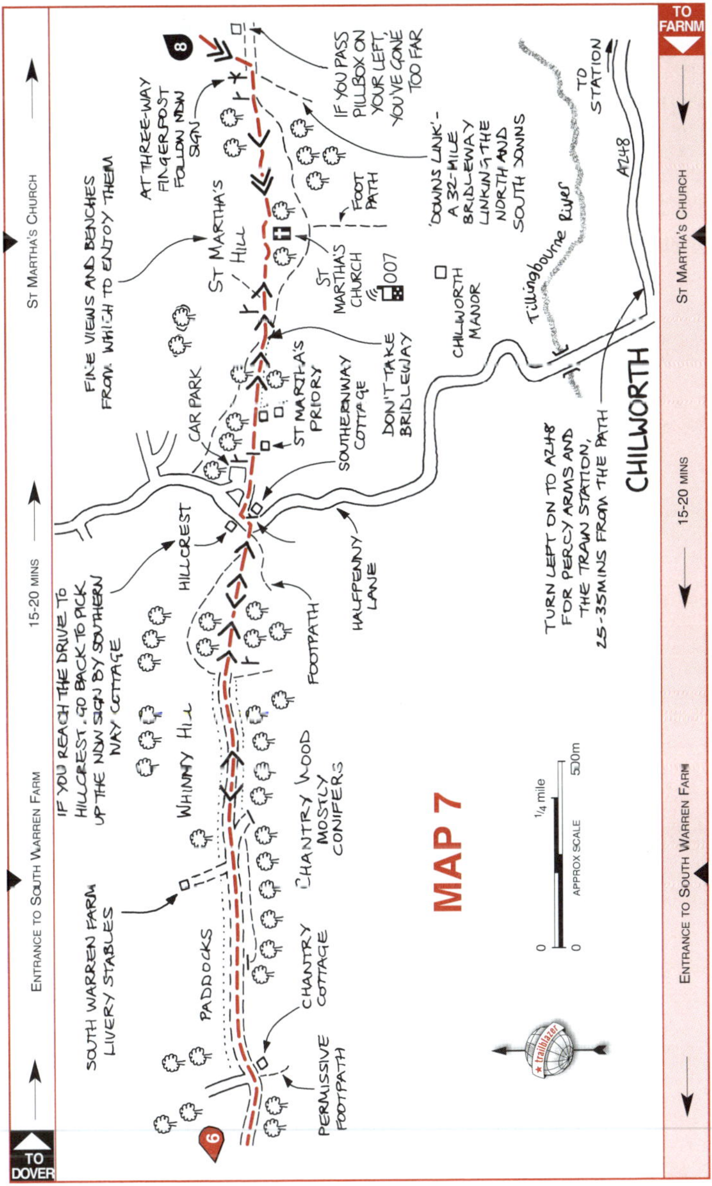
MAP 7
TO DOVER
TO FARNM
ENTRANCE TO SOUTH WARREN FARM
15-20 MINS
ST MARTHA'S CHURCH
APPROX SCALE
0
1/4 mile
500m
trailblazer
PERMISSIVE FOOTPATH
CHANTRY COTTAGE
SOUTH WARREN FARM LIVERY STABLES
PADDOCKS
CHANTRY WOOD MOSTLY CONIFERS
WHINNY HILL
IF YOU REACH THE DRIVE TO HILLCREST, GO BACK TO PICK UP THE NDW SIGN BY SOUTHERN WAY COTTAGE
FOOTPATH
HILLCREST
HALFPENNY LANE
SOUTHERNWAY COTTAGE
CAR PARK
ST MARTHA'S PRIORY
FINE VIEWS AND BENCHES FROM WHICH TO ENJOY THEM
DON'T TAKE BRIDLEWAY
ST MARTHA'S HILL
ST MARTHA'S CHURCH
007
CHILWORTH MANOR
FOOT PATH
AT THREE-WAY FINGERPOST FOLLOW NDW SIGN
8
6
IF YOU PASS PILLBOX ON YOUR LEFT, YOU'VE GONE TOO FAR
'DOWNS LINK' - A 32-MILE BRIDLEWAY LINKING THE NORTH AND SOUTH DOWNS
Tillingbourne River
A248
TO STATION
TURN LEFT ON TO A248 FOR PERCY ARMS AND THE TRAIN STATION, 25-35MINS FROM THE PATH
CHILWORTH

church that shares its name. It is believed that pilgrims visited the church on the way to Canterbury, so it is often referred to as the Pilgrims' Church, though it's debatable whether there was ever only one route pilgrims followed. Nevertheless, it's likely that they found the church a convenient place to stop and rest. And few are those who don't find their spirits soaring when they visit, for even if the sermons within the church fail to rouse, the panorama over the Surrey Hills outside it surely will; it's a lovely spot to rest for a few minutes and enjoy the view over nearby **Chilworth** and, further east, **Albury**.

CHILWORTH [off MAP 7, p81]

Reached by turning right off the trail (down Halfpenny Lane) before St Martha's Hill, Chilworth straggles along the A248 but has a good pub, ***The Percy Arms*** (☎ 01483-561765, 🖳 thepercyarms.net; 1T or D/4D, all en suite; ☕; 🐕 bar area only), with a rather incongruous South African theme. Nevertheless the rooms (**B&B** £57.50-67.50pp, sgl occ room rate) are pretty opulent and the **food** (Mon-Fri noon-3pm & 6-10pm, Sat noon-10pm & Sun noon-9pm; booking essential) is renowned, particularly the steaks (£23.95 for the 10oz rump).

GWR's Reading to Redhill service (see box pp42-3) calls at the **railway station**. Compass Travel and the No 32 **bus service** (Guildford to Dorking/Redhill) stops at the station; see pp44-7 for details.

ALBURY [off MAP 8]

Albury is an estate village belonging to the Duke of Northumberland and estate buildings are painted in green trim. Mentioned in the Domesday Book under its original name, Eldeberie, it was said to consist of one church, one mill and woodland worth 30 hogs; little has changed since. Well known locally for its highly decorative **Pugin** chimneys, the estate yard also has a restored **dovecote**. The estate is now also home to the **Silent Pool gin distillery** (🖳 silentpooldistillers.com).

Ten minutes east on the A248 is the **Catholic Apostolic Church** (not open) and the **Saxon Old Church, Albury Park** (daily 10am-5pm or dusk), which is worth a visit for its Pugin mortuary chapel.

For **supplies** there's Pratt's Stores & **post office** (☎ 01483-202123; Mon-Fri 8am-5pm, Sat to noon) and Albury Village Stores (Mon-Sat 7am-7.30pm, Sun 8am-2pm). There are **rooms** at the smart and sumptuous ***Drummond at Albury*** (☎ 01483-202039, 🖳 thedrummondatalbury.co.uk; 4D/6T/1Qd, all en suite; ☕; 🐕 bar area only) from £50pp (sgl occ full room rate). **Food** is served (daily 8-11am plus Mon-Fri noon-2.45pm & 6-8.45pm, Sat noon-8.45pm, Sun noon-8pm), with mains from £15 and the delightful beer garden borders the Tillingbourne River.

The No 32 **bus service** (Guildford to Dorking/Redhill) stops by The Drummond; see pp44-7 for details.

Tearing yourself away from the views, as you eventually must, you'll find more benches along **Albury Downs** before you gain the North Downs Way ridgeline at busy **Newlands Corner**.

NEWLANDS CORNER [MAP 8]

The views from here are spectacular on a clear day and this beauty spot was the scene of the 10-day disappearance of Agatha Christie, the mystery writer, (see box p84) in December 1926.

The trail passes to the front of **Surrey Wildlife Trust Countryside Centre** (daily 9am to around 4.30pm), which has an informative display on the flora and fauna of this part of the Downs.

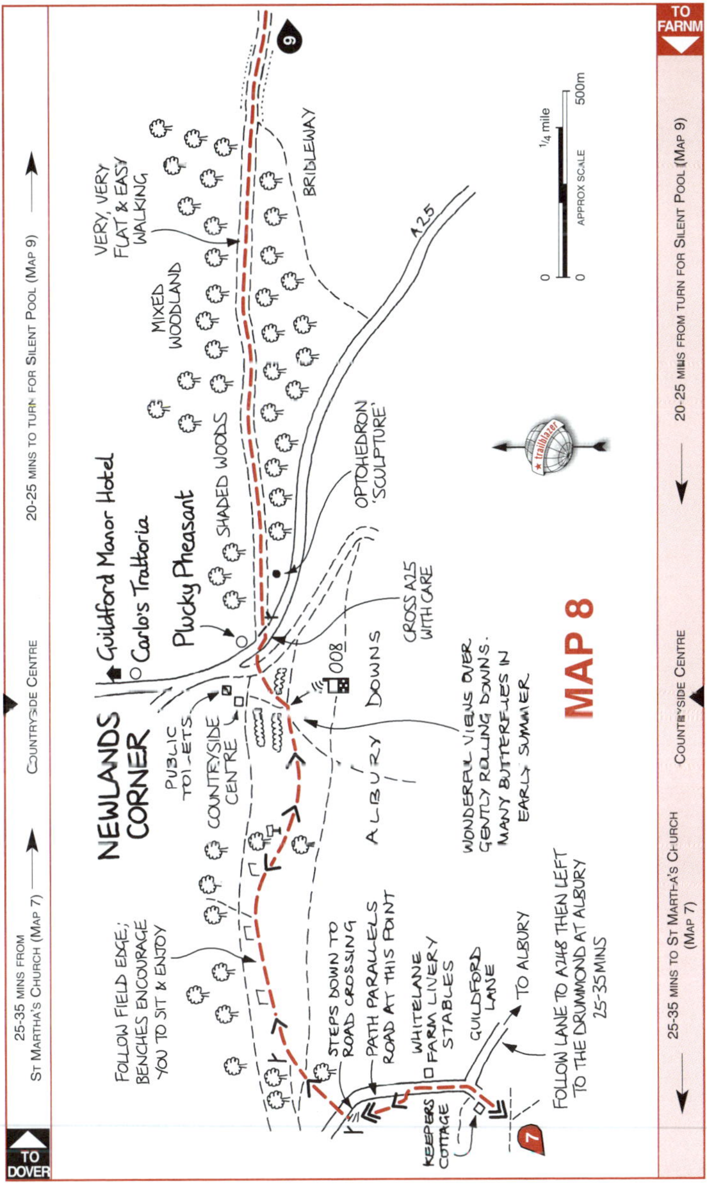
TO DOVER
TO FARNM
25-35 mins from St Martha's Church (Map 7)
Countryside Centre
20-25 mins to turn for Silent Pool (Map 9)
20-25 mins from turn for Silent Pool (Map 9)
Countryside Centre
25-35 mins to St Martha's Church (Map 7)
NEWLANDS CORNER
Guildford Manor Hotel
Carlo's Trattoria
Plucky Pheasant
SHADED WOODS
MIXED WOODLAND
VERY, VERY FLAT & EASY WALKING
BRIDLEWAY
A25
9
OPTOHEDRON 'SCULPTURE'
CROSS A25 WITH CARE
PUBLIC TOILETS
COUNTRYSIDE CENTRE
008
ALBURY DOWNS
WONDERFUL VIEWS OVER GENTLY ROLLING DOWNS. MANY BUTTERFLIES IN EARLY SUMMER
MAP 8
trailblazer
0 1/4 mile
0 500m
APPROX SCALE
FOLLOW FIELD EDGE; BENCHES ENCOURAGE YOU TO SIT & ENJOY
STEPS DOWN TO ROAD CROSSING
PATH PARALLELS ROAD AT THIS POINT
WHITELANE FARM LIVERY STABLES
KEEPERS COTTAGE
GUILDFORD LANE
TO ALBURY
FOLLOW LANE TO A248 THEN LEFT TO THE DRUMMOND AT ALBURY 25-35 MINS
7

There is a small **eatery** here but you're probably better off crossing the road to ***The Plucky Pheasant*** (☎ 01483-225222, 🖳 thepluckypheasant.com; summer Mon-Fri 8.30am-4.30pm, Sat & Sun to 5pm, winter closing 30 mins earlier; 🐕). This place is often crowded, especially at the weekend, with people feasting on the views and the expensive but hearty fare, with hot breakfast options in the range of £5-13.50.

A short walk down the busy A25 (no pavement) is ***Carlo's Trattoria*** (☎ 01483-224180, 🖳 carlostrattoria.com; Tue-Sat noon-2.30pm & 6-10pm, Sun noon-3pm); Italian food at its best.

If you can go no further after that the smart ***Guildford Manor Hotel*** (☎ 01483-222624, 🖳 guildfordmanor.com; 51 rooms, all en suite; ◗) charges from £59.50pp (sgl occ from £99) including breakfast; rates without breakfast are also available.

The only **bus** service is the limited No 25 (Cranleigh to Guildford); see pp44-7 for details.

❑ AGATHA CHRISTIE AND THE MYSTERIOUS AFFAIR AT NEWLANDS CORNER

When Agatha Christie disappeared from here in December 1926 she was on the best-seller lists so was well known; thus her disappearance had thousands out searching for her. She abandoned her car here on a Friday evening. Since it was close to Silent Pool (off Map 9) it prompted fears that she had committed suicide. The pool was dredged but no body was found. It turned out that she had travelled to Harrogate, the Yorkshire spa town.

Did she get there by train and was it from Chilworth, Gomshall or nearby Guildford? We shall never know as she refused to talk about her 'lost days'. She booked into a hotel under the name Neele, her husband's mistress's name, and was eventually found when guests recognised her from newspaper photographs.

On her return the story was put about that she suffered amnesia following her mother's death. But why did she do what she did? Were they the actions of someone unhinged by jealousy, or were they pre-planned to embarrass her husband and get away from a bad marriage? Perhaps someone else was in on it and helped her travel from deepest Surrey to Yorkshire? Maybe it's time to call Poirot.

Those extensive views disappear as suddenly as Agatha Christie did in 1926 (see box above) as you strike east along a drove road to undertake perhaps the most extensive stretch of woodland walking of any national trail, a stretch that continues, on and off, all the way to Ranmore Common. That said, few and foolish are those who don't take a break from all this sylvan strolling by turning off the trail at Hollister Farm to visit Surrey's prettiest village, **Shere**. The path joins a by-way, crosses the A25 and enters Shere by the car park.

SHERE [MAP 9a, p86]

Described as the prettiest village in Surrey, Shere suffers as a result and perhaps should claim the title as one of the busiest. But it's packed with picturesque 15th- and 16th-century **timbered buildings** and attractive cottages.

At the 12th-century parish **church of St James** (open daily), the lychgate was designed by Lutyens (see box p86).

Shere Museum (☎ 01483-202769, 🖳 exploringsurreyspast.org.uk; free; Sat & Sun 2-5pm plus Apr-Oct Tue & Thur 10am-3pm) focuses on local history.

You can withdraw cash at the **post office** (Mon-Tue & Thur-Fri 8am-10pm, Wed 8am-6pm, Sat & Sun 9am-6pm) in the **Welcome** convenience store (Mon-Fri 7am-10pm, Sat/Sun 8am-10pm).

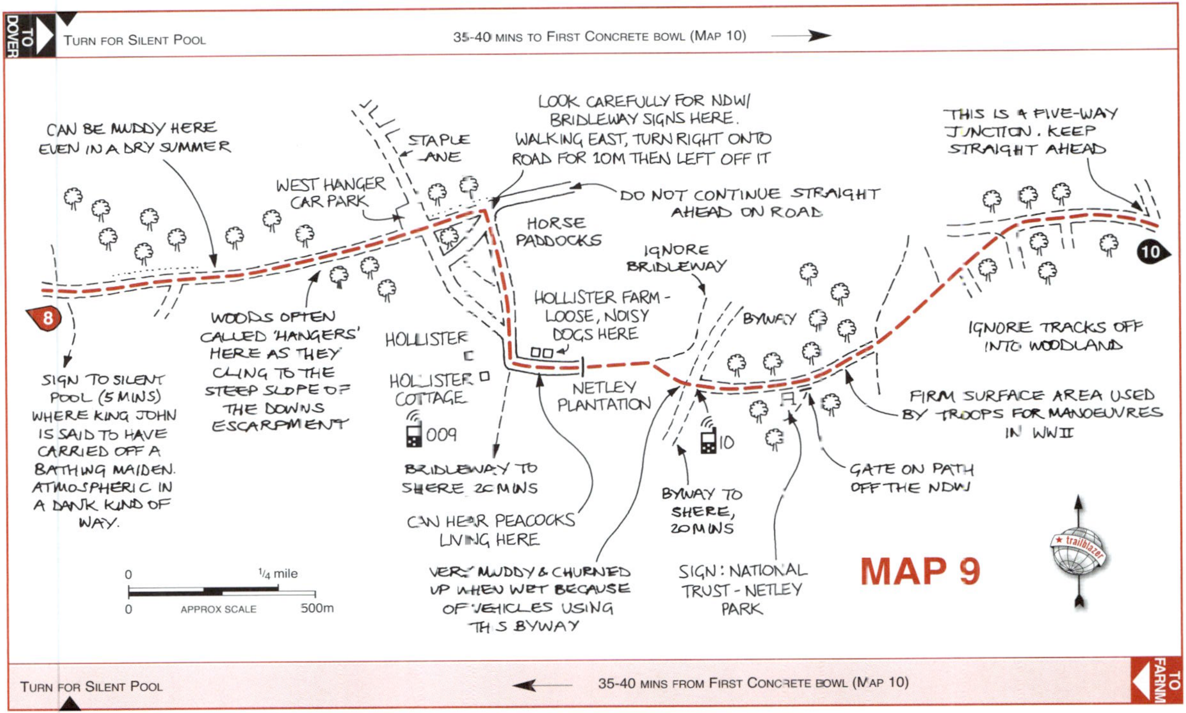
TO DOVER
TURN FOR SILENT POOL
35-40 MINS TO FIRST CONCRETE BOWL (MAP 10)
CAN BE MUDDY HERE EVEN IN A DRY SUMMER
STAPLE LANE
WEST HANGER CAR PARK
LOOK CAREFULLY FOR NDW/ BRIDLEWAY SIGNS HERE. WALKING EAST, TURN RIGHT ONTO ROAD FOR 10M THEN LEFT OFF IT
DO NOT CONTINUE STRAIGHT AHEAD ON ROAD
HORSE PADDOCKS
THIS IS A FIVE-WAY JUNCTION. KEEP STRAIGHT AHEAD
IGNORE BRIDLEWAY
HOLLISTER FARM - LOOSE, NOISY DOGS HERE
BYWAY
10
8
SIGN TO SILENT POOL (5 MINS) WHERE KING JOHN IS SAID TO HAVE CARRIED OFF A BATHING MAIDEN. ATMOSPHERIC IN A DANK KIND OF WAY.
WOODS OFTEN CALLED 'HANGERS' HERE AS THEY CLING TO THE STEEP SLOPE OF THE DOWNS ESCARPMENT
HOLLISTER
HOLLISTER COTTAGE
009
NETLEY PLANTATION
IGNORE TRACKS OFF INTO WOODLAND
FIRM SURFACE AREA USED BY TROOPS FOR MANOEUVRES IN WWII
BRIDLEWAY TO SHERE 20 MINS
10
GATE ON PATH OFF THE NDW
BYWAY TO SHERE, 20 MINS
CAN HEAR PEACOCKS LIVING HERE
0
¼ mile
0
APPROX SCALE
500m
VERY MUDDY & CHURNED UP WHEN WET BECAUSE OF VEHICLES USING THIS BYWAY
SIGN: NATIONAL TRUST - NETLEY PARK
MAP 9
trailblazer
TURN FOR SILENT POOL
35-40 MINS FROM FIRST CONCRETE BOWL (MAP 10)
TO FARNM

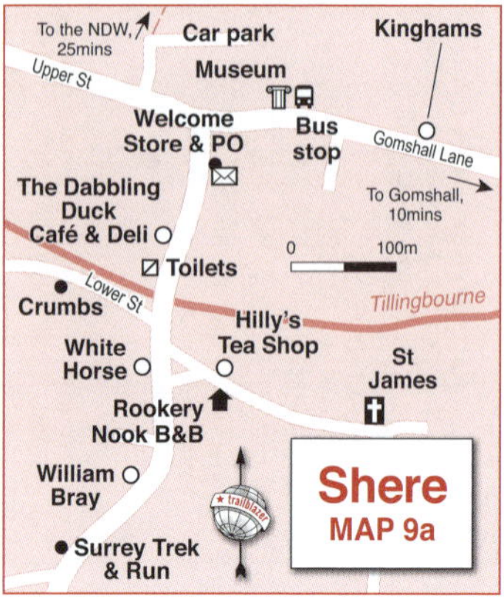

You'll find the village rather expensive but **Crumbs Bakery** (Tue-Thur 8am-2pm, Sat 8-11am) does the best-value food.

A little surprisingly, Shere also has its own **trekking outfitter**, Surrey Trek & Run (☎ 01483-209559, 💻 surreytrekandrun.co.uk; Mon 10.30am-3pm, Tue & Fri to 4pm, Sat to 5pm, Sun 11am-3pm) on Shere Lane.

The only **accommodation** option is near the centre on The Square, ***Rookery Nook*** (☎ 07946-756344, 💻 rookerynook.info; 1D, private bathroom; ◓) is a bit of a tourist attraction in its own right, a 15th-century Grade II listed cottage with original wattle-and-daub walls. **B&B** costs from £80pp (sgl occ from £110).

There is more choice for **food**. The popular ***White Horse*** (☎ 01483-202518, 💻 chefandbrewer.com; food Mon-Thur 11.30am-9pm, Fri-Sun 9.30am-9pm; 🐕) is perhaps the most reasonably priced. It's a lovely beamed pub, with an open fire and an extensive menu (mains from £13.29) of burgers, pies, steaks and pub classics.

Just up the road, ***William Bray*** (aka ***The Bray***; ☎ 01483-202275, 💻 thebray.net; food daily from 11am; 🐕 bar area) has some lovely outside seating and a highly regarded kitchen (pizzas from £14, other mains £17-19, sandwiches £11-13).

Kinghams (☎ 01483-202168, 💻 kinghams-restaurant.co.uk; Tue-Sat noon-2pm & 7-9pm, Sun noon-2.15pm; booking essential) is an altogether more formal experience, packed with the great and the good of Surrey. Prices start at around the £18 for mains such as salt-baked beetroot with braised lentils, chicory and homemade ricotta. Even if not eating there do walk past the terraced garden dining room in summer – it's glorious.

If the menu at ***The Dabbling Duck Café & Deli*** (☎ 01483-205791, 💻 thedabblingduck.uk.com; Mon-Fri 9am-5pm, Sat & Sun to 5.30pm, winter hours vary; 🐕) seems familiar, that's because it's the sister café of the ***Plucky Pheasant*** at Newlands Corner (there is a circular walk between the two). Again, it isn't cheap but is very likeable nevertheless, with mains from £14 (for tart of the day with salad) up to £17.50 for the burger, though sandwiches are from £9.

Upmarket ***Hilly's Tea Shop*** (☎ 01483-346550, 💻 hillysteashop.com; Tue-Sun 8.30am-4pm) has some lovely light bites including a cheese and herb scone with salmon and cream cheese (from £10).

The No 25 and 32 **bus** services stop near the Village Hall. The No 22 calls here on schooldays only (1/day). See pp44-7 for more details.

❑ SIR EDWIN LUTYENS (1869-1944) AND THE SURREY STYLE

Surrey saw a revival in vernacular architecture – the architecture of ordinary buildings – in the late 19th and early 20th century. Lutyens favoured the distinctive Surrey style using materials that would blend in with existing buildings and the surrounding countryside. This was typically oak framing, white plaster infilling, or brick and hanging clay tiles decorating the walls of the first floor. Dormer windows were used and chimneys tended to be large and separately built. His first commission was for the lychgate of **St James's Church** in Shere. Early on in his career he met and collaborated with the well-connected doyenne of English garden design, Gertrude Jekyll.

For more on this prolific and celebrated architect see 💻 lutyenstrust.org.uk.

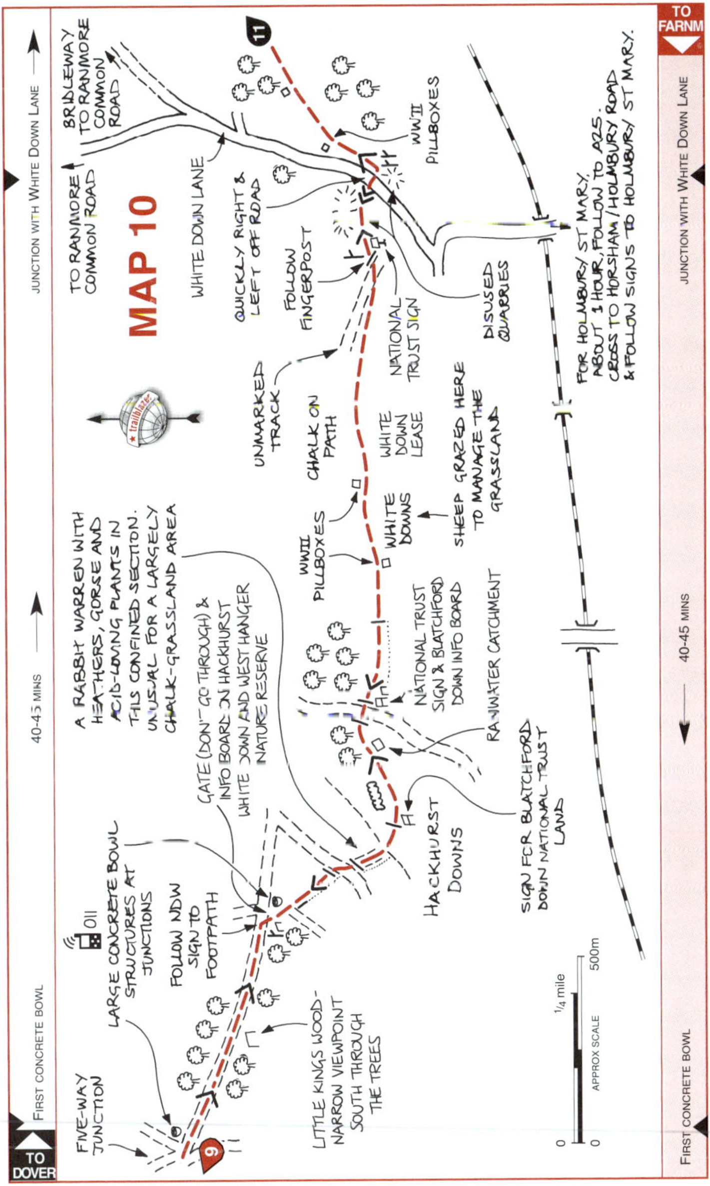
MAP 10
JUNCTION WITH WHITE DOWN LANE
40-43 MINS
FIRST CONCRETE BOWL
TO DOVER
TO FARNM
40-45 MINS
TO RANMORE COMMON ROAD
BRIDLEWAY TO RANMORE COMMON ROAD
WHITE DOWN LANE
QUICKLY RIGHT & LEFT OFF ROAD
FOLLOW FINGERPOST
WWII PILLBOXES
NATIONAL TRUST SIGN
DISUSED QUARRIES
FOR HOLMBURY ST MARY, ABOUT 1 HOUR, FOLLOW TO A25. CROSS TO HORSHAM/HOLMBURY ROAD & FOLLOW SIGNS TO HOLMBURY ST MARY.
UNMARKED TRACK
CHALK ON PATH
WHITE DOWN LEASE
WHITE DOWNS
SHEEP GRAZED HERE TO MANAGE THE GRASSLAND
WWII PILLBOXES
A RABBIT WARREN WITH HEATHERS, GORSE AND ACID-LOVING PLANTS IN THIS CONFINED SECTION. UNUSUAL FOR A LARGELY CHALK-GRASSLAND AREA
GATE (DON'T GO THROUGH) & INFO BOARD ON HACKHURST WHITE DOWN AND WEST HANGER NATURE RESERVE
NATIONAL TRUST SIGN & BLATCHFORD DOWN INFO BOARD
RAINWATER CATCHMENT
HACKHURST DOWNS
SIGN FOR BLATCHFORD DOWN NATIONAL TRUST LAND
LARGE CONCRETE BOWL STRUCTURES AT JUNCTIONS
FOLLOW NDW SIGN TO FOOTPATH
FIVE-WAY JUNCTION
LITTLE KINGS WOOD - NARROW VIEWPOINT SOUTH THROUGH THE TREES
9
11
0
1/4 mile
0
500m
APPROX SCALE
JUNCTION WITH WHITE DOWN LANE
40-45 MINS
FIRST CONCRETE BOWL

Back on the trail, you may occasionally pass large concrete water storage bowls, built by the Canadians during WWII while on manoeuvres. Continuing on, you emerge from beneath the forest canopy at Ranmore Common to pass the Gothic-style **church of St Barnabas** (Map 12; see box p90).

There's little reason to tarry in **Ranmore Common**, particularly now the YHA Tanners Hatch hostel is currently available for exclusive hire only (sleeps 15 in 3 rooms), and the bus service is no more. From Ranmore Common it is a mere hop and a skip to the **Denbies Estate** (Map 13), England's largest vine-

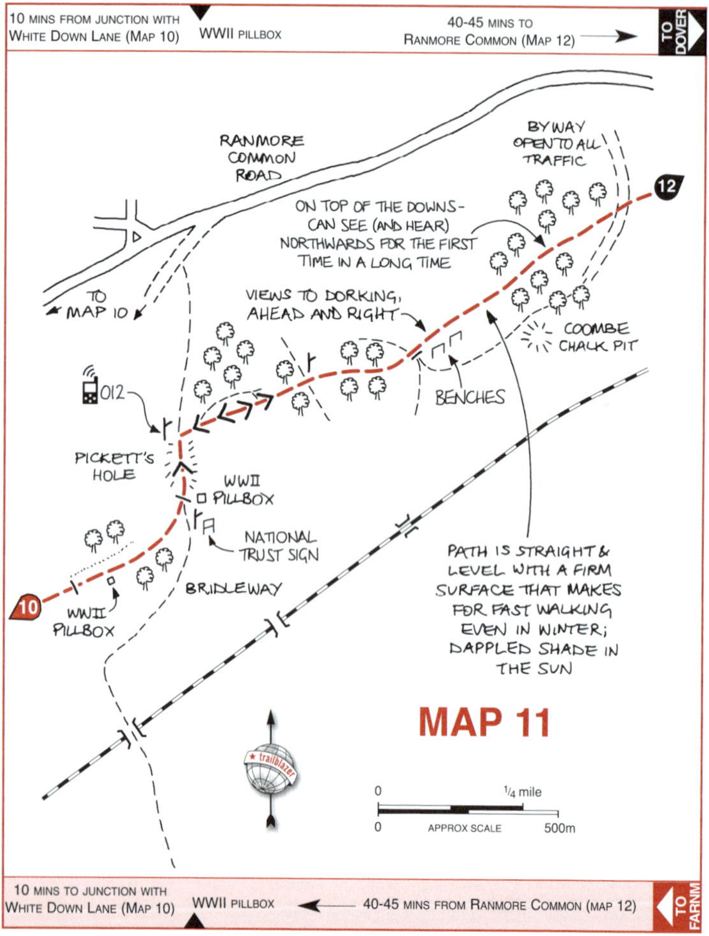

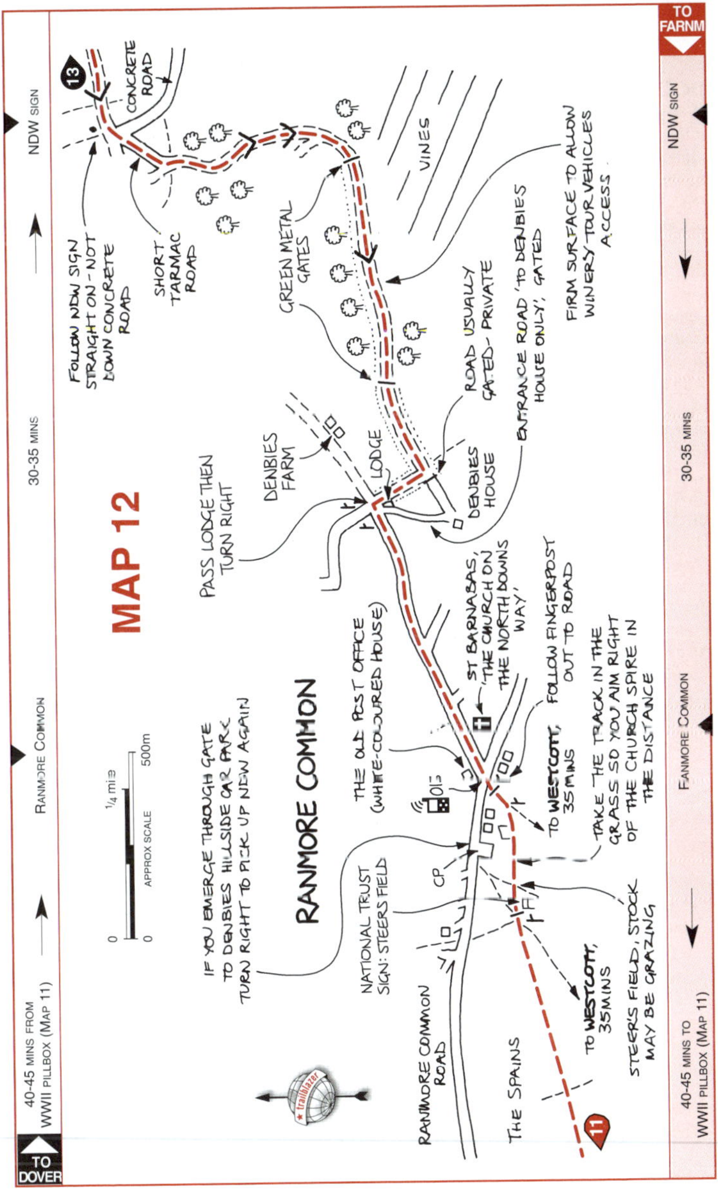

MAP 12
TO DOVER
40-45 MINS FROM WWII PILLBOX (MAP 11)
RANMORE COMMON
30-35 MINS
NDW SIGN
TO FARNM
40-45 MINS TO WWII PILLBOX (MAP 11)
FANMORE COMMON
30-35 MINS
NDW SIGN
0 1/4 mile
0 APPROX SCALE 500m
RANMORE COMMON
RANMORE COMMON ROAD
THE SPAINS
IF YOU EMERGE THROUGH GATE TO DENBIES HILLSIDE CAR PARK TURN RIGHT TO PICK UP NDW AGAIN
NATIONAL TRUST SIGN: STEERS FIELD
CP
THE OLD POST OFFICE (WHITE-COLOURED HOUSE)
ST BARNABAS, 'THE CHURCH ON THE NORTH DOWNS WAY'
FOLLOW FINGERPOST OUT TO ROAD
TO WESTCOTT, 35MINS
TAKE THE TRACK IN THE GRASS SO YOU AIM RIGHT OF THE CHURCH SPIRE IN THE DISTANCE
TO WESTCOTT, 35MINS
STEER'S FIELD, STOCK MAY BE GRAZING
PASS LODGE THEN TURN RIGHT
DENBIES FARM
LODGE
DENBIES HOUSE
ROAD USUALLY GATED - PRIVATE
ENTRANCE ROAD 'TO DENBIES HOUSE ONLY'; GATED
GREEN METAL GATES
FIRM SURFACE TO ALLOW WINERY TOUR VEHICLES ACCESS
VINES
FOLLOW NDW SIGN STRAIGHT ON - NOT DOWN CONCRETE ROAD
SHORT TARMAC ROAD
CONCRETE ROAD
13
11

yard, situated on the outskirts of Dorking. A short diversion to the visitor centre (see below) and the winery tour are recommended.

DENBIES WINE ESTATE [MAP 13]

With your thirst sharpened along the 13-mile stage, a detour to England's largest vineyard, Denbies (☎ 01306-876616, 🖳 denbies.co.uk), could be in order. A tour of the vines costs £10.95 and can be booked at the **visitor centre** (daily 9.30am-5pm).

The stylish ***Gallery Restaurant*** (Wed-Sun noon-3.30pm; mains from £20; booking essential) on the third floor has panoramic views of the vineyard. The ***Conservatory Restaurant*** (daily 9.30am-4pm) is the cheaper, more informal option with a wide range of salads and sandwiches as well as a decent breakfast, and they now also have the ***Hatch on the Lawn*** takeaway (daily 9.30am-2.30pm).

Surrey Hills Brewery (☎ 01306-883603; 🖳 surreyhills.co.uk) is also based on the estate (pre-booked tour £15pp).

B&B is offered at ***Denbies Vineyard Hotel*** (☎ 01306-876777, 🖳 denbies.co.uk/accommodation; 5D/1Tr/1Qd in the original farmhouse, 2T/8D in the converted barn, Brokes, next door, all en suite; ▾; 🐕) for £124-150pp in high season (sgl occ £169-199), with some rooms offering great views over the vineyard.

Another option nearby is the luxurious ***Burford Bridge Hotel*** (☎ 020-7660 0684, 🖳 all.accor.com; 57D, all en suite; ▾; 🐕; £62-77pp; sgl occ room rate). Nelson is said to have stayed here before departing for Trafalgar and reputedly Keats completed his poem *Endymion* here.

For **food**, head to walker- and dog-friendly country pub ***Stepping Stones*** (☎ 01306-889932, 🖳 steppingstonesdorking.co.uk; food Mon-Thur 8.30am-8.30pm, Fri to 9pm, Sat 11am-9pm, Sun noon-6pm; 🐕 bar area), at Westhumble. It has a range of sandwiches (£11.95) and burgers (around £15) plus other familiar pub fare.

And if you want fast food before tackling Box Hill there is ***Ryka's Café*** (🖳 rykas.co.uk; Mon & Tue 8am-5pm, Wed-Sun 8am-7pm), popular with the burger and biker crowd since the 1920s! Breakfast buns here start at £5.50. Or if you're more in the mood for pizza they have that covered too with their ***Pizza Shed*** (Wed-Fri 2-9pm, eat in or takeaway).

Box Hill & Westhumble **railway station** is a couple of minutes' walk away from Stepping Stones pub and has services to both London Waterloo (South Western Railway) and Victoria (Southern Railway); see box pp42-3.

TfL's No 465 **bus** service (Kingston-upon-Thames to Dorking) stops on the A24; see pp44-7 for details.

❑ ST BARNABAS – THE CHURCH ON THE NORTH DOWNS WAY

St Barnabas (Map 12) was built by Sir George Gilbert Scott in 1859 for the Cubitt family, then owners of the nearby Denbies Estate. Scott also designed the Albert Memorial and the enormous Grand Midland Hotel at St Pancras Station in London, while his grandson, Sir Giles, designed the original Battersea Power Station (now redeveloped into high-end residential and retail units), Bankside (now the Tate Modern) and the iconic red phone boxes that were once so common all over Britain.

Described as being one of Sir George Gilbert Scott's 'original gems with his fingerprints all over it', it has also been called a 'cathedral in the woods' by former Bishop of Guildford, Christopher Hill.

Although it is known as the 'Church on the North Downs Way', it is not, of course, the only one – you passed lovely St Martha's (see pp81-2), which bagged the title 'Pilgrims' Church', earlier on this stage.

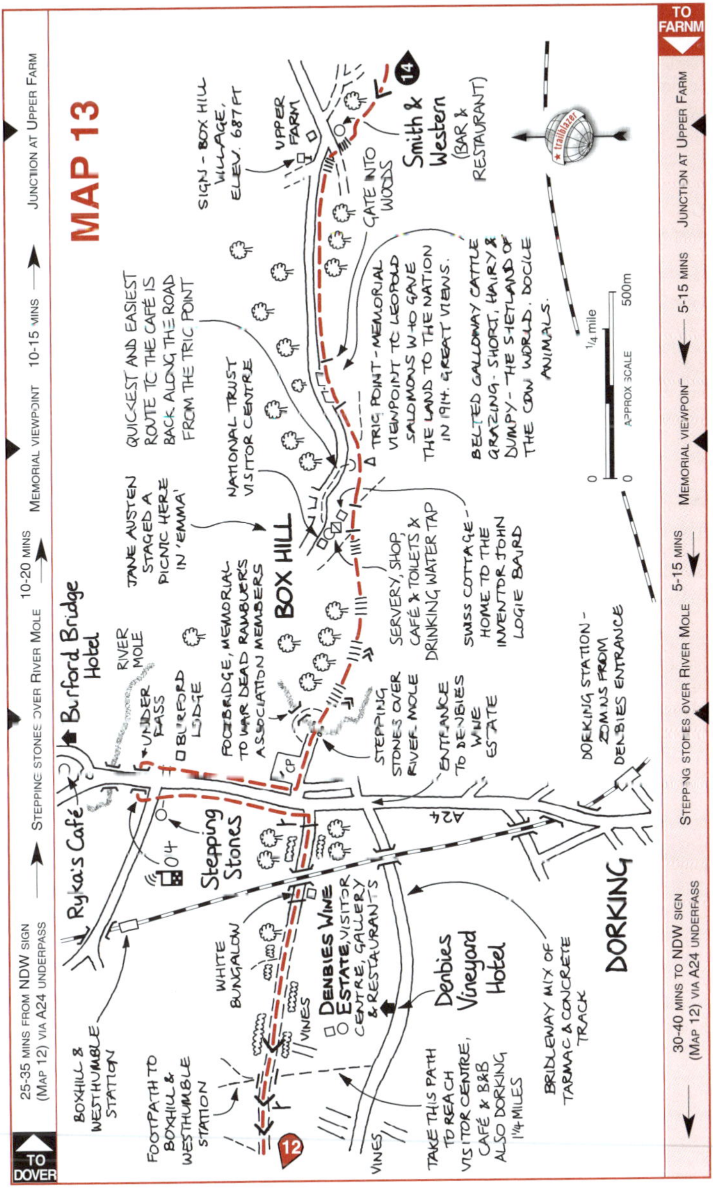
MAP 13
TO FARNM
TO DOVER
25-35 MINS FROM NDW SIGN (MAP 12) VIA A24 UNDERPASS
STEPPING STONES OVER RIVER MOLE
10-20 MINS
MEMORIAL VIEWPOINT
10-15 MINS
JUNCTION AT UPPER FARM
30-40 MINS TO NDW SIGN (MAP 12) VIA A24 UNDERPASS
5-15 MINS
5-15 MINS
APPROX SCALE
0
0
1/4 mile
500m
14
12
SMITH & WESTERN (BAR & RESTAURANT)
GATE INTO WOODS
SIGN - BOX HILL VILLAGE, ELEV. 687 FT
UPPER FARM
QUICKEST AND EASIEST ROUTE TO THE CAFÉ IS BACK ALONG THE ROAD FROM THE TRIG POINT
NATIONAL TRUST VISITOR CENTRE
TRIG POINT - MEMORIAL VIEWPOINT TO LEOPOLD SALOMONS WHO GAVE THE LAND TO THE NATION IN 1914. GREAT VIEWS.
BELTED GALLOWAY CATTLE GRAZING. SHORT, HAIRY & DUMPY - THE SHETLAND OF THE COW WORLD. DOCILE ANIMALS.
JANE AUSTEN STAGED A PICNIC HERE IN 'EMMA'
BOX HILL
SERVERY, SHOP, CAFÉ & TOILETS & DRINKING WATER TAP
SWISS COTTAGE - HOME TO THE INVENTOR JOHN LOGIE BAIRD
FOOTBRIDGE, MEMORIAL TO WAR DEAD RAMBLERS ASSOCIATION MEMBERS
Burford Bridge Hotel
RIVER MOLE
UNDER PASS
BURFORD LODGE
CP
STEPPING STONES OVER RIVER MOLE
ENTRANCE TO DENBIES WINE ESTATE
DORKING STATION - 20 MINS FROM DENBIES ENTRANCE
A24
Ryka's Café
04
Stepping Stones
DORKING
BOXHILL & WESTHUMBLE STATION
FOOTPATH TO BOXHILL & WESTHUMBLE STATION
WHITE BUNGALOW
VINES
DENBIES WINE ESTATE, VISITOR CENTRE, GALLERY & RESTAURANTS
Denbies Vineyard Hotel
BRIDLEWAY MIX OF TARMAC & CONCRETE TRACK
TAKE THIS PATH TO REACH VISITOR CENTRE, CAFÉ & B&B ALSO DORKING 1¼ MILES
VINES

The end of the estate is marked by the horribly busy A24. Tempting as it may be to try to run straight across the road, we urge you not to. Instead, turn north for 350m to take the underpass; or, even better, head south to **Dorking**, which has plenty of accommodation options and good transport links. You can walk along the A24, though that's not a pleasant option; instead, we recommend you take the turn-off from the trail marked on Map 13.

DORKING [MAP 13a]

Dorking is a thriving town at the foot of the North Downs' chalk ridge and Box Hill. It is reputed to have more antique shops per head of population than any other town in England, but even if you don't fancy wandering around the shops – and remember: a full-size Victorian mahogany wardrobe is not the easiest thing to carry on the North Downs Way – there's still enough good eateries and accommodation to warrant a visit.

What to see and do

Volunteer-run **Dorking Museum** (🖳 dorkingmuseum.org.uk; Thur 1-4pm, Fri-Sat 10am-4pm; free entry) has exhibits of the town's history and there is memorabilia of composer **Ralph Vaughan Williams** who lived locally; there is now a statue of him outside **Dorking Halls**, at the eastern end of the High St. At 26 Wathen Rd, a blue plaque commemorates **Sir Lawrence Olivier** who was born there.

Pre-booking is required for visits to **Dorking Caves**, the maze of passages under South St which were used as warehouses, smugglers' dens and for illegal cock-fighting in the past. There are guided tours in the summer months; to check the dates and make a booking (£8) visit the Dorking Museum website.

West Street is the centre of the antique trade; by the sign to the museum notice the plaque above the former home of **William Mullins** (at No 58), a shoemaker who joined the Pilgrim Fathers and sailed on the *Mayflower* to America in 1620.

Dorking Traditional **Market** (including clothes, mobile phones for sale too, but with local produce also available is held every Friday at St Martin's Walk, off High St.

Services

Tourist information for Dorking is available online at 🖳 visitdorking.com.

There are **three supermarkets** in the town centre, Marks & Spencer (Mon-Fri 8.30am-7pm, Sat from 8am, Sun 10am-4pm), Sainsbury's (Mon-Sat 7am-8pm, Sun 10am-4pm) and Waitrose (Mon-Fri 8am-9pm, Sat 8am-8pm, Sun 10am-4pm). There is also a Boots **chemist** (Mon-Sat 8.30am-5.30pm, Sun 10am-4pm) on the High St and a couple of outdoor shops: **SC Fuller** (☎ 01306-882177, 🖳 scfuller.co.uk; Mon-Sat 9am-5pm), 28-32 South St, which claims to be the oldest in Dorking; and a branch of **Millets** (Mon-Sat 9am-6pm, Sun 10am-4pm) on St Martin's Walk.

There are several **ATMs** on West St and High St. The main **post office** (Mon-Fri 9am-5.30pm, Sat 9am-12.30pm) is on High St. For **shoe repairs** there's Timpson (Mon-Fri 9am-5.30pm, Sat to 5pm).

Transport

There are three **railway stations**: Dorking (sometimes referred to as Dorking North) is used by South Western Railway (for London Waterloo) and Southern Railway (London Victoria to Horsham); GWR's services (Gatwick Airport/Redhill to Reading) call at Dorking West and Dorking Deepdene. See box pp42-3 for details.

Metrobus's **bus** services No 21 (Crawley to Epsom), 22 (Crawley to Holmbury St Mary) and No 32 (Guildford to Dorking/Redhill) all stop by the White Horse Hotel (see Where to stay) and at Dorking railway station. Tfl's No 465 (to Kingston-upon-Thames via Denbies) also calls at the station. See pp44-7.

For a **taxi** call Dorking Taxis (☎ 01306-885533, 🖳 dorkingtaxis.co.uk).

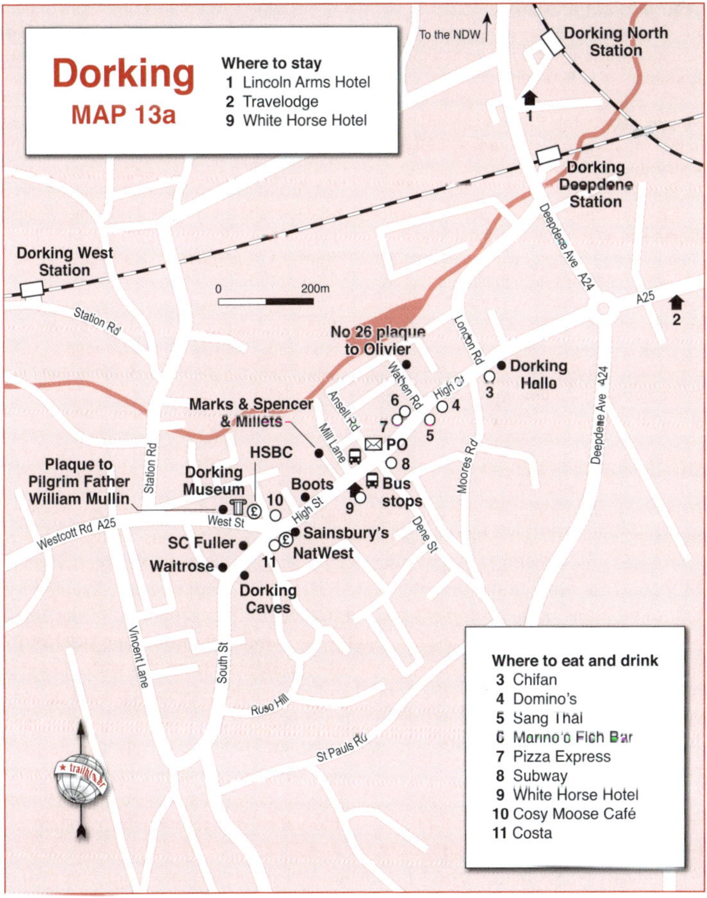

Where to stay

Coming into town off the A24, about 300m to the east along the A25, is a ***Travelodge*** (☎ 0871-984 6026, 🖳 travelodge.co.uk; 55 rooms, all en suite; ☛; 🐕; see also p21).

Centrally located on the High St is the characterful 13th century ***White Horse Hotel*** (☎ 01306-881138, 🖳 whitehorse dorking.com; 9S/25D/19D or T, 3 luxury rooms, all en suite; 🐕) with room only prices varying but in the range of £49.50 to £79.50pp (sgl occ full room rate).

If your legs just won't carry you any further coming into town along the A24 from the trail there is always ***The Lincoln Arms Hotel*** (☎ 01306-882820, 🖳 lincoln arms.co.uk; 4S/3D/10T/3Tr, all en suite; ☛) next to Dorking Station. It's seen a few incarnations but has always been a station hotel. Room only rates are from £30pp (sgl from £45).

Where to eat and drink

In addition to that ubiquitous coffee provider, ***Costa*** (Mon-Fri 7am-5.30pm, Sat from 8am, Sun 9am-4pm) there are several quirky cafés too. Our favourite is ***Cosy Moose*** (**fb**; Mon-Fri 8.30am-4pm, Sat 9am-4.30pm, Sun 9am-4pm), at 1 High St, which does only coffee and cake, but does them well.

Superior pub food is available at ***White Horse Hotel*** (see Where to stay; food Mon-Thur noon-9.15pm, Fri & Sat to 10pm, Sun to 9pm) which has an à la carte menu featuring standard British-style food and daily specials (mains from £15.25).

For evening dining there's a Chinese restaurant, ***Chifan*** (☎ 01306-889918, 🖳 chinesedorking.co.uk; Mon & Wed-Sat noon-2.30pm & 5.30-11pm, Sun noon-10pm), and the ever-popular ***Sang Thai*** (☎ 01306-888237, 🖳 sangthairestaurant.com; daily noon-2pm & 6-10.30pm), a Thai restaurant with set menus from £23.90.

Nearby is a branch of ***Pizza Express*** (☎ 01306-888236, 🖳 pizzaexpress.com/dorking; Sun-Thur 11.30am-10pm, Fri & Sat to 11pm). They offer a takeaway service, too, though if you'd like more local fare there's a decent chippy, ***Marino's Fish Bar*** (aka ***Superdish;*** ☎ 01306-887760, **fb**; Mon-Sat 11.30am-2pm & 4.30-9pm).

For takeaway-only fare you have ***Subway*** (Mon-Fri 8am-8.30pm, Sat to 9pm, Sun 10am-8pm) and ***Domino's*** (Sun-Thur 11am-midnight, Fri & Sat to 1am).

DORKING TO OXTED [MAPS 13-21]

In the introduction to this book we talked about how the North Downs Way fights a not infrequent battle against the relentless incursions of the modern world and it is something of a wonder that the trail manages to plot such a beautiful course through a region so dissected, despoiled, choked and corrupted by the trepidations of *homo sapiens* and, in particular, the cacophony of the combustion engine. Well, it is on this lengthy **18.2-mile/29.4km stage (4¾hrs to 6¾hrs)** that this conflict is most keenly fought, and in truth the path, in some places, struggles to maintain the upper-hand against the incessant tumult of traffic. The A24, M25 and its diminutive but equally noisy sibling the A25, the A217, A23, M23, M25 (again) and A22 all scream for your attention at various points throughout this lengthy stage. Thankfully, the national trail has a clever way of distracting you from all the hubbub by cramming this section with as many sights, panoramas, and points of interest as possible – and by being as pretty as it possibly can be in the circumstances too.

Indeed, no sooner do you trip off the A24 than you encounter one of the stage's highlights, the National Trust-owned **Stepping Stones** that convey you across the River Mole. Having successfully negotiated them, you then find yourself confronted by the biggest climb on the North Downs Way, a sweaty, sweltering slog up a steep, slippery slope. Encourage yourself by thinking of the rewards that await you at the top including yet more lovely views and, even more welcome, a National Trust café (see p96) with plenty of outdoor seating.

> *'Mole, that like a nousling mole doth make*
> *His way still underground, til Thames he*
> *overtake'*
> **Edmund Spenser**, ***The Faerie Queene***

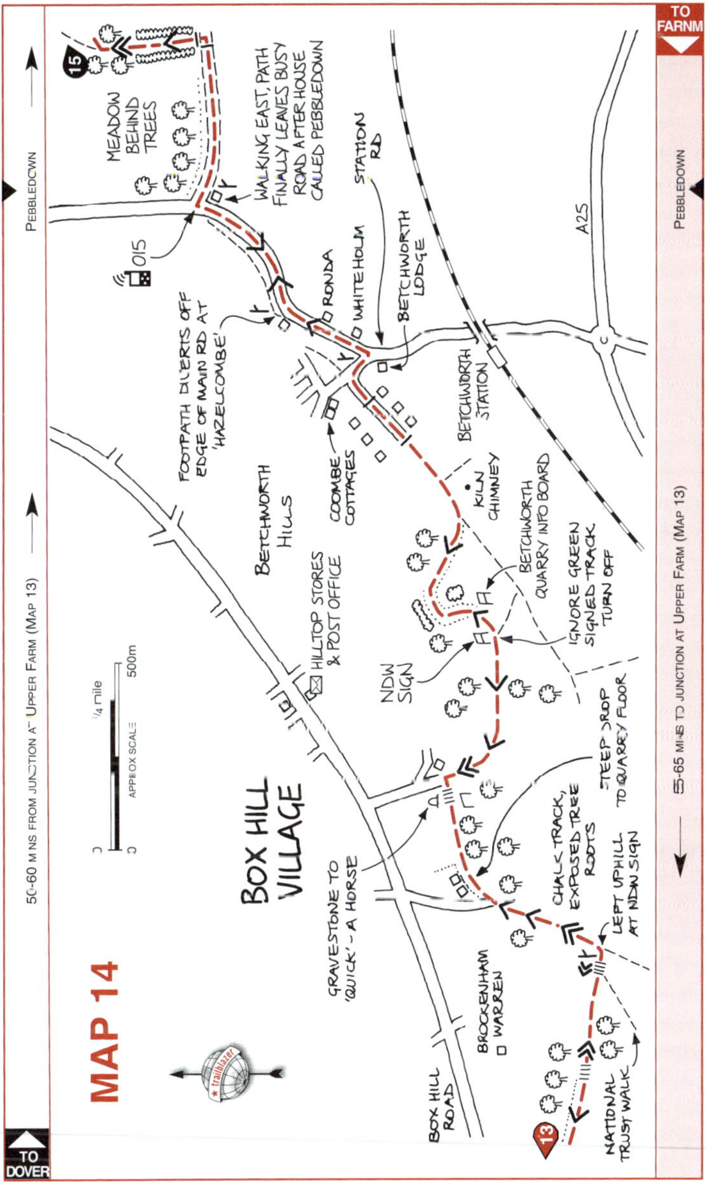
MAP 14
TO DOVER
TO FARNM
50-60 MINS FROM JUNCTION AT UPPER FARM (MAP 13)
PEBBLEDOWN
55-65 MINS TO JUNCTION AT UPPER FARM (MAP 13)
PEBBLEDOWN
0
0
¼ mile
500m
APPROX SCALE
trailblazer
BOX HILL VILLAGE
15
13
MEADOW BEHIND TREES
WALKING EAST, PATH FINALLY LEAVES BUSY ROAD AFTER HOUSE CALLED PEBBLEDOWN
STATION RD
015
FOOTPATH DIVERTS OFF EDGE OF MAIN RD AT 'HAZELCOMBE'
RONDA
WHITE HOLM
BETCHWORTH LODGE
BETCHWORTH STATION
A25
BETCHWORTH HILLS
COOMBE COTTAGES
KILN CHIMNEY
BETCHWORTH QUARRY INFO BOARD
IGNORE GREEN SIGNED TRACK TURN OFF
HILLTOP STORES & POST OFFICE
NDW SIGN
STEEP DROP TO QUARRY FLOOR
CHALK TRACK, EXPOSED TREE ROOTS
LEFT UPHILL AT NDW SIGN
GRAVESTONE TO 'QUICK' - A HORSE
BROCKENHAM WARREN
BOX HILL ROAD
NATIONAL TRUST WALK

Appropriately for a hill called Box, the man who invented the most significant 'box' of them all, the television, lived up here for four years (1929-32). That man was John Logie Baird who lived at Swiss Cottage (closed to the public) and carried out some of his most important experiments here. Rather than being named after the goggle box, however, the name **Box Hill** (Map 13) is believed to have been derived from the box trees that flourish up here. Now in the care of the National Trust, having been gifted to the nation by Leopold Salomons (whose memorial you'll pass on the trail after the café), much of the hill is an SSSI (see p55), with two-thirds of Britain's butterfly species having been recorded here; it's also home to important chalk grassland plants, see pp61-2.

> *'They had a very fine day for Box Hill … Nothing was wanting but to be happy when they got there. Seven miles were travelled in expectation of enjoyment, and every body had a burst of admiration on first arriving…'* **Jane Austen, *Emma***

The hill is also an important burial site with two Bronze Age barrows close to Salomons' Memorial. A further grave of note is that of Peter Labilliere (misspelt Labelliere on the grave) an 18th-century political agitator, peace campaigner and eccentric who would come here to meditate, but whose rather low standards of personal hygiene led to his nickname of 'The Walking Dung Hill'.

BOX HILL & BOX HILL VILLAGE [MAP 13, p91 & MAP 14, p95]

The ***servery*** (Map 13; daily 8am-3pm) has a big menu of snacks including cakes, pasties and a daily homemade soup with crusty bread. There is also a popular **café-cum-gift shop** (daily 9 or 10am-4.30pm) with a similar menu.

Further on, and opposite Upper Farm – though it's all but hidden by trees in full leaf in summer – is ***Smith & Western*** (Map 13; ☎ 01737-841666, 💻 smith-western.co.uk/boxhill; Sun-Thur noon-9pm, Fri & Sat to 11pm) an American-themed diner where the portions are huge though it's rather expensive, with burgers amongst the cheaper options (from £16.95).

A mile down Box Hill Rd in the **village** there is **Hilltop Stores** (Map 14; Mon-Thur & Sat 7.30am-6.30pm, Fri to 7.30pm, Sun 8.30am-12.30pm), incorporating the **post office** (Mon-Fri 9am-1.30pm & 3.30-5pm, Sat 9am-noon).

Metrobus's No 21 **bus** service (Crawley to Epsom; see pp44-7) stops at the National Trust Visitor Centre and at Upper Farm.

Note that although Boxhill & Westhumble **railway station** (Map 13) is a couple of miles from the village, it is less than half a mile from the North Downs Way (see p90).

Plunging back into woodland soon after Salomons' Memorial, the trail now runs past a couple of former lime quarries, climbing short but steep hills to **Juniper Hill** (Map 15).

With the noise of the M25 now encroaching from the north, the Ridgeline is gained at Colley Hill. The path is punctuated by masts, a water tower, a **monument to Lt Col Inglis** (Map 16), who gave this land to public use, a **memorial to a plane** that crashed on the hill during WWII, a couple of **pillboxes** and

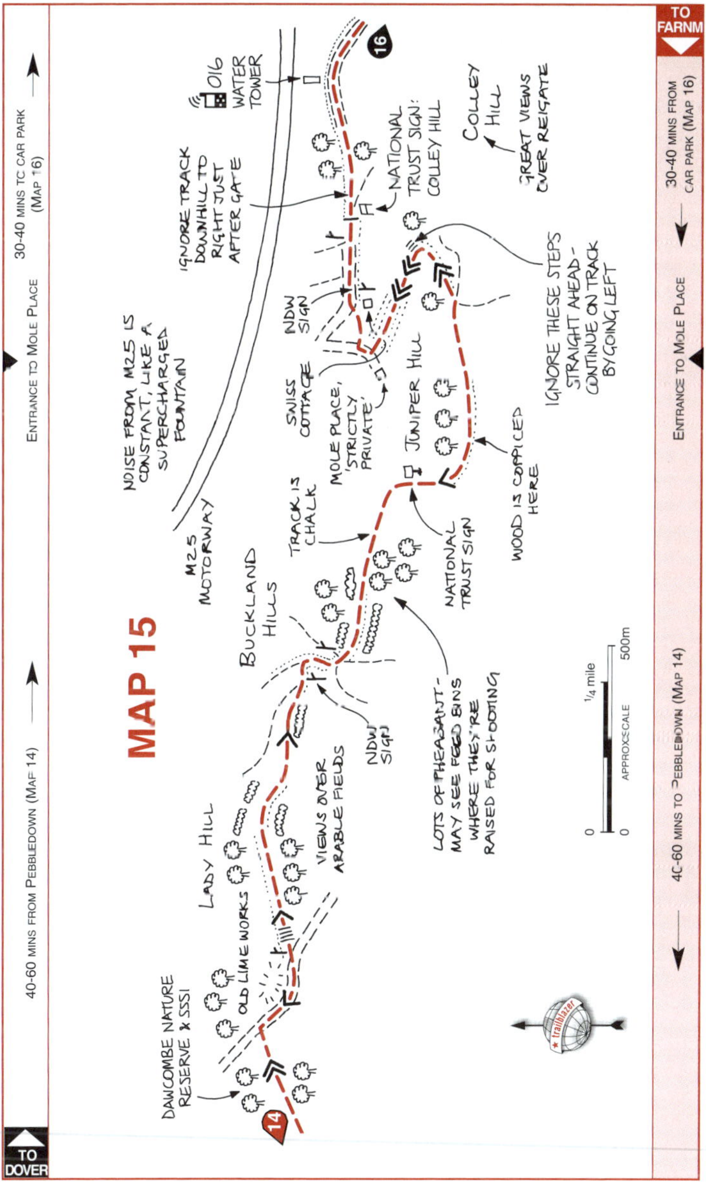
MAP 15
40-60 MINS FROM PEBBLEDOWN (MAP 14)
ENTRANCE TO MOLE PLACE
30-40 MINS TO CAR PARK (MAP 16)
TO DOVER
TO FARNM
30-40 MINS FROM CAR PARK (MAP 16)
ENTRANCE TO MOLE PLACE
40-60 MINS TO PEBBLEDOWN (MAP 14)
14
16
DAWCOMBE NATURE RESERVE & SSSI
OLD LIME WORKS
LADY HILL
VIEWS OVER ARABLE FIELDS
NDW SIGN
BUCKLAND HILLS
M25 MOTORWAY
NOISE FROM M25 IS CONSTANT, LIKE A SUPERCHARGED FOUNTAIN
TRACK IS CHALK
LOTS OF PHEASANT - MAY SEE FEED BINS WHERE THEY'RE RAISED FOR SHOOTING
NATIONAL TRUST SIGN
WOOD IS COPPICED HERE
JUNIPER HILL
MOLE PLACE, 'STRICTLY PRIVATE'
SWISS COTTAGE
NDW SIGN
IGNORE THESE STEPS STRAIGHT AHEAD - CONTINUE ON TRACK BY GOING LEFT
IGNORE TRACK DOWNHILL TO RIGHT JUST AFTER GATE
NATIONAL TRUST SIGN: COLLEY HILL
COLLEY HILL
GREAT VIEWS OVER REIGATE
016 WATER TOWER
0 1/4 mile
0 500m
APPROX SCALE
trailblazer

Napoleonic Reigate Fort (see box below) – enough distractions, I think you'll agree, to draw your attention away from both the M25's rumble and any weariness you may be feeling after all that climbing today.

REIGATE HILL [MAP 16]

The path passes above and behind ***The Bridge House Hotel*** (☎ 07736-816618, 🖳 bridgehousereigate.com; 8S/23D/6T/2Tr, all en suite; ♥). Room rates vary but are around £28-55pp (sgl/sgl occ from £50); with breakfast an extra £7.50pp if booked in advance. The attached ***restaurant*** is open daily noon-3pm and 6.30-9.30pm. To reach the hotel you need to cross the footbridge over the A217 to the snack bar and car park, and then cross the A217 itself.

The ***Junction 8*** **snack bar** (daily 8am-4pm) is conveniently situated at the top of Reigate Hill with a nice line in smoothies and a decent selection of wraps and ciabattas. Below the car park is Wray Lane leading to Redhill, though be careful on this pavement-less winding road; you may find it easier to walk on to Merstham and get a bus back from there if Redhill is your destination.

❑ WARTIME DEFENCES – SURREY'S MAGINOT LINE

Reigate Fort (see Map 16) was built in 1898 as one of 13 installations forming a defence chain over 70 miles of the Downs escarpment to protect London from invasion from the south and east. At the time France was considered the greatest potential threat. The structures were not forts in the ordinary sense but large gun encampments. At the time they were cutting-edge military tactics – a static defence line facing the enemy along the ridge of the North Downs. The same methods were adopted in WWII with pillboxes creating a Surrey Maginot Line – Maginot was the French General who devised the tactic.

The tank traps and pillboxes seen along the trail (see Map 6 p75, Map 10 p87, and Map 11 p88) are remnants of defence thinking in the inter-war years. The concrete boxes, complete with machine-gun slits and 17-inch thick walls, dotting the route in Surrey were part of a three-tier system of national defence – coastal defences on beaches, stop lines inland and finally a fixed line of tank traps and pillboxes 50 miles behind the south and east coasts.

REDHILL [MAP 16a, p100]

Although not exactly the most charismatic of places you'll visit on your walk, this commuter town does at least have some useful services and good transport links. The central area around High St, Station Rd and the Harlequin Centre is pedestrianised.

Services

In the **Belfry Centre** (🖳 redhillbelfry.co.uk) there is an **outdoor shop**, Trespass (Mon-Sat 9am-5.30pm, Sun 10.30am-4.30pm), Boots **pharmacy** (Mon-Fri 9am-6pm, Sat 9am-5pm, Sun 10.30am-4pm) and a Timpson's **shoe repairers** (Mon-Sat 9am-5.30pm, Sun 10.30am-4.30pm) next door.

The Sainsbury's **supermarket**, north of the Harlequin Centre, is open daily (Mon-Sat 7am-10pm, Sun 10am-4pm) and there's a branch of (cheaper) Iceland (Mon-Sat 8am-7pm, Sun 10am-4pm). The town centre has an open-air **market** (every Thur, Fri & Sat) and a farmers' market (2nd Fri of month).

There are several banks with **ATMs** on Station Rd and a **post office** (Mon-Sat 9am-5.30pm) in the branch of WH Smith in the Belfry Centre.

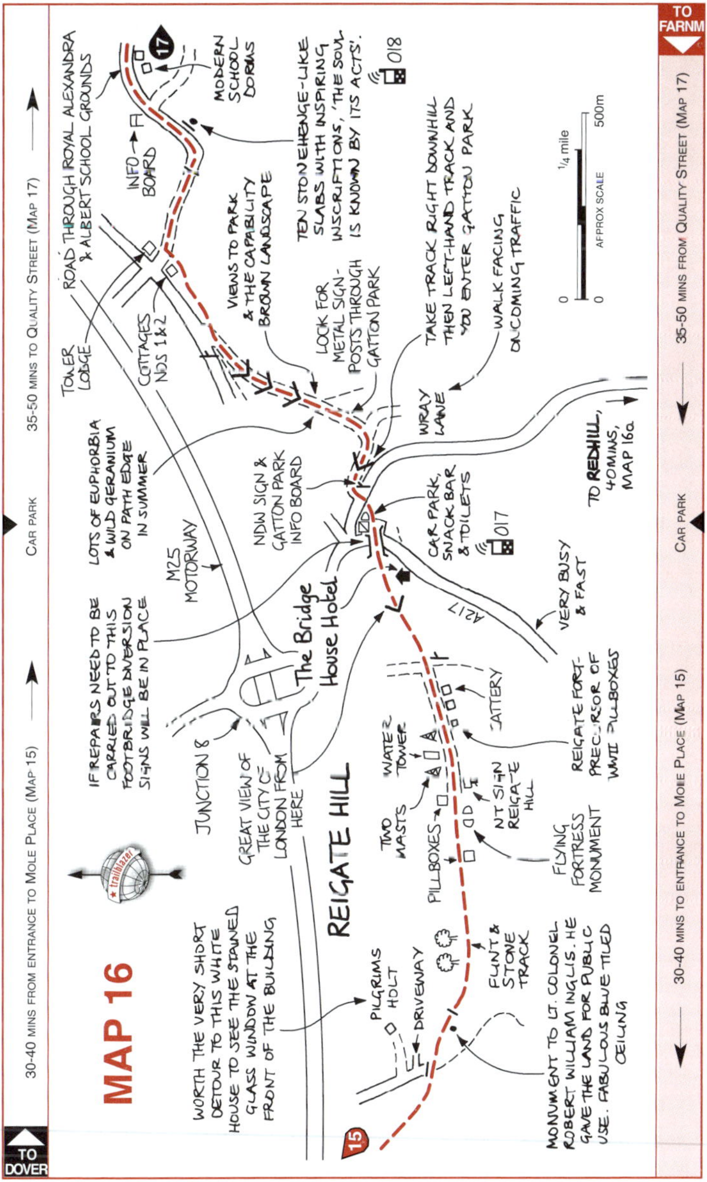
MAP 16
30-40 MINS FROM ENTRANCE TO MOLE PLACE (MAP 15)
CAR PARK
35-50 MINS TO QUALITY STREET (MAP 17)
TO DOVER
TO FARNM
30-40 MINS TO ENTRANCE TO MOLE PLACE (MAP 15)
CAR PARK
35-50 MINS FROM QUALITY STREET (MAP 17)
trailblazer
WORTH THE VERY SHORT DETOUR TO THIS WHITE HOUSE TO SEE THE STAINED GLASS WINDOW AT THE FRONT OF THE BUILDING
IF REPAIRS NEED TO BE CARRIED OUT TO THIS FOOTBRIDGE DIVERSION SIGNS WILL BE IN PLACE
JUNCTION 8
GREAT VIEW OF THE CITY OF LONDON FROM HERE
REIGATE HILL
PILGRIMS HOLT
DRIVEWAY
LOTS OF EUPHORBIA & WILD GERANIUM ON PATH EDGE IN SUMMER
M25 MOTORWAY
The Bridge House Hotel
TOWER LODGE
COTTAGES NOS 1 & 2
ROAD THROUGH ROYAL ALEXANDRA & ALBERT SCHOOL GROUNDS
INFO BOARD
MODERN SCHOOL DORMS
17
VIEWS TO PARK & THE CAPABILITY BROWN LANDSCAPE
TEN STONEHENGE-LIKE SLABS WITH INSPIRING INSCRIPTIONS, 'THE SOUL IS KNOWN BY ITS ACTS'.
018
LOOK FOR METAL SIGN-POSTS THROUGH GATTON PARK
NDW SIGN & GATTON PARK INFO BOARD
TAKE TRACK RIGHT DOWNHILL THEN LEFT-HAND TRACK AND YOU ENTER GATTON PARK
WALK FACING ONCOMING TRAFFIC
WRAY LANE
CAR PARK, SNACK BAR & TOILETS
017
A217
VERY BUSY & FAST
TO REDHILL, 40MINS, MAP 16a
TWO MASTS
WATER TOWER
PILLBOXES
BATTERY
NT SIGN REIGATE HILL
REIGATE FORT - PRECURSOR OF WWII PILLBOXES
FLYING FORTRESS MONUMENT
FLINT & STONE TRACK
MONUMENT TO LT. COLONEL ROBERT WILLIAM INGLIS. HE GAVE THE LAND FOR PUBLIC USE. FABULOUS BLUE TILED CEILING
15
0
1/4 mile
0
500m
APPROX SCALE

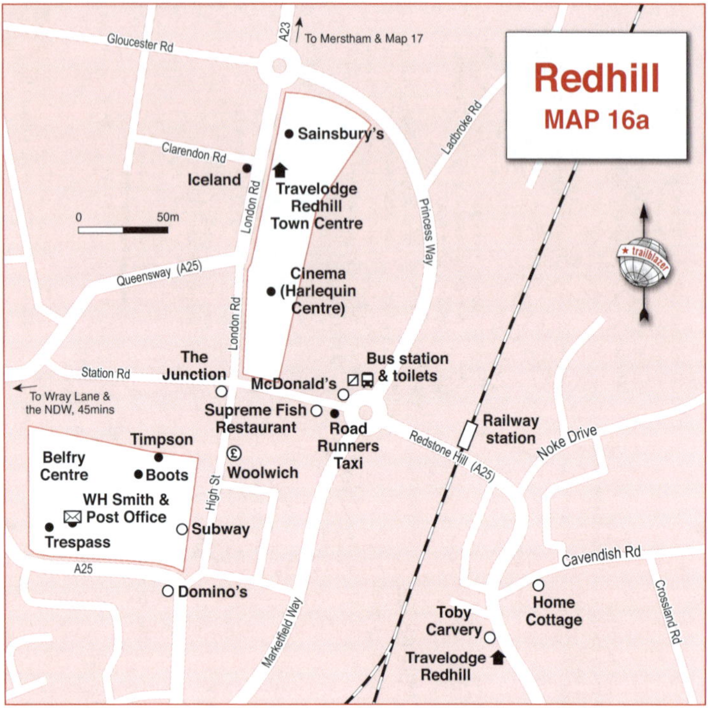

Transport

The most useful **bus** services are: Metrobus's No 400 (East Grinstead to Caterham), No 420 (Crawley to Sutton via Reigate), Nos 430/435 (to Merstham) and No 460 (Epsom to Crawley); Compass's and Metrobus's No 32 (to Guildford); and Arriva's No 405 (to West Croydon). See pp44-7 for details.

The main bus station is opposite the **railway station**; Southern Railway, GWR and Thameslink operate train services to a number of destinations in the south of England; see box pp42-3.

Road Runners **taxis** (☎ 01737-760076), 💻 roadrunnersgatwick.co.uk can always drop you back on the trail.

Where to stay, eat & drink

The ***Travelodge*** chain has two branches in Redhill, ***Travelodge Redhill Town Centre*** above Sainsbury's at 26 London Rd (☎ 08719-846516, 💻 travelodge.co.uk; 68 en suite rooms; ☕; 🐕) and ***Travelodge Redhill*** on Redstone Hill at No 2 (☎ 08715-591843, 💻 travelodge.co.uk; 37 en suite rooms ☕; 🐕). See also p21.

The best of the culinary bunch in the heart of the town is ***The Junction*** (☎ 01737-762357, 💻 thejunctionredhill.com; 🐕), a pub which welcomes dogs and has a fine menu with food (Mon-Fri 11.30am-3pm & 5.30-9pm, Sat 11.30am-4pm & 5.30-9pm) including pub classics (£13.95-16.95) and several dishes from Asia (around £15). Note that the kitchen is closed on Sundays, though the bar is open (noon-5pm).

Good pub grub is on offer at ***Home Cottage*** (☎ 01737-762771, 💻 homecottage redhill.com; food Mon-Sat noon-10pm,

Sun to 9pm; 🐕 bar area only), a Victorian pub serving Young's on Redstone Hill; it's probably the most charming place in town to eat at and the food is reasonable (mains £16-18.50).

Toby Carvery (☎ 01737-768434; food daily 9am-10pm), next to the Travelodge (see Where to stay), dishes up breakfasts (£6.49 for the full English. £6.99 at weekends) in addition to its better-known roast dinners.

The spotless chippy ***Supreme Fish Restaurant*** (☎ 01737-766872; Mon-Thur 11am-midnight, Fri & Sat to 1am, Sun to 10pm), on Station Rd, is popular.

For fast food you're spoilt for choice with, most conveniently of all, a 24-hour ***McDonald's*** by the bus station and a ***Domino's*** (☎ 01737-773737, 💻 dominos.co.uk; Mon-Thur 11am-midnight, Fri & Sat to 1am, Sun to 11pm) at 37 High St.

Separating you from the first settlement of any note actually on the trail since Puttenham is a saunter down the Capability Brown designed landscape of **Gatton Park** (Map 16), a chicane through school grounds and a saunter across **Reigate Hill Golf Club** (Map 17), where you're likely to find skylarks pouring out their song as they spiral skyward from the rough. The North Downs Way enters **Merstham** by the quaintly named Quality Street and its diverse collection of 18th-century houses.

MERSTHAM [MAP 17, p102]

There is no accommodation in Merstham – you'll have to catch a bus or train down to Redhill for that – but there are a few other facilities. There's an **ATM** about 500m from the southern end of Quality St on Nutfield Rd. The Esso petrol station's Londis **shop** is open 24 hours a day and has an ATM on the outside wall (£1.99 charge).

Across the busy road is ***The Feathers*** (☎ 01737-645643, 💻 pubanddining.co.uk/feathers-hotel-redhill; food Mon-Wed 11am-9pm, Thur-Sat to 10pm, Sun noon-9pm; 🐕), with a diverse and good-value menu with mains in the £12-16 range and sandwiches from £8.50.

There is also a **newsagent** (Mon-Sat 5.30am-9pm), and Station Cars **taxi** (☎ 01737-767676) based at the station.

Arriva London's **bus** service No 405 (West Croydon to Redhill) runs along the main street (the A23) and stops by The Feathers. You'll need to walk to the south of town to catch Metrobus's No 430 or 435 (circular route to Redhill station). See pp44-7 for details.

Merstham is also a stop on Thameslink's St Pancras International to Horsham **railway** service; see box pp42-3.

Crossing the M25 and M23 in quick succession, the path climbs steadily to the ridgeline where the traffic noise recedes. The level track continues past **Quarry Hangers Nature Reserve** (Map 18), a chalk grassland habitat managed by Surrey Wildlife Trust (see box p56).

The track then leads to **Whitehill Tower** (see box p104), a folly, from where it is a short walk to ***The Harrow Inn*** (Map 18; ☎ 01883-331218, 💻 harrowcaterham.co.uk; food Mon-Sat noon-9pm, Sun noon-4.30pm; 🐕 bar area). The menu includes pub favourites such as bangers & mash (£17.50) as well as a decent range of burgers (£15.50-17.50).

(cont'd on p104)

ROUTE GUIDE AND MAPS

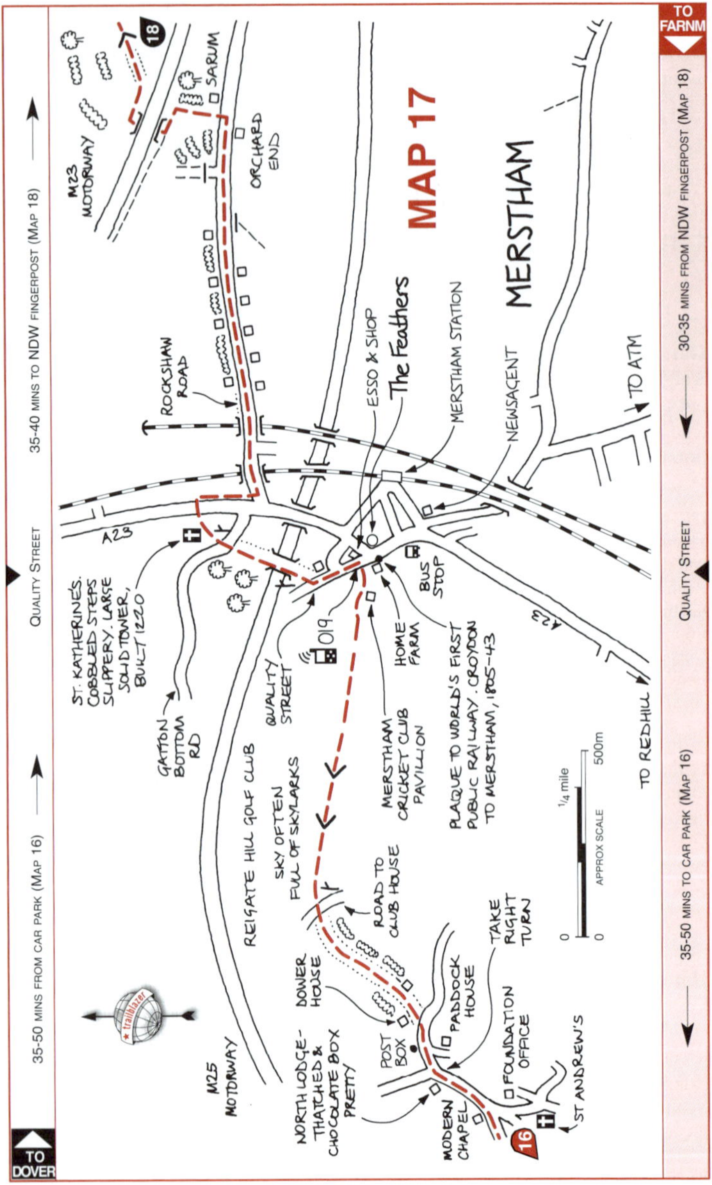
35-50 MINS FROM CAR PARK (MAP 16)
QUALITY STREET
35-40 MINS TO NDW FINGERPOST (MAP 18)
TO DOVER
TO FARNM
35-50 MINS TO CAR PARK (MAP 16)
QUALITY STREET
30-35 MINS FROM NDW FINGERPOST (MAP 18)
MAP 17
MERSTHAM
trailblazer
M25 MOTORWAY
M23 MOTORWAY
18
16
SARUM
ORCHARD END
ROCKSHAW ROAD
A23
ESSO & SHOP
The Feathers
MERSTHAM STATION
NEWSAGENT
TO ATM
ST. KATHERINE'S. COBBLED STEPS SLIPPERY. LARGE SOLID TOWER, BUILT 1220
GATTON BOTTOM RD
QUALITY STREET
019
HOME FARM
BUS STOP
MERSTHAM CRICKET CLUB PAVILION
PLAQUE TO WORLD'S FIRST PUBLIC RAILWAY. CROYDON TO MERSTHAM, 1805-43
TO REDHILL
REIGATE HILL GOLF CLUB
SKY OFTEN FULL OF SKYLARKS
ROAD TO CLUB HOUSE
TAKE RIGHT TURN
DOWER HOUSE
PADDOCK HOUSE
POST BOX
FOUNDATION OFFICE
NORTH LODGE - THATCHED & CHOCOLATE BOX PRETTY
MODERN CHAPEL
ST ANDREW'S
APPROX SCALE
0
1/4 mile
0
500m

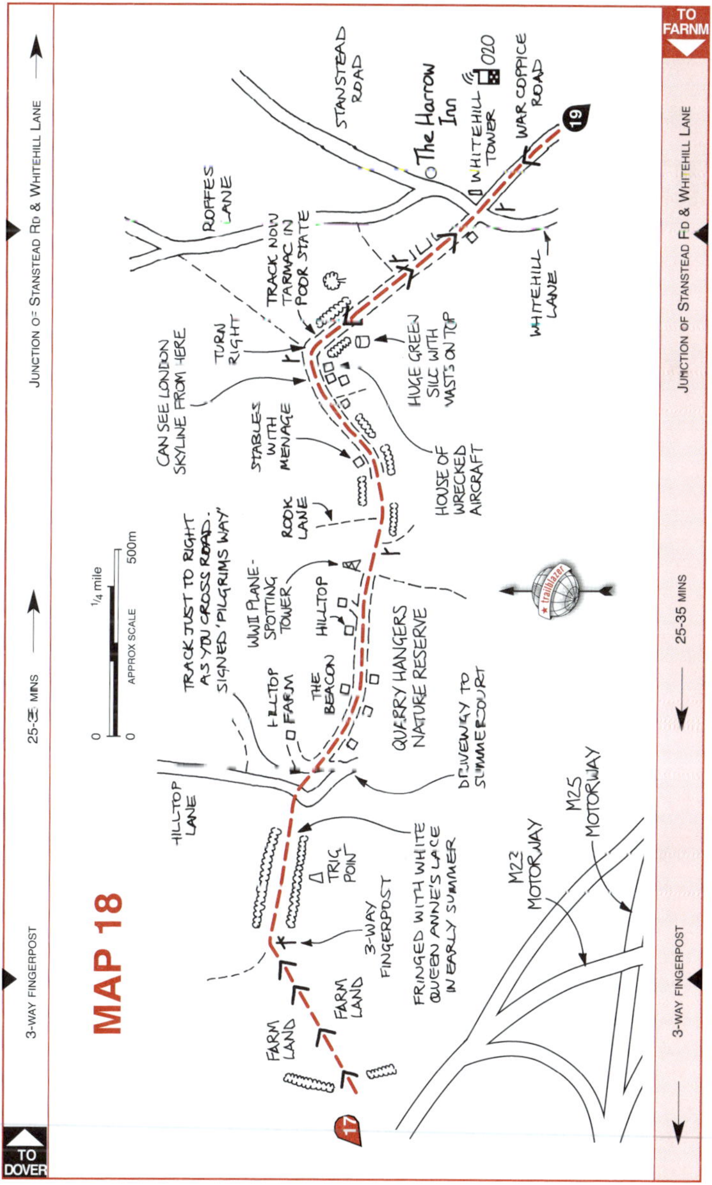
MAP 18
TO DOVER
TO FARNM
3-WAY FINGERPOST
25-35 MINS
JUNCTION OF STANSTEAD RD & WHITEHILL LANE
3-WAY FINGERPOST
25-35 MINS
JUNCTION OF STANSTEAD RD & WHITEHILL LANE
0
1/4 mile
0
APPROX SCALE
500m
FARM LAND
FARM LAND
3-WAY FINGERPOST
TRIG POINT
FRINGED WITH WHITE QUEEN ANNE'S LACE IN EARLY SUMMER
M23 MOTORWAY
M25 MOTORWAY
HILLTOP LANE
HILLTOP FARM
THE BEACON
DRIVEWAY TO SUMMERCOURT
QUARRY HANGERS NATURE RESERVE
TRACK JUST TO RIGHT AS YOU CROSS ROAD. SIGNED 'PILGRIMS WAY'
WWII PLANE-SPOTTING TOWER
HILLTOP
ROOK LANE
STABLES WITH MENAGE
CAN SEE LONDON SKYLINE FROM HERE
HOUSE OF WRECKED AIRCRAFT
TURN RIGHT
HUGE GREEN SILO WITH MASTS ON TOP
TRACK NOW TARMAC IN POOR STATE
ROFFES LANE
WHITEHILL LANE
STANSTEAD ROAD
The Harrow Inn
WHITEHILL TOWER
020
WAR COPPICE ROAD
17
19
trailblazer

A short section of road walking and a stretch in dense woodland leads to **Caterham Viewpoint** (Map 19) and the A22.

Once again a section of tree-lined trekking follows as you haul your wearying carcass up to the top of **Tandridge Hill** (Map 20), only then to descend just as sharply via wooden steps to **Oxted Downs** (Map 21), a chalk grassland habi-

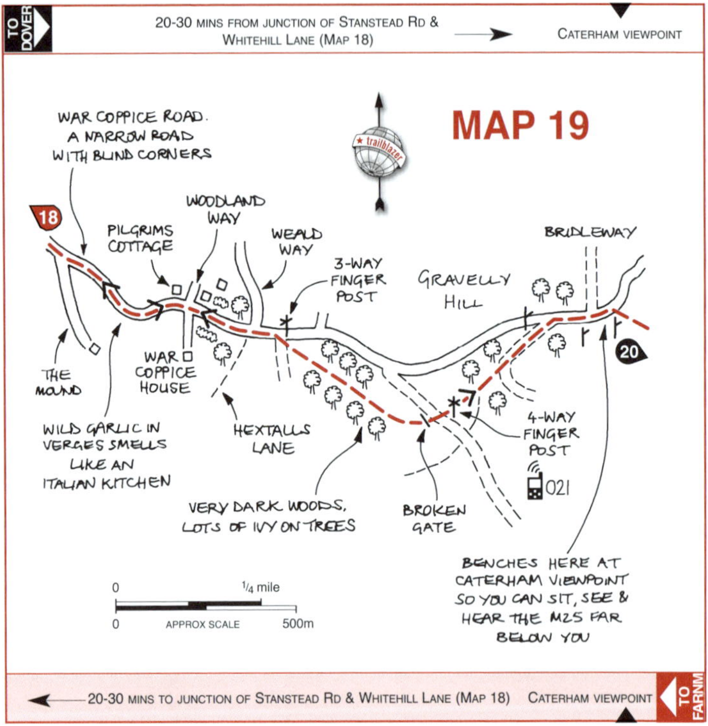

❑ WHITEHILL TOWER

Follies, bizarre and quirky buildings with no apparent practical use or purpose, were built by the grieving, the eccentric, and the out-and-out bonkers. Whitehill Tower (Map 18) is also known as Whitehill Folly Tower and the Sight Tower. Built in 1862 by Jeremiah Long, after his son was killed at sea, supposedly you are able to see the sea from the top. A fourth floor was reputedly added after the trees around the tower grew.

The bible on follies is *Follies, Grottoes and Garden Buildings*, Headley & Meulenkamp, Aurum Press, or visit The Folly Fellowship website: 🖳 follies.org.uk.

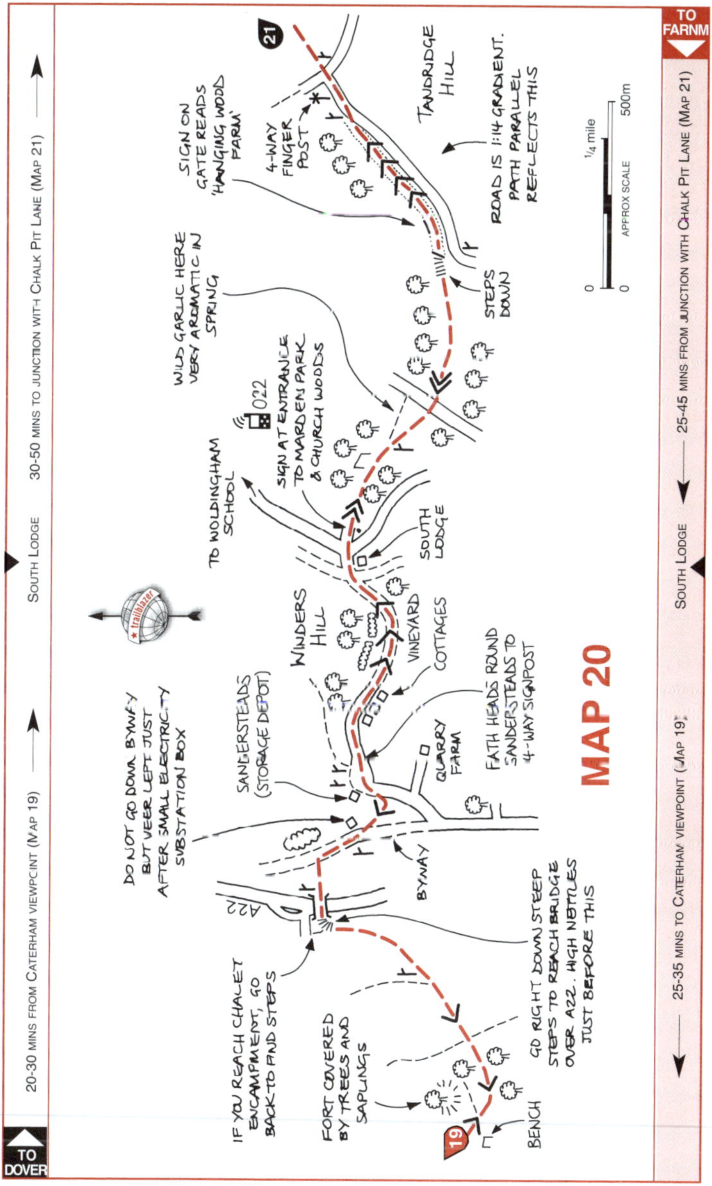
20-30 MINS FROM CATERHAM VIEWPOINT (MAP 19)
SOUTH LODGE
30-50 MINS TO JUNCTION WITH CHALK PIT LANE (MAP 21)
TO DOVER
TO FARNM
25-35 MINS TO CATERHAM VIEWPOINT (MAP 19)
SOUTH LODGE
25-45 MINS FROM JUNCTION WITH CHALK PIT LANE (MAP 21)
MAP 20
19
21
trailblazer
IF YOU REACH CHALET ENCAMPMENT, GO BACK TO FIND STEPS
FORT COVERED BY TREES AND SAPLINGS
BENCH
GO RIGHT DOWN STEEP STEPS TO REACH BRIDGE OVER A22. HIGH NETTLES JUST BEFORE THIS
A22
DO NOT GO DOWN BYWAY BUT VEER LEFT JUST AFTER SMALL ELECTRICITY SUBSTATION BOX
BYWAY
SANDERSTEADS (STORAGE DEPOT)
QUARRY FARM
PATH HEADS ROUND SANDERSTEADS TO 4-WAY SIGNPOST
WINDERS HILL
VINEYARD
COTTAGES
SOUTH LODGE
TO WOLDINGHAM SCHOOL
022
SIGN AT ENTRANCE TO MARDEN PARK & CHURCH WOODS
WILD GARLIC HERE VERY AROMATIC IN SPRING
STEPS DOWN
SIGN ON GATE READS 'HANGING WOOD FARM'
4-WAY FINGER POST
TANDRIDGE HILL
ROAD IS 1:14 GRADIENT. PATH PARALLEL REFLECTS THIS
0
1/4 mile
0
APPROX SCALE
500m

tat and SSSI (see p55) packed with wildflowers in spring and such a counterpoint to the M25 running below it. Cattle are grazed to conserve the downland habitat and prevent trees taking over. The trail then cuts across the grassland to **Chalk Pit Lane** from where it's a 25-minute or so walk to **Oxted**. Call Station Taxis (see below) if you prefer the thought of a lift.

OXTED [MAP 21a, p109]

Oxted is separated from Old Oxted by the A25 and divided east and west by the railway line with a parade of shops either side of the station. Though Old Oxted and its high street is undoubtedly the most photogenic part, for something other than a pub keep to the streets near the station where you'll find pretty much everything you might need.

Services

For **tourist information** see 🖳 loveoxted.co.uk. There are a couple of **ATMs** on Station Rd East, others at the supermarkets, and a **post office** (Mon-Fri 9am-5.30pm, Sat to 12.30pm) on Station Rd West.

Morrisons' **supermarket** (Mon-Sat 7am-10pm, Sun 10am-4pm) is the largest in town but there's also Waitrose (Mon-Fri 7am-9pm, Sat 7am-8pm, Sun 10am-4pm), Sainsbury's (daily 7am-11pm) and Co-op (daily 7am-10pm) all on Station Rd East. Boots the **chemist** (Mon-Sat 8.30am-6pm, Sun 10am-4pm) is on the same strip. For **boot repairs** there's a Timpson (Mon-Sat 9am-5.30pm).

For a bit of escapism, the quirky Everyman **cinema** chain (🖳 everymancinema.com) has a branch in Oxted – it's a lovely place to relax and immerse yourself in something other than walking.

Transport

The railway station is a stop on Southern Railway's frequent **train services** (see box pp42-3) between London Victoria and East Grinstead and London Bridge to/from Uckfield.

Bus services include: Metrobus's No 410 (Redhill to Hurst Green) which stops on Station Rd East (near Oxted station), as do their No 236 (to East Grinstead) and 594/595 (to Westerham). See pp44-7.

For a **taxi** contact Station Cars Oxted (☎ 01883-3776000, 🖳 stationcarsoxted.co.uk).

Where to stay, eat & drink

Meads (☎ 01883-730115, 🖳 bandbmeads.co.uk; 1T/1D, both en suite; ☕; min 2 nights at peak times), 23 Granville Rd, is a substantial 1920s Tudor-style house where **B&B** costs £55pp (sgl occ from £85); note that they don't accept credit cards.

There are **cafés** aplenty and you should find one that's to your taste. ***Café Papillon*** (☎ 01883-717031, 🖳 cafepapillon.co.uk; Mon-Sat 8am-5pm) is a popular place to the west of the station with good breakfasts (egg Benedict £7.95), decent baguettes and sandwiches and hot meals for the rest of the day (all mains around £11-14).

Coughlan's (☎ 01883-716972; Mon-Fri 7.30am-4.30pm, Sat 8am-4pm) is a regional bakery chain that's been going since the thirties.

Finally in this category, there are also outlets of the ubiquitous ***Costa*** (Mon-Sat 6.30am-6pm, Sun to 5pm) and ***Caffè Nero*** (Mon-Fri 6.30am-6pm, Sat 7.30am-6pm, Sun 8am-5pm) chains.

For lunches, all the above are good choices as is ***Brisk Burgers*** (☎ 01883-717071, 🖳 briskburgers.com; Mon & Wed-Fri noon-2.30pm & 4-9pm, Sat noon-9pm, Sun noon-8pm, closed Tue), a top-notch

❑ Important note – walking times

All times in this book refer only to the time spent walking. You will need to add 20-30% to allow for rests, photography, checking the map, drinking water etc.

ROUTE GUIDE AND MAPS

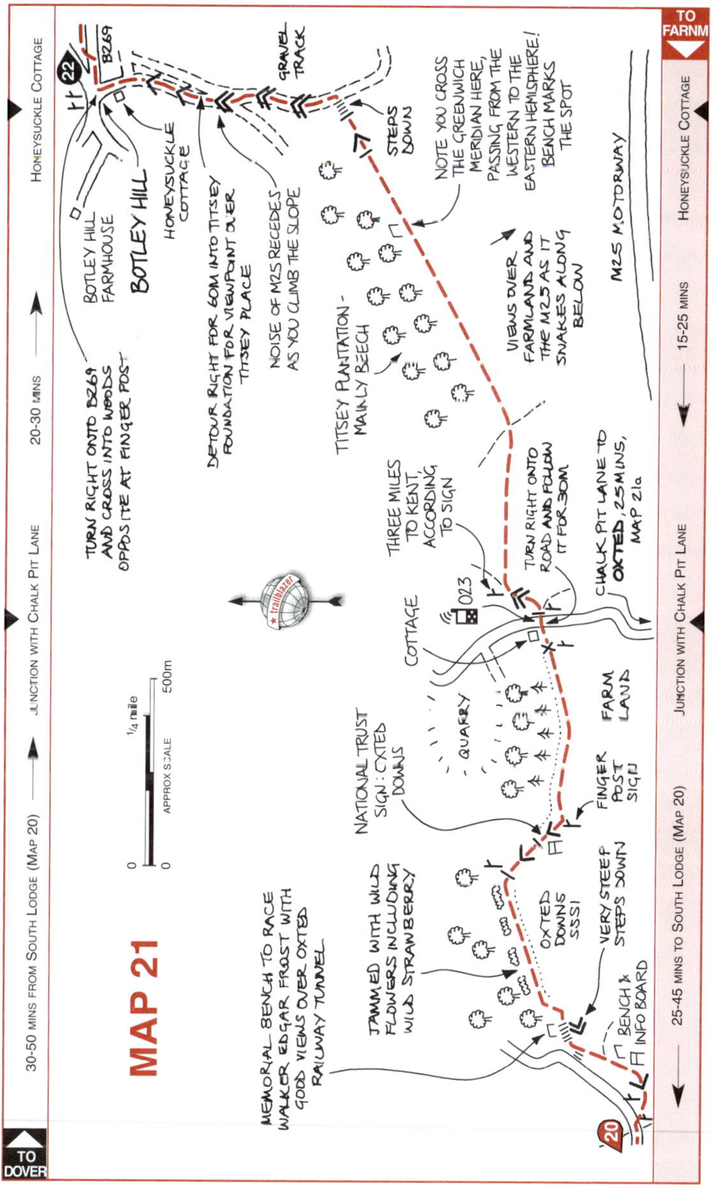
MAP 21
TO DOVER
30-50 MINS FROM SOUTH LODGE (MAP 20)
JUNCTION WITH CHALK PIT LANE
20-30 MINS
HONEYSUCKLE COTTAGE
TO FARNM
25-45 MINS TO SOUTH LODGE (MAP 20)
JUNCTION WITH CHALK PIT LANE
15-25 MINS
HONEYSUCKLE COTTAGE
APPROX SCALE
0 1/4 mile
0 500m
MEMORIAL BENCH TO RACE WALKER EDGAR FROST WITH GOOD VIEWS OVER OXTED RAILWAY TUNNEL
JAMMED WITH WILD FLOWERS INCLUDING WILD STRAWBERRY
OXTED DOWNS SSSI
VERY STEEP STEPS DOWN
BENCH & INFO BOARD
20
NATIONAL TRUST SIGN: OXTED DOWNS
QUARRY
FINGER POST SIGN
FARM LAND
COTTAGE
023
trailblazer
THREE MILES TO KENT, ACCORDING TO SIGN
TURN RIGHT ONTO ROAD AND FOLLOW IT FOR 30M
CHALK PIT LANE TO OXTED, 25MINS, MAP 21a
TURN RIGHT ONTO B269 AND CROSS INTO WOODS OPPOSITE AT FINGER POST
DETOUR RIGHT FOR 60M INTO TITSEY FOUNDATION FOR VIEWPOINT OVER TITSEY PLACE
TITSEY PLANTATION - MAINLY BEECH
VIEWS OVER FARMLAND AND THE M25 AS IT SNAKES ALONG BELOW
M25 MOTORWAY
NOISE OF M25 RECEDES AS YOU CLIMB THE SLOPE
BOTLEY HILL FARMHOUSE
BOTLEY HILL
HONEYSUCKLE COTTAGE
NOTE YOU CROSS THE GREENWICH MERIDIAN HERE, PASSING FROM THE WESTERN TO THE EASTERN HEMISPHERE! BENCH MARKS THE SPOT
STEPS DOWN
GRAVEL TRACK
B269
22

burger (from £8.45) and beer bar with friendly staff.

In the evening, for **pub grub** you can try the Wetherspoons-owned ***Oxted Inn*** (☎ 01883-723440, 🖳 jdwetherspoon.com; food daily 8am-11pm), by the station, but for a place with a bit more character you're better off heading to **Old Oxted**, to the far west of the station across the A25, where there are three pubs, two of which do food.

If you just want a pint, you could try ***The Wheatsheaf*** (daily from 3pm), the first place you reach walking from the station.

Continuing along High St, next is ***The Crown*** (☎ 01883-717853, 🖳 crowninnold oxted.com; food Mon-Sat noon-2.30pm & 7-9pm, Sun noon-6pm; WI-FI intermittent; 🐕) a 17th-century dog-friendly place with a pleasant beer garden, serving big plates of pub grub; mains start at £11.50 for a tofu salad, and burgers start from £12.50.

A little further on, ***The Old Bell*** (☎ 01883-712181, 🖳 chefandbrewer.com; food Mon-Thur 11.30am-9pm, Fri-Sun 9.30am-9pm; 🐕) serves food all day and a popular roast on Sundays (from £14.99).

For **international food** you're spoilt for choice. Oxted is home to a couple of Chinese restaurants – the smart ***Golden Palace*** (☎ 01883-715323; Tue-Sun noon-2pm & 5-10pm), to the west of the station, and ***China Garden*** (☎ 01883-730754; daily 5-11pm) on Station Rd East. Also here are subcontinental eateries ***Golden Bengal*** (☎ 01883-717373, 🖳 bengal-oxted.co.uk; Wed-Sun 5-10pm) and ***Gurkha Kitchen*** (☎ 01883-722621, 🖳 gurkhakitchen.co.uk; Mon 5.30-10.30pm, Tue-Sat noon-2.30pm & 5.30-10.30pm, Sun noon-9.30pm) with mains £9-14.

For smart Italian food head to ***Cucina Italiana*** (☎ 01883-713988, 🖳 cucinaoxted .co.uk; Mon-Fri noon-2.30pm & 5-10.30pm, Sat noon-10.30pm, Sun noon-9.30pm), which has great risotto (£14.95-16.95). There's also ***Pizza Express*** (☎ 01883-723142; Mon-Thur 11.30am-10pm, Fri & Sat to 11pm, Sun noon-10pm) with pizzas from £11.75 for a classic margherita.

All these also offer some sort of **take-away** service, as does ***Oxted Kebab House*** (☎ 01883-722675; Mon-Sat 11.30am-10pm, Sun 12.30-10pm), and the upmarket chippy, ***Deep Blue*** (☎ 01883-722666, 🖳 deepbluerestaurants.com; daily 4-8.30pm for takeaway), at the bottom of the hill on Station Rd East, with attached restaurant (Mon-Wed 11.30am-2.30pm & 4-8pm, Thur-Sat 11.30am-9pm, Sun 4-9pm.

❑ THE SOCIETY OF SUNDAY TRAMPS

'*Sunrays, leaning on our wild southern hills and lighting*
wild cloud-mountains that drag the hill along,
Oft ends the day of your shifting brilliant laughter
Chill as a dull face frowning on a song.'
George Meredith (1828-1909), ***Love in the Valley***.

Meredith lived in Mickleham and was one of the founders of The Society of Sunday Tramps, a group of friends who would meet up to walk along the North Downs together. Their number included such literary luminaries as Robert Louis Stevenson, Rudyard Kipling, Henry James and JM Barrie.

OXTED (CHALK PIT LANE) TO OTFORD [MAPS 21-26]

This **11.6-mile/18.6km** (**3¾hrs-5¼hrs**) hike encompasses several milestones of importance to walkers. For this is the stage where you reach the **highest point of the North Downs Way** at **Botley Hill** (269.6m/885ft). On this stage you also **cross the county border** separating Surrey from its North Downs neighbour,

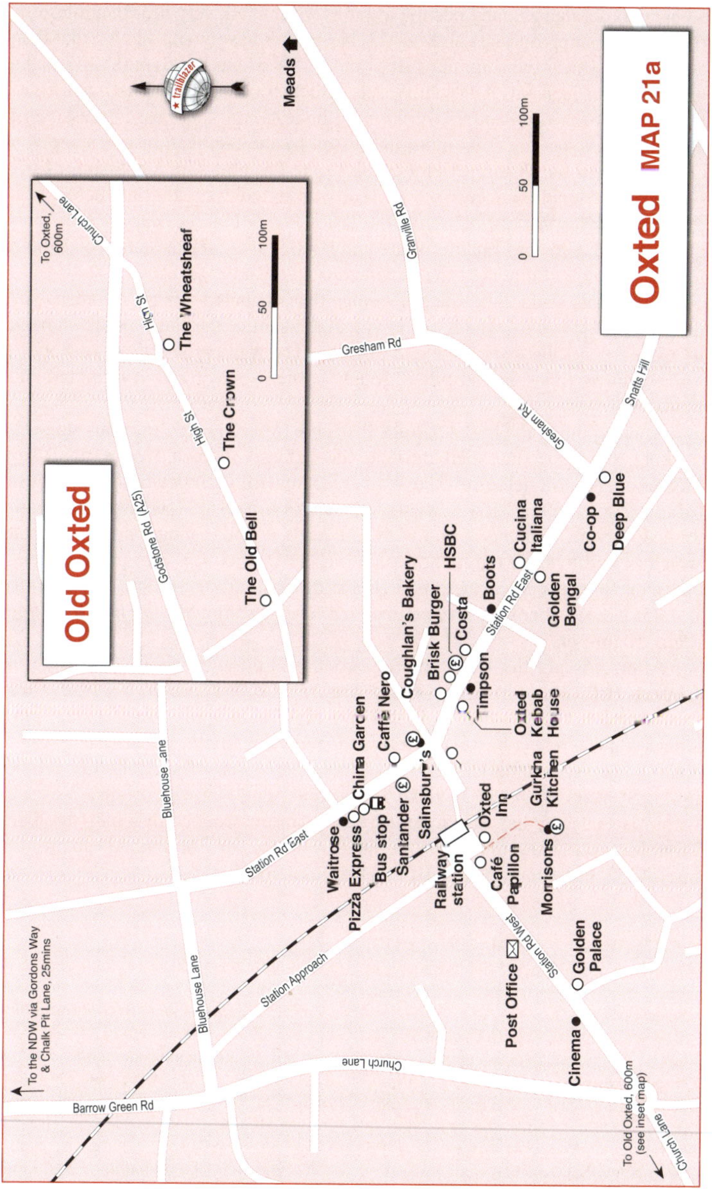

ROUTE GUIDE AND MAPS

Kent, a border that actually occurs, as far as we can tell, very near the milestone (which seems appropriate) on Map 23. No sooner have you achieved that than you then pass near the summit of Betsom's Hill – which, at 251m (823ft), is the **highest point in Kent**. And while such parochial concerns may perhaps be of little interest to you – and 251m is, in all honesty, not the most impressive of altitudes – maybe you'll be more impressed by the fact that on this stage you also pass from the Western Hemisphere to the Eastern, with a **crossing of the Greenwich Meridian** occurring very early on in today's walk (just before you join the track leading north through the Titsey Plantation; see Map 21, to be precise). Indeed, Greater London is only a few miles away at times and you should be able to catch glimpses of the skyline during the day.

Milestones aside, this is another stage that's haunted – but not ruined – by the whine of the M25, which greets you at the start of the stage and is on hand to wave you off just before the end of it too. The walking is also, to be honest, a little dull at times as you pass through a patchwork of arable farmland and fields of horses.

After rejoining the trail at **Chalk Pit Lane** (Map 21), you start this stage by walking alongside and then through the extensive beech woods of Titsey Plantation. A short detour off the Way at Botley Hill is ***Botley Hill Farmhouse*** (Map 21; ☎ 01959-577154, 💻 botleyhill-farmhouse.co.uk; food Wed-Sat noon-3pm & 6-9pm, Sun noon-6pm; 🐕 on lead) a 16th-century pub-restaurant which is said to sit at the highest point on the Downs. It's very popular especially on Sundays when there is a choice of roasts from £19.95 (nut roast) to £27.25 (lamb) so booking is recommended. They also run ***Sheep Shed Tea Shop*** (daily 10am-4pm).

After crossing the B269 the trail continues through woods to emerge at **Church Hill** (Map 22) below ***Titsey Brewing Co & Taproom*** (💻 titseybrewingco.com, **fb**; Thur noon-9pm, Fri & Sat 9.30am-9pm, Sun 9.30am-7pm) where you can rest your weary limbs and enjoy a hearty breakfast, sandwiches, soups, burgers and other dishes – or simply a cup of tea. Nearby and just off the trail is **St Mary's Church**, a small 11th-century building with original Norman windows that may have been built by William the Conqueror's half- brother. From here you can saunter past the massive houses of Chestnut Avenue to the busy A233 and, should you wish it, a diversion to Westerham.

WESTERHAM [MAP 23a, p113]

Westerham lies on the A25 but it remains an attractive town with historic connections (see box p114).

There are banks with **ATMs** on Market Square. Services include a couple of **convenience stores**: Co-op (daily 7am-10pm) and a **Nisa** (Mon-Fri 6am-8pm, Sat 7am-9pm, Sun 7am-8pm). There's also a newsagent with a **post office** (Mon-Fri 9am-5.30pm, Sat 9am-12.30pm) and a Day Lewis **pharmacy** (Mon-Fri 9am-6pm, Sat 9am-1pm).

There are a couple of **accommodation** options: ***Kings Arms Hotel*** (☎ 01959-562990, 💻 greenekinginns.co.uk; 3S/2T/8D/1Tr/3Qd, all en suite; ☕; 🐕), on Market Sq, can be good value with rates from £31.50pp, though this can rise to £75pp (sgl from £49.50). Food is also available here every day (Mon-Sat noon-9pm,

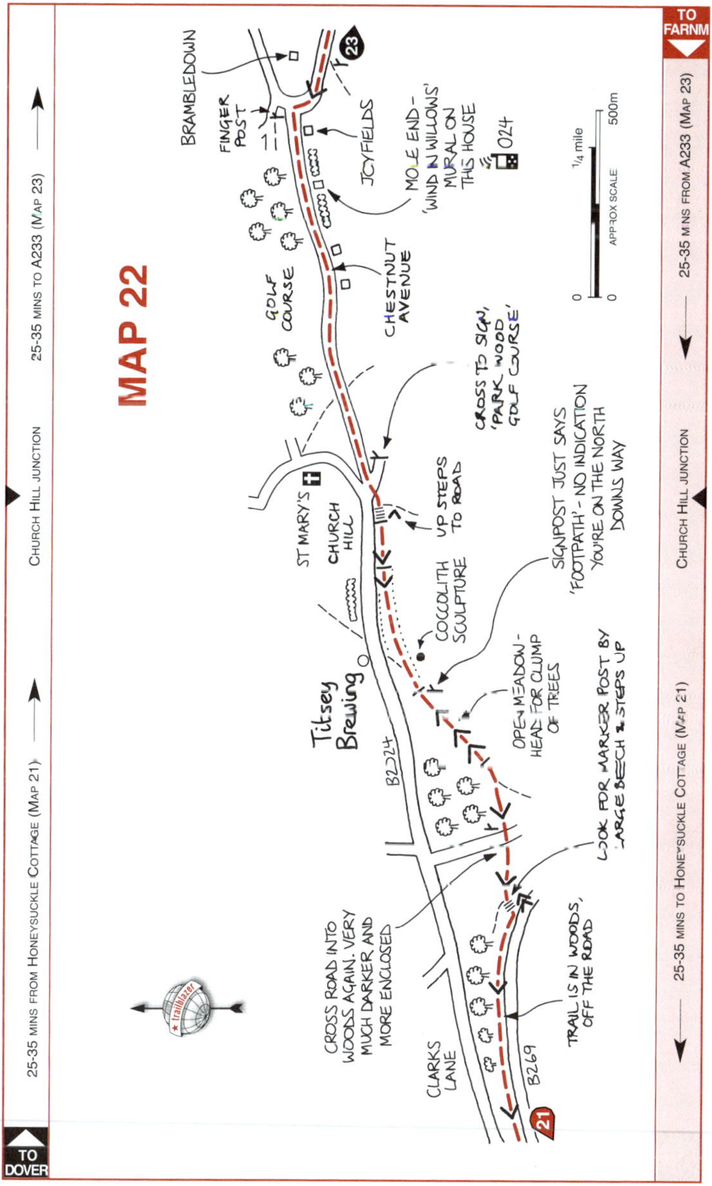
MAP 22
25-35 MINS FROM HONEYSUCKLE COTTAGE (MAP 21)
CHURCH HILL JUNCTION
25-35 MINS TO A233 (MAP 23)
TO DOVER
TO FARNM
25-35 MINS TO HONEYSUCKLE COTTAGE (MAP 21)
CHURCH HILL JUNCTION
25-35 MINS FROM A233 (MAP 23)
23
BRAMBLEDOWN
FINGER POST
IVYFIELDS
MOLE END - 'WIND IN WILLOWS' MURAL ON THIS HOUSE
024
1/4 mile
0
0
500m
APPROX SCALE
GOLF COURSE
CHESTNUT AVENUE
CROSS TO SIGN, 'PARK WOOD GOLF COURSE'
ST MARY'S
CHURCH HILL
UP STEPS TO ROAD
SIGNPOST JUST SAYS 'FOOTPATH' - NO INDICATION YOU'RE ON THE NORTH DOWNS WAY
COCCOLITH SCULPTURE
Titsey Brewing
B2024
OPEN MEADOW - HEAD FOR CLUMP OF TREES
LOOK FOR MARKER POST BY LARGE BEECH & STEPS UP
CROSS ROAD INTO WOODS AGAIN. VERY MUCH DARKER AND MORE ENCLOSED
CLARKS LANE
B269
TRAIL IS IN WOODS, OFF THE ROAD
21
trailblazer

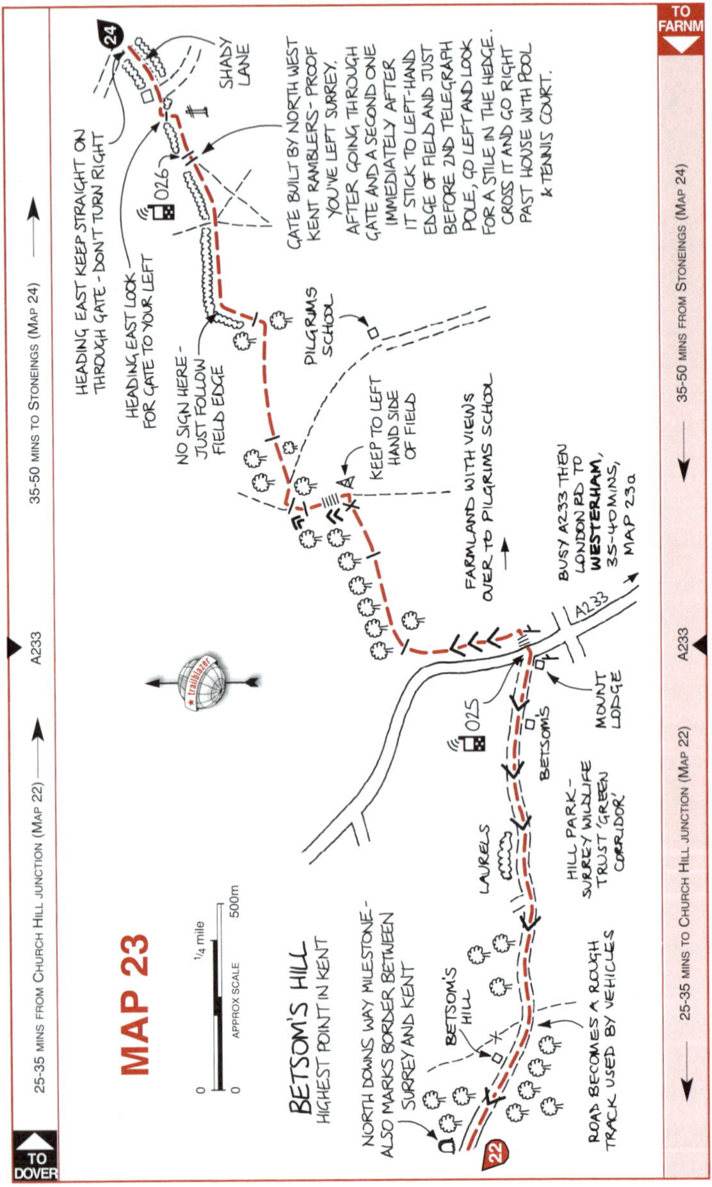
MAP 23
0 1/4 mile
0 APPROX SCALE 500m
TO DOVER
TO FARNM
25-35 MINS FROM CHURCH HILL JUNCTION (MAP 22)
A233
35-50 MINS TO STONEINGS (MAP 24)
25-35 MINS TO CHURCH HILL JUNCTION (MAP 22)
A233
35-50 MINS FROM STONEINGS (MAP 24)
22
24
trailblazer
BETSOM'S HILL
HIGHEST POINT IN KENT
NORTH DOWNS WAY MILESTONE - ALSO MARKS BORDER BETWEEN SURREY AND KENT
BETSOM'S HILL
ROAD BECOMES A ROUGH TRACK USED BY VEHICLES
LAURELS
HILL PARK - SURREY WILDLIFE TRUST 'GREEN CORRIDOR'
BETSOM'S
025
MOUNT LODGE
A233
BUSY A233 THEN LONDON RD TO WESTERHAM, 35-40MINS, MAP 23a
FARMLAND WITH VIEWS OVER TO PILGRIMS SCHOOL
KEEP TO LEFT HAND SIDE OF FIELD
NO SIGN HERE - JUST FOLLOW FIELD EDGE
PILGRIMS SCHOOL
HEADING EAST LOOK FOR GATE TO YOUR LEFT
HEADING EAST KEEP STRAIGHT ON THROUGH GATE - DON'T TURN RIGHT
026
SHADY LANE
GATE BUILT BY NORTH WEST KENT RAMBLERS - PROOF YOU'VE LEFT SURREY. AFTER GOING THROUGH GATE AND A SECOND ONE IMMEDIATELY AFTER IT STICK TO LEFT-HAND EDGE OF FIELD AND JUST BEFORE 2ND TELEGRAPH POLE, GO LEFT AND LOOK FOR A STILE IN THE HEDGE. CROSS IT AND GO RIGHT PAST HOUSE WITH POOL & TENNIS COURT.

Sun to 8pm) with a tempting menu (mains from £10.50) including crispy Asian pork belly (£18).

Part of the small Bel & The Dragon chain of 'modern English inns', ***The George & Dragon*** (☎ 01959-928414; 💻 georgeanddragonwesterham.co.uk; 9D/3D or T/1Qd; all en suite; ▼) is one of the smarter places to stay in town, with 13 elegant rooms, including a family room with a king-size bed plus bunk beds. Prices start at £62.50pp (sgl occ full room rate). They also serve food (daily noon-8pm; 🐕), with mains from £13 including crab linguine (£21).

You won't go hungry or thirsty in Westerham. Nor will you suffer from coffee withdrawal, with several places dedicated to the bean with the caffeine. In addition to a branch of the ***Costa*** chain (Mon-Fri 7am-5pm, Sat & Sun 8am-5pm) there are several local and more 'individual' places including: the popular ***Deli Di Luca*** (Mon-Sat 7am-5pm), historic ***Tudor Rose Tearooms*** (**fb**; Mon-Fri 10am-4pm, Sat & Sun 9am-4.30pm) for a traditional afternoon tea; and ***No 21*** (**fb**; Wed-Sat 9.30am-4.30pm, Sun 9am-3pm).

Moving onto evening dining, if you're craving Italian our favourite is ***Napoli è*** (☎ 01959-561688, **fb**; Tue-Sun noon-3pm & 6-11pm), at 18 Market Square; it is certainly the best choice for pizzas (from £13).

Perhaps the smartest place to eat in town is ***Rendezvous Brasserie*** (☎ 01959-561408, 💻 rendezvousbrasserie.co.uk; Mon-Sat 10am-4pm & 6-10pm, Sun & bank hols 9.30am-5pm), serving imaginative fare from across the Channel including a lovely beef bourguignon (£19.50).

For simpler meals, ***Westerham Fish & Chips and Chinese Take Away*** (☎ 01959-562462; Tue-Sun 11.45am-11pm) leaves you in no doubt what it does and ***Sultan Kebab House*** (☎ 01959-565589; daily 11.30am-11.30pm) is next door.

Metrobus' 594/595 **bus services** (to Oxted) and their No 236 (Oxted to East Grinstead) call here by the King's Arms. TfL/Stagecoach's No 246 and Go Bus's No 1 (to Sevenoaks) stop at The Green. See pp44-7 for details.

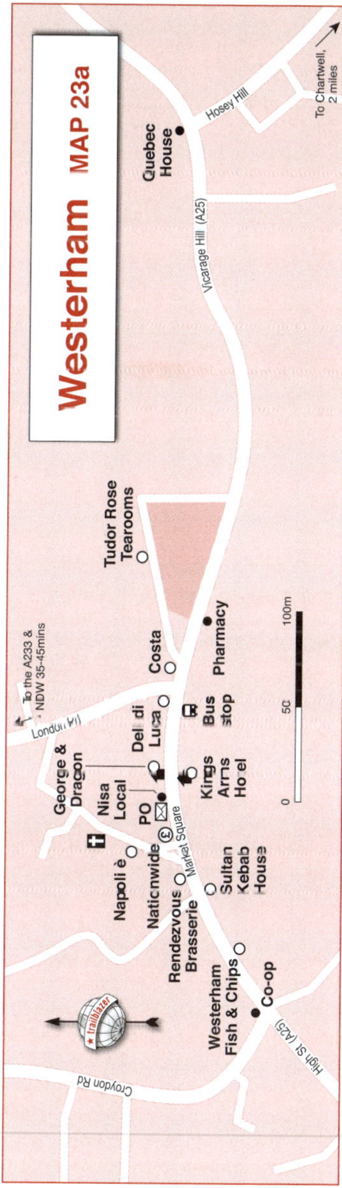

❏ WESTERHAM'S HISTORIC CONNECTIONS

Quebec House, Chartwell & Emmetts Garden ☎ *01732-868381;* 💻 *nationaltrust .org.uk)*

The childhood home of General James Wolfe, who captured Quebec from the French in 1759 only to die a few days later of gunshot wounds, **Quebec House** (Map 23a) is open to visitors (Mar-Oct Wed-Sun & bank hol Mons, Nov-Dec weekends only; house 11am-2pm, garden 11am-4pm; £7). The house contains Georgian memorabilia as well as a Battle of Quebec exhibition.

Sir Winston Churchill's former home, **Chartwell** (off Map 23a; Mar-Oct house daily 11am-3.40pm; garden daily 10am-5pm; house & garden/garden & studio £20/14) is one of the National Trust's most popular properties. Winston Churchill lived here from 1924 till the end of his life and the house is still much as he left it. Parts of the garden were created by him and his wife. Timed tickets for the house are issued on arrival (though afternoon tickets can be pre-booked on the website) so it could be a while before you get in.

Emmetts Garden (Mar-Oct daily 10am-5pm; Nov-Feb to 4pm; £13), an old Edwardian estate with panoramic views over the Weald, can be reached via a path from Chartwell.

Chartwell is about three miles south of the trail; TfL/Stagecoach's **bus** No 246 (Bromley to Westerham) calls here; see also pp44-7.

Continuing along the trail, you soon reach **Chevening Lane** (Map 25) and the turn-off to **Knockholt Pound**.

KNOCKHOLT POUND

[off MAP 25, p116]

The Three Horseshoes (☎ 01959-532102, 💻 3shoesknockholt.co.uk; food Mon noon-3pm, Tue-Thur noon-3pm & 6-8pm, Fri to 9pm, Sat noon-9pm, Sun to 5pm; 🐕 bar area) is about 15 minutes down Chevening Lane; it's a fine old place though with a surprisingly modern restaurant area; mains are about £15-18. Its only real rival lies up the road at ***The Harrow Inn*** (☎ 01959-928926, 💻 harrowknockholt.co.uk; food Tue-Fri 5-8pm, Sat & Sun 4-8pm; 🐕 on lead) specialising in pizzas (£7-15). Note food is not served here on Mondays, although the bar is open from 4pm.

Go Bus's No 3 **bus service** (see pp44-7 for details) calls here en route between Sevenoaks and Orpington; it also calls at Knockholt station which is a stop on South Eastern Railway's Charing Cross to Sevenoaks **rail** service (see box pp42-3).

The North Downs Way skirts the mixed woodland of the grounds of Chevening House, the Foreign Secretary's country residence, and descends quickly with views over to the M25/M26 interchange. **Chevening** is not on the trail, the house is not open to the public and the church, St Botoph's, is often locked, so there is no real reason to go there.

When you reach the **Sevenoaks Ramblers Association bench** (Map 25) you have a choice. Straight on is the official NDW route to Sundridge Lane, where you would then turn right to visit ***Eat'n'Mess*** (💻 eatnmesscakes.co.uk; Tue-Sat 8am-5pm, Sun 9am-4pm), a bakery and cake-maker with a café selling

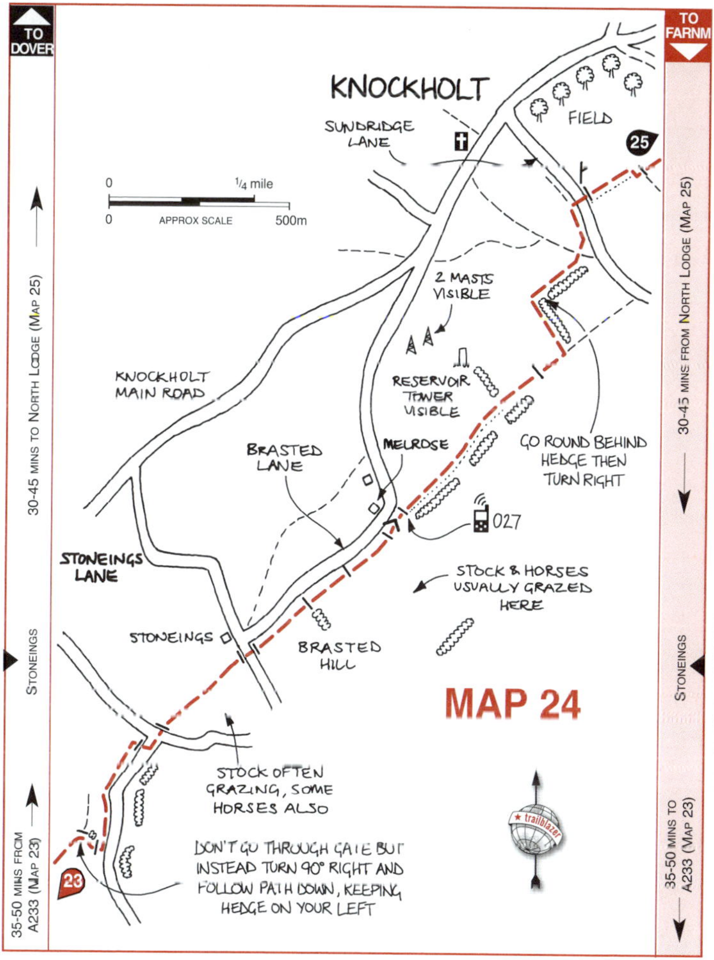

lunches including sarnies and toasties, pancakes, soups, buns and 'crumpins'. However, rejoining the official trail then requires a terrifying 100m shuffle along the pavement-less Sundridge Lane to a crossing of the M25 and Dunton Green. If you are not visiting the ***Eat'n'Mess*** café, we recommend that instead you **turn left** at the Sevenoaks Ramblers Association bench to take the public footpath marked on Map 25, which emerges where the pavement begins. It's by far the safer option.

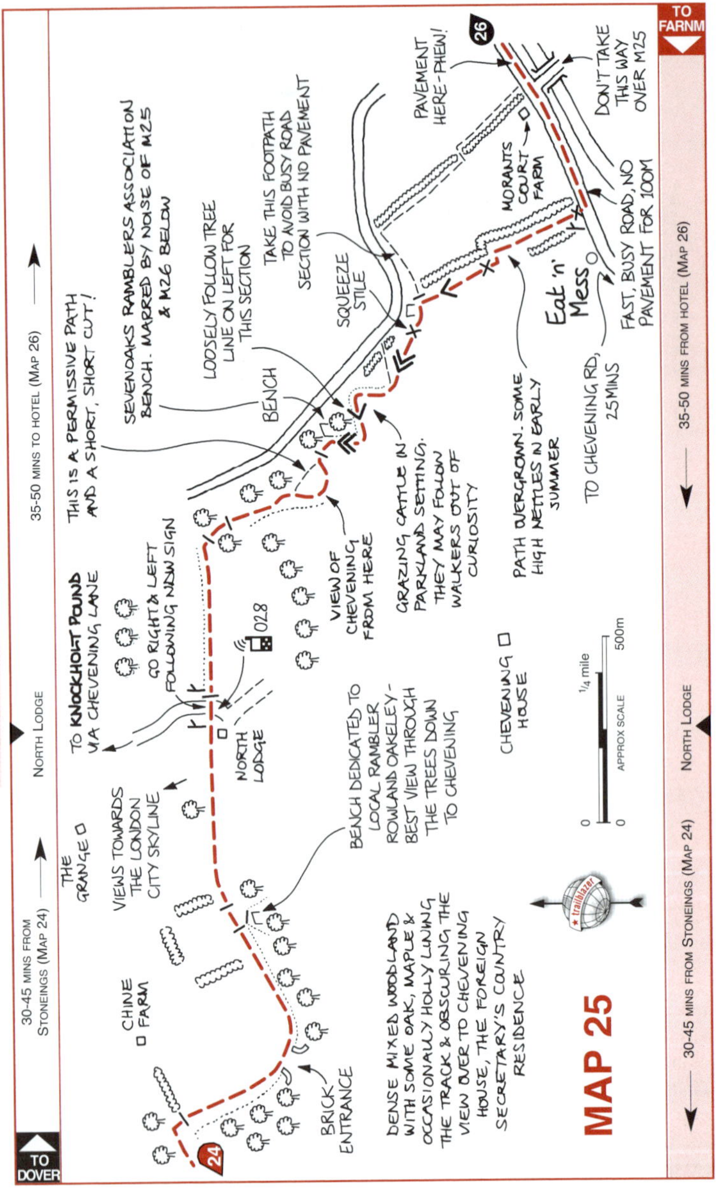
MAP 25
TO DOVER
TO FARNM
30-45 MINS FROM STONEINGS (MAP 24)
NORTH LODGE
35-50 MINS TO HOTEL (MAP 26)
35-50 MINS FROM HOTEL (MAP 26)
30-45 MINS FROM STONEINGS (MAP 24)
24
26
CHINE FARM
THE GRANGE
VIEWS TOWARDS THE LONDON CITY SKYLINE
TO KNOCKHOLT POUND VIA CHEVENING LANE
GO RIGHT & LEFT FOLLOWING NDW SIGN
028
NORTH LODGE
THIS IS A PERMISSIVE PATH AND A SHORT, SHORT CUT!
SEVENOAKS RAMBLERS ASSOCIATION BENCH. MARRED BY NOISE OF M25 & M26 BELOW
LOOSELY FOLLOW TREE LINE ON LEFT FOR THIS SECTION
BENCH
TAKE THIS FOOTPATH TO AVOID BUSY ROAD SECTION WITH NO PAVEMENT
SQUEEZE STILE
PAVEMENT HERE-PHEW!
MORANTS COURT FARM
DON'T TAKE THIS WAY OVER M25
FAST, BUSY ROAD, NO PAVEMENT FOR 100M
Eat 'n' Mess
TO CHEVENING RD, 25MINS
PATH OVERGROWN. SOME HIGH NETTLES IN EARLY SUMMER
GRAZING CATTLE IN PARKLAND SETTING. THEY MAY FOLLOW WALKERS OUT OF CURIOSITY
VIEW OF CHEVENING FROM HERE
CHEVENING HOUSE
BENCH DEDICATED TO LOCAL RAMBLER ROWLAND OAKELEY - BEST VIEW THROUGH THE TREES DOWN TO CHEVENING
BRICK ENTRANCE
DENSE MIXED WOODLAND WITH SOME OAK, MAPLE & OCCASIONALLY HOLLY LINING THE TRACK & OBSCURING THE VIEW OVER TO CHEVENING HOUSE, THE FOREIGN SECRETARY'S COUNTRY RESIDENCE
0
1/4 mile
0
500m
APPROX SCALE
trailblazer

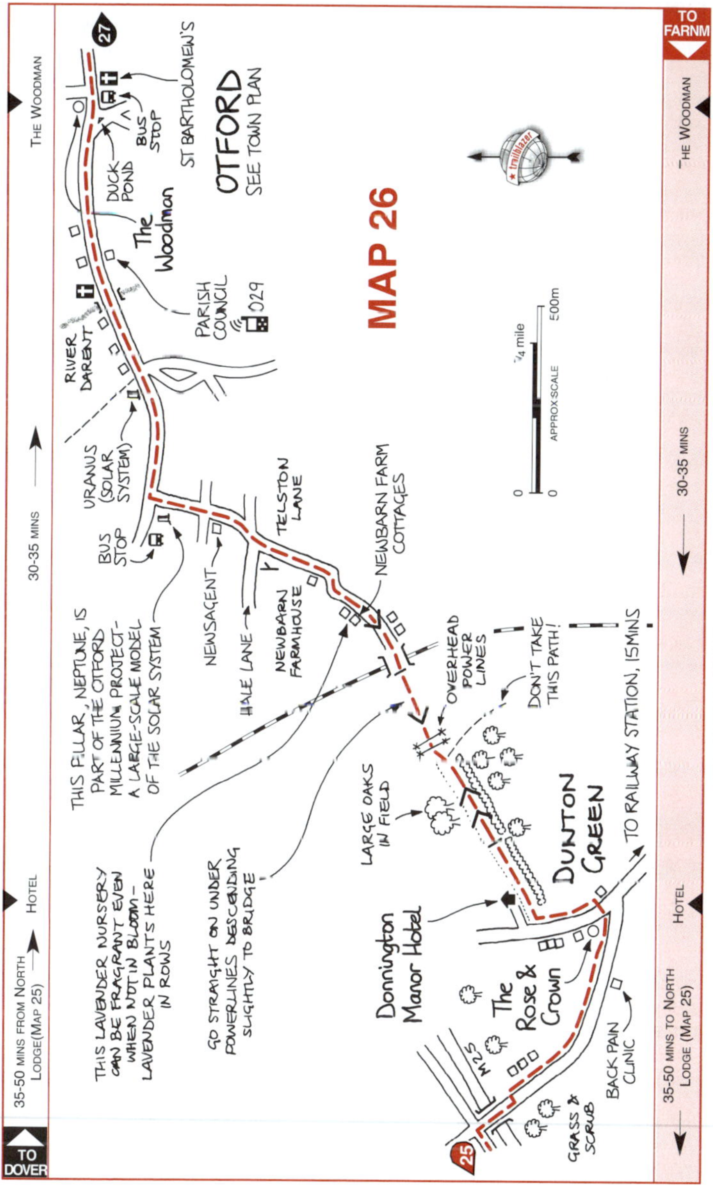
MAP 26
TO DOVER
TO FARNM
35-50 MINS FROM NORTH LODGE (MAP 25)
HOTEL
30-35 MINS
THE WOODMAN
35-50 MINS TO NORTH LODGE (MAP 25)
THIS LAVENDER NURSERY CAN BE FRAGRANT EVEN WHEN NOT IN BLOOM – LAVENDER PLANTS HERE IN ROWS
GO STRAIGHT ON UNDER POWERLINES DESCENDING SLIGHTLY TO BRIDGE
THIS PILLAR, NEPTUNE, IS PART OF THE OTFORD MILLENNIUM PROJECT – A LARGE-SCALE MODEL OF THE SOLAR SYSTEM
BUS STOP
URANUS (SOLAR SYSTEM)
RIVER DARENT
DUCK POND
ST BARTHOLOMEW'S
OTFORD
SEE TOWN PLAN
The Woodman
PARISH COUNCIL
029
NEWSAGENT
HALE LANE
TELSTON LANE
NEWBARN FARMHOUSE
NEWBARN FARM COTTAGES
OVERHEAD POWER LINES
DON'T TAKE THIS PATH!
TO RAILWAY STATION, 15MINS
LARGE OAKS IN FIELD
DUNTON GREEN
Donnington Manor Hotel
The Rose & Crown
M25
GRASS & SCRUB
BACK PAIN CLINIC
APPROX SCALE
¼ mile
500m
25
27

DUNTON GREEN [MAP 26, p117]

Well it probably won't be the most memorable detour of your trip but Dunton Green has a few facilities (off Map 26) including a railway station about half a mile from the path on the London Rd.

However, on the Way is ***The Rose & Crown*** (Map 26; ☎ 01732-462343, 💻 vintageinn.co.uk; food Mon-Sat noon-10pm, Sun to 9.30pm; 🐕), where a two-course fixed price lunch is £19.50, or it's £23.50 for three courses.

For **accommodation** consider 15th century ***Donnington Manor Hotel*** (Map 26; ☎ 01732-462681, 💻 donningtonmanorhotel.co.uk; 63D or T, all en suite), also right on the path and boasting a wide range of rooms charging at least £75pp (sgl occ rates on request).

Near the railway station (off Map 26) there's a clutch of shops including a **newsagent** (Mon-Sat 7am-8pm, Sun 8am-8pm). There's also a Tesco **supermarket** (Mon-Sat 6am-midnight, Sun 10am-4pm), a quarter of a mile due south at the roundabout.

Places to eat (off Map 26) include a café, ***Bojangles Coffee House*** (☎ 01732 455511, 💻 bojanglescoffeehouse.co.uk; Mon-Sat 8.30am-4pm) with reasonably priced sandwiches and paninis; a Chinese takeaway, ***Hei's*** (☎ 01732-462335; Mon 5-10pm, Tue-Thur noon-2pm & 5-10pm, Fri & Sat noon-2pm & 5-10.30pm); and ***Taj Tandoori*** (☎ 01732-462277, 💻 tajtandoori.co.uk; daily noon-2pm & 6-11pm; eat in or takeaway) which optimistically rises above the ordinariness of the area with curries starting at £7.50.

Train-wise (see box pp42-7), Dunton Green is a stop on South Eastern Railway's Charing Cross to Sevenoaks service.

Go **bus** No 3 stops by The Dukes Head on its way to Sevenoaks; see pp44-7.

Back on the route, you say a temporary ta-ta to the tarmac for the time being by **Donnington Manor Hotel** (see above). From here it is a pleasant walk through fields, then along a hard track through a **lavender nursery** before rejoining the pavement to cross over the **River Darent** and arrive at Otford's picturesque duck pond.

❑ OTFORD'S SOLAR SYSTEM MODEL

As part of Otford Parish Council's Millennium celebrations the world's largest scale model of the solar system was built in Otford (💻 otford.org.uk/solarsystem). Starting at the recreation ground, pillars mark the position of the planets at midnight on 1 January 2000. See the website above for a map and 'walk' the solar system if you have time, bearing in mind that every millimetre you walk represents 4595.7km in space!

There are a couple of pillars – Neptune and Uranus – actually on the North Downs Way (see Map 26).

OTFORD [MAP 26a]

Called Otta's Ford by the Anglo-Saxons, Otford is a lovely village with the **ruins** of an archbishop's palace, which fell into decay following its surrender to Henry VIII, and the world's largest scale **model of the solar system** (see box above).

The **pharmacy** (☎ 01959-522072; Mon-Fri 8.35am-6.30pm, Sat 9am-1pm & 2.15-5pm) is by the roundabout. There is an **ATM** outside the **One Stop** (daily 7am-10pm) convenience store and the **post office** (Mon-Fri 9am-5pm, Sat 9am-2.30pm) is down the road from that.

The nearest place to stay is actually in neighbouring **Kemsing**. ***Up the Downs B&B*** (see p120) is only a 10-minute walk

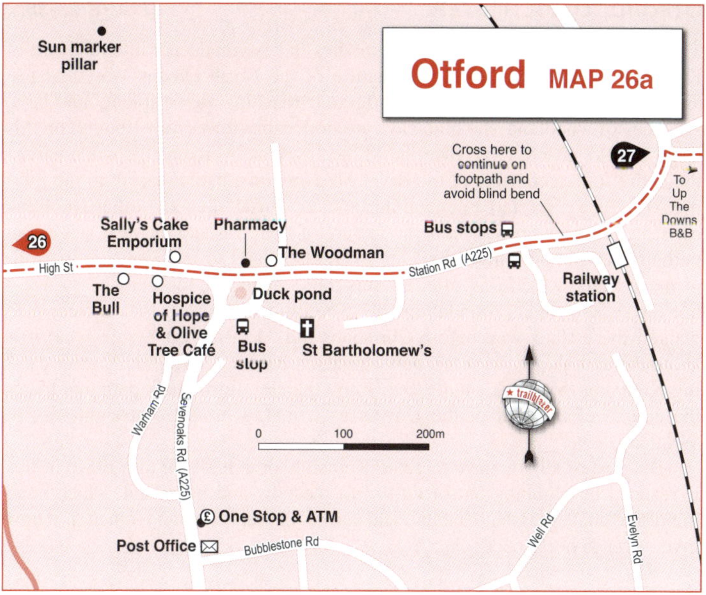

from Otford railway station. To reach it, continue along the Pilgrims Way East a little further to Tudor Drive, turning right down here to look for a public footpath on your left between houses. This leads all the way to Dynes Rd in Kemsing, which in turn leads to Northdown Rd.

The pink palace that is ***Sally's Cake Emporium*** (☎ 01959-928447, 🖳 sallyscakemporium.co.uk; Tue-Sat 9am-4.30pm, Sun from 10am) is certainly the most eye-catching place in the village and, as you'd expect, has a wide selection of cakes as well as breakfast (eggs Benedict £7.95) and sandwiches, wraps and bagels (from £7.25). However, we prefer the more peaceful ***Olive Tree Bistro & Tea Room*** (**fb**; Mon-Sat 9am-4pm, Sun 10.30am-3.30pm) at the rear of the Hospice of Hope charity shop. The menu is simple (scones, jacket potatoes, sandwiches) but the place is very likeable, and they allow dogs in the small outdoor seating area. They have occasional live music evenings in the summer.

At ***The Bull*** (☎ 01959-580585, 🖳 greeneking.co.uk; 🐕 bar area; food daily noon-8pm), the fireplace is reputedly 16th century and said to have come from the ruined archbishop's palace. It's an atmospheric place with decent pub grub (mains from £11.45, burgers from £13.95).

The Woodman (☎ 01959-522195; 🐕; daily from 11.30am) is a friendly enough place but there's no food on offer.

Otford is a stop on South Eastern Railway's **train** services to London Victoria and also Thameslink Railway's line to West Hampstead; see box pp42-3.

Go **bus** No 2 (Sevenoaks to Swanley) calls here. See pp44-7 for details.

❑ **Walk side by side and on healthy grass** In other words where possible don't walk in single file or on worn areas in order to protect the fragile earth.

OTFORD TO ROCHESTER [MAPS 26-36a]

This **17.8-mile/28.6km stage (5¼hrs6¾hrs)** takes you deeper into the heart of Kent and, as it does so, the very nature of the North Downs Way changes. While this section of the trail still offers far-reaching views aplenty and large stretches of woodland, the highways are noticeably fewer now (though on this stage you do have to cross over the M20 as well as overcome the worst part of the entire trail, a crossing of the River Medway on a path adjacent to the roaring M2). You also start to encounter ancient burial sites and other Neolithic constructions that are very much a feature of both this and the next stage. But perhaps most importantly of all, the path also starts to feel like a proper pilgrimage trail – which was, after all, this trail's main role for many centuries, if not the reason for its foundation (the Neolithic sites prove that ancient man walked these trails way before Christians did). I'm not quite sure what it is about the path that gives it this new character, but we felt it initially after passing **Kemsing** (Map 27), on the lovely cow-parsley-lined chalk path that traces the course of the foot of the Downs as it makes its arrow-straight way to Wrotham.

But first of all you have to get to Kemsing, or at least the turn-off to it; this is reached by climbing out of Otford to meadow and woodland, which is an important chalk grassland habitat, and across pleasant farmland, much of it now given over to horse paddocks.

KEMSING [MAP 27]

There is only one **accommodation** option in pretty, historical Kemsing (if you are walking west to east, you can reach it via a short cut from Otford, see p118-9).

Up The Downs B&B (☎ 07759 268115, ☎ 01959-526869, 💻 upthedowns.com; 1D en suite, 1T private bathroom; 🍽; Mar-end Oct) sits at the end of a quiet cul-de-sac about halfway between the centre of Kemsing and Otford Station. Rates are £49-51.50pp in the twin, £52-54.50pp in the double (sgl occ from £65).

In Kemsing itself there is **food** at ***The Bell*** (☎ 01732-761550, 💻 thebellkemsing.com; bar Mon-Sat from 11am, Sun from noon; food Wed-Sat noon-3pm & 6-9pm, Sun noon-4pm; 🍽; 🐕) where a decent roast on Sunday costs £16.50/18.50. Round the corner, ***Kemsing Italian Deli*** (☎ 01732-761581; **fb**; Tue-Fri 9am-3.30pm, Sat 9.30am-3pm, Sun 10am-3pm) is a **deli** and coffee shop with superior coffee. They occasionally have a pizza van outside on Friday evenings and Sundays in summer.

The **railway** station is about 20 minutes to the south of the village; South Eastern Railway's services between London Victoria and Ashford International (with onward connections from there to Folkestone and Dover) call here except on Sundays.

Go **bus** No 6 serves Sevenoaks and stops by Kemsing; see pp44-7.

Back on the trail, and having survived any equine or bovine encounters, and having resisted the temptation to divert from the path to the pretty ***Rising Sun*** (Map 28; ☎ 01959-522683) and its ice creams, which are advertised along the trail, you will find yourself dropping steeply to land on the chalk path leading to **Wrotham**.

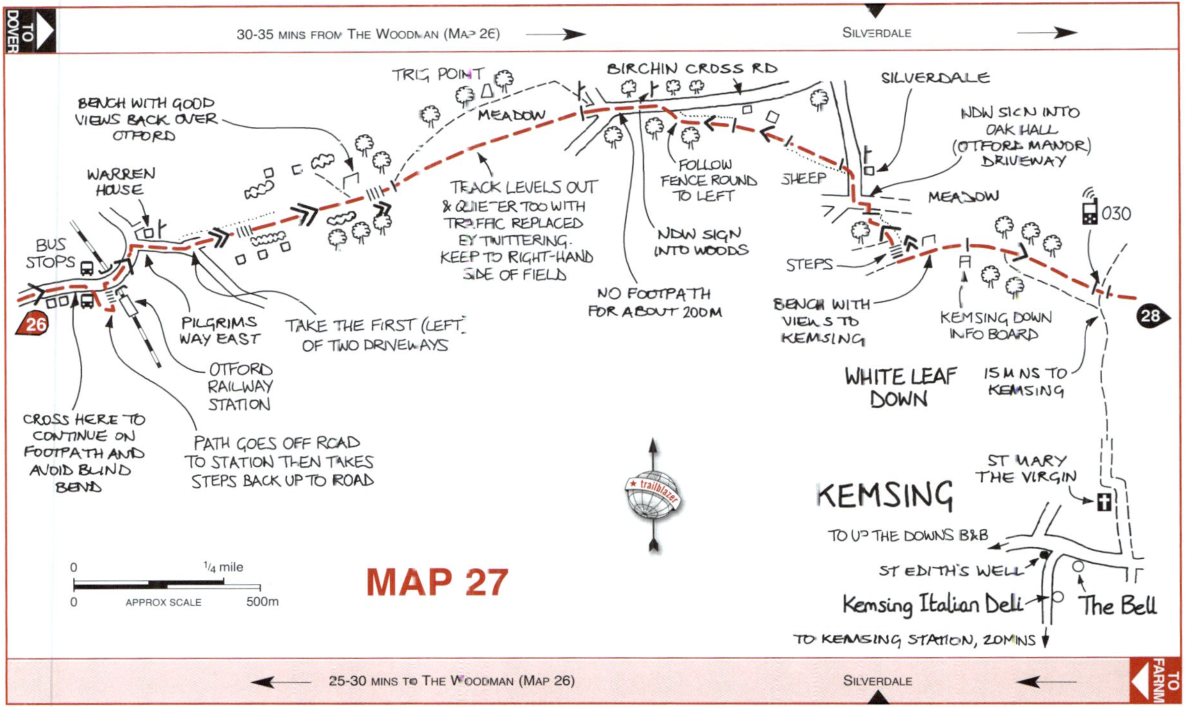
TO DOVER
30-35 MINS FROM THE WOODMAN (MAP 26)
SILVERDALE
BENCH WITH GOOD VIEWS BACK OVER OTFORD
WARREN HOUSE
BUS STOPS
TRIG POINT
MEADOW
BIRCHIN CROSS RD
SILVERDALE
NDW SIGN INTO OAK HALL (OTFORD MANOR) DRIVEWAY
TRACK LEVELS OUT & QUIETER TOO WITH TRAFFIC REPLACED BY TWITTERING. KEEP TO RIGHT-HAND SIDE OF FIELD
FOLLOW FENCE ROUND TO LEFT
SHEEP
MEADOW
030
NDW SIGN INTO WOODS
STEPS
NO FOOTPATH FOR ABOUT 200M
BENCH WITH VIEWS TO KEMSING
KEMSING DOWN INFO BOARD
28
26
PILGRIMS WAY EAST
TAKE THE FIRST (LEFT) OF TWO DRIVEWAYS
OTFORD RAILWAY STATION
WHITE LEAF DOWN
15 MINS TO KEMSING
CROSS HERE TO CONTINUE ON FOOTPATH AND AVOID BLIND BEND
PATH GOES OFF ROAD TO STATION THEN TAKES STEPS BACK UP TO ROAD
trailblazer
ST MARY THE VIRGIN
KEMSING
TO UP THE DOWNS B&B
ST EDITH'S WELL
Kemsing Italian Deli
The Bell
TO KEMSING STATION, 20MINS
0
1/4 mile
0
APPROX SCALE
500m
MAP 27
25-30 MINS TO THE WOODMAN (MAP 26)
SILVERDALE
TO FARNM

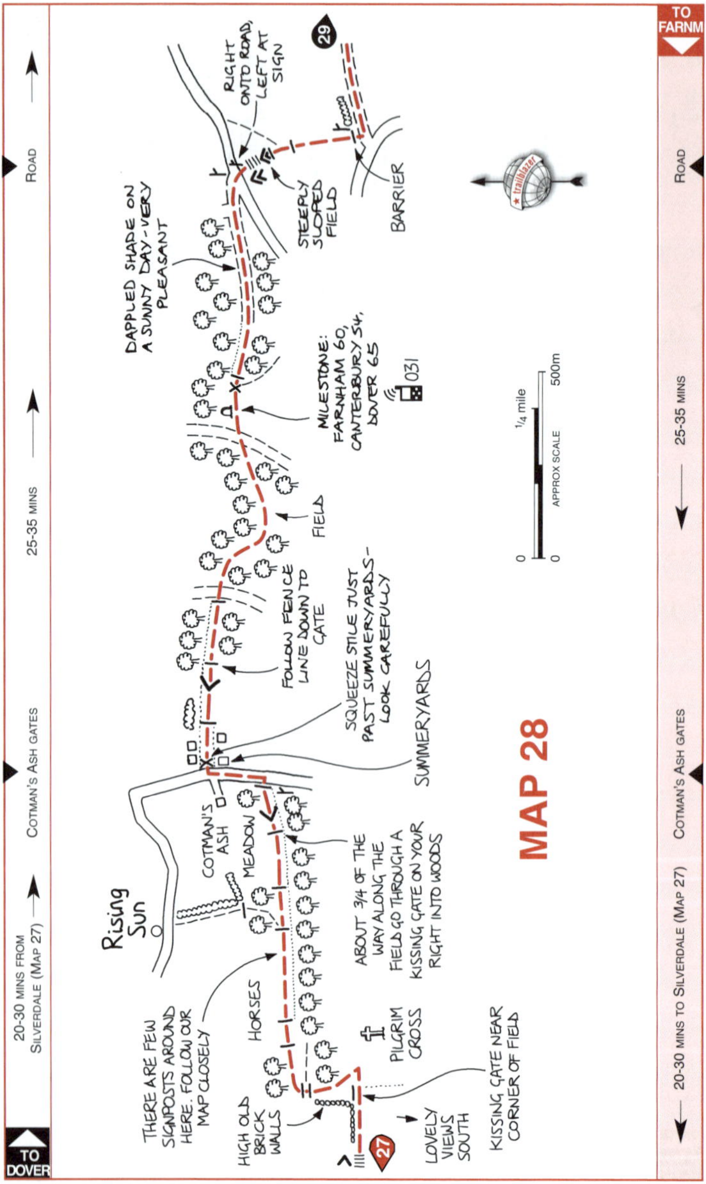
TO DOVER
20-30 mins from Silverdale (Map 27)
Cotman's Ash Gates
25-35 mins
Road
TO FARNM
20-30 mins to Silverdale (Map 27)
Cotman's Ash Gates
25-35 mins
Road
MAP 28
27
29
There are few signposts around here. Follow our map closely
High old brick walls
Horses
Rising Sun
Cotman's Ash
Meadow
Pilgrim Cross
Lovely views south
Kissing gate near corner of field
About 3/4 of the way along the field go through a kissing gate on your right into woods
Summeryards
Squeeze stile just past Summeryards - look carefully
Follow fence line down to gate
Field
Milestone: Farnham 60, Canterbury 54, Dover 65
031
Dappled shade on a sunny day - very pleasant
Steeply sloped field
Barrier
Right onto road, left at sign
0
1/4 mile
0
Approx scale
500m
trailblazer

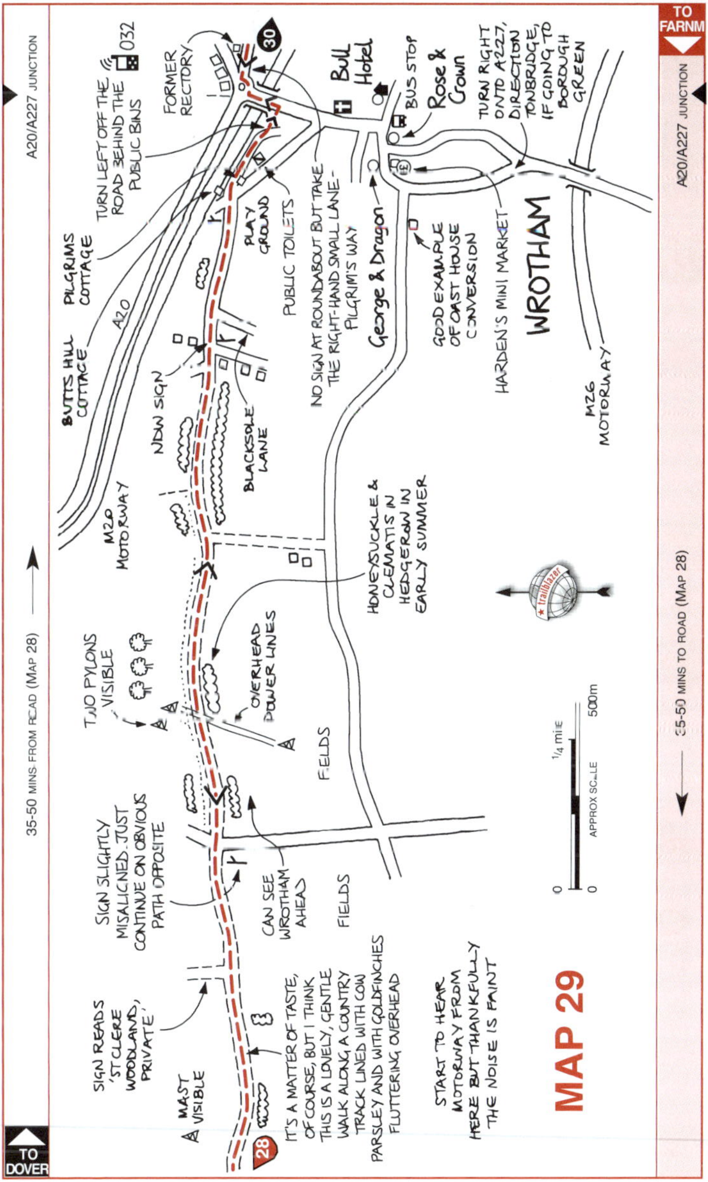

TO DOVER
A20/A227 JUNCTION
35-50 MINS FROM ROAD (MAP 28)
TO FARNM
A20/A227 JUNCTION
35-50 MINS TO ROAD (MAP 28)
MAP 29
28
30
MAST VISIBLE
SIGN READS 'ST CLERE WOODLANDS, PRIVATE'
IT'S A MATTER OF TASTE, OF COURSE, BUT I THINK THIS IS A LOVELY, GENTLE WALK ALONG A COUNTRY TRACK LINED WITH COW PARSLEY AND WITH GOLDFINCHES FLUTTERING OVERHEAD
START TO HEAR MOTORWAY FROM HERE BUT THANKFULLY THE NOISE IS FAINT
SIGN SLIGHTLY MISALIGNED. JUST CONTINUE ON OBVIOUS PATH OPPOSITE
CAN SEE WROTHAM AHEAD
FIELDS
TWO PYLONS VISIBLE
OVERHEAD POWER LINES
FIELDS
M20 MOTORWAY
HONEYSUCKLE & CLEMATIS IN HEDGEROW IN EARLY SUMMER
BLACKSOLE LANE
NDW SIGN
BUTTS HILL COTTAGE
A20
PILGRIMS COTTAGE
PLAY GROUND
PUBLIC TOILETS
NO SIGN AT ROUNDABOUT BUT TAKE THE RIGHT-HAND SMALL LANE - PILGRIM'S WAY
George & Dragon
GOOD EXAMPLE OF OAST HOUSE CONVERSION
HARDEN'S MINI MARKET
WROTHAM
M26 MOTORWAY
TURN LEFT OFF THE ROAD BEHIND THE PUBLIC BINS
032
FORMER RECTORY
Bull Hotel
BUS STOP
Rose & Crown
TURN RIGHT ONTO A227, DIRECTION TONBRIDGE, IF GOING TO BOROUGH GREEN
trailblazer
APPROX SCALE
0
1/4 mile
0
500m

WROTHAM **[MAP 29, p123]**

Pronounced 'Root ham', the relatively unspoilt village sits below the M20/A20 interchange and above the M26. The remains of an archbishop's palace lies east of the squat old church.

Harden's Mini Market (daily 8am-8pm) has an **ATM** (£1.60 fee) and sells all the lunch supplies you'd need.

Accommodation is thin on the ground in Wrotham and even the **campsite**, ***Gate House Wood Touring Park*** (☎ 01732-843062, 💻 sellersleisure.com; adults only; 🐕), is really in Wrotham Heath, about a 40-minute walk from the trail. Rates here are from £30.

Back in Wrotham itself, **rooms** are

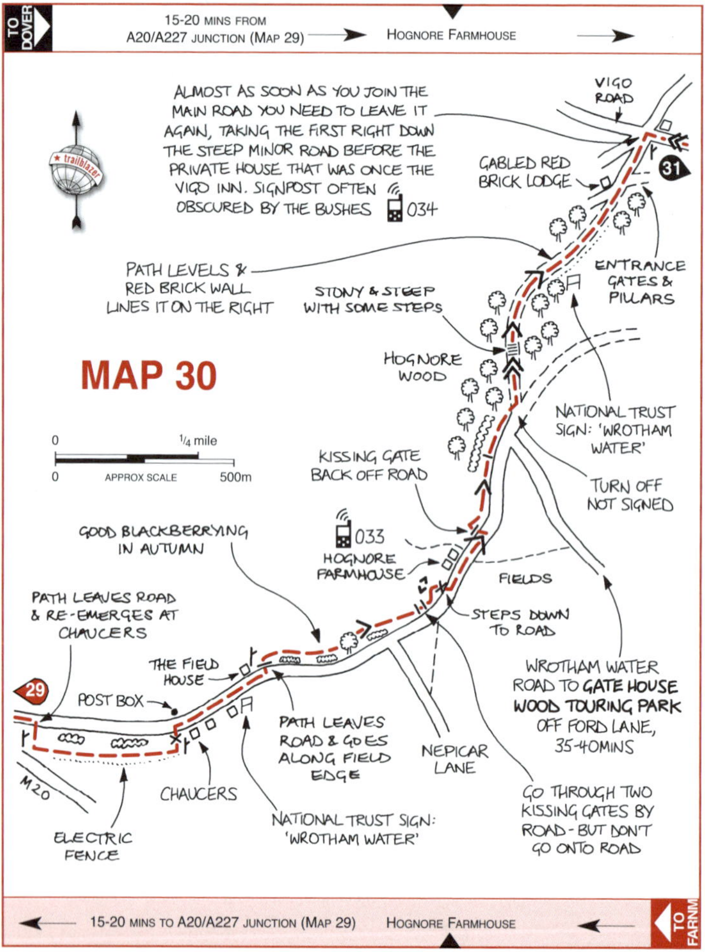

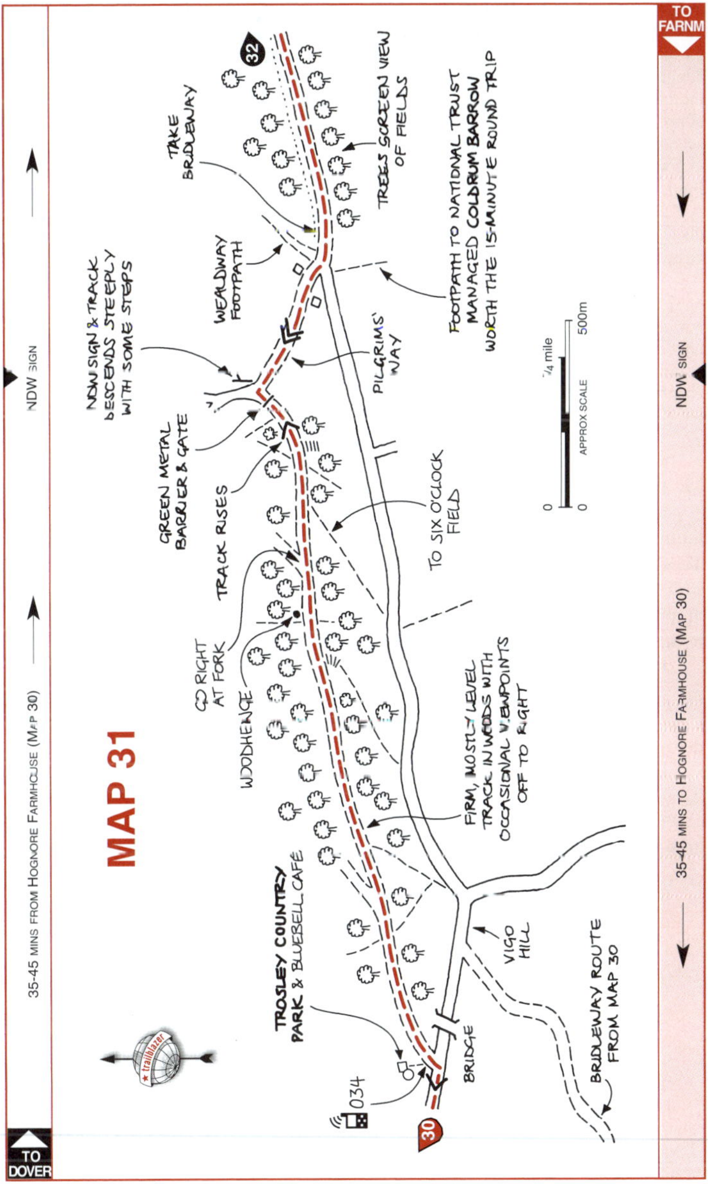

ROUTE GUIDE AND MAPS

available at ***The Bull Hotel*** (☎ 01732-789800, 🖳 thebullhotel.com; 1T/10D, all en suite; ☛; 🐕), an upmarket choice with attention to detail and décor appropriate to the historic inn. Room rates (around £40-60pp, sgl occ full room rate less £10) vary according to the day of the week on which you wish to stay; breakfast is £10 extra. For **food** (Mon-Tue 6-9pm, Wed-Fri noon-2.30pm & 6-9pm, Sat noon-9pm, Sun noon-6pm), main dishes start at £16 for a basic pasta dish.

The ***George & Dragon*** (☎ 01732-884298, 🖳 www.georgeanddragonwrotham.co.uk; 🐕 bar area only) serves standard pub lunches (Mon-Wed & Fri-Sat noon-9pm, Sun noon-2.30pm, Thur no food). Nearby, ***The Rose & Crown*** (☎ 01732-885839, 🖳 roseandcrownwrotham.co.uk, **fb**; 🐕 on lead) is a lovely friendly place but the only food they do is fish & chips on Fridays (6-9pm, booking essential).

Some of Autocar's **bus** No 222 (to Tonbridge) services continue to/start from opposite the Bull Hotel; see pp44-7.

The nearest **railway station** to Wrotham is a 20-minute walk away in Borough Green. The station is called Borough Green & Wrotham and is a stop on South Eastern Railway's rail services (see box pp42-3) between London Victoria and Ashford International and also London Charing Cross to Maidstone East.

For a **taxi** between Wrotham and Borough Green, Borough Green Taxis (☎ 01732-882020, 🖳 boroughgreentaxi.co.uk) have an office at the station.

Leaving Wrotham the first obstacle to overcome is the noisy M20. Mercifully you're largely unaware it's there until you come upon it and it disappears from both your view and your conscience fairly shortly afterwards too, though its roar reminds you of its presence until – almost – the entrance to **Trosley Country Park** (Map 31). Here you'll find the Visitors Centre and its welcome **café** (term time Mon-Fri 10am-3pm, weekends & school holidays to 4pm; 🐕 outside only) with plenty of outside seating. Red Route Bus Nos 306 & 308 (see pp44-7) stop at Trosley Country Park.

Progress through the country park is straightforward, the firm track allowing for fast walking, before the trail eventually descends sharply to meet the Pilgrims' Way. At this point a short detour to **Coldrum Long Barrow** (see box below) is in order.

Back on the North Downs Way, the path continues its eastward line to the bridleway leading south to **Ryarsh** (off Map 32), where the ***Duke of Wellington*** (☎ 01732-842318, 🖳 dukeofwellingtonryarsh.com; food Mon-Wed noon-2pm & 6-9pm, Thur-Sat noon-9pm, Sun noon-6pm; 🐕) pub has polished wood floors and cosy snugs and offers tapas (dishes £3.95-8.95) as well as regular pub fare.

❑ COLDRUM LONG BARROW (off Map 31, p125)

Owned and managed by the National Trust (🖳 nationaltrust.org.uk), this Neolithic site is a largely intact long barrow burial site or tomb. The structure dates from 3985-3855BC (so is around 1000 years older than Stonehenge) when agriculture was developing in Europe, stone tools were used and metal ones had yet to be invented. In the 1900s the bones of 22 people were excavated. Many visitors hang lucky charms and gifts in the trees surrounding the stones and it's said that the name derives from the old Cornish word *Galdrum* or 'place of enchantments'. It's certainly a pretty location at the foot of the Downs overlooking farmland toward Blue Bell Hill and east to the Medway valley.

ROUTE GUIDE AND MAPS

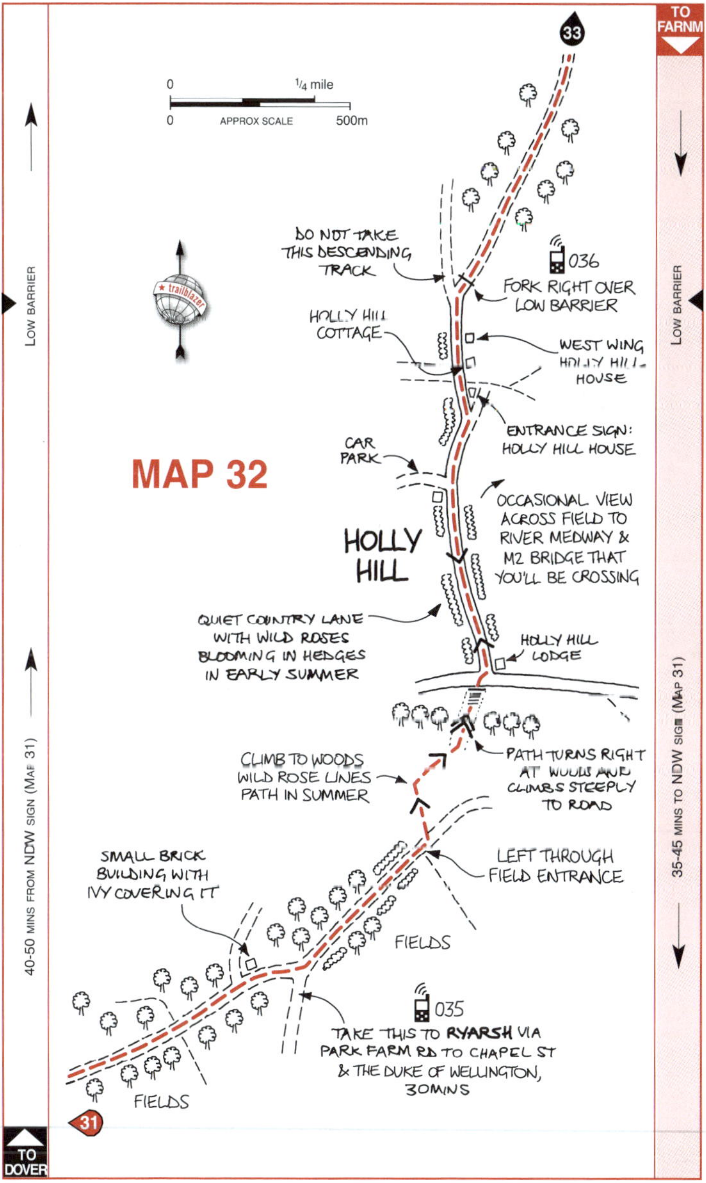
TO FARNM
33
0 1/4 mile
0 APPROX SCALE 500m
trailblazer
DO NOT TAKE THIS DESCENDING TRACK
036
FORK RIGHT OVER LOW BARRIER
HOLLY HILL COTTAGE
WEST WING HOLLY HILL HOUSE
ENTRANCE SIGN: HOLLY HILL HOUSE
CAR PARK
MAP 32
OCCASIONAL VIEW ACROSS FIELD TO RIVER MEDWAY & M2 BRIDGE THAT YOU'LL BE CROSSING
HOLLY HILL
QUIET COUNTRY LANE WITH WILD ROSES BLOOMING IN HEDGES IN EARLY SUMMER
HOLLY HILL LODGE
CLIMB TO WOODS WILD ROSE LINES PATH IN SUMMER
PATH TURNS RIGHT
CLIMBS STEEPLY
TO ROAD
LEFT THROUGH FIELD ENTRANCE
SMALL BRICK BUILDING WITH IVY COVERING IT
FIELDS
035
TAKE THIS TO **RYARSH** VIA PARK FARM RD TO CHAPEL ST & THE DUKE OF WELLINGTON, 30MINS
FIELDS
31
TO DOVER
LOW BARRIER
40-50 MINS FROM NDW SIGN (MAP 31)
LOW BARRIER
35-45 MINS TO NDW SIGN (MAP 31)

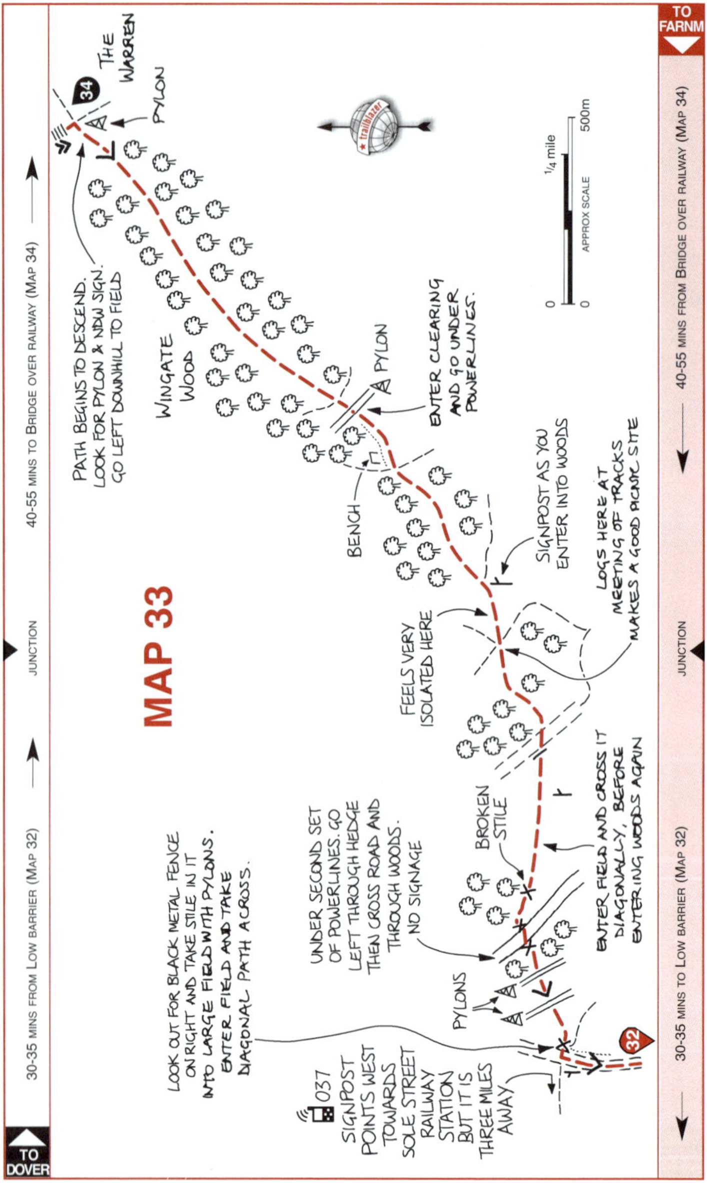

MAP 33
40-55 MINS TO BRIDGE OVER RAILWAY (MAP 34)
JUNCTION
30-35 MINS FROM LOW BARRIER (MAP 32)
TO DOVER
TO FARNM
40-55 MINS FROM BRIDGE OVER RAILWAY (MAP 34)
JUNCTION
30-35 MINS TO LOW BARRIER (MAP 32)
34
THE WARREN
PYLON
PATH BEGINS TO DESCEND. LOOK FOR PYLON & NDW SIGN. GO LEFT DOWNHILL TO FIELD
WINGATE WOOD
PYLON
ENTER CLEARING AND GO UNDER POWERLINES.
BENCH
SIGNPOST AS YOU ENTER INTO WOODS
LOGS HERE AT MEETING OF TRACKS MAKES A GOOD PICNIC SITE
FEELS VERY ISOLATED HERE
BROKEN STILE
ENTER FIELD AND CROSS IT DIAGONALLY, BEFORE ENTERING WOODS AGAIN
UNDER SECOND SET OF POWERLINES. GO LEFT THROUGH HEDGE THEN CROSS ROAD AND THROUGH WOODS. NO SIGNAGE
PYLONS
LOOK OUT FOR BLACK METAL FENCE ON RIGHT AND TAKE STILE IN IT INTO LARGE FIELD WITH PYLONS. ENTER FIELD AND TAKE DIAGONAL PATH ACROSS.
037
SIGNPOST POINTS WEST TOWARDS SOLE STREET RAILWAY STATION BUT IT IS THREE MILES AWAY
32
trailblazer
APPROX SCALE
0
1/4 mile
0
500m

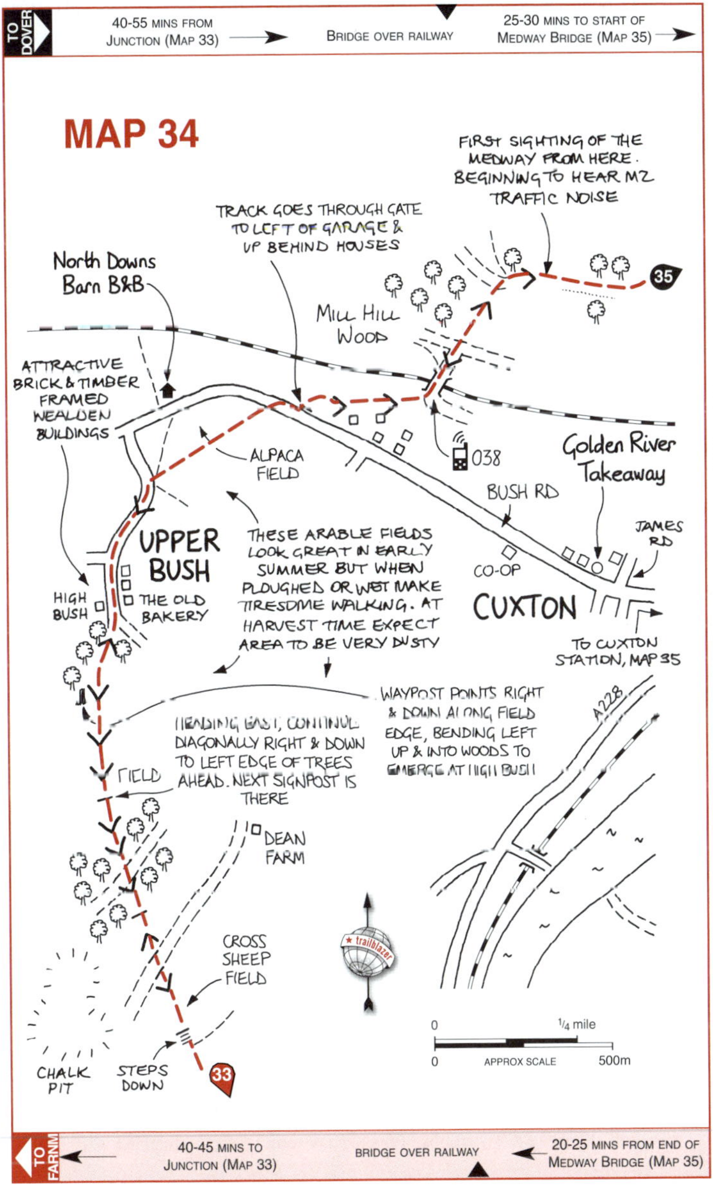
TO DOVER
40-55 MINS FROM JUNCTION (MAP 33)
BRIDGE OVER RAILWAY
25-30 MINS TO START OF MEDWAY BRIDGE (MAP 35)
MAP 34
FIRST SIGHTING OF THE MEDWAY FROM HERE. BEGINNING TO HEAR M2 TRAFFIC NOISE
TRACK GOES THROUGH GATE TO LEFT OF GARAGE & UP BEHIND HOUSES
North Downs Barn B&B
MILL HILL WOOD
35
ATTRACTIVE BRICK & TIMBER FRAMED WEALDEN BUILDINGS
ALPACA FIELD
038
Golden River Takeaway
BUSH RD
JAMES RD
UPPER BUSH
THESE ARABLE FIELDS LOOK GREAT IN EARLY SUMMER BUT WHEN PLOUGHED OR WET MAKE TIRESOME WALKING. AT HARVEST TIME EXPECT AREA TO BE VERY DUSTY
CO-OP
CUXTON
HIGH BUSH
THE OLD BAKERY
TO CUXTON STATION, MAP 35
WAYPOST POINTS RIGHT & DOWN ALONG FIELD EDGE, BENDING LEFT UP & INTO WOODS TO EMERGE AT HIGH BUSH
A228
HEADING EAST, CONTINUE DIAGONALLY RIGHT & DOWN TO LEFT EDGE OF TREES AHEAD. NEXT SIGNPOST IS THERE
FIELD
DEAN FARM
CROSS SHEEP FIELD
trailblazer
0
1/4 mile
0
APPROX SCALE
500m
CHALK PIT
STEPS DOWN
33
TO FARNM
40-45 MINS TO JUNCTION (MAP 33)
BRIDGE OVER RAILWAY
20-25 MINS FROM END OF MEDWAY BRIDGE (MAP 35)

Now bending north-easterly to ascend **Holly Hill**, (Map 32) it feels wonderfully isolated and peaceful along this section even though the industrial towns of the Medway valley are only a couple of miles away. You get little sense of that as the trail eventually drops down through a series of undulating arable fields, through the attractive hamlet of **Upper Bush** (Map 34) to arrive at **Cuxton**.

CUXTON [MAP 34, p129 & MAP 35]

On Bush Rd there is a **Co-op** (Map 34; daily 7am-10pm).

Most will stay overnight in **Rochester** (Map 36a), which is worth the detour, but there is one **accommodation** option just off the North Downs Way between Upper Bush and Cuxton: the luxurious ***North Downs Barn*** (☎ 01634-296829, 💻 northdowns barn.co .uk; 1D or T/2D, en suite; ☕; Ⓛ), a sympathetic barn conversion. B&B costs £55-60pp (sgl occ £80).

There are a couple of options for a meal. Further down Bush Rd there's a Chinese takeaway, ***Golden River*** (☎ 01634-296888, **fb**; Mon-Thur 5-9.30pm, Fri & Sat 4.30-9.30pm). Or continue on towards Cuxton station for the ***White Hart*** (Map 35; ☎ 01634-789969, 💻 whitehartcuxton.co .uk; food Tue-Fri noon-3pm & 6-9pm, Sat noon-9pm, Sun noon-5.30pm; 🐕) which does filling pub grub, including a fair range of burgers (from £14.50), and has a pleasant beer garden (though it's marred by the noise of the traffic). Note that the pub is closed on Mondays.

South Eastern Railway operates **rail** services (see box pp42-3) between Strood and Paddock Wood via Cuxton; change at Paddock Wood for Tonbridge and at Strood Thameslink offers services to St Pancras (London).

Only some of Nu-Venture's No 151 (Chatham to West Malling) **bus** services stop at the end of Bush Rd by the White Hart, so check in advance; see pp44-7.

❑ ROCHESTER THROUGH DICKENS' EYES

'*On the left of the spectator lay the ruined wall, broken in many places, and in some overhanging the narrow beach below in rude and heavy masses. ... Behind it rose the ancient castle, its towers roofless, and its massive walls crumbling away, but telling us proudly of its old might and strength ... On either side the banks of the Medway, covered with cornfields and pastures, with here and there a windmill or a distant church, stretched away as far as the eye could see, presenting a rich and varied landscape, rendered more beautiful by the changing shadows which passed swiftly across it, as the thin and half-formed clouds skimmed away in the light of the morning sun.*'

Charles Dickens, ***Pickwick Papers***

Growing up in nearby Chatham, Charles John Huffam Dickens (1812-1870) used local settings in his novels such as *The Mystery of Edwin Drood*, *The Uncommercial Traveller* and *Pickwick Papers*. Indeed, Dickens also asked to be buried in the moat of Rochester Castle! His associations with the North Downs Way are not confined to Rochester, however; Canterbury was the setting of one of his classic works, *David Copperfield*, and he described the walk from Maidstone to Rochester – a track that would follow a pretty similar course to the North Downs Way from Rochester over Blue Bell Hill (see p137) – as one of the most beautiful walks in England.

TO DOVER → START OF MEDWAY BRIDGE ▼ 15-20 MINS TO END OF PEDESTRIAN ROUTE OVER BRIDGE (MAP 36) →

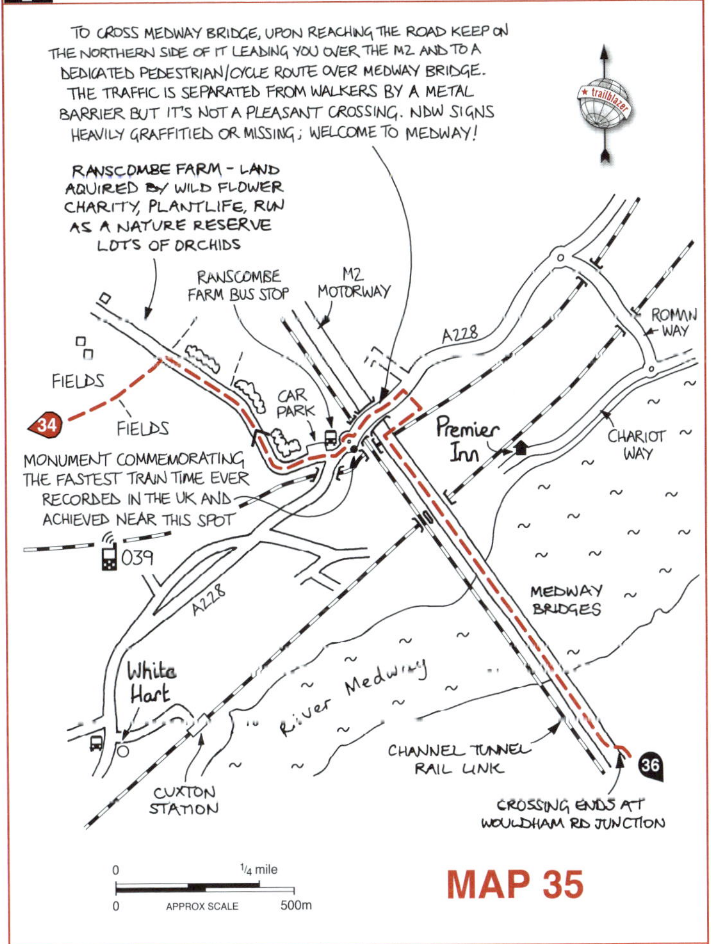

TO FARNM ← END OF MEDWAY BRIDGE ▲ ← 15-20 MINS FROM START OF PEDESTRIAN ROUTE OVER BRIDGE (MAP 36)

❑ Important note – walking times

All times in this book refer only to the time spent walking. You will need to add 20-30% to allow for rests, photography, checking the map, drinking water etc.

Climbing behind Cuxton, with views over the Medway, the trail emerges to cross the Medway Bridge. There are in fact two – a road bridge carrying the M2 and another carrying the Channel Tunnel rail link. There is a dedicated pedestrian and cycle crossing running alongside the M2. It's horrible, to be sure, the scream of traffic is loud enough to shake your fillings loose and make your ears bleed, but distract yourself from the noise and fumes by looking instead at the river below and the outline of **Rochester**, with its cathedral and castle, in the distance.

ROCHESTER [MAP 36a, p135]

As you've just passed the halfway point – and have also reached the most northerly point on the trail – it's a good excuse to visit Rochester, a 40-minute walk off the path, and perhaps celebrate with a day off and a good meal.

Sometimes referred to as the city of Great Expectations, the great Victorian novelist, **Charles Dickens** (see box p130), is to Rochester what Mickey Mouse is to Disney.

With two Dickens' festivals a year, in July and December, accommodation goes fast. But this commercialism aside there's plenty to see including a Norman castle, England's second oldest cathedral and a wonderful Restoration house.

What to see and do

For **tourist information**, 💻 visitmedway.org is useful and has links to all the essential sights of Rochester, including:

Rochester Castle (Tue-Sun & bank hols 10am-6pm; £8.50) is reckoned to be one of the country's best-preserved Norman castles. Started in the 11th century by Bishop Gundolf there are excellent views from the top of the 113ft tower over the Medway and the cathedral.

Guildhall Museum (☎ 01634-332900, Tue-Sat 10am-5pm; £5) is strong on local Medway history.

On the High St, **Eastgate House** (£6.50) is a Grade 1 listed 16th century townhouse whose gardens host Charles Dickens' Swiss chalet which was moved from one of his previous residences in the nearby village of Higham. The house is occasionally open to the public at some weekends.

Rochester Cathedral (💻 rochestercathedral.org; Mon-Sat 10am-4pm, Sun 1-3pm) was founded in AD604 and is the second oldest cathedral in England (after Canterbury Cathedral). It has a pleasant **café** (see Where to eat).

Also well worth seeing is the **Restoration House & Gardens** (☎ 01634-848520, 💻 restorationhouse.co.uk; mid Jun-Sep Thur & Fri only, 10am-5pm; £12, garden only £6) at 17-19 Crow Lane. The house, a 17th-century mansion house, takes its name from King Charles II's stay there on the eve of the Restoration. It's privately owned and superbly maintained, filled with period furniture and a good collection of English portraits. It is said to have been Dickens' inspiration for Satis House in *Great Expectations*.

Finally, there's a **Huguenot Museum** (☎ 01634-789347, 💻 huguenotmuseum.org; Tue-Sat 11am-4pm, Bank Hol Mons 10am-4pm; £5.50) on the first floor of the former tourist office; the office has shut but the museum, for the time being, clings on.

Services

The **post office** (Mon-Fri 9am-5.30pm, Sat to 4.30pm, Sun 10am-1pm) is in the newsagent's at 190-192 High St.

For any ailments there is **Paydens Chemists** (☎ 01634-842838; Mon-Fri 9am-5.30pm, Sat 9am-1pm).

For **food provisions**, Austen's of Rochester (**fb**; Mon-Sat 9am-4.30pm, Sun 10.30am-4pm) is a traditional greengrocer's; while in Strood, over the ornate 'Lion Bridge' at the northern end of the High St, is a Tesco **supermarket** (Mon-Sat 6am-midnight, Sun 10am-4pm).

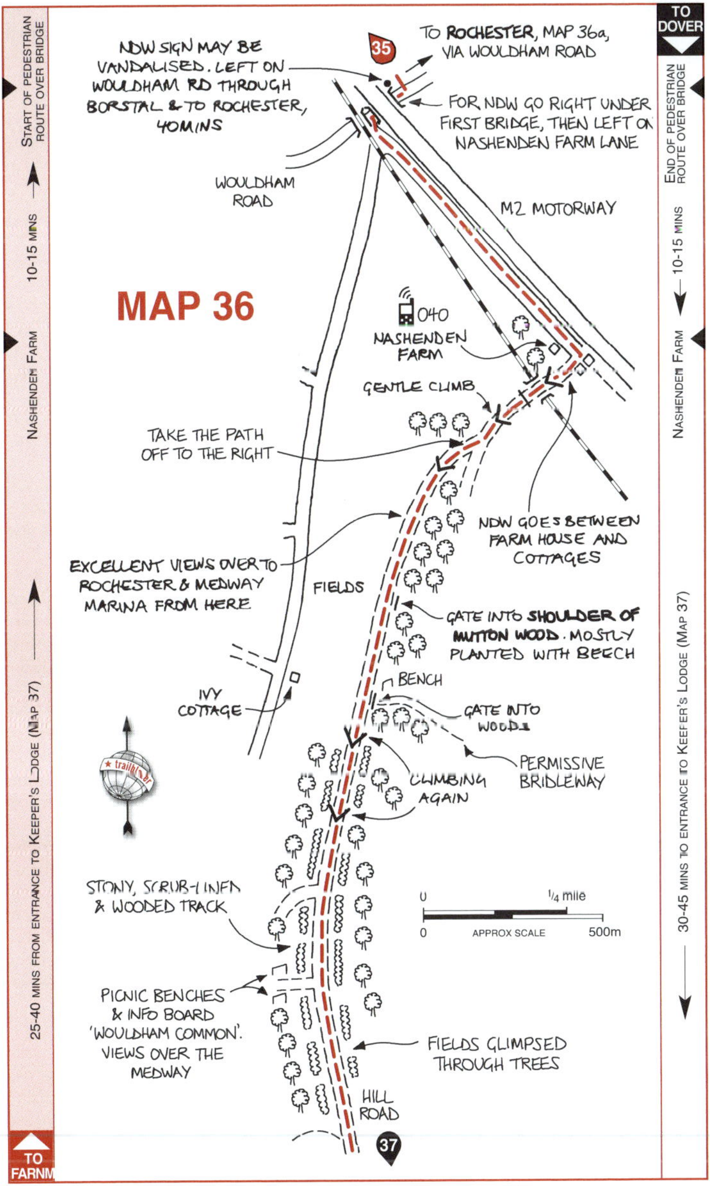
TO DOVER
TO FARNM
START OF PEDESTRIAN ROUTE OVER BRIDGE
10-15 MINS
NASHENDEN FARM
25-40 MINS FROM ENTRANCE TO KEEPER'S LODGE (MAP 37)
END OF PEDESTRIAN ROUTE OVER BRIDGE
10-15 MINS
NASHENDEN FARM
30-45 MINS TO ENTRANCE TO KEEPER'S LODGE (MAP 37)
MAP 36
35
37
TO ROCHESTER, MAP 36a, VIA WOULDHAM ROAD
NDW SIGN MAY BE VANDALISED. LEFT ON WOULDHAM RD THROUGH BORSTAL & TO ROCHESTER, 40MINS
FOR NDW GO RIGHT UNDER FIRST BRIDGE, THEN LEFT ON NASHENDEN FARM LANE
WOULDHAM ROAD
M2 MOTORWAY
040
NASHENDEN FARM
GENTLE CLIMB
TAKE THE PATH OFF TO THE RIGHT
NDW GOES BETWEEN FARM HOUSE AND COTTAGES
EXCELLENT VIEWS OVER TO ROCHESTER & MEDWAY MARINA FROM HERE
FIELDS
GATE INTO SHOULDER OF MUTTON WOOD. MOSTLY PLANTED WITH BEECH
BENCH
IVY COTTAGE
GATE INTO WOODS
PERMISSIVE BRIDLEWAY
CLIMBING AGAIN
STONY, SCRUB-LINED & WOODED TRACK
0
1/4 mile
0
APPROX SCALE
500m
PICNIC BENCHES & INFO BOARD 'WOULDHAM COMMON'. VIEWS OVER THE MEDWAY
FIELDS GLIMPSED THROUGH TREES
HILL ROAD

The Blue Boar Lane car park hosts the monthly **Farmers' Market**, on the third Sunday of each month.

Transport

The **railway station** has regular services (operated by Southeastern Railway and Thameslink) to several London stations, as well as to Canterbury East and Dover Priory; see box pp42-3 for details.

Arriva's **bus** No 155 (Chatham to Borstal) calls at Warden Rd and Star Hill. Nu-Venture's No 142 stops on Delce Rd and their Nos 151, 172 & 173, which also serve Chatham, stop at the railway station. See pp42-7 for details.

For a taxi call **Vokes** (☎ 01634-222222, 🖳 vokestaxis.co.uk).

Where to stay

Travelodge and Premier Inn both have branches serving Rochester, with rooms starting at around £30. ***Travelodge*** (☎ 08719 846555, 🖳 travelodge.co.uk; 81 en suite rooms; ◗; 🐕) is the most convenient for the city, east of the railway just three minutes from the main centre on Cory's Rd. ***Premier Inn*** (Map 35; ☎ 0333 321 8451, 🖳 premierinn. com; 161 en suite rooms; ◗), on the other hand, lies north of the River Medway (Rochester Medway Valley Leisure Park) and is more convenient for the trail itself: heading east, rather than taking the turn-off leaving the A228 to cross the Medway Bridge, instead continue along the A228 to a second roundabout and turn right here to join Roman Way, before taking another right at the river to take you back west along Chariot Way by the river to the Premier Inn.

In the centre of Rochester there's Grade II listed ***Gordon House Hotel*** (☎ 01634-831000; 2T/9T/2Qd, all en suite; ◗; WI-FI some rooms). Rooms cost £37.50-42.50pp (sgl occ full room rate).

There's also a Wetherspoons pub, ***The Golden Lion*** (☎ 01634-405402, 🖳 jdwetherspoon.com; 6D/3D or T, all en suite; ◗), further along the High St at 147-151. Room-only rates, starting at £31.25pp (sgl occ full room rate), are reasonable given the central location, and a comprehensive breakfast menu is available downstairs in the bar for an additional cost (from £2.35 for a bacon butty).

Where to eat and drink

There are several good independent cafés in town in addition to the usual ***Costa*** outlet (Mon-Fri 6.30am-7.30pm, Sat from 7am, Sun 7.30am-6pm). Our favourite is ***Leonards*** (☎ 01634-843881; Mon-Sat 10.30am-4.30pm, Sun 11am-3.30pm; 🐕) at the back of the gallery-cum-bookshop, Store 104. The lunch menu usually consists of just a few items but they serve the best coffee in town and their cake cabinet includes such delights as a lemon-and-meringue 'cruffin' (a muffin made with croissant pastry; £4.50). It's a real find.

Another good option is ***Deaf Cat Coffee*** (Mon-Sat 9am-5pm, Sun 10am-5pm) at 83 High St. It doesn't offer much in the way of food except a few pre-made sandwiches and other snacks but what it does, it does well, namely some first-rate coffees and teas.

Around the corner from the High St in an enviable location near the cathedral and with outside seating, ***Jaggers*** (☎ 01634-7806455, 🖳 jaggersrochester.co.uk; Thur & Sun 10am-5pm, Fri & Sat to 11pm, takeaway only for orders after 7pm) has transformed itself from a crêperie into a cocktail bar and coffee house, though one with a substantial and diverse menu too including tapas, salads and sandwiches as well as the crêpes and waffles in which they originally specialised.

Try the traditional ***Peggotty's Parlour*** (🖳 peggottysparlour.co.uk; Tue-Fri 10am-4pm, Sat to 4.30pm, Sun 11am-4pm); it's easy to miss, being located on the first floor, but while the menu is largely traditional and the food is fine (sandwiches from £6), it's the elevated location opposite the cathedral that is the biggest draw.

For somewhere that's both right in the heart of Rochester, and yet an escape from it, the cathedral's own ***Café in the Crypt*** (🖳 rochestercathedral.org/cafe; Mon-Sat 10am-4pm) offers handmade sandwiches, jacket potatoes and an array of cakes that are, appropriately enough, quite heavenly.

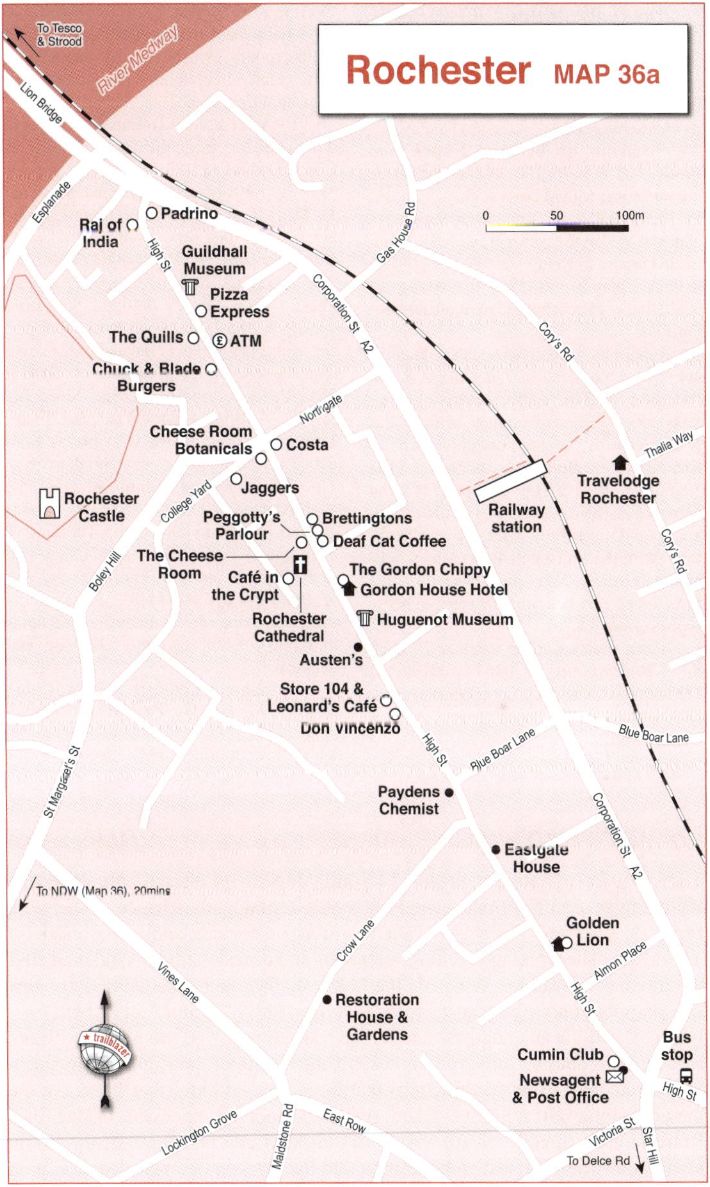
Rochester MAP 36a
To Tesco & Strood
River Medway
Lion Bridge
Esplanade
0 50 100m
Padrino
Raj of India
High St
Guildhall Museum
Pizza Express
The Quills
ATM
Chuck & Blade Burgers
Gas House Rd
Corporation St A2
Cory's Rd
Northgate
Cheese Room Botanicals
Costa
Jaggers
College Yard
Rochester Castle
Peggotty's Parlour
Brettingtons
Deaf Cat Coffee
The Cheese Room
Café in the Crypt
Rochester Cathedral
The Gordon Chippy
Gordon House Hotel
Huguenot Museum
Railway station
Thalia Way
Travelodge Rochester
Cory's Rd
Boley Hill
Austen's
Store 104 & Leonard's Café
Don Vincenzo
High St
Blue Boar Lane
Blue Boar Lane
St Margaret's St
Paydens Chemist
Eastgate House
Corporation St A2
To NDW (Map 36), 20mins
Crow Lane
Golden Lion
Almon Place
Vines Lane
High St
Restoration House & Gardens
trailblazer
Bus stop
Cumin Club
Newsagent & Post Office
High St
Lockington Grove
Maidstone Rd
East Row
Victoria St
Star Hill
To Delce Rd

The Quills (☎ 01634-407402, 🖳 thequills.co.uk; Mon-Thur 9am-9.30pm, Fri & Sat to 11pm, Sun to 8.30pm), towards the northern end of the High St, lists some great burgers on its menu starting at £12.99 for its cheeseburger.

Speaking of burgers, ***Chuck and Blade*** (☎ 01634-780190, 🖳 chuckandbladeburgers.com; Mon-Thur 11.30am-9pm, Fri to 10pm, Sat 9am-10pm, Sun 9am-9pm) claim to make the 'juiciest, filthiest hand-made burgers in Kent', starting at £9 for the halloumi burger and rising to £16 for the quadzilla, a cheeseburger of monster proportions.

Unsurprisingly, cheese also features heavily on the menu of ***The Cheese Room*** (☎ 01634-845270, 🖳 thecheeseroomrochester.co.uk). This establishment actually has two premises, a restaurant known as Cheese Room Botanicals at No 60 (Tue 10am-5pm, Wed & Thur to 10pm, Fri & Sat 9am-11pm, Sun 9am-5pm) which does great (and thankfully cheese-free) breakfasts, with the Full English £11, and a deli-cum-café (daily 9am-4pm; 🐕) with some great bread and delicious takeaway cheese scones (from £1.30).

For a meaty slap-up meal, at 79 High St is ***Brettingtons*** (☎ 01634-400192, 🖳 brettingtons.com; daily noon-9pm), a steak and lobster bar with steaks from £30 for a 10oz sirloin.

At the other end of the price range, food at ***The Golden Lion*** (see Where to stay; daily 8am-midnight) is, as with all Wetherspoons-owned places, unquestionably great value, though remember than dogs aren't allowed.

There are several **Italian** restaurants in town, ranging from the familiar, such as ***Pizza Express*** (21-23 High St; ☎ 01634-812171, 🖳 pizzaexpress.com; Sun-Wed 11.30am-10pm, Thur-Sat to 11pm), to the independent one-offs, such as the smart ***Don Vincenzo*** (☎ 01634-408373, 🖳 donvincenzo.co.uk; Mon noon-3pm & 6-9pm, Tue-Fri noon-3pm & 6-10pm, Sat noon-4pm & 6-10pm, Sun noon-8pm) with pizzas from £11.50 and, at the end of the street opposite the bridge, ***Padrino*** (☎ 01634-553370, 🖳 padrino-pizza.com; Mon, Tue & Thur 4-10pm, Fri to 11pm, Sat 10am-11pm, Sun 11am-8pm), with pizzas from £10. They also do takeaway and delivery.

There is a good **Indian** restaurant, the sophisticated ***Cumin Club*** (☎ 01634-400880, 🖳 cuminclub.com; Tue-Sun & bank hols 5-10.30pm) at the southern end of the High St; and, at the northern end, ***Raj of India*** (☎ 01634-844489, 🖳 rajofindiarochester.co.uk; daily noon-2pm & 6pm-midnight). Both also do takeaway and delivery.

For more traditional **takeaway** fare there's ***The Gordon Chippy*** (🖳 gordonchippy.co.uk; Tue-Thur noon-9pm, Fri & Sat to 10pm, Sun to 8pm).

ROCHESTER TO HOLLINGBOURNE [MAPS 36-42]

There's a lot of interest on this **14.8-mile/23.8km** (**4½hrs to 6hrs**) section including several Neolithic sites, Kent's oldest village, the chance to stay with friars at Aylesford Friary and visit the ruins of a motte-and-bailey castle at Thurnham. The walking is seldom strenuous and occasionally blissful, and after the traumas of walking alongside the M2 yesterday, you'll be pleased to know that there are only two A roads to cross today (the A229 and A249), both easily negotiated via an underpass and bridge respectively. And though their distant roar remains audible for several miles, it's the beauty of the Kent countryside – and the ancient stone constructions that lie hidden within – that lingers in the memory long after you've taken off your boots at the end of the day. Refreshments directly on (or very near) the trail can be found at: the Robin Hood pub (Map 37), just an hour or so into the stage; at the petrol station shop by the A229 (Map 38); and then at Detling (Map 40), nearly nine miles into the day. Or take the lengthy detour to Aylesford where further refreshments await.

The day begins with a climb along the edge of **Shoulder of Mutton Wood** (Map 36), eventually emerging on a tarmac road to pass within view of the ***Robin Hood*** pub (Map 37; ☎ 01634-861500, 💻 robinhood-pub.co.uk; food Wed-Thur noon-10pm, Fri & Sat noon-11pm, Sun noon-6.30pm; 🐕). This section of the Way is popular with cyclists, most of whom are pleasant and civil but, as with life in general, you'll always get one or two who think the path is for their own personal use only. Just smile sweetly.

Continuing on the same path eventually brings you out at **Blue Bell Hill** picnic site (Map 38), from where you drop down along a surfaced bridleway to pass **Kit's Coty** (see box p138). If you're worn out already you can divert off to ***Kit's Coty Glamping*** (off Map 38; see p139) which has bell tents, a cabin and a shepherd's hut.

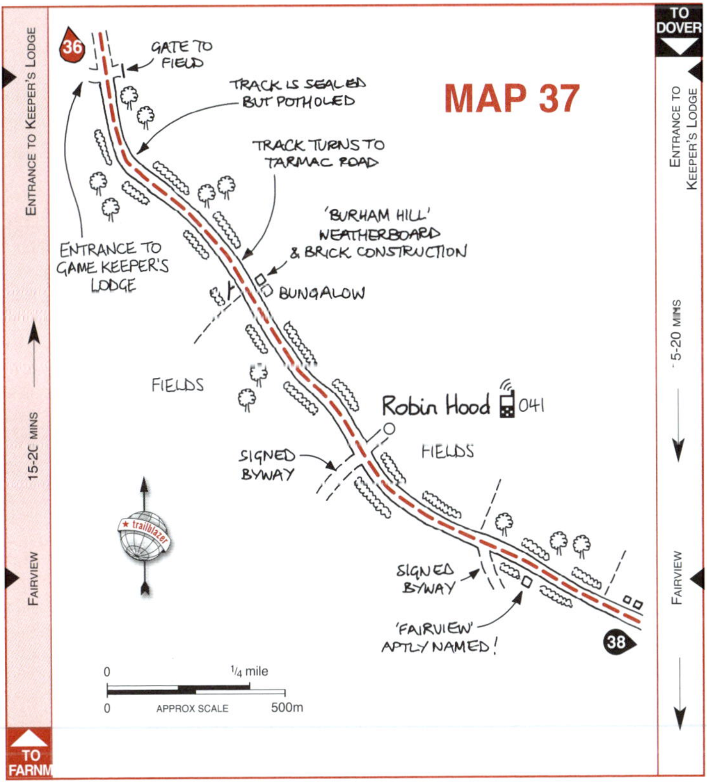

❑ MEDWAY BURIAL TOMBS

Kit's Coty is a Neolithic burial site built between 3500BC and 2500BC near Aylesford consisting of three upright stones and a capstone across the top standing about 15ft high. The structure is thought to have been at the entrance to a long barrow burial chamber about 200ft long running east to west. The site is now railed off and managed by English Heritage.

The **White Horse Stone** (see Map 38), further along the trail, is also thought to be a Neolithic burial site. Between the two and just off the trail – is **Little Kit's Coty** (Map 38) – also known as the **Countless Stones**. The latter name derives from the legend that, if you were to try to count how many there are, you'd end up with a different figure each time. That said, another superstition associated with them is that those who do try to count them will endure bad luck afterwards. The stones lie a couple of hundred metres off the path, in the field on the left-hand side of Rochester Rd, though the sign pointing to them is often obscured by the vegetation. Alternatively stay on the Way and after crossing the road, look to your right through the trees. The stones lie beyond the first pylon, though the fence that surrounds them is often overgrown so you may not be able to see much.

At the bottom of the lane, the modern world crashes back into yours as you have to negotiate a crossing of the busy Rochester Road. If you're feeling peckish (or just plain knackered), head down to **Aylesford** (Map 38a) following our directions below for the safest route.

THE SAFEST ROUTE TO AYLESFORD [MAP 38]

If you're heading down to **Aylesford**, rather than taking the direct route along pavement-less Rochester Road – a prospect simply too terrifying to contemplate – continue on the trail along a tree-shrouded bridleway that takes you, eventually, to an underpass under the A229. Before you reach the underpass you'll come to a path on the right. Take this path which will lead you onto Pratling Street (also pavement-less but much quieter). Continue until Beddow Way, turning left here to march through the industrial estate and onto Forstal Way, then turn right. It's a slightly longer walk, but much safer, and saner too.

AYLESFORD [MAP 38a, p140]

Pronounced 'ales ford' and reputedly one of the oldest villages in Kent, with the buildings along the narrow High St stacked tightly together above the River Medway.

The **village store** (Mon-Sat 7.30am-6pm, Sun 8am-2pm) has a range of snacks, drinks and groceries, but there are few other amenities in the village for walkers save for a couple of places to eat and stay.

Glamping fans can divert off the trail before the turn-off to Aylesford (see Map 38) to ***Kit's Coty Glamping*** (off Map 38; ☎ 01634-685862, 💻 kitscotyglamping.co.uk; Apr-end Sep) which offers a cabin, a shepherd's hut and three bell tents for weary, wealthy walkers. One of the **tents** sleeps two people (from £120) in a double bed and the others sleep four/six people (£170/210) all in single beds; the **shepherd's hut** sleeps two in a double bed (£120), and the **cabin** sleeps two adults and two children (double bed plus bunk beds; from £125). They offer a cream tea on arrival (from £7.50pp), breakfast hampers

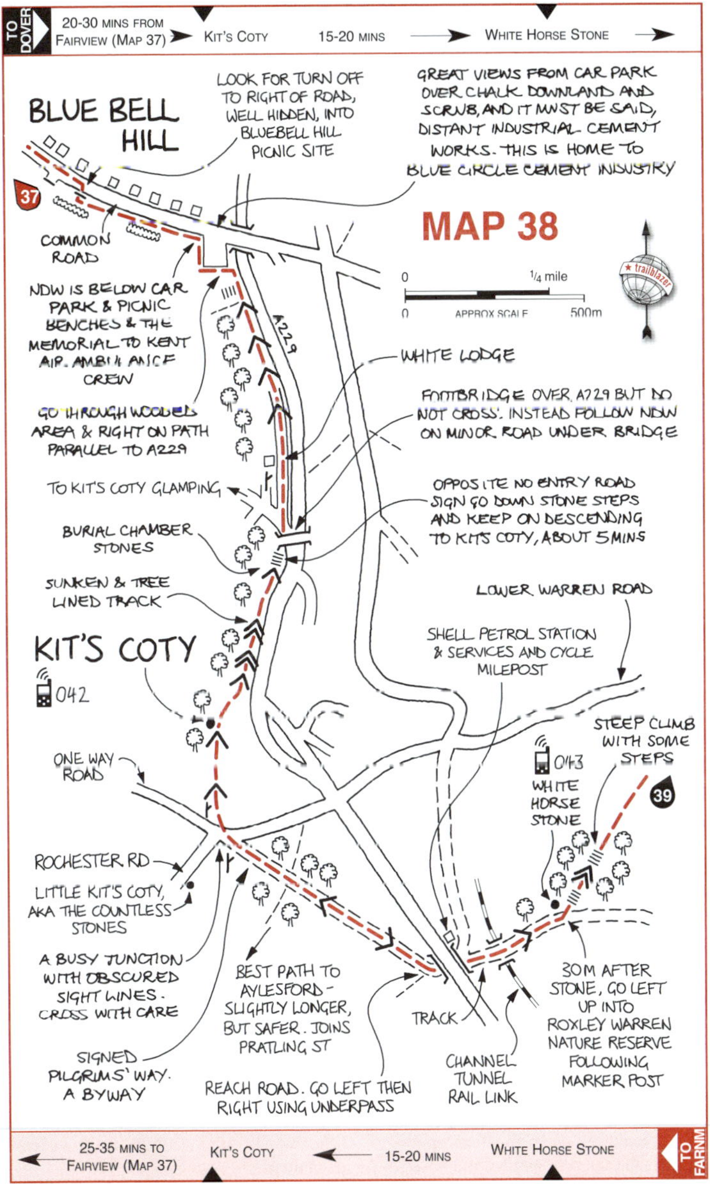
TO DOVER
20-30 MINS FROM FAIRVIEW (MAP 37)
KIT'S COTY
15-20 MINS
WHITE HORSE STONE
BLUE BELL HILL
37
LOOK FOR TURN OFF TO RIGHT OF ROAD, WELL HIDDEN, INTO BLUEBELL HILL PICNIC SITE
GREAT VIEWS FROM CAR PARK OVER CHALK DOWNLAND AND SCRUB, AND IT MUST BE SAID, DISTANT INDUSTRIAL CEMENT WORKS. THIS IS HOME TO BLUE CIRCLE CEMENT INDUSTRY
MAP 38
0
1/4 mile
0
APPROX SCALE
500m
trailblazer
COMMON ROAD
NDW IS BELOW CAR PARK & PICNIC BENCHES & THE MEMORIAL TO KENT AIR AMBULANCE CREW
A229
WHITE LODGE
GO THROUGH WOODED AREA & RIGHT ON PATH PARALLEL TO A229
FOOTBRIDGE OVER A229 BUT DO NOT CROSS. INSTEAD FOLLOW NDW ON MINOR ROAD UNDER BRIDGE
TO KIT'S COTY GLAMPING
OPPOSITE NO ENTRY ROAD SIGN GO DOWN STONE STEPS AND KEEP ON DESCENDING TO KIT'S COTY, ABOUT 5 MINS
BURIAL CHAMBER STONES
SUNKEN & TREE LINED TRACK
LOWER WARREN ROAD
KIT'S COTY
042
SHELL PETROL STATION & SERVICES AND CYCLE MILEPOST
STEEP CLIMB WITH SOME STEPS
043
WHITE HORSE STONE
39
ONE WAY ROAD
ROCHESTER RD
LITTLE KIT'S COTY, AKA THE COUNTLESS STONES
A BUSY JUNCTION WITH OBSCURED SIGHT LINES. CROSS WITH CARE
BEST PATH TO AYLESFORD - SLIGHTLY LONGER, BUT SAFER. JOINS PRATLING ST
TRACK
30M AFTER STONE, GO LEFT UP INTO ROXLEY WARREN NATURE RESERVE FOLLOWING MARKER POST
SIGNED PILGRIMS' WAY. A BYWAY
REACH ROAD. GO LEFT THEN RIGHT USING UNDERPASS
CHANNEL TUNNEL RAIL LINK
25-35 MINS TO FAIRVIEW (MAP 37)
KIT'S COTY
15-20 MINS
WHITE HORSE STONE
TO FARNM

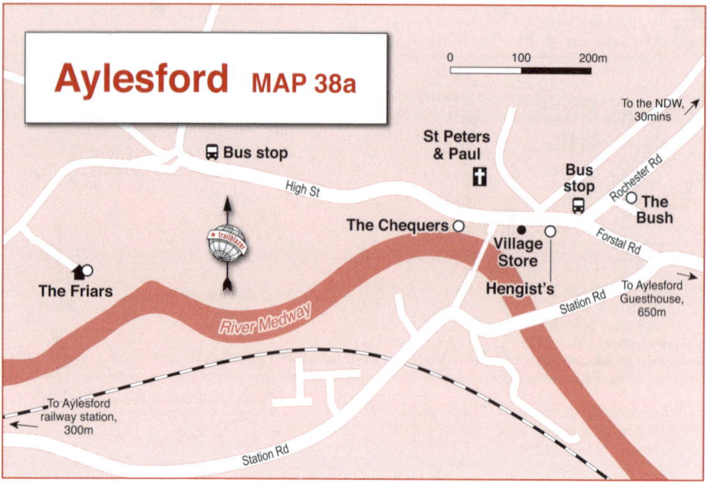

and local takeaways deliver to them which is ideal for walkers. They also have a small **shop** (daily 4-8.30pm). To get there, having left the minor road off the A229, turn right at the end of the large wooden fence and walk straight along Collingwood Rd for approximately 600m to the end.

In Aylesford itself, The Carmelite Friary was founded in 1242, subsequently dissolved by Henry VIII and then re-established in 1949. ***The Friars*** (☎ 01622-717272, 💻 thefriars.org.uk; 27S/31D/7Tr/1Qd, some en suite, most shared facilities; ☕; some WI-FI) offer a great welcome with simple rooms and communal facilities. Rates are from £50pp (sgl/sgl occ from £60) for B&B, and it's £16.50 extra for an en suite room. It's a large and busy complex complete with **tea room** (summer daily 10am-5pm, winter hours vary), chapels and shrines. Judging by the calendar of events they've cornered the market in retreats and pilgrimage. The friars are also know as Whitefriars because as Carmelites they wear white robes; Dominicans wear black. Non-residents can eat here (book at least 48hrs ahead; light supper £12, 3-course lunch £26.20, breakfast £11.80).

The other accommodation option in town is the friendly and helpful ***Aylesford Guesthouse*** (☎ 01622-717208; 4D or T, all en suite), at 29a Forstal Cottages on Forstal Rd, about 10-15 minutes east from the High St. Rates are from a very reasonable £27.50-30pp (sgl occ £40-45), though note that breakfast is *not* included.

Food-wise, filling pub grub is available at ***The Bush*** (☎ 01622-717446; closed Mon, food Wed-Sat noon-9pm, Sun noon-4pm; 🐕 on a lead) on Rochester Rd, the first eatery you come to and the cheaper option. Newly refurbished, ***The Chequers*** (☎ 07885-144422; **fb**; 🐕; Mon-Thur 11am-10pm, Fri & Sat 9am-11.30pm, Sun 9am-10pm) serves classic pub favourites (from £16) plus their ever-popular Sunday lunch, as well as bar snacks such as bang-bang chicken wings (£8).

For upmarket cuisine there is ***The Hengist*** (☎ 01622-947930, 💻 thehengist restaurant.com; Sun & Tue noon-11pm, Wed-Sat 9am-11pm, Mon closed) but unless you carry stylish glad rags in your pack you'll probably feel out of place at this elegant restaurant and cocktail bar.

Southeastern Railway's **train** services (see box pp42-3) between Strood and Paddock Wood) call here; change at Paddock Wood for Tonbridge and at Strood Thameslink offers services to St Pancras (London).

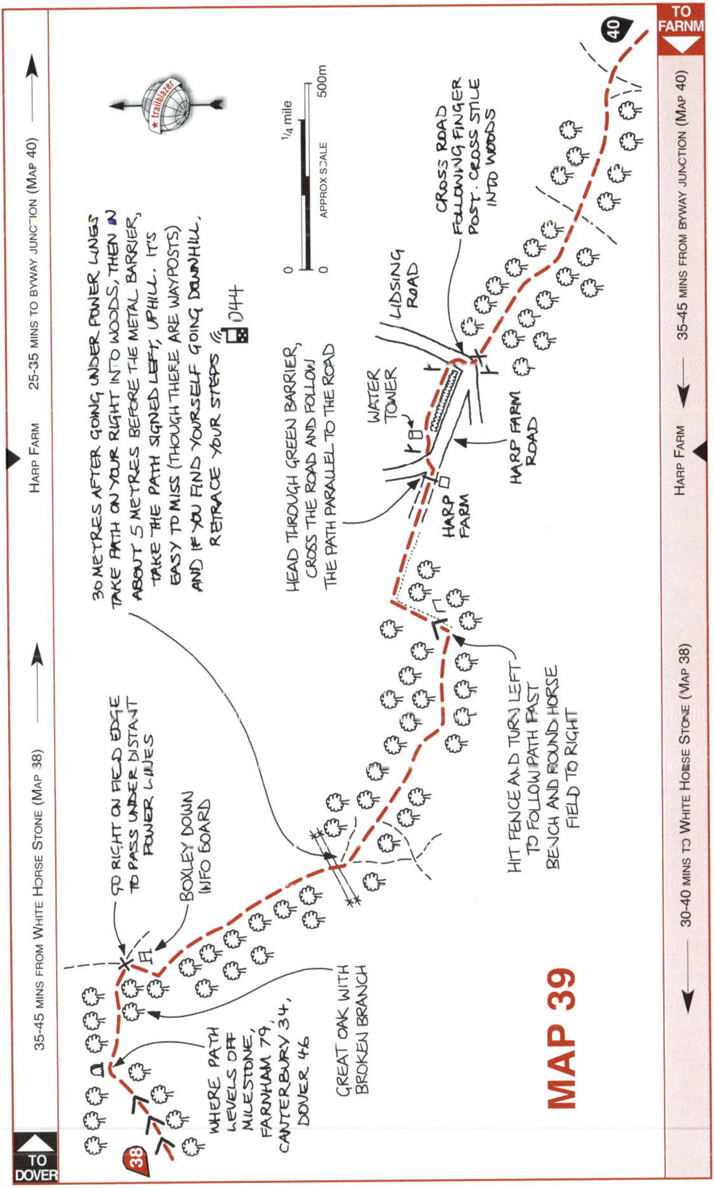
MAP 39
35-45 MINS FROM WHITE HORSE STONE (MAP 38)
HARP FARM
25-35 MINS TO BYWAY JUNCTION (MAP 40)
30-40 MINS TO WHITE HORSE STONE (MAP 38)
35-45 MINS FROM BYWAY JUNCTION (MAP 40)
TO DOVER
TO FARNM
38
40
trailblazer
0
1/4 mile
0
500m
APPROX SCALE
30 METRES AFTER GOING UNDER POWER LINES TAKE PATH ON YOUR RIGHT INTO WOODS, THEN IN ABOUT 5 METRES BEFORE THE METAL BARRIER, TAKE THE PATH SIGNED LEFT, UPHILL. IT'S EASY TO MISS (THOUGH THERE ARE WAYPOSTS) AND IF YOU FIND YOURSELF GOING DOWNHILL, RETRACE YOUR STEPS
044
HEAD THROUGH GREEN BARRIER, CROSS THE ROAD AND FOLLOW THE PATH PARALLEL TO THE ROAD
WATER TOWER
LIDSING ROAD
CROSS ROAD FOLLOWING FINGER POST. CROSS STILE INTO WOODS
HARP FARM
HARP FARM ROAD
GO RIGHT ON FIELD EDGE TO PASS UNDER DISTANT POWER LINES
BOXLEY DOWN INFO BOARD
WHERE PATH LEVELS OFF MILESTONE, FARNHAM 79, CANTERBURY 34, DOVER 46
GREAT OAK WITH BROKEN BRANCH
HIT FENCE AND TURN LEFT TO FOLLOW PATH PAST BENCH AND ROUND HORSE FIELD TO RIGHT

Back at Rochester Road and the trail, Nu-Venture's **bus** No 142 operates from Chatham to Kit's Coty via Rochester and Blue Bell Hill Village; see pp44-7 for details.

At the end of the underpass, the trail passes the 24-hour Shell petrol station **shop** with snacks and drinks, before climbing via the insignificant-looking **White Horse Stone** (easily missed) and into **Roxley Warren Nature Reserve**, remaining substantially in woodland until emerging above Detling.

DETLING [MAP 40]

Though lacking accommodation, Detling does boast the pleasant **Detling Community Store** (🖳 detlingcommunitystore.co.uk, **fb**; Mon, Tue & Thur-Sat 8am-4pm, Wed to noon, Sun 9am-1pm) with **post office** (open same as store Mon-Sat, closed Sun), operating out of an old shipping container. The staff are friendly, dog-mad and can rustle up hot drinks, pasties and sausage rolls in their **coffee shop**.

There's also a popular pub, ***Cock Horse Inn*** (☎ 01622-730144, 🖳 cockhorsedetling.co.uk, **fb**; food Tue-Sat noon-3pm & 5-8pm, Sun noon-3.30pm; 🐕 bar area only & on lead), a friendly place and one that, delightfully, is right on the trail. The food is tasty, with a simple and good value menu with mains starting at £11.50 for the three-bean chilli nachos. Note that the pub is closed on Mondays.

Regaining the ridgeline the trail strikes out for the overgrown **ruins of Thurnham Castle** (Map 40). It's known as a 'motte and bailey' fortification, basically a mound surrounded by an enclosure, and dates from the Norman period. Souvenir hunters pilfered most of the stone work and quarrying damaged what remains but it was once a large garrison – about 70 metres in diameter – and remains a nice place to sit and have a picnic lunch and admire the scenery below.

THURNHAM [MAP 40]

Accommodation and food are available at ***The Black Horse Inn*** (off Map 40; ☎ 01622-737185, 🖳 blackhorsekent.co.uk; 20D/4T/3Qd, all en suite; ☕; 🐕) on Thurnham Lane, a very attractive dark-beamed, candle-strewn country pub just off the trail. **B&B** rates are from £50pp (sgl occ from £80), with a slight increase at weekends; breakfast is £12pp extra. Their kitchen (Mon-Thur noon-9.30pm, Fri & Sat to 10pm, Sun to 8pm) serves a range of lunchtime sandwiches (from £10) and mains such as ham, egg and chips (from £14.50).

Following the fence line up through fields the trail crosses Coldblow Lane, so named after the Saxon for 'crossing of the ways' though it's hard not to credit the sometimes chill wind whipping across the Downs ridge for the name. Shortly afterwards **the path divides** (Map 41) for a short while; the lower route is the classic North Downs Way, but the upper route takes you past a **viewpoint** with a wooden sculpture and picnic benches. With the latter now the popular route (and deservedly so), the official North Downs Way is actually becoming a little underused and overgrown; given this, we advise that you take the 'Viewpoint' route; the two trails meet back again about fifteen minutes later.

After crossing mostly open fields on a fairly well-defined track the Way drops down to **Hollingbourne**. The path passes the wonderfully named but

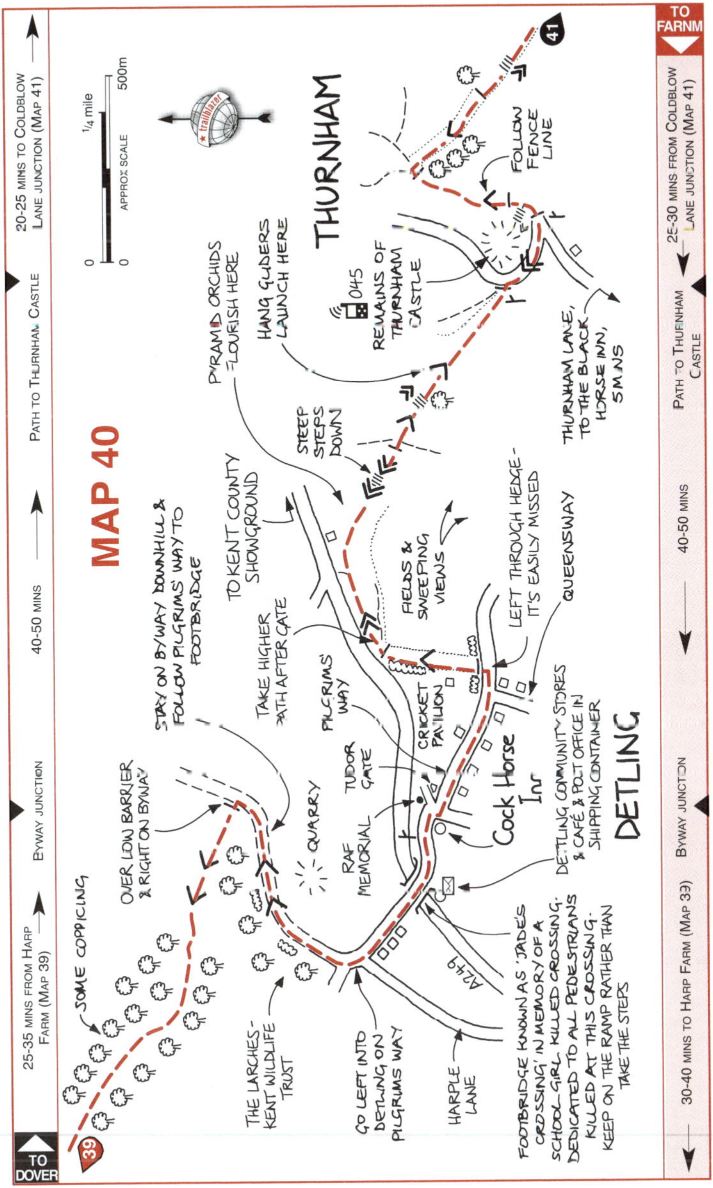

ROUTE GUIDE AND MAPS

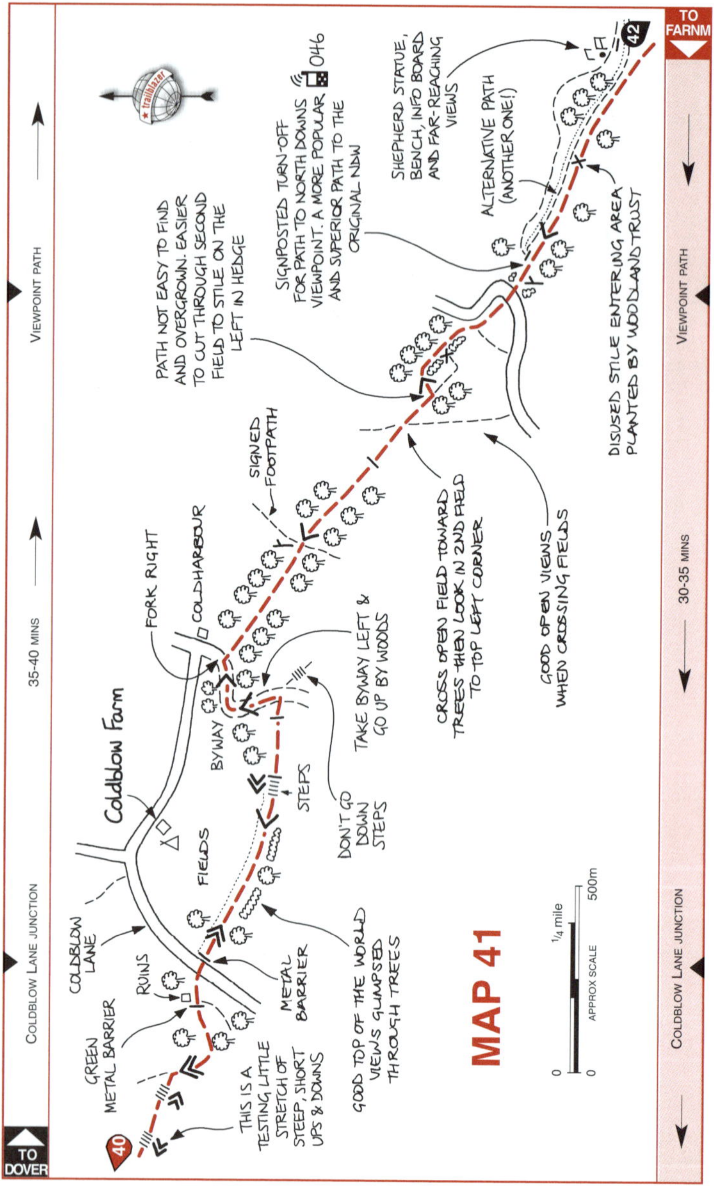

TO DOVER
TO FARNM
42
40
COLDBLOW LANE JUNCTION
35-40 MINS
VIEWPOINT PATH
30-35 MINS
MAP 41
APPROX SCALE
0
1/4 mile
0
500m
trailblazer
GREEN METAL BARRIER
THIS IS A TESTING LITTLE STRETCH OF STEEP, SHORT STEEP, SHORT UPS & DOWNS
RUINS
COLDBLOW LANE
METAL BARRIER
GOOD TOP OF THE WORLD VIEWS GLIMPSED THROUGH TREES
FIELDS
Coldblow Farm
STEPS
DON'T GO DOWN STEPS
BYWAY
FORK RIGHT
COLDHARBOUR
TAKE BYWAY LEFT & GO UP BY WOODS
SIGNED FOOTPATH
CROSS OPEN FIELD TOWARD TREES THEN LOOK IN 2ND FIELD TO TOP LEFT CORNER
GOOD OPEN VIEWS WHEN CROSSING FIELDS
PATH NOT EASY TO FIND AND OVERGROWN. EASIER TO CUT THROUGH SECOND FIELD TO STILE ON THE LEFT IN HEDGE
SIGNPOSTED TURN-OFF FOR PATH TO NORTH DOWNS VIEWPOINT. A MORE POPULAR AND SUPERIOR PATH TO THE ORIGINAL NDW
046
DISUSED STILE ENTERING AREA PLANTED BY WOODLAND TRUST
ALTERNATIVE PATH (ANOTHER ONE!)
SHEPHERD STATUE, BENCH, INFO BOARD AND FAR-REACHING VIEWS

temporarily closed ***Dirty Habit*** (Map 42; ☎ 01622-880880, 💻 elitepubs.com/venue/the-dirty-habit), which is due to reopen in Spring 2025 after the fire in October 2022.

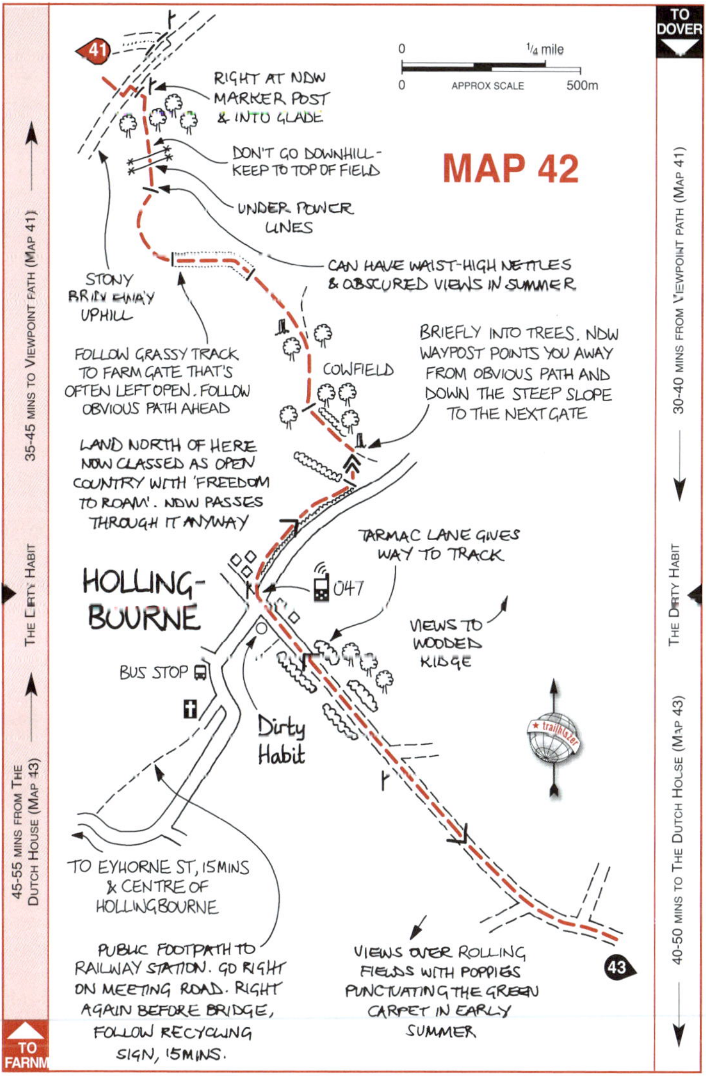

HOLLINGBOURNE

[off MAP 42, p145]

Hollingbourne is an attractive little village, more vibrant than some, though you've got a long walk from the trail to reach its heart. The church is 300m from the trail; the station is at least 1000m beyond that, and the village itself is about 400m beyond the turn-off to the station. Take the path by the church for the prettiest and shortest route.

There are two lovely traditional pubs here. **Rooms** are available at ***The Windmill*** (☎ 01622-889000, 🖳 thewindmillhollingbourne.co.uk; 5D en suite), a smart place with rates from £41pp room only; breakfast is available for £10pp. They also serve top notch **food** (Mon-Thur noon-3pm & 6-9pm, Fri noon-3pm & 5-9pm, Sat noon-9pm, Sun noon-8pm; WI-FI; 🐕 bar area only) with mains around the £17-30 mark, though £35 and beyond for a steak. Alternatively, friendly ***Sugar Loaves*** (☎ 01622-880220, 🖳 sugarloaveshollingbourne.com; food Mon-Sat noon-3pm & 6-9pm, Sun noon-5pm; 🐕) has mains such as chilli prawn linguine (£12.95).

Hollingbourne **railway station**, on Eyhorne St, is a stop on Southeastern Railway's London Victoria to Ashford service (see box pp42-3).

Nu-Venture operates the No 13 and 14 **bus services**; buses depart from the church and these useful services stop on Eyhorne St at the post office and at Leeds Castle's main entrance on the way to Maidstone. Stagecoach's No 10X (Maidstone to Ashford) also stops in Hollingbourne; see pp44-7 for details.

HOLLINGBOURNE TO BOUGHTON LEES [MAPS 42-49]

A long-ish stage of **12.6 miles/20.3km (3½hrs to 5¼hrs)**, necessarily so due to the lack of any accommodation in Charing. Campers can reduce the length of this stage by stopping in Westwell at the campsite there (see p154; for a total of 10.6 miles/17.1km); while those with unlimited funds may want to stop at Eastwell and stay at the Manor Hotel there (see p156; for a total of 11.8 miles/19km). Otherwise, Boughton Lees is a sensible place to end the stage: it's right on the trail, it's got a B&B, a pub and a campsite – which all happen to be the same place – and there's a bus to Ashford too, for those who want to escape back to London. It is also the nearest village to the point where the North Downs Way divides – see box, p156 for details.

As for the walking itself on this stage – well it's very pleasant and straightforward. If you weren't feeling like a pilgrim before now, you certainly will once you join this route. For today you pass plenty of evidence that this route has been used by pilgrims for centuries. Setting off from Dirty Habit – a reference, of course, to the clothes of monks who would have made up a large proportion of those walking to Canterbury for their faith – on the way you also pass Pilgrim Lodge and Pilgrim Cottage on a path that's been officially called Pilgrims' Way (see box p166). Indeed, there's a rather good wooden sculpture of a pilgrim sitting on a bench just after the Harrietsham turn-off! And just to emphasise the spiritual purpose of this path, each of the several ancient villages that line the Pilgrims' Way have their own centuries-old church, that would once have served the pilgrims as they made their way to Canterbury – and which still perform this function to a degree today; the first is at **Harrietsham**, home to the 12th-century St John the Baptist Church.

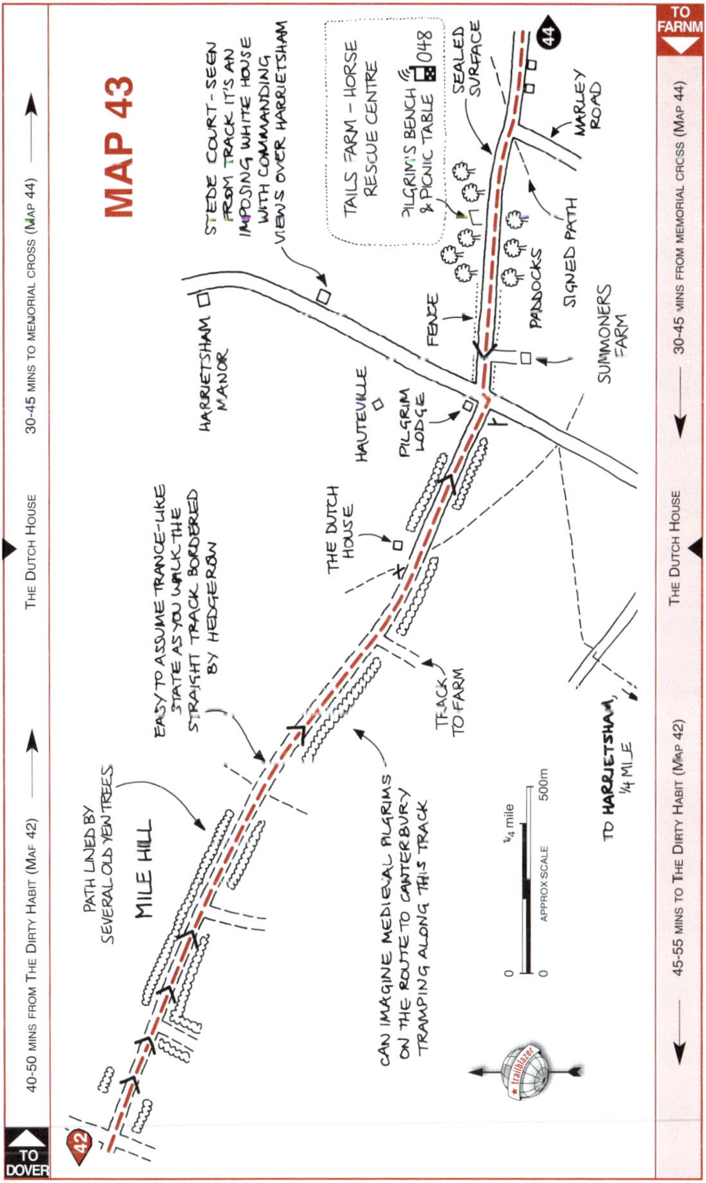
MAP 43
40-50 MINS FROM THE DIRTY HABIT (MAP 42)
THE DUTCH HOUSE
30-45 MINS TO MEMORIAL CROSS (MAP 44)
TO DOVER
TO FARNM
42
44
STEDE COURT - SEEN FROM TRACK IT'S AN IMPOSING WHITE HOUSE WITH COMMANDING VIEWS OVER HARRIETSHAM
TAILS FARM – HORSE RESCUE CENTRE
PILGRIM'S BENCH & PICNIC TABLE
048
SEALED SURFACE
MARLEY ROAD
SIGNED PATH
PADDOCKS
FENCE
SUMMONERS FARM
HARRIETSHAM MANOR
HAUTEVILLE
PILGRIM LODGE
THE DUTCH HOUSE
EASY TO ASSUME TRANCE-LIKE STATE AS YOU WALK THE STRAIGHT TRACK BORDERED BY HEDGEROW
TRACK TO FARM
TO HARRIETSHAM, ¼ MILE
PATH LINED BY SEVERAL OLD YEW TREES
MILE HILL
CAN IMAGINE MEDIEVAL PILGRIMS ON THE ROUTE TO CANTERBURY TRAMPING ALONG THIS TRACK
0
¼ mile
0
500m
APPROX SCALE
trailblazer
45-55 MINS TO THE DIRTY HABIT (MAP 42)
THE DUTCH HOUSE
30-45 MINS FROM MEMORIAL CROSS (MAP 44)

HARRIETSHAM [off MAP 43, p147]

Though not as charming as many of its neighbouring villages, Harrietsham does have a few amenities including a **post office** (Mon, Tue, Thur & Fri 9am-1pm); and further down a **Village Store** (Mon-Sat 7am-8.30pm, Sun 7.30am-7pm), at the far end of the village from the trail. If you can be bothered, there's more choice across the busy A20 at the Co-op **convenience store** (daily 7am-10pm).

There's currently nowhere to stay in the village but there are a couple of dining options including a pub, ***Percival's Rest*** (☎ 01622-587 518, 🖳 percivalsrest.com; food Wed-Sat noon-9pm, Sun to 5pm; bar Tue-Sun from noon) with lots of live music and mains starting at a tenner for a small bowl of mussels and fries; and a Bangladeshi restaurant, ***The Taste of Bengal*** (☎ 01622-859461, 🖳 www.thetasteofbengal.com; daily noon-2pm & 5.30-10.30pm).

Southeastern Railway's London Victoria to Ashford service (see box pp42-3) calls at the **railway station**.

Stagecoach's **bus** service No 10X (Maidstone to Ashford) stops by The Roebuck; see pp44-7.

By now you will have come to the conclusion that the Pilgrims' Way itself is really rather a straight and level track, mostly bordered by hedges with occasional views over vast arable fields. This makes for fast walking on a mostly firm track below the ridge line and at times it's all too easy to drift into a trance-like state as the miles slip by – until before you know it, the turn-off to **Lenham.** Here there's a better choice of accommodation and dining options – all huddled around the main village square.

LENHAM [MAP 44a]

In many ways Lenham is your typical North Downs Way settlement. A handsome village with a long history, it is filled with venerable, vernacular buildings and enough eateries, accommodation and other services to lure the trekker off the trail.

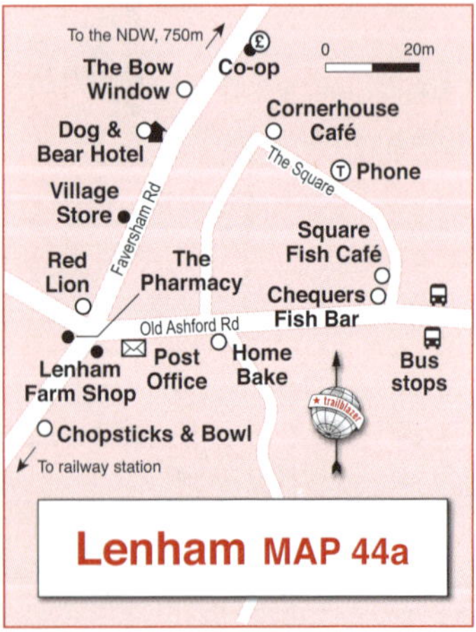

The first shop you reach is a Co-op **supermarket** (daily 7am-10pm) with **ATM**, though there's a **Village Store** (Mon-Sat 7am-8pm, Sun 10am-6pm) in the village centre as well as the ***Lenham Farm Shop*** (Tue-Sat 9am-5pm), selling mainly local produce. You can also withdraw cash at the **post office** (Mon-Fri 9am-2.45pm, Sat to 12.30pm) on The Square. Opposite is a **pharmacy** (🖳 saxonwarriorpharmacy.com; Mon-Fri 9am-5.30pm, Sat to 12.30pm).

On the second Sunday of every month in the main square there's a **farmers' market**.

Offering **accommodation**, ***Dog and Bear Hotel*** (☎ 01622-858219, 🖳 dogandbearlenham.co.uk; 1S/12D/8D or T/1Tr/2Qd, all en suite; ☕; 🐕) started life as a 15th-century coaching inn. B&B costs £40-50pp (sgl from £60) in this friendly establishment. They also serve good food (Mon-Sat noon-9.30pm, Sun noon-9pm) with sausages and new potatoes for £15.50.

ROUTE GUIDE AND MAPS

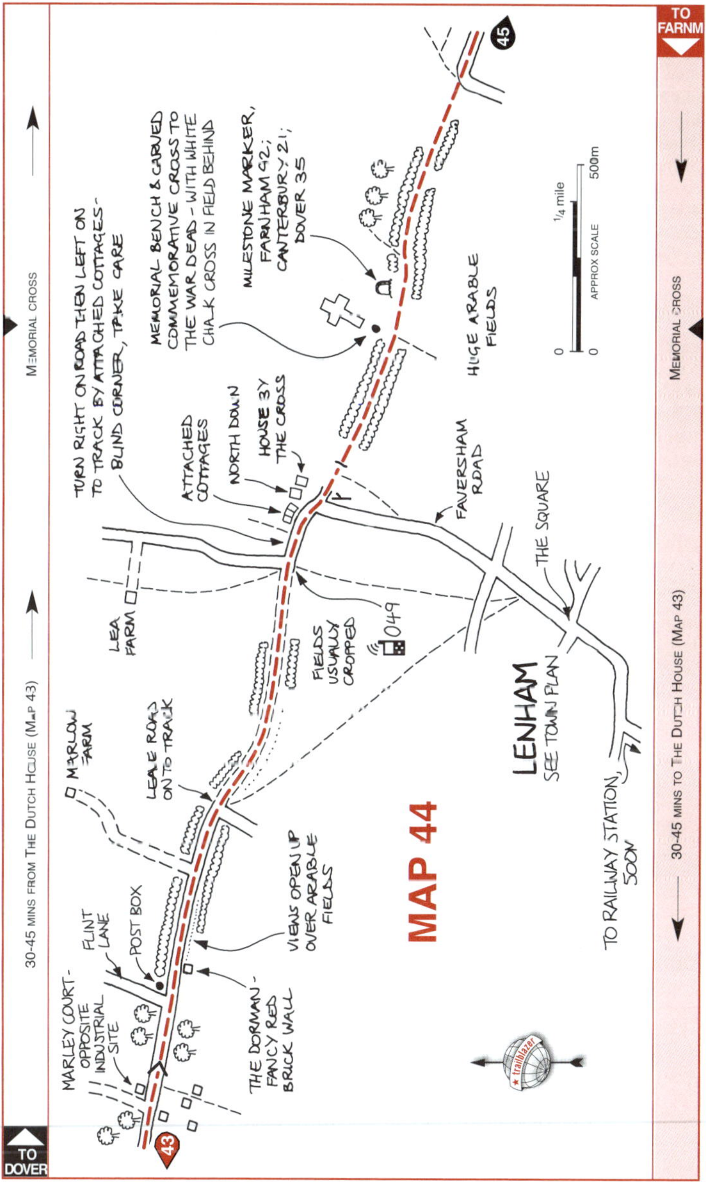
TO DOVER
30-45 MINS FROM THE DUTCH HOUSE (MAP 43)
MEMORIAL CROSS
TO FARNM
MEMORIAL CROSS
30-45 MINS TO THE DUTCH HOUSE (MAP 43)
MAP 44
43
45
MARLEY COURT - OPPOSITE INDUSTRIAL SITE
FLINT LANE
POST BOX
THE DORMAN - FANCY RED BRICK WALL
VIEWS OPEN UP OVER ARABLE FIELDS
MARLOW FARM
LEAVE ROAD ONTO TRACK
LEA FARM
FIELDS USUALLY CROPPED
049
TURN RIGHT ON ROAD THEN LEFT ON TO TRACK BY ATTACHED COTTAGES - BLIND CORNER, TAKE CARE
ATTACHED COTTAGES
NORTH DOWN
HOUSE BY THE CROSS
FAVERSHAM ROAD
THE SQUARE
LENHAM
SEE TOWN PLAN
TO RAILWAY STATION, 500m
MEMORIAL BENCH & CARVED COMMEMORATIVE CROSS TO THE WAR DEAD - WITH WHITE CHALK CROSS IN FIELD BEHIND
MILESTONE MARKER, FARNHAM 92; CANTERBURY 21; DOVER 35
HUGE ARABLE FIELDS
0
1/4 mile
0
APPROX SCALE
500m
trailblazer

The first eatery you come to is ***The Bow Window*** (☎ 01622-850802, 🖳 the bowwindowcafe.co.uk; Tue-Sat 9am-4pm, Sun 10am-3pm; 🐕), which has pretty much everything a walker requires including a welcoming attitude towards dogs and some tasty offerings, with toasties and panini (both £7.50). ***Cornerhouse Café*** (Mon-Sat plus 2nd Sun of month, 9am-4pm), on The Square, has a few hot dishes (fish pie £8.95) as well as sandwiches and cakes. Opposite, ***Home Bake*** (Mon-Fri 8am-5pm, Sat 7.30am-2pm) is the best option for takeaway lunches (pasties from £2.20).

The centre of The Square is dominated by two very different fish restaurants. ***Chequers Fish Bar*** (☎ 01622-859878, 🖳 chequersfishbar.co.uk; Mon-Fri 8am-2.30pm & 4-10pm, Sat 8am-10pm, Sun & Bank Hols 10am-9pm) works long hours to keep its punters fed with fish and kebabs. Backing onto it is the fancy ***Square Fish Café*** (☎ 01622-858268, 🖳 thesquarefish cafe.co.uk; Tue-Sat noon-3pm and 5-11pm), a restaurant in all but name and cooks up some really lovely dishes including a divine seafood linguine (£26.95).

Chinese food is available from ***Chopsticks & Bowl*** (☎ 01622-858416; Tue 5-11pm, Wed-Sun noon-2pm & 5-11pm) to eat in or take away.

For good pub grub try ***The Red Lion*** (☎ 01622-858531, 🖳 redlionlenhampub.co .uk; food Tue-Fri noon-2.30pm & 6-8.30pm, Sat noon-8pm, Sun to 6pm; 🐕) with menus consisting largely of pub standards such as ham, egg and chips (£11.50).

The **railway station** is a stop on Southeastern Railway's London Victoria to Ashford International service (see box pp42-3).

Stagecoach's **bus** No 10X (Maidstone to Ashford) stops by The Square; see pp44-7 for details.

After Lenham the North Downs Way passes under a large **chalk cross** (Map 44). While this may feel like another example of the Christian pilgrimage nature of this walk, it's actually a memorial to local soldiers who died in WWII. You then follow a byway with little evidence of much vehicle use. With views over large arable fields the trail passes through woodland and descends to the A252, with **Charing** just a short distance away.

❑ A PLACE OF SOME IMPORTANCE

Charing again was the last convenient halt in any rich man's journey...It is something under 16 miles from Canterbury, following the track of the Old Road and even the poor upon the pilgrimages would have halted there... Charing, therefore, was designed by its every character to be a place of some importance, and was a very conscious little town.'

Hilaire Belloc, *The Old Road*

CHARING [MAP 46, p152]

Even today you can tell just what an important village Charing must have been. Many of the buildings are rather grand, a few are half timbered and the **church** (St Peter & St Paul) has a fine tower.

Right next to it and just off the High St there are also the **ruins** of a former archbishop's palace, which are well worth a look.

On the High Street, Wady & Brett (Mon-Sat 8am-6pm, Sun 9am-4pm) is part of the Londis chain of **convenience stores**.

Unfortunately, like so many villages around here, Charing is suffering from decline. Where once there were five pubs, for example, today there is just the one drinks-only micro-pub, ***The Charing Bar Company*** (formerly The Bookmakers

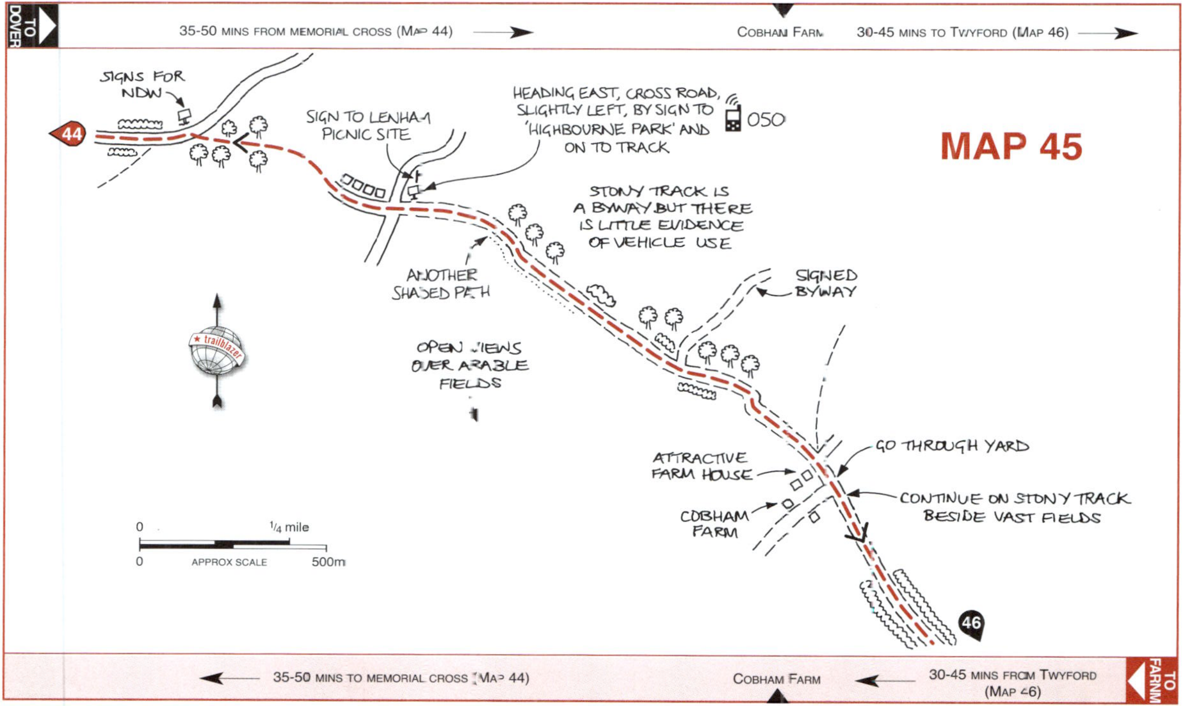
TO DOVER
35-50 MINS FROM MEMORIAL CROSS (MAP 44)
COBHAM FARM
30-45 MINS TO TWYFORD (MAP 46)
MAP 45
44
SIGNS FOR NDW
SIGN TO LENHAM PICNIC SITE
HEADING EAST, CROSS ROAD, SLIGHTLY LEFT, BY SIGN TO 'HIGHBOURNE PARK' AND ON TO TRACK
050
STONY TRACK IS A BYWAY BUT THERE IS LITTLE EVIDENCE OF VEHICLE USE
ANOTHER SHADED PATH
SIGNED BYWAY
OPEN VIEWS OVER ARABLE FIELDS
trailblazer
ATTRACTIVE FARM HOUSE
COBHAM FARM
GO THROUGH YARD
CONTINUE ON STONY TRACK BESIDE VAST FIELDS
46
0
1/4 mile
0
APPROX SCALE
500m
35-50 MINS TO MEMORIAL CROSS (MAP 44)
COBHAM FARM
30-45 MINS FROM TWYFORD (MAP 46)
TO FARNM

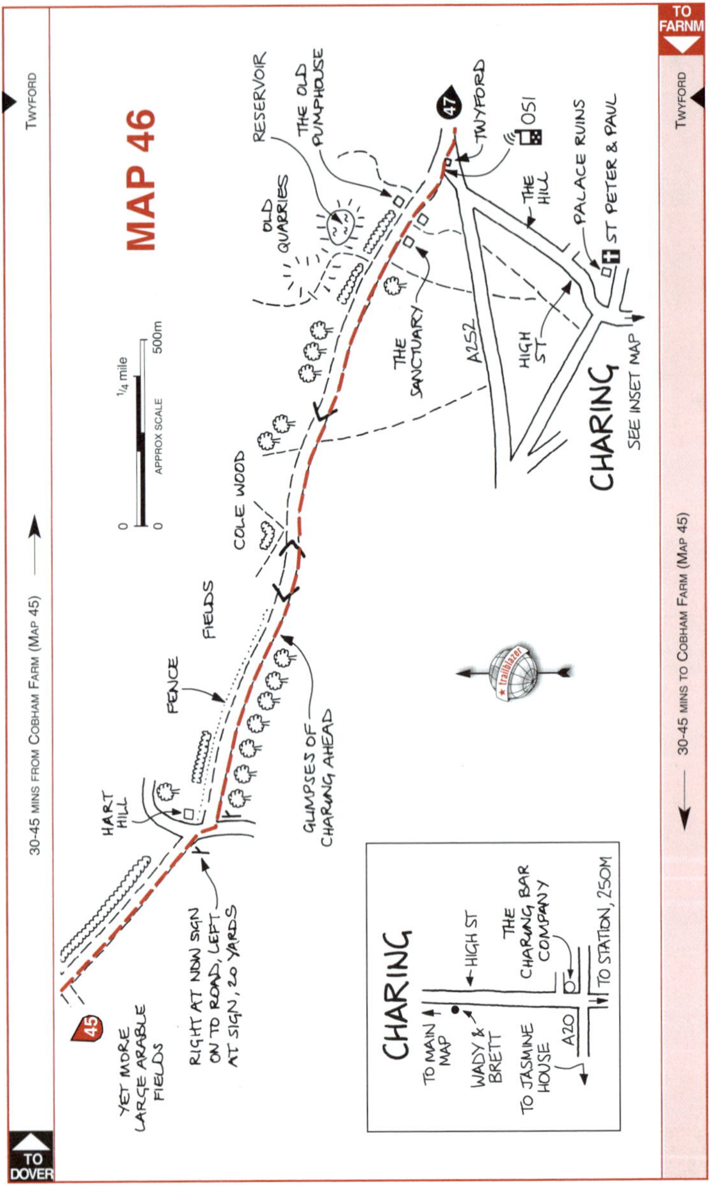

MAP 46
TWYFORD
30-45 MINS FROM COBHAM FARM (MAP 45)
0
1/4 mile
0
APPROX SCALE
500m
RESERVOIR
THE OLD PUMPHOUSE
OLD QUARRIES
47
TWYFORD
051
THE HILL
PALACE RUINS
ST PETER & PAUL
THE SANCTUARY
A252
HIGH ST
CHARING
SEE INSET MAP
COLE WOOD
FIELDS
FENCE
HART HILL
GLIMPSES OF CHARING AHEAD
45
YET MORE LARGE ARABLE FIELDS
RIGHT AT NDW SIGN ON TO ROAD, LEFT AT SIGN, 20 YARDS
trailblazer
CHARING
TO MAIN MAP
HIGH ST
THE CHARING BAR COMPANY
WADY & BRETT
TO JASMINE HOUSE
A20
TO STATION, 250M
TO FARNM
TWYFORD
30-45 MINS TO COBHAM FARM (MAP 45)
TO DOVER

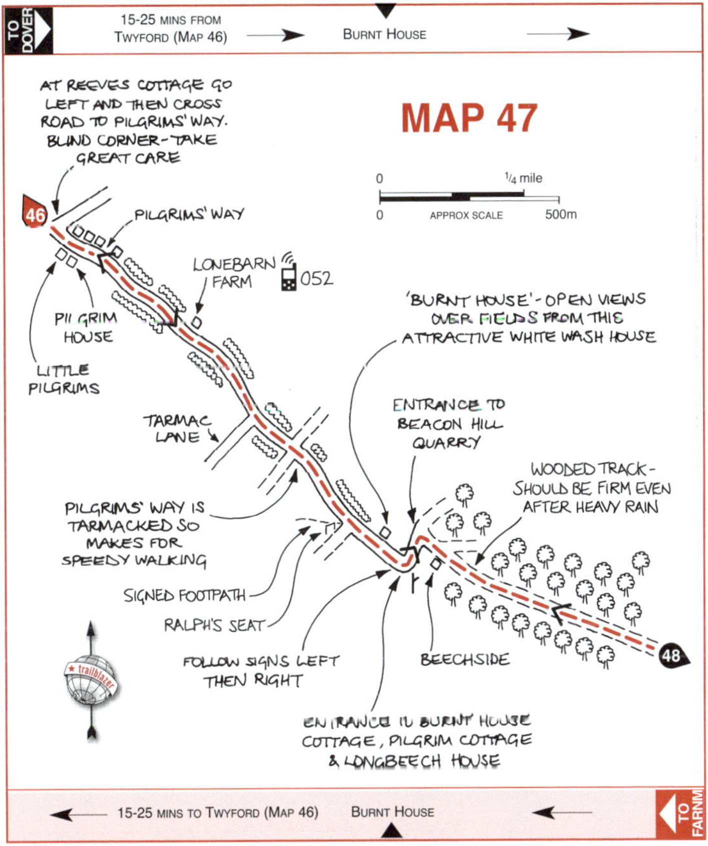

Arms; **fb**; Tue-Thur 7-11pm, Fri & Sat from 5pm, Sun 2-10.30pm).

There are no B&Bs left either but should you need to find a meal in the evening, ***Jasmine House*** (☎ 01233-714988, 💻 jasminehousekent.com; Mon & Wed-Thur 3-10.15pm, Fri & Sat to 10.45pm, Sun 1.30-9.45pm) is a smart and cavernous Chinese restaurant about 600m west of the High St just past the main roundabout on the A20. Meals are reasonably priced (from £9 for a veggie main).

Southeastern Railway operates services (see box pp42-3) to London Victoria and Ashford International from the **railway station**.

Stagecoach's **bus** No 10X (Maidstone to Ashford) stops here; see pp44-7.

After Charing the path continues to follow the route of the Pilgrims' Way, now hurtling headlong into the dense woods of **Westwell Downs** (Map 48), before arriving at the village that shares its name.

WESTWELL [MAP 48]

There's not much here but **campers** will find pitches for £10pp at the fair and friendly ***Dunn Street Farm*** (🖳 dunnstreetfarm.co.uk, bookings preferred; well behaved 🐕 on leads); the route passes in front of the farm gates. It's on a lovely friendly livestock farm with showers, drinking water taps and washing-up facilities – and it's so refreshing to find a campsite positioned right on the trail. They also have a '**living wagon**' (from £60pp, min 2 nights) which sleeps up to four in a double bed plus two single bunk-beds.

From Westwell a fairly lengthy crossing of a couple of vast arable fields follows as you make your way to the tranquil park landscape of **Eastwell**. Don't miss the 30-second diversion to the **ruined church of St Mary's** (Map 49 and see box below) and its lakeside setting – truly one of the most magical locations on the entire path. The church was actually destroyed by a V2 bomber in WWII, but is still consecrated ground and holds the grave of the last of the Plantagenets.

From here, it's a straightforward amble through the grounds of ***Eastwell Manor Hotel*** (see p156). The path cuts across the driveway of the hotel before crossing one more field on its way to **Boughton Lees** and its large village green.

❑ ST MARY'S CHURCH AND THE LAST OF THE PLANTAGENETS

Though today St Mary's Eastwell (Map 49) is closed to the public, inside it is said to be the tomb of Richard Plantagenet, the man who claimed to be the illegitimate son of Richard III (reigned 1452-1485).

Despite the king refusing to officially recognise Richard as his own, he was raised by teachers who taught in Latin and he received regular sums of money from an anonymous donor. At the time the boy had no idea who his father was and the king and his son remained strangers throughout Richard's childhood.

All that changed on the eve of the Battle of Bosworth, when the king summoned Richard, then 16, to tell him of his royal lineage and to say that, should the battle be won, the king would acknowledge Richard as his son; but if he lost, the son should flee for his own safety.

The king, of course, was defeated and ended up interred beneath a car park in Leicester. Taking his father's advice, the young Richard subsequently chose to live anonymously as a bricklayer and mason. His identity was only discovered by Sir Thomas Moyle, who had hired him to build his manor at Eastwell and who found him reading a book in Latin. Though Sir Thomas offered Richard the chance to live at his manor once it was completed, Richard, by then nearly 70, refused, instead building a one-room cottage in the grounds. (A building called Plantagenet Cottage still stands on the site of the original; the manor, incidentally, was demolished in the 1920s.) There he resided until his death at the age of 81 – the last of the Plantagenet dynasty that had ruled England for over 300 years.

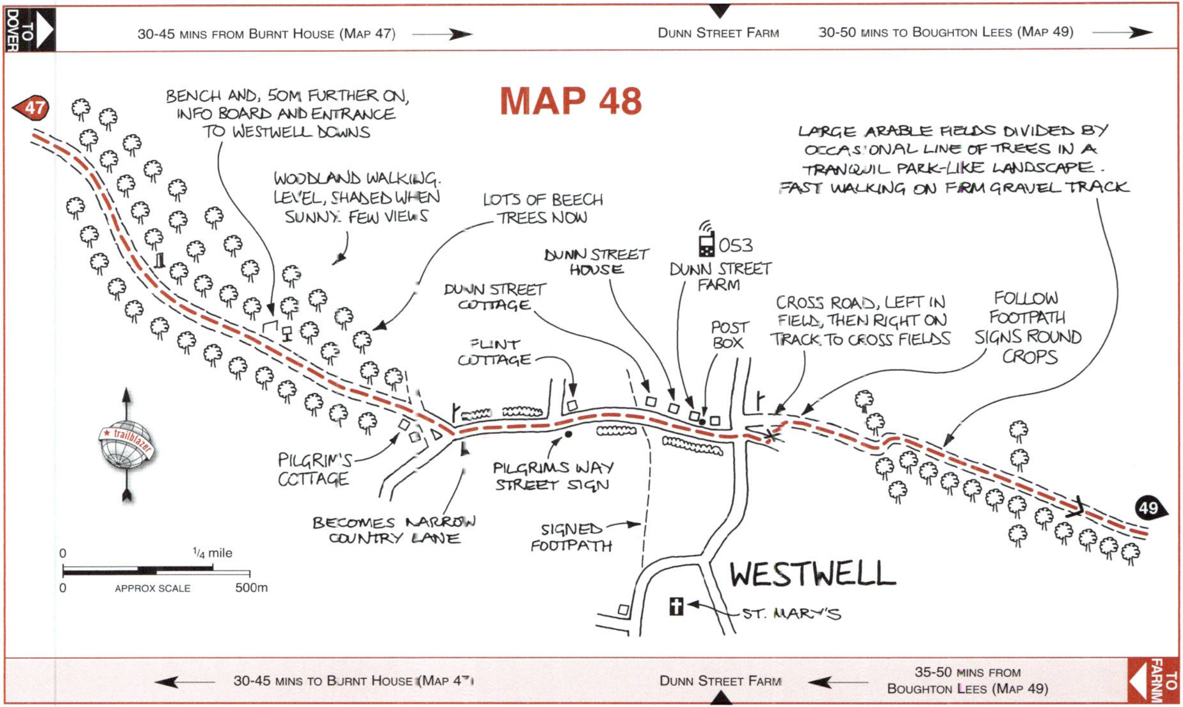
TO DOVER
30-45 MINS FROM BURNT HOUSE (MAP 47)
DUNN STREET FARM
30-50 MINS TO BOUGHTON LEES (MAP 49)
MAP 48
47
BENCH AND, 50M FURTHER ON, INFO BOARD AND ENTRANCE TO WESTWELL DOWNS
WOODLAND WALKING. LEVEL, SHADED WHEN SUNNY. FEW VIEWS
LOTS OF BEECH TREES NOW
DUNN STREET COTTAGE
FLINT COTTAGE
DUNN STREET HOUSE
053
DUNN STREET FARM
POST BOX
LARGE ARABLE FIELDS DIVIDED BY OCCASIONAL LINE OF TREES IN A TRANQUIL PARK-LIKE LANDSCAPE. FAST WALKING ON FIRM GRAVEL TRACK
CROSS ROAD, LEFT IN FIELD, THEN RIGHT ON TRACK TO CROSS FIELDS
FOLLOW FOOTPATH SIGNS ROUND CROPS
PILGRIM'S COTTAGE
BECOMES NARROW COUNTRY LANE
PILGRIMS WAY STREET SIGN
SIGNED FOOTPATH
WESTWELL
ST. MARY'S
49
trailblazer
0
1/4 mile
0
APPROX SCALE
500m
30-45 MINS TO BURNT HOUSE (MAP 47)
DUNN STREET FARM
35-50 MINS FROM BOUGHTON LEES (MAP 49)
TO FARNM

EASTWELL PARK & BOUGHTON LEES [MAP 49]

Close by the NDW, ***Eastwell Manor Hotel*** (☎ 0343-2241700, 🖳 champneys.com; 23D or T, all en suite; ●) is top-hole, luxury spa, glossy brochure stuff, carved panelled rooms with baronial-stone fireplaces. You'll pay from £94pp (sgl occ rates on request) for B&B. Some rooms have four posters. There's a **restaurant** here too.

Leaving the grounds of the hotel, you find yourself in the village of Boughton Lees. The wonderful ***Flying Horse Inn*** (☎ 01233-620914, 🖳 theflying.horse; **fb**; 4D, all en suite; ●) is a lovely spot with both accommodation and food. They offer **B&B** (£47.50pp, sgl occ £95), though try to avoid the room directly above the bar as it can get very noisy. They even have a basic **campsite** (🐕), which is free as long as you book to eat in the **restaurant** (food Tue-Sat noon-3pm & 6-9pm, Sun noon-4.30pm; 🐕 bar area only). Food offerings include their 'Proper Pies' in a choice of sizes from £15.

Stagecoach's No 666 **bus** between Ashford and Faversham calls at the village green; see pp44-7.

❑ NORTHERN OR SOUTHERN ROUTE?

Look at a geological map of Kent and you'll notice that the chalk swathe of the North Downs that cuts through the county becomes slightly broader at its eastern end. It is perhaps for this reason that the trail authorities decided to divide the trail into two as it approaches Dover – to cover in greater detail the Downs at this eastern extremity.

The 30-mile (48.2km) **northern route** (described from p159), the better-known of the two paths, heads north-east after Boughton Lees to travel via **Canterbury** to Dover; while the 24.3-mile (39.1km) **southern route** (described from p186) takes a more south-easterly direction to visit **Wye** and brush alongside **Folkestone**, before travelling north along the coastal cliffs to a reunion with the other trail and the end of the path.

The obvious question for Way walkers to ask, therefore, is which trail should you take? The National Trail website remains resolutely neutral on this matter, treating each of the two branches equally. Indeed, if you study their website you would think that in order to complete the trail you need to do *both* routes! For example, throughout the website they describe the trail as being 153 miles long – which is about right only if you take both paths (though we actually think the total figure is nearer 155.9 miles/250.9km).

Northern route

Whilst it's true that the more northerly route via Canterbury enjoys greater popularity, it can only be assumed that this is largely due to the fame of Canterbury itself, rather than through any aesthetic considerations. For it must be said that while the path between Boughton Lees and Canterbury is wonderful, passing as it does through that most quintessential of Kentish sceneries, an undulating terrain of orchards and oast-houses, the path after Canterbury could be considered a little mundane.

Southern route

The southern route, on the other hand, is a pretty and interesting walk the whole way, taking in the handsome village of Wye as well as some lovely, sumptuous landscapes on the way to the coast. This southern trail also finishes with an extensive stretch of coastal clifftop walking that provides a suitably grand finale to the National Trail, arguably preferable to the route from Canterbury to Dover, dribbling as it does via road and field before finally limping to the coast.

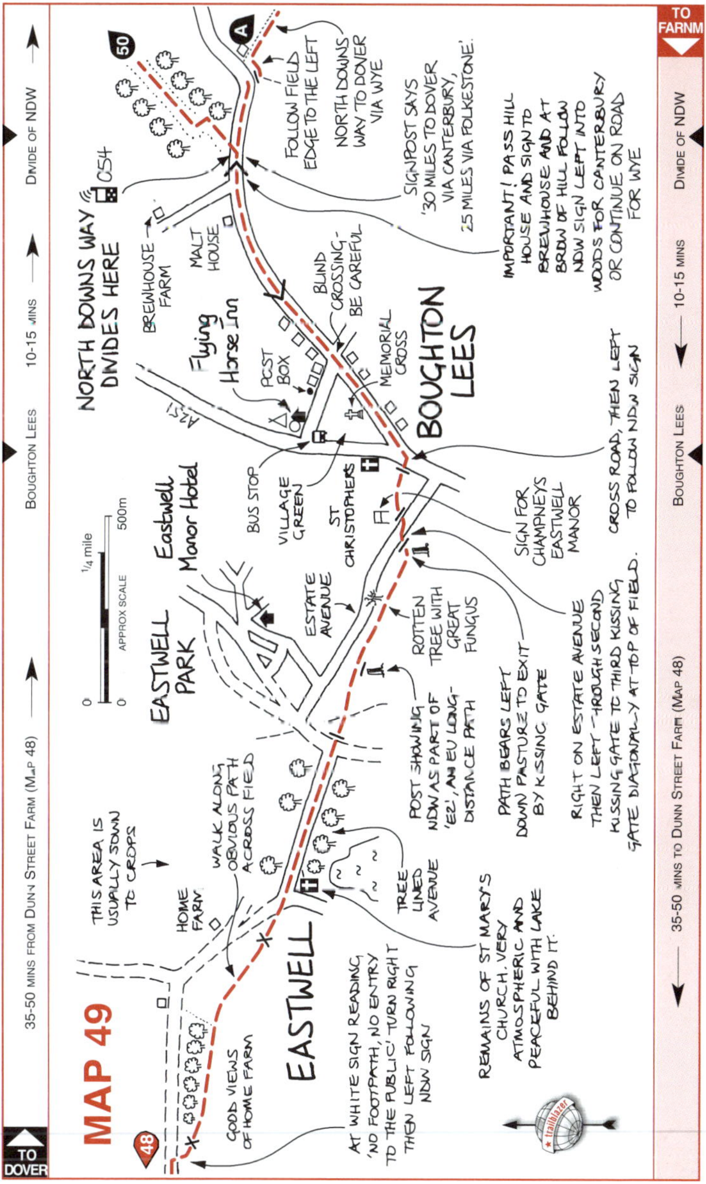
MAP 49
TO DOVER
TO FARNM
35-50 MINS FROM DUNN STREET FARM (MAP 48)
BOUGHTON LEES
10-15 MINS
DIVIDE OF NDW
35-50 MINS TO DUNN STREET FARM (MAP 48)
BOUGHTON LEES
10-15 MINS
DIVIDE OF NDW
48
50
A
NORTH DOWNS WAY DIVIDES HERE
C54
BREWHOUSE FARM
MALT HOUSE
Flying Horse Inn
POST BOX
A251
BUS STOP
VILLAGE GREEN
ST CHRISTOPHERS
BLIND CROSSING - BE CAREFUL
MEMORIAL CROSS
BOUGHTON LEES
FOLLOW FIELD EDGE TO THE LEFT
NORTH DOWNS WAY TO DOVER VIA WYE
SIGNPOST SAYS '30 MILES TO DOVER VIA CANTERBURY, 25 MILES VIA FOLKESTONE'
IMPORTANT! PASS HILL HOUSE AND SIGN TO BREWHOUSE AND AT BROW OF HILL FOLLOW NDW SIGN LEFT INTO WOODS FOR CANTERBURY OR CONTINUE ON ROAD FOR WYE
SIGN FOR CHAMPNEYS EASTWELL MANOR
CROSS ROAD, THEN LEFT TO FOLLOW NDW SIGN
Eastwell Manor Hotel
0 1/4 mile
0 500m
APPROX SCALE
EASTWELL PARK
ESTATE AVENUE
ROTTEN TREE WITH GREAT FUNGUS
POST SHOWING NDW AS PART OF 'E2', AN EU LONG-DISTANCE PATH
PATH BEARS LEFT DOWN PASTURE TO EXIT BY KISSING GATE
RIGHT ON ESTATE AVENUE THEN LEFT THROUGH SECOND KISSING GATE TO THIRD KISSING GATE DIAGONALLY AT TOP OF FIELD.
THIS AREA IS USUALLY SOWN TO CROPS
WALK ALONG OBVIOUS PATH ACROSS FIELD
HOME FARM
TREE LINED AVENUE
EASTWELL
GOOD VIEWS OF HOME FARM
AT WHITE SIGN READING 'NO FOOTPATH, NO ENTRY TO THE PUBLIC' TURN RIGHT THEN LEFT FOLLOWING NDW SIGN
REMAINS OF ST MARY'S CHURCH. VERY ATMOSPHERIC AND PEACEFUL WITH LAKE BEHIND IT.
trailblazer

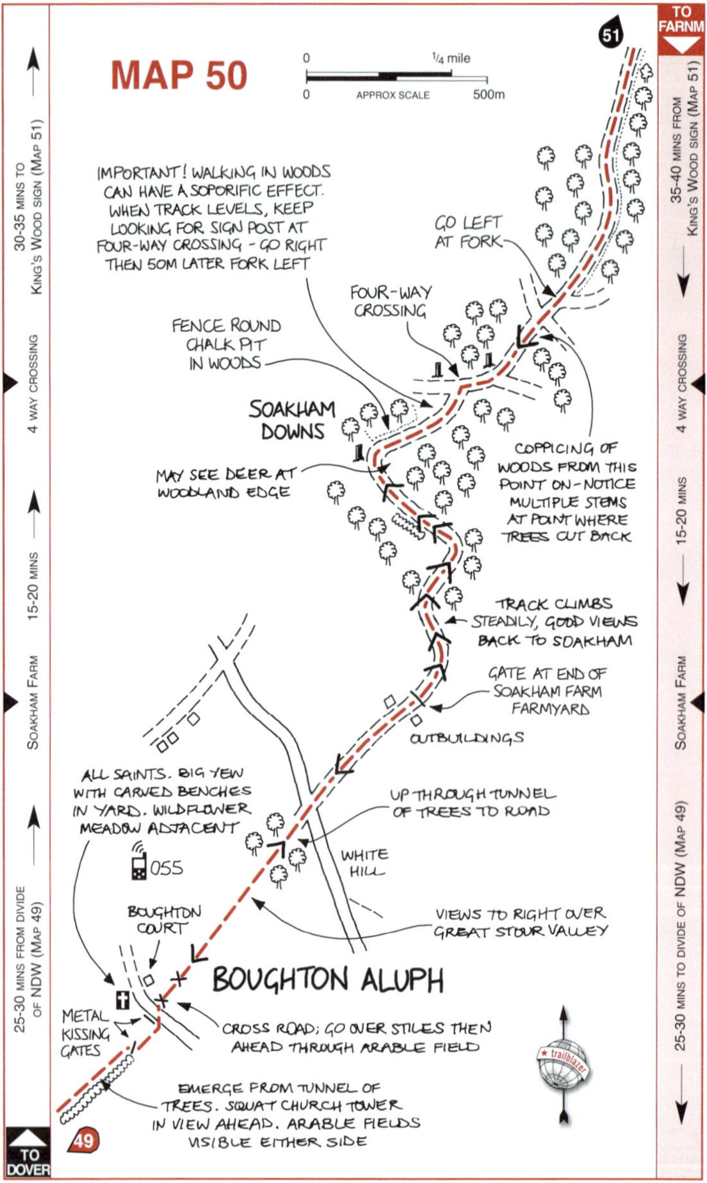
MAP 50
0 1/4 mile
0 APPROX SCALE 500m
TO FARNM
51
35-40 MINS FROM KING'S WOOD SIGN (MAP 51)
4 WAY CROSSING
15-20 MINS
SOAKHAM FARM
25-30 MINS TO DIVIDE OF NDW (MAP 49)
30-35 MINS TO KING'S WOOD SIGN (MAP 51)
4 WAY CROSSING
15-20 MINS
SOAKHAM FARM
25-30 MINS FROM DIVIDE OF NDW (MAP 49)
IMPORTANT! WALKING IN WOODS CAN HAVE A SOPORIFIC EFFECT. WHEN TRACK LEVELS, KEEP LOOKING FOR SIGN POST AT FOUR-WAY CROSSING - GO RIGHT THEN 50M LATER FORK LEFT
GO LEFT AT FORK
FOUR-WAY CROSSING
FENCE ROUND CHALK PIT IN WOODS
SOAKHAM DOWNS
COPPICING OF WOODS FROM THIS POINT ON - NOTICE MULTIPLE STEMS AT POINT WHERE TREES CUT BACK
MAY SEE DEER AT WOODLAND EDGE
TRACK CLIMBS STEADILY, GOOD VIEWS BACK TO SOAKHAM
GATE AT END OF SOAKHAM FARM FARMYARD
OUTBUILDINGS
ALL SAINTS. BIG YEW WITH CARVED BENCHES IN YARD. WILDFLOWER MEADOW ADJACENT
UP THROUGH TUNNEL OF TREES TO ROAD
055
WHITE HILL
BOUGHTON COURT
VIEWS TO RIGHT OVER GREAT STOUR VALLEY
BOUGHTON ALUPH
METAL KISSING GATES
CROSS ROAD; GO OVER STILES THEN AHEAD THROUGH ARABLE FIELD
trailblazer
EMERGE FROM TUNNEL OF TREES. SQUAT CHURCH TOWER IN VIEW AHEAD. ARABLE FIELDS VISIBLE EITHER SIDE
49
TO DOVER

NORTHERN ROUTE: BOUGHTON LEES TO CHILHAM [MAPS 49-52]

The path divides not long after Boughton Lees on this short-but-sweet stage of **5.9 miles/9.5km** (**1¾hrs to 2½hrs**). Having marched along the tarmac for about half a mile you reach a signpost, where the northern and southern routes (see p156) part company.

> *'I walk'd along a stream, for pureness rare,*
> *Brighter than sunshine; for it did acquaint*
> *The dullest sight with all glorious prey*
> *That in the pebble-paved channel lay'*
> **Christopher Marlowe**, ***The Stream***,
> about the River Stour

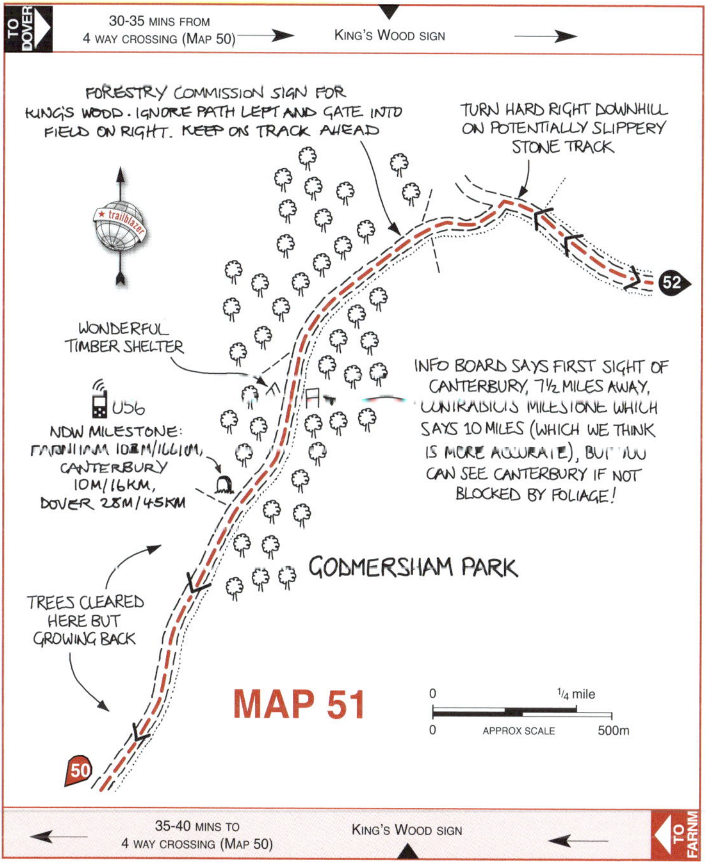

For the northern route via Canterbury (30 miles according to the signpost) and its World Heritage cathedral, the path leaves the tarmac to the left and heads through a tree tunnel to the lovely little church at **Boughton Aluph** (see Map 50), from where the trail cuts through the yard of Soakham Farm, in a lovely setting with uninterrupted views over the Great Stour Valley. The trail climbs steeply on to **Soakham Downs** and then through an attractive beech and chestnut forest for the next hour or so, before following a quiet tarmac road past **Chilham Castle** (Map 52) and into the village which it overlooks.

CHILHAM [MAP 52]

Pretty Chilham is overlooked by a Jacobean castle, now a private residence but visible through the fence. At the heart of the village is the medieval square bordered by black and white half-timbered buildings, some faced with brick.

The friendly **post office shop** (Mon, Tue, Thur & Fri 9am-1pm & 2-5.30pm, Wed & Sat 9am-1pm) has snacks and drinks.

The Old Alma (☎ 01227-731913, 💻 theoldalma.co.uk; 4D/1T, all en suite), a former pub turned **B&B**, charges £40-45pp (sgl occ from £55). It's the closest to the railway station and on the A28.

Probably the most historic place is the ivy-clad ***Bagham Farmhouse*** (☎ 01227-730306; 2D/2T, all en suite; min 2 nights), built in 1470 and now standing off the A28. B&B costs from £43pp (from £60 sgl occ).

The excellent ***Woolpack Inn*** (☎ 01227-730351, 💻 woolpackchilham.co.uk; 1S/5D/3T/rm sleeps 6, all en suite or private facilities; ▼; 🐕) has very comfortable **rooms** (about £65-105pp, sgl £100, sgl occ room rate). The **food** (Mon-Sat 11am-9pm, Sun noon-5pm) here is top notch with big portions (mains starting at £17, lunchtime sandwiches £10-12).

The ***White Horse Inn*** (☎ 01227-730355, 💻 thewhitehorse.pub; food Mon-Thur noon-3pm & 5-9pm, Fri & Sat noon-10pm, Sun noon-8pm; 🐕) boasts a cheaper menu (£12.95-16.95) and has regular music nights.

There is a great traditional tearoom too. ***The Church Mouse*** (☎ 01227-730303, 💻 thechurchmouse.info; Thur-Tue 9.30am-4pm; 🐕), crammed into a small beamed house, has a great array of cakes as well as sandwiches, teacakes and light meals.

Chilham **railway** station is a stop on Southeastern's services between London Charing Cross and Ramsgate; see box pp42-3. Stagecoach's **bus** No 1X (Ashford to Canterbury) calls here; see pp44-7.

❑ OAST-HOUSES AND HOP GARDENS

Oast-houses are basically huge ovens used to dry hops, an ingredient in beer production. Now most have been converted into houses and occasionally B&Bs. Usually consisting of four rooms, the oven and the store room downstairs, the drying room and the cooling room upstairs, when converted they make a spacious living area. The characteristic conical roof and pointed chimneys were designed to draw extra air through the kiln, increasing the amount of hops that could be dried in one go. Often oast-houses were built near ponds – combining fire and wood is a risky business.

The hop is a climbing plant and was traditionally grown on a system of poles and strings up to 20ft high. The female flower, or cone, is what gives beer a 'hoppy' bitter taste. At the height of the Kent hop industry up to 80,000 pickers would descend on the county for the September harvest but modern plants grow as 8ft hedges and now the crop is easily harvested by machine.

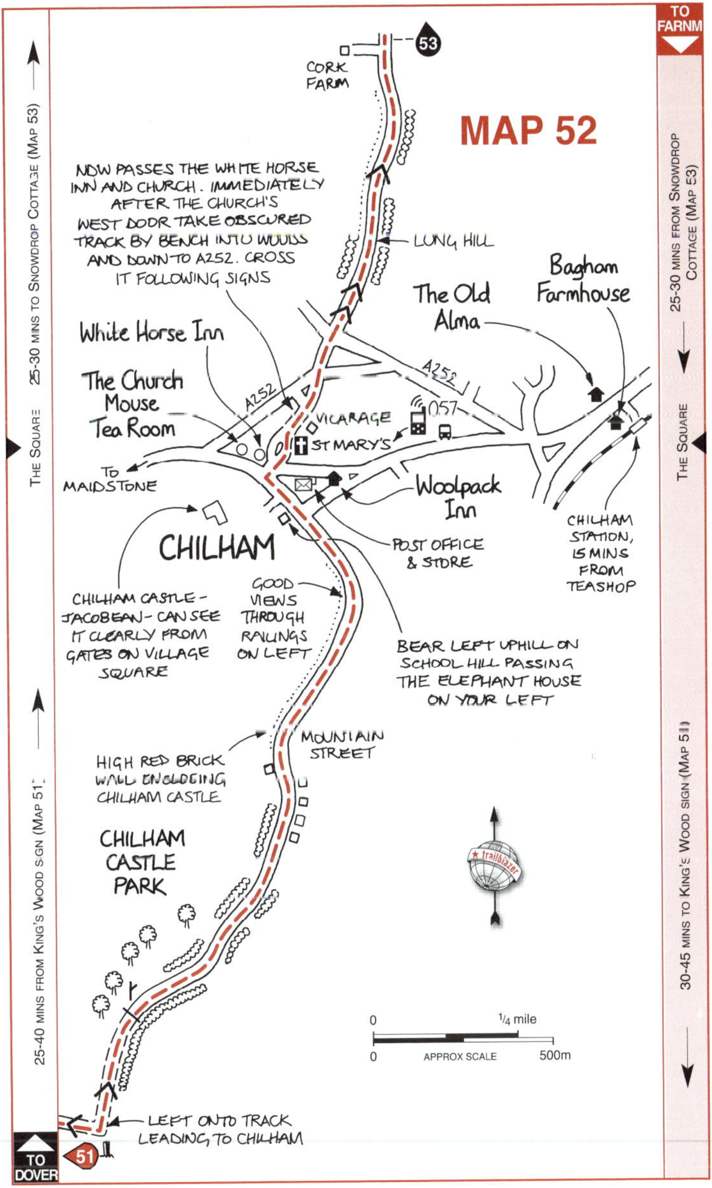
TO FARNM
MAP 52
53
CORK FARM
NOW PASSES THE WHITE HORSE INN AND CHURCH. IMMEDIATELY AFTER THE CHURCH'S WEST DOOR TAKE OBSCURED TRACK BY BENCH INTO WOODS AND DOWN TO A252. CROSS IT FOLLOWING SIGNS
LONG HILL
Bagham Farmhouse
The Old Alma
White Horse Inn
The Church Mouse Tea Room
A252
A252
057
VICARAGE
ST MARY'S
TO MAIDSTONE
Woolpack Inn
CHILHAM
POST OFFICE & STORE
CHILHAM STATION, 15 MINS FROM TEASHOP
CHILHAM CASTLE - JACOBEAN - CAN SEE IT CLEARLY FROM GATES ON VILLAGE SQUARE
GOOD VIEWS THROUGH RAILINGS ON LEFT
BEAR LEFT UPHILL ON SCHOOL HILL PASSING THE ELEPHANT HOUSE ON YOUR LEFT
MOUNTAIN STREET
HIGH RED BRICK WALL ENCLOSING CHILHAM CASTLE
CHILHAM CASTLE PARK
trailblazer
0 1/4 mile
0 APPROX SCALE 500m
LEFT ONTO TRACK LEADING TO CHILHAM
51
TO DOVER
THE SQUARE 25-30 MINS TO SNOWDROP COTTAGE (MAP 53)
25-40 MINS FROM KING'S WOOD SIGN (MAP 51)
25-30 MINS FROM SNOWDROP COTTAGE (MAP 53) THE SQUARE
30-45 MINS TO KING'S WOOD SIGN (MAP 51)

NORTHERN ROUTE: CHILHAM TO CANTERBURY [MAPS 52-56]

Oast-houses and orchards, history and hops, apples and inns – today's **6.4-mile/10.3km walk (2¼hrs to 3hrs)** from the prettiest village on the North Downs Way to its largest and most fascinating city is a showcase for much of the clichéd glories of Kent – and it's quite delightful.

Leaving Chilham through the grounds and graveyard of St Mary's (where the oldest grave dates from 1638) the trail climbs gently but purposefully past orderly orchards to the curiously named **Old Wives Lees** (Map 53). A sharp right turn at the junction leads you out of the village (eventually) past oast-houses and yet another orchard – this one run on a more industrial scale, with the workers' accommodation forming its own mobile-home village by the railway bridge – and onto the village of **Chartham Hatch** (Map 54), though this no longer has any services.

If you need to get away from all this bucolic beauty, a 20-minute walk down Hatch Lane will bring you to the railway station at Chartham.

CHARTHAM [MAP 54, p164]

For food in the evening your only option lies beyond the railway station at ***The Artichoke*** (☎ 01227-738316, 💻 artichoke chartham.co.uk; food Mon-Fri noon-2.30pm & 6-8.30pm, Sat noon-8.30pm, Sun noon-4pm; 🐕), a handsome timber-framed pub with a history dating back almost 700 years, serving pub classics from £11.95.

Chartham **railway** station is a stop on South Eastern Railway's services (see box pp42-3) between London Charing Cross and Ramsgate.

Stagecoach's **bus** Nos 1A & 1X (Ashford to Canterbury) stop opposite the railway station; see pp44-7.

Back on the trail, the final stretch of your pilgrimage for this stage is a pleasant stroll through **No Man's Orchard** (see box below) followed by a lengthy schlep through woodland, before a crossing of the A2 signals the start of the suburbs of **Canterbury**, gaining entrance to the city centre via the West Gate to arrive at its revered and venerable cathedral.

❑ NO MAN'S ORCHARD – A COMMUNITY ORCHARD

This orchard (see Map 54; 💻 kentishstour.org.uk) was planted in 1947 and purchased by Chartham and Harbledown parish councils, becoming a community orchard in 1995. Orchards and fruit farms featured prominently in the landscape of Kent; with its mild climate and rich, deep soils the county came to be known as the garden of England. But experts reckon that 90% of its orchards have been lost in the last 50 years. No Man's Orchard is traditionally planted with tall stemmed, large trees in contrast to modern dwarf varieties which are easier to harvest mechanically. The orchard is managed to attract birds with trees left to blossom and windfall fruit left on the ground to attract wildlife.

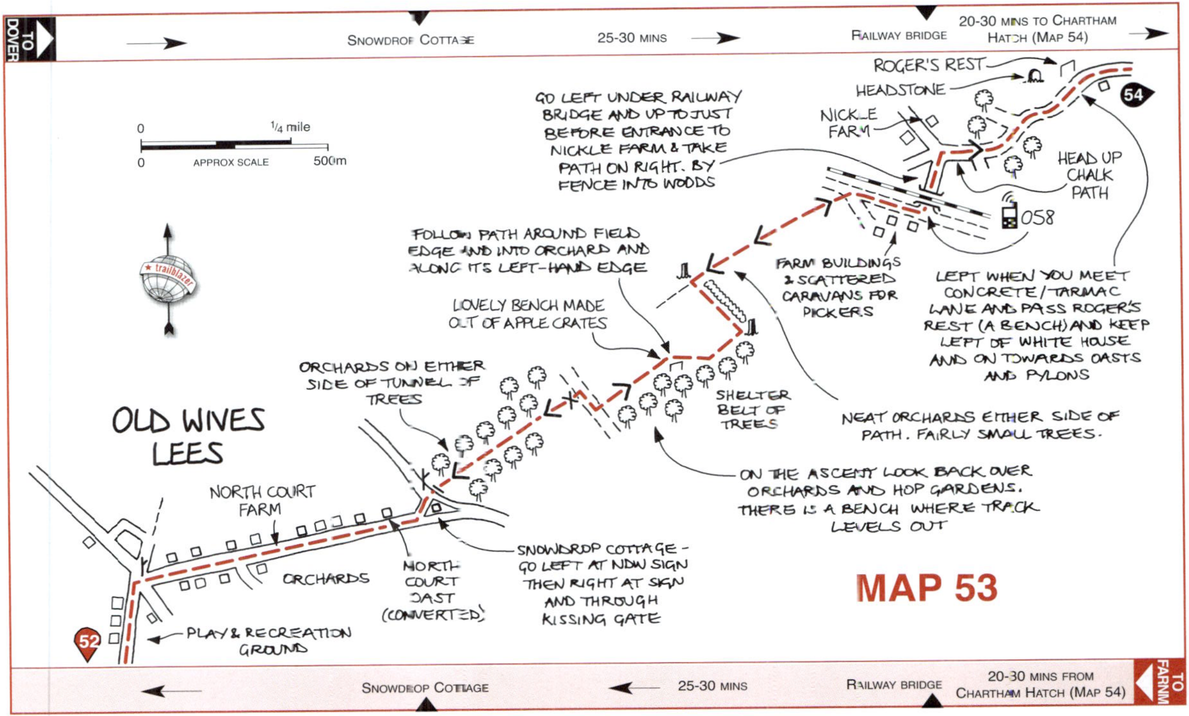

TO DOVER
SNOWDROP COTTAGE
25-30 MINS
RAILWAY BRIDGE
20-30 MINS TO CHARTHAM HATCH (MAP 54)
0 1/4 mile
0 APPROX SCALE 500m
ROGER'S REST
HEADSTONE
NICKLE FARM
GO LEFT UNDER RAILWAY BRIDGE AND UP TO JUST BEFORE ENTRANCE TO NICKLE FARM & TAKE PATH ON RIGHT. BY FENCE INTO WOODS
HEAD UP CHALK PATH
058
54
FOLLOW PATH AROUND FIELD EDGE AND INTO ORCHARD AND ALONG ITS LEFT-HAND EDGE
FARM BUILDINGS & SCATTERED CARAVANS FOR PICKERS
LEFT WHEN YOU MEET CONCRETE/TARMAC LANE AND PASS ROGER'S REST (A BENCH) AND KEEP LEFT OF WHITE HOUSE AND ON TOWARDS OASTS AND PYLONS
LOVELY BENCH MADE OUT OF APPLE CRATES
ORCHARDS ON EITHER SIDE OF TUNNEL OF TREES
SHELTER BELT OF TREES
NEAT ORCHARDS EITHER SIDE OF PATH. FAIRLY SMALL TREES.
OLD WIVES LEES
NORTH COURT FARM
ON THE ASCENT LOOK BACK OVER ORCHARDS AND HOP GARDENS. THERE IS A BENCH WHERE TRACK LEVELS OUT
SNOWDROP COTTAGE - GO LEFT AT NDW SIGN THEN RIGHT AT SIGN AND THROUGH KISSING GATE
NORTH COURT OAST (CONVERTED)
ORCHARDS
MAP 53
52
PLAY & RECREATION GROUND
SNOWDROP COTTAGE
25-30 MINS
RAILWAY BRIDGE
20-30 MINS FROM CHARTHAM HATCH (MAP 54)
TO FARNM

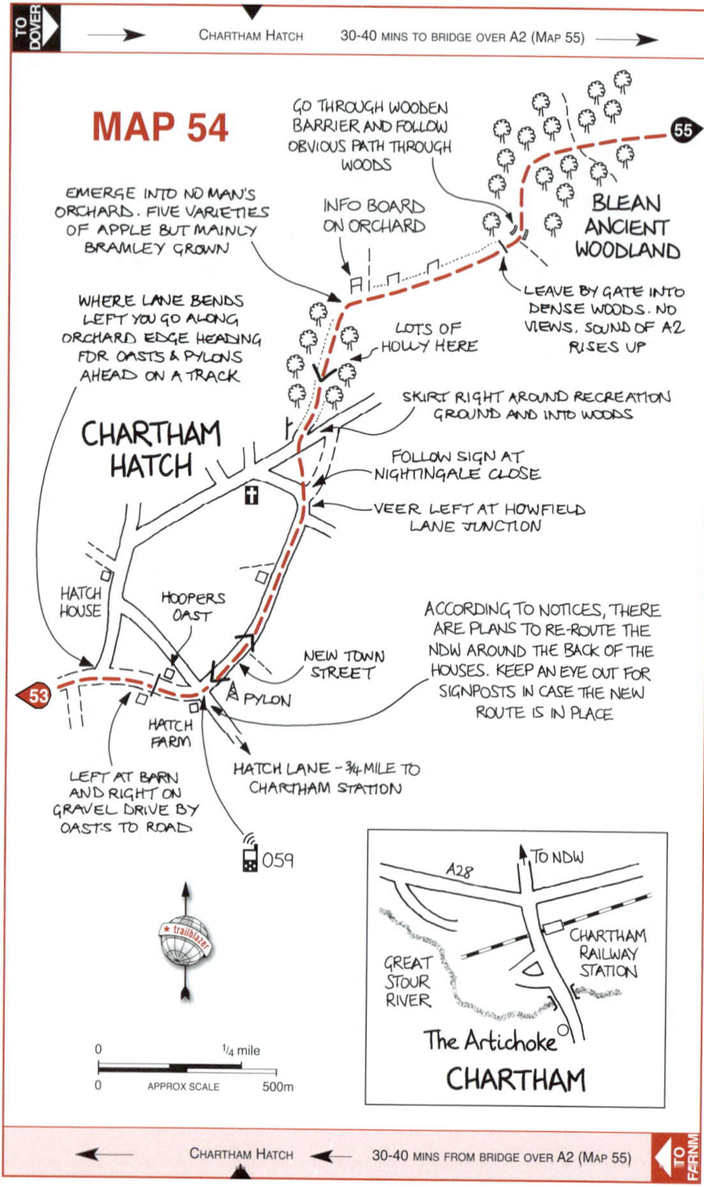
TO DOVER
CHARTHAM HATCH
30-40 MINS TO BRIDGE OVER A2 (MAP 55)
MAP 54
GO THROUGH WOODEN BARRIER AND FOLLOW OBVIOUS PATH THROUGH WOODS
55
EMERGE INTO NO MAN'S ORCHARD. FIVE VARIETIES OF APPLE BUT MAINLY BRAMLEY GROWN
INFO BOARD ON ORCHARD
BLEAN ANCIENT WOODLAND
WHERE LANE BENDS LEFT YOU GO ALONG ORCHARD EDGE HEADING FOR OASTS & PYLONS AHEAD ON A TRACK
LOTS OF HOLLY HERE
LEAVE BY GATE INTO DENSE WOODS. NO VIEWS, SOUND OF A2 RISES UP
SKIRT RIGHT AROUND RECREATION GROUND AND INTO WOODS
CHARTHAM HATCH
FOLLOW SIGN AT NIGHTINGALE CLOSE
VEER LEFT AT HOWFIELD LANE JUNCTION
HATCH HOUSE
HOOPERS OAST
ACCORDING TO NOTICES, THERE ARE PLANS TO RE-ROUTE THE NDW AROUND THE BACK OF THE HOUSES. KEEP AN EYE OUT FOR SIGNPOSTS IN CASE THE NEW ROUTE IS IN PLACE
NEW TOWN STREET
53
PYLON
HATCH FARM
HATCH LANE – ¾ MILE TO CHARTHAM STATION
LEFT AT BARN AND RIGHT ON GRAVEL DRIVE BY OASTS TO ROAD
059
trailblazer
0
¼ mile
0
APPROX SCALE
500m
A28
TO NDW
CHARTHAM RAILWAY STATION
GREAT STOUR RIVER
The Artichoke
CHARTHAM
CHARTHAM HATCH
30-40 MINS FROM BRIDGE OVER A2 (MAP 55)
TO FARNM

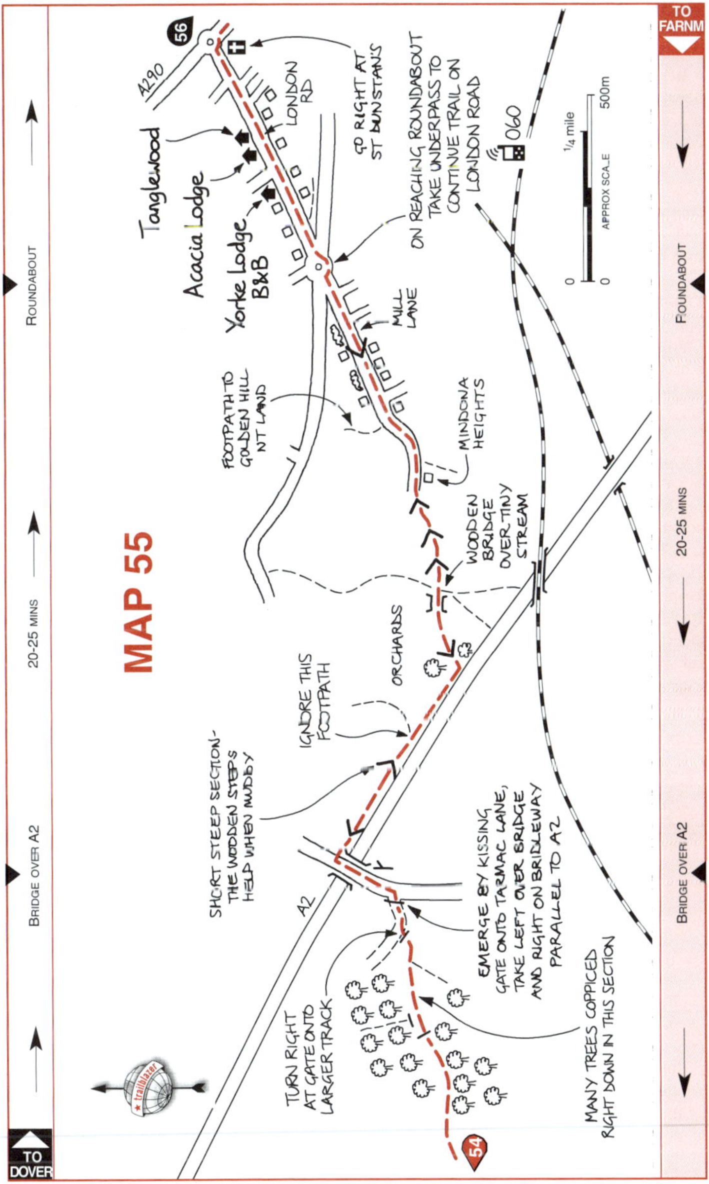
MAP 55
TO DOVER
TO FARNM
BRIDGE OVER A2
20-25 MINS
ROUNDABOUT
56
54
A290
Tanglewood
Acacia Lodge
Yorke Lodge B&B
LONDON RD
GO RIGHT AT ST DUNSTAN'S
ON REACHING ROUNDABOUT TAKE UNDERPASS TO CONTINUE TRAIL ON LONDON ROAD
MILL LANE
FOOTPATH TO GOLDEN HILL NT LAND
MINDONA HEIGHTS
WOODEN BRIDGE OVER TINY STREAM
ORCHARDS
IGNORE THIS FOOTPATH
SHORT STEEP SECTION - THE WOODEN STEPS HELP WHEN MUDDY
A2
EMERGE BY KISSING GATE ONTO TARMAC LANE, TAKE LEFT OVER BRIDGE AND RIGHT ON BRIDLEWAY PARALLEL TO A2
TURN RIGHT AT GATE ONTO LARGER TRACK
MANY TREES COPPICED RIGHT DOWN IN THIS SECTION
060
0
$^{1}/_{4}$ mile
0
500m
APPROX SCALE

CANTERBURY [MAP 56, pp168-9]

Canterbury, home of the Mother Church for Anglicans, shrine of the martyr St Thomas à Becket and the destination of Chaucer's bawdy pilgrims, is worth at least a full day's visit and makes an ideal stop-over before the final leg to Dover.

As one of England's top visitor attractions the demand for rooms is always high so book well ahead. The centre is car-free with a **medieval street pattern** surrounded by a ring road.

> *'And specially from every shire's end*
> *Of England they to Canterbury went,*
> *The holy blessed martyr there to seek*
> *Who helped them when they lay so ill*
> *and weak'* **Geoffrey Chaucer,**
> ***The Canterbury Tales***

What to see and do

Top of the must-see list are Canterbury Cathedral, the ruins of St Augustine's Abbey and St Martin's church which make up the city's **UNESCO World Heritage site** (see box opposite).

Greyfriars (Easter to end Sep Mon-Sat 2-4pm; free), in the gardens off Stour St, was the first Franciscan chapel and was founded in 1267; it is so named for the colour of the friars' habits.

Today the private areas of **Eastbridge Hospital** (☎ 01227-471688, 💻 eastbridgehospital.org.uk), on St Peter's St, provide warden-assisted accommodation for the elderly of Canterbury. Originally a hospital for pilgrims, the Chantry chapel, the Pilgrims' Chapel and the medieval undercroft are fascinating though it's closed for renovations until summer 2025.

The 1000-year-old **St Dunstan's Church** (open Mon-Sat 9.30am-3pm, Sun after service to 3pm) is the first church passed on the way into Canterbury before West Gate. Reputedly the head of Sir Thomas More lies in a lead vault in this church. More, a Catholic and Lord Chancellor of England, refused to swear an oath of supremacy recognising Henry VIII as head of the church in England. In 1535 on the orders of Henry he was charged with treason and beheaded.

Canterbury Guided Tours (☎ 01227-459779, 💻 canterburyguidedtours.com) offer daily walking tours lasting 90 minutes, departing from the Buttermarket (Easter-Oct 11am & 2pm, rest of year 11am only; £15).

ROUTE GUIDE AND MAPS

❑ THE PILGRIMS' WAY

On 29 December 1170, Archbishop Thomas à Becket was murdered in Canterbury Cathedral by four knights, their swords scattering his brains on the floor. He had been appointed by Henry II to bring the Church under the influence of the monarchy but set about defending its rights and paid the price. The spot where he was killed went on to become a shrine drawing thousands of pilgrims following Becket's swift elevation by the Pope to sainthood in 1173 and for the remainder of the Middle Ages it was one of the most popular and wealthiest of shrines.

It's doubtful that there was ever only one route by which pilgrims came to venerate at the cathedral and it was only after 1860 that the name 'Pilgrims' Way' appeared on Ordnance Survey maps. The pilgrimages reached their height of popularity towards the end of the 14th century, at a time when Geoffrey Chaucer wrote *Canterbury Tales*. The North Downs Way coincides with the so-called Pilgrims' Way for much of its length in Kent. At Detling (Map 40, p143) the Way is also marked by the traditional symbol of pilgrimage, the scallop shell, and behind the Tudor gate is thought to have been a pilgrim hospital or shelter for medieval pilgrims on their journey to Canterbury.

❑ CANTERBURY'S UNESCO WORLD HERITAGE SITE

Many visitors will be aghast to discover that they have to pay to even enter the precincts of their own mother church, but others will argue that at least **Canterbury Cathedral** (☎ 01227-762862, 🖳 canterbury-cathedral.org; Mon-Sat 9am-5pm, Sun 11.30am-5pm; £17) is worth the money. It was founded in AD597 by St Augustine, a Catholic and the cathedral's first archbishop. It's now the seat of the Mother Church of the Anglican Communion, officially titled 'The Cathedral and Metropolitical Church of Christ, Canterbury' and is famously the crime scene for the murder of Thomas à Becket (see box opposite) in 1170.

The cathedral has a wonderful Romanesque crypt, 12th-century quire and stained glass and of course the site and shrine of St Thomas à Becket's martyrdom. A guided tour (Mon-Sat 10.30am, noon & 1pm, but 2pm in winter, Sun 1pm; 1hr; £5) is the best way to appreciate such history. Tickets are available from the cathedral's Welcome Centre on the day.

English Heritage (EH) manages the **ruins of St Augustine's Abbey** (☎ 01227-767345; daily summer 10am-6pm, to 5pm in Oct, Nov-Mar Sat & Sun 10am-4pm; £7.70-11.80); founded in AD598, it was thoroughly smashed by Henry VIII on the dissolution of the monasteries. There's a good audio tour.

Off Longport lies England's oldest parish church and the oldest church in continuous use in the English-speaking world, **St Martin's** (☎ 01227-768072, 🖳 martinpaul.org/stmartin-html; Wed-Sun 11am-3pm except during services), having been 'a community of prayer and welcome in the name of Jesus Christ since before 547AD'.

ROUTE GUIDE AND MAPS

Services

The **tourist information centre** (TIC; ☎ 01227-862162, 🖳 canterburymuseums.co.uk/the-beaney/visitor-information; Mon-Wed & Fri-Sat 10am-5pm, Thur to 6pm, Sun 11am-4pm) resides in The Beaney House of Art & Knowledge at 18 High St.

There are several banks with **ATMs** on the High St, particularly clustered near the corner of St Margaret's St, and a **post office** (Mon-Sat 9am-5.30pm, Sun 10am-2pm) in the branch of WH Smith on St George's St.

There are several **outdoor shops**: Blacks (Mon-Sat 9am-6pm, Sun 11am-5pm), 44 Burgate St; Mountain Warehouse (Mon-Sat 9am-6pm, Sun 11am-5pm) on The Parade. You'll also find an **army surplus store**, Golding Surplus Limited (☎ 01227-787899, 🖳 goldingsurplus.co.uk; Mon, Wed, Fri & Sat 9.30am-5pm, Sun noon-4pm) at 25 Palace St (aka King's Mile). On the same street is Rohan (Mon-Sat 9am-5pm), while on the High St there's a branch of Trespass (Mon-Sat 9am-6pm, Sun 10am-4pm).

Boots **pharmacy** (Mon-Fri 9am-5.30pm, Sat to 6pm, Sun 11am-5pm) is on Whitefriars opposite the bus station. Just next to it is a **supermarket**, Tesco (Mon-Sat 7am-10pm, Sun 11am-5pm), while opposite that is a Marks & Spencer (Mon-Sat 8am-7pm, Sun 11am-5pm).

A general **market** is held every Wednesday and Friday at St George's St and a farmers market is held every third Saturday in Westgate Hall; see also The Goods Shed p171.

Transport

There are two **railway stations**: **Canterbury West** is a stop on Southeastern Railways' services to London Charing Cross and Ramsgate; **Canterbury East** is a stop on the London Victoria to Dover Priory line. See box pp42-3 for details.

The **bus station** is on St George's Lane. As you'd expect, there are many buses serving many destinations from here; perhaps most useful are Stagecoach's bus: Nos 16 & 17 (to Folkestone); the No 18 to

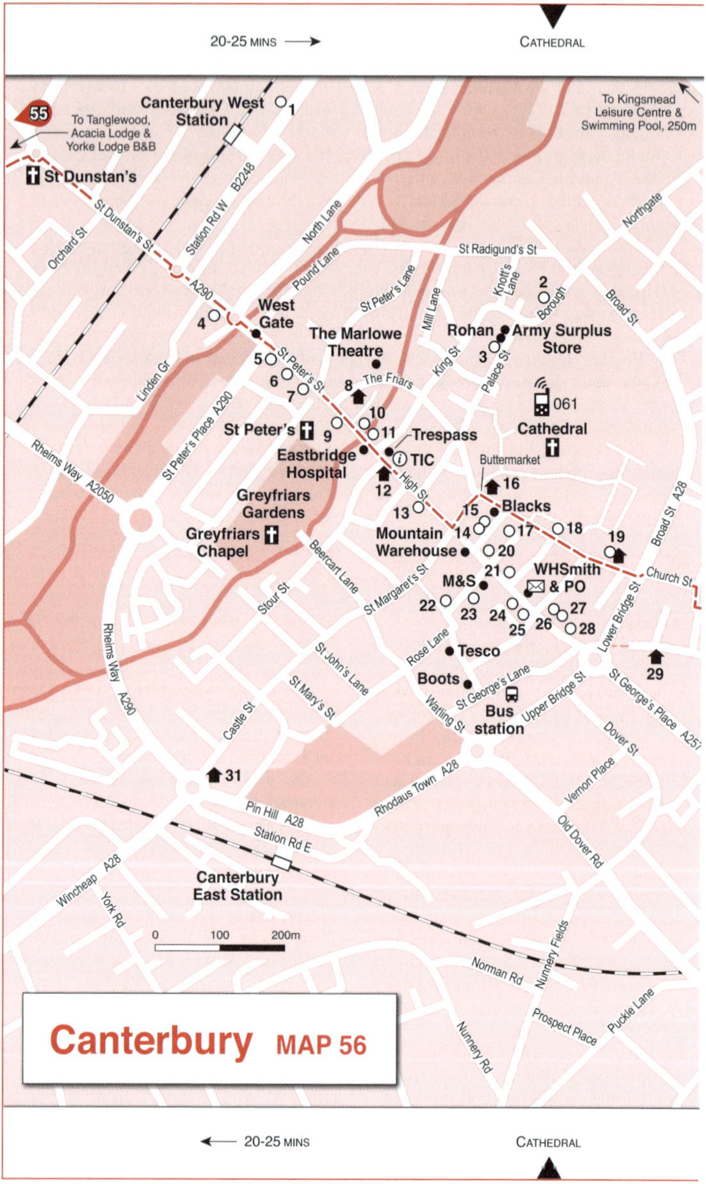

ROUTE GUIDE AND MAPS

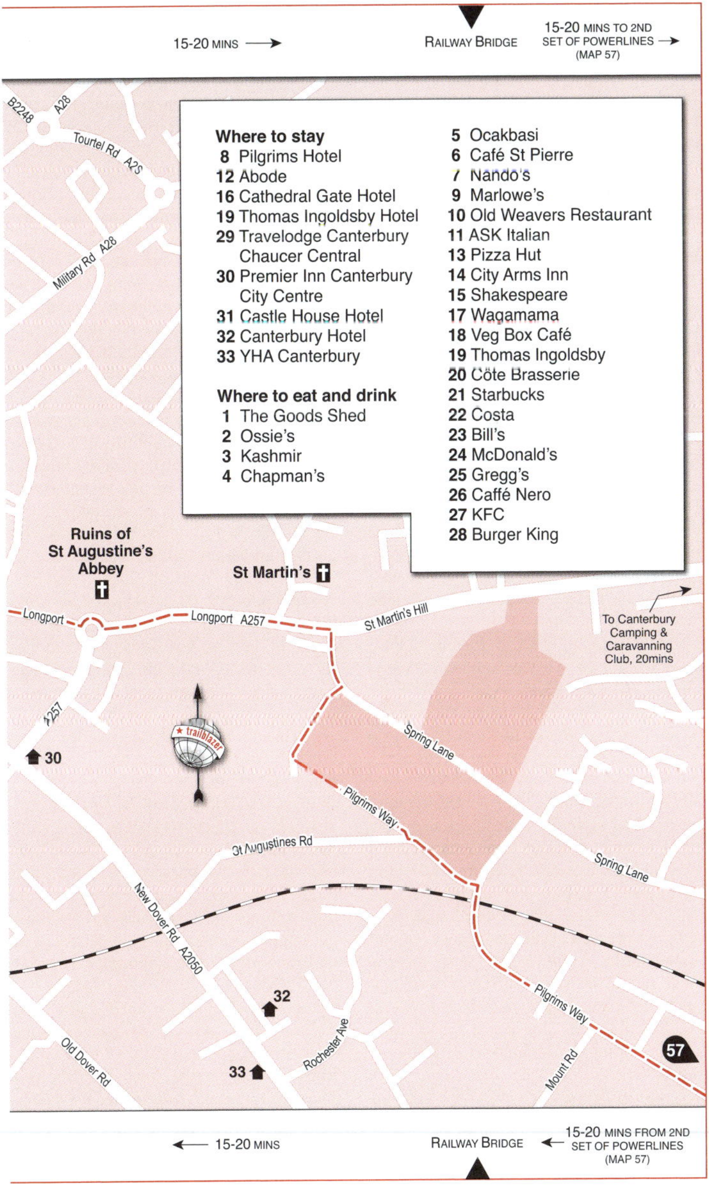
15-20 MINS →
RAILWAY BRIDGE
15-20 MINS TO 2ND SET OF POWERLINES → (MAP 57)
Where to stay
8 Pilgrims Hotel
12 Abode
16 Cathedral Gate Hotel
19 Thomas Ingoldsby Hotel
29 Travelodge Canterbury Chaucer Central
30 Premier Inn Canterbury City Centre
31 Castle House Hotel
32 Canterbury Hotel
33 YHA Canterbury
Where to eat and drink
1 The Goods Shed
2 Ossie's
3 Kashmir
4 Chapman's
5 Ocakbasi
6 Café St Pierre
7 Nando's
9 Marlowe's
10 Old Weavers Restaurant
11 ASK Italian
13 Pizza Hut
14 City Arms Inn
15 Shakespeare
17 Wagamama
18 Veg Box Café
19 Thomas Ingoldsby
20 Côte Brasserie
21 Starbucks
22 Costa
23 Bill's
24 McDonald's
25 Gregg's
26 Caffé Nero
27 KFC
28 Burger King
B2248
A28
Tourtel Rd A28
Military Rd A28
Ruins of St Augustine's Abbey
St Martin's
Longport
Longport A257
St Martin's Hill
To Canterbury Camping & Caravanning Club, 20mins
A257
30
trailblazer
Spring Lane
Pilgrims Way
St Augustines Rd
Spring Lane
New Dover Rd A2050
32
33
Old Dover Rd
Rochester Ave
Pilgrims Way
Mount Rd
57
← 15-20 MINS
RAILWAY BRIDGE
← 15-20 MINS FROM 2ND SET OF POWERLINES (MAP 57)

Hythe; the Nos 1A/1X (to Ashford and Chartham); and the 15 (to Dover). See pp44-7 for more information.

Canterbury is a stop on National Express **coach** services (see p40) between London Victoria Coach Station and Dover/ Deal (NX007) and Ramsgate (NX022).

You can pick up a **taxi** from the southern end of the High St, or call Galaxy Taxis (☎ 01227-450150).

Where to stay

There is a campsite serving Canterbury but it's about a mile east of town. ***Canterbury Camping and Caravanning Club Site*** (☎ 01227-463216, 🖳 campingandcaravanning club.co.uk; 🐕 on lead) never turns away a backpacker (it's the Caravan Club rules); prices are variable but make sure you ask for their backpacker rate; a solo trekker with a small tent can expect to pay around £11. To reach it, continue along the North Downs Way out of the city, but instead of dropping down Spring Lane carry on along the A257 (see Map 56) for three-quarters of a mile, turning right onto Bekesbourne Lane. It's about a 20-minute walk from the city walls to the site.

Non-camping budget travellers have several choices. To the south-east of the city is ***YHA Canterbury*** (☎ 0345-371 9010, 🖳 yha.org.uk/hostel/yha-canterbury; sleeps 68 in 15 rooms, range of room sizes sleep 2-6, some en suite; WI-FI communal area), 54 New Dover Rd. The rates are variable but start from about £30 for a private room, or £40-120 in an en suite. They also have three 'hobbit houses' in their back garden – well-appointed wooden **cabins** (sleeping up to five; £80-160; 🐕) furnished with a kitchenette area that houses a fridge, microwave, sink, kettle and crockery and shower/toilet facilities; they also provide bedding and, best of all, the cabins are one of the few places in the city where your dog is allowed to stay. There is a self-catering kitchen although breakfast is available in the hostel.

You'd expect a city the size of Canterbury to have both a Premier Inn and a Travelodge and you wouldn't be wrong; they're both conveniently situated to just outside the city walls to the east. ***Premier Inn Canterbury City Centre*** (☎ 0333-321 9298, 🖳 premierinn.com; 120 en suite rooms; ◗) is at 1-7 Dover Road, while ***Travelodge Canterbury Chaucer Central*** (☎ 08719 846471, 🖳 travelodge.co.uk; 59 en suite rooms; ◗; 🐕) is on nearby Ivy Lane. Both have rooms starting at just £30.

Speaking of national chains offering good value accommodation, the city's Wetherspoons, ***Thomas Ingoldsby*** (01227 463339, 🖳 jdwetherspoons.com; 13 en suite rooms; ◗) offers rooms from £88 per night (room only), with breakfast available (additional charge) in the pub downstairs.

Arriving in the city the trail passes a few **B&Bs** on London Rd (Map 55), which is convenient for Canterbury West station (see p167). Standing out are ***Acacia Lodge & Tanglewood*** (☎ 07769-0213976, 🖳 aca cialodge.co.uk; 3D/2T in total over the two houses, all en suite or private bathroom), two Victorian cottages operated as one B&B at 39 & 40 London Rd; B&B at both costs from £40pp (sgl occ from £75).

Down the road at No 50, luxurious ***Yorke Lodge*** (☎ 01227-451243, 🖳 yorke lodge.com; 1S/3T/5D, all en suite; ◗; 🐕) is one of the very few B&Bs in Canterbury to accept dogs. Well appointed and immaculately clean and tidy, rates in this relaxing B&B are £80pp (sgl/sgl occ from £85/110).

Three conveniently located city centre hotels belong to the same small group (🖳 hotelscanterbury.co.uk/hotels). At 28 Castle St, part of ***Castle House Hotel*** (☎ 01227-761897; 7D/2D or T/1Tr/5Qd, all en suite; ◗) formed the medieval city walls, now near the busy Wincheap roundabout. Large rooms start from around £57.50pp in the high summer season (sgl occ £105), with a two-night minimum stay at weekends. A little further out is ***The Canterbury Hotel*** (☎ 01227-768433; 2S/12D/1Tr/1Qd, all en suite; ◗; 🐕) with B&B rates from £42.50pp (sgl £85). They also have some self-catering cottages for longer stays. Right in the centre near the Marlowe Theatre is the ***Pilgrims Hotel*** (☎ 01277-464531; 1S/3D/1D or T/1Qd, all en suite; ◗; 🐕) with rates from £40pp (sgl £70), including a continental breakfast.

❑ THE NORTH DOWNS WAY ROUTE THROUGH CANTERBURY
[MAP 56, pp168-9]

The path enters the city by West Gate and after the river keeps straight on to the pedestrianised High St. After passing the tourist office look out for Mercery Lane on your left, take it towards the cathedral, then turn right when you reach the cathedral entrance to cross over Lower Bridge St, part of the busy 'ring road' surrounding the old city. Keep straight on till you can turn right onto Monastery St then left along Burgate and on to Longport St.

Turn left at the roundabout onto the A257 (the direction marked is Littlebourne), keeping the ruins of St Augustine's Abbey on your left. Walk up the road and then turn right down Spring Lane past the sign to St Martin's, then right again onto Pilgrims' Way, opposite EKC Canterbury College.

Follow the North Downs Way marker post and pass the playing fields. Turn right over the railway bridge and follow the road (still called the Pilgrims' Way) as it bends left. The road becomes a rough track at the end of the row of houses and continues bordered by hedges to Barton Farm Business Park (Map 57).

The ***Cathedral Gate Hotel*** (☎ 01227-464381, 💻 cathgate.co.uk; 4S/42D shared/2T en suite/10D en suite; ☕) next to the Cathedral has a real medieval feel to it with sloping floors, low doorways and the hustle and bustle from the street below. Continental breakfast is included (a full English breakfast costs an extra £9.50pp) and the rates are £50pp in a double or twin with shared facilities, £60pp en suite (sgl/sgl occ from £75).

The former County Hotel has now been transformed into the luxurious designer ***Abode Canterbury*** (☎ 01227-766266, 💻 abodecanterbury.co.uk; 63D/9T, all en suite; ☕), 30 High St, with rooms graded (by the hotel itself) as 'Comfortable', 'Desirable', 'Enviable', 'Most Enviable' and 'Fabulous'. B&B costs £40-62.50pp (sgl occ room rate) for the 'Comfortable' rooms and up to £175-250pp (sgl occ room rate) for those labelled 'Fabulous'.

Where to eat and drink

There are some quirky little cafés on the main drag and around the Cathedral. For unpretentious, honest French fare look no further than the long-established ***Café St Pierre*** (☎ 01227-456791, **fb**; Mon-Sat 8am-6pm, Sun 9am-5.30pm) at the northern end of the main road running through the heart of the old city (known, at this end, as St Peter's St). All baguettes are £7.15.

For vegetarians there's ***Veg Box Café*** (☎ 01227-456654, 💻 thevegboxcafe.co.uk; Mon-Sat 8.30am-5pm, Sun 9am-4pm), where they try to use only local, organic and Fairtrade produce in their meals. Breakfasts start at £5.95 for toast with beans or tofu, though they're more renowned for their frittatas (from £12.95).

Veg Box isn't the only place using locally sourced ingredients. ***The Goods Shed*** (☎ 01227-459153, 💻 thegoodsshed.co.uk; Tue-Wed & Sun noon-3pm, Thur-Sat noon-3pm & 5.30-9pm) is England's first full-time farmers' market restaurant, housed in a revamped Victorian engine shed with high oak-beamed ceilings and huge windows. Bringing the kitchen to the market, the menu constantly changes (dinner mains around £18-25) using the produce available on the day so you can get the likes of Jerusalem artichokes, shallots, lentils, goats curd and hazelnut (£18.50).

As you'd expect from a major city, Canterbury is awash with the big brands of cafés, fast-food outlets and restaurants. There's a whole slew of them at the southern end of St George's St), including ***Caffè Nero*** (Mon-Fri 7am-6.30pm, Sat & Sun from 7.30am), ***Starbucks*** (Mon-Sat 7.30am-7pm, Sun 8am-5.30pm), and ***Costa*** (actually south-west of the main drag on

Rose Lane; Mon-Fri 7am-6.30pm, Sat to 7pm, Sun 8am-5pm).

Back on St George's St, the fast-food restaurant chains have also infested this strip, including ***McDonald's*** (24 hours), ***Burger King*** (daily 10am-10pm), ***KFC*** (daily 10.30am-11pm) and ***Gregg's*** (Mon-Sat 6am-8.30pm, Sun 7.30am-5.30pm).

There are also branches of the more 'upmarket' eatery chains such as ***Côte Brasserie*** (☎ 01227-786386, 💻 cote.co.uk; Mon-Sat 9am-10pm, Sun 9am-9.30pm) at 2 Longmarket, with mains from £12.95 for the quiche. ***Wagamama*** (☎ 01227-454307, 💻 wagamama.com; Sun-Thur 11am-10pm, Fri & Sat to 11pm), is just behind them at 7-9 Longmarket; ***Nando's*** (☎ 01227-766261, 💻 nandos.co .uk; daily 11.30am-10pm), at 46 St Peter's St, serves peri peri chicken from £5.50; and ***Bill's*** (☎ 01227-479552, 💻 bills-website.co.uk; Mon-Wed 8am-10pm, Thur-Sat to 11pm, Sun 8am-10pm) is on the way to Tesco on Rose Lane.

On the main drag are branches of those well-known Italian pizzeria joints, ***Ask Italian*** (☎ 01227-767617, 💻 askitalian.co .uk; Mon-Thur 11.30am-9.30pm, Fri & Sat to 11pm, Sun to 10pm; pizzas from £10.20) at 24 High St and ***Pizza Hut*** (☎ 01227-451049, 💻 pizzahut.co.uk; daily 11am-10pm) at No 39.

More traditional fare can be found at ***Marlowe's*** (☎ 01227-462194, 💻 marlowes restaurant.co.uk; Mon-Sat 11am-10pm, Sun to 9pm; 55 St Peter St), one of the best-value eateries with mains from £12.95 for the halloumi burger. Nearby, ***The Old Weavers Restaurant*** (☎ 01227-464660, 💻 weaversrestaurant.co.uk; Mon-Sat 10am-midnight, Sun to 11pm), just before the bridge on St Peter's St, deserves a mention for its pleasant riverside seating and its top selection of pies (£15.95 up to £19.95 for duck and apricot pie).

For **pub food**, Butchery Lane has a couple of decent options including ***The City Arms Inn*** (☎ 01227-637171, 💻 thecity armsinnpub.co.uk; food Tue-Sun 11am-5pm), and ***Shakespeare*** (☎ 01227-463252, 💻 shakespearecanterbury.com; food Mon-Thur noon-9pm, Fri-Sun to 8pm) – more a restaurant and wine bar than a proper boozer, though they do some great gourmet burgers from £14. There's also the Wetherspoons-owned ***Thomas Ingoldsby*** (see Where to stay; food daily 8am-11pm) with their usual good-value menu, right on the trail at the end of Burgate.

Smarter, more formal dining options include the fish restaurant ***Chapman's*** (☎ 01227-780749, 💻 chapmansincanterbury .co.uk; Tue 5-9pm, Wed-Sat 12-2.30pm & 5-9pm), just outside the city walls on St Dunstan's, with mains from £15.90 for the nut roast up to £33.90 for the lobster and hake Goan curry.

Takeaway outlets tend to be gathered around West Gate, including the kebab house ***Ocakbasi*** (☎ 01227-784019, 💻 ocak basiofkent.net; Mon-Thur 3pm-3am, Fri-Sun noon-3am). Nearer the cathedral there's a chippy, ***Ossie's*** (☎ 01227-462187; Mon-Sat 11am-10pm) at 7 Borough; and an Indian, ***Kashmir*** (☎ 01227-462050, 💻 kashmirtandoori.co.uk; Mon-Sat noon-2pm & 5-11.30pm, Sun noon-11.30pm; eat in or take away) at 20 Palace St.

❑ CHITTY CHITTY BANG BANG

The fine Palladian house at **Higham Park and Gardens** (see Map 58; not open to public) is glimpsed from the North Downs Way and has Italianate gardens designed by Harold Peto. It was here in the 1920s that Polish count and dashing racing-car driver Louis Zborowski built three racing cars powered by aero engines and all called Chitty Chitty Bang Bang. Inspired by the count and his cars, Ian Fleming, who at the time lived at nearby Bekesbourne, wrote the children's story *Chitty Chitty Bang Bang* in 1964 and Roland Emett, sculptor and cartoonist, worked up the model of the car in the 1968 movie of the same name adapted from Roald Dahl's screenplay. One of the count's cars is displayed at the National Motor Museum, Beaulieu, Hampshire.

ROUTE GUIDE AND MAPS

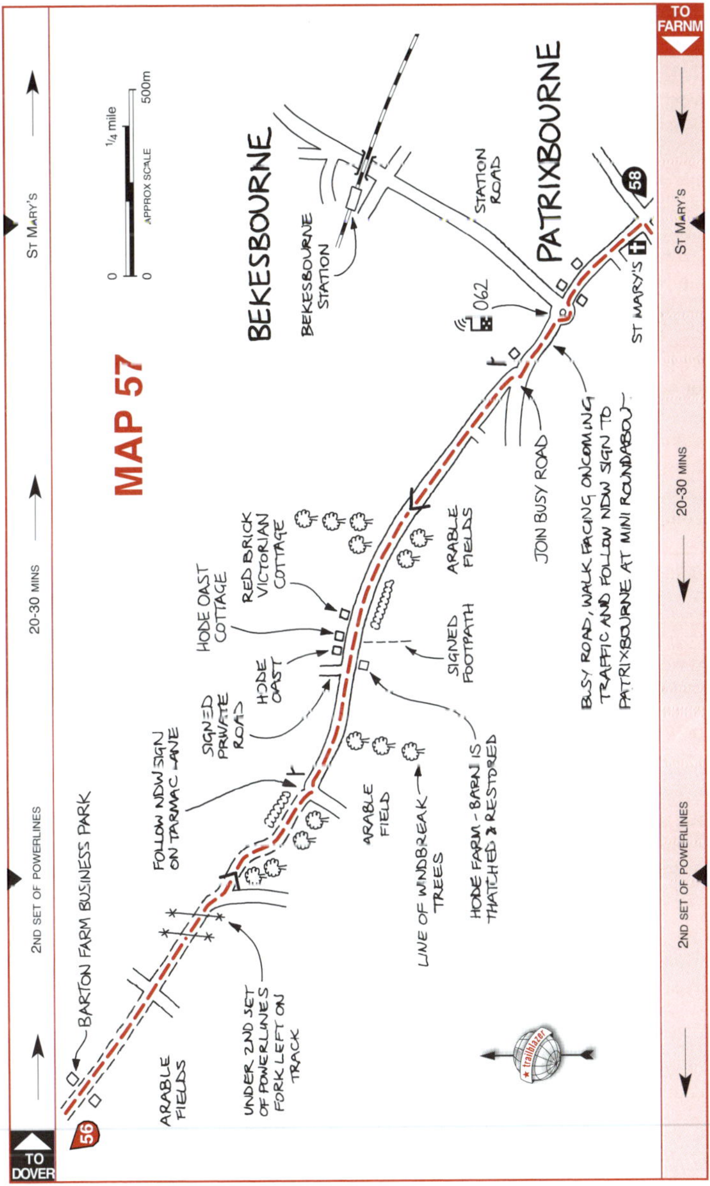
MAP 57
TO DOVER
56
TO FARNM
58
ST MARY'S
20-30 MINS
2ND SET OF POWERLINES
0 1/4 mile
0 APPROX SCALE 500m
BARTON FARM BUSINESS PARK
ARABLE FIELDS
UNDER 2ND SET OF POWERLINES FORK LEFT ON TRACK
FOLLOW NDW SIGN ON TARMAC LANE
SIGNED PRIVATE ROAD
HODE OAST
HODE OAST COTTAGE
RED BRICK VICTORIAN COTTAGE
ARABLE FIELD
LINE OF WINDBREAK TREES
HODE FARM - BARN IS THATCHED & RESTORED
SIGNED FOOTPATH
ARABLE FIELDS
JOIN BUSY ROAD
BUSY ROAD, WALK FACING ONCOMING TRAFFIC AND FOLLOW NDW SIGN TO PATRIXBOURNE AT MINI ROUNDABOUT
BEKESBOURNE
BEKESBOURNE STATION
STATION ROAD
PATRIXBOURNE
062
ST MARY'S
trailblazer

NORTHERN ROUTE: CANTERBURY TO SHEPHERDSWELL [MAPS 56-62]

After leaving Canterbury along Pilgrims' Way you spend a long time crossing very large arable fields on this **10.8-mile/17.4km (2¾hrs to 3½hrs)** stage. Not the most fascinating part of the North Downs Way, for a large stretch of this trek the A2 is an unwelcome, noisy companion. Walkers should thus find pleasure where they can to distract themselves from the constant blast of traffic, be it in the tiny yet gorgeous hamlets of Patrixbourne and Womenswold, the lovely wildflower meadows that spring up where the farmer leaves the ground untouched, and the butterflies that flit above them, including the **marble white butterfly** – common in these fields but seldom encountered elsewhere on the trail.

Note that at the time of research there were no B&Bs in Shepherdswell so be prepared to march on a further 8.6 miles/13.8km) to Dover, or hop on a bus or train.

Having negotiated your way through Canterbury it's not long before you come to the quaint village of **Patrixbourne** (Map 57), a huddle of houses built higgledy-piggledy around handsome St Mary's Church. At the end of the village the trail turns off the road to walk parallel to the A2, unless you want to continue along the road to the village of **Bridge** (Map 58).

BRIDGE [MAP 58]

There are a few services in Bridge and a couple of options for a meal.

The Bridgeway Stores **convenience store** (Mon-Fri 7am-7pm, Sat 8am-7pm, Sun 8am-5pm) has an outdoor **ATM** (£1.99 for withdrawals). There's a twice-weekly **post office** (Wed & Fri 9-11am) service in the ***Red Lion*** pub (see below).

Gastro-pub the ***Red Lion*** (☎ 01227-832213, 💻 redlionbridge.co.uk; **food** Mon-Fri noon-3pm & 5-8.30pm, Sat noon-8.30pm, Sun noon-7pm; 🐕) has smart offerings such as duck breast with hoisin gravy (£18.95) as well as takeaway pizzas (Wed-Thur 5-7pm; from £11.50).

The ***Bridge Arms*** (☎ 01227-286534, 💻 bridgearms.co.uk; food Wed-Sat noon-2.30pm & 6-9pm, Sun noon-5pm; 🐕) is more of a restaurant than a pub, and one whose food and ambience have been rewarded with a Michelin star. Expect to pay anything from £26 to £70 for a main course (plus extra for side dishes).

Stagecoach's **bus** service No 17 (Canterbury to Folkestone) stops by the Bridge Arms; see pp44-7 for details.

The path passes the entrance to **Higham Park and Gardens** (see box p172 and Map 58), before crossing huge arable fields to arrive at the quaint village of **Womenswold** (Map 60).

A further march through fields will take you to **Woolage Village** (Map 60), built for colliery workers in the Kent coalfields. After Woolage the trail climbs through a **tunnel of trees and hedgerows** (Map 61), before dropping along a country lane and farm track to arrive in **Shepherdswell** (Map 62).

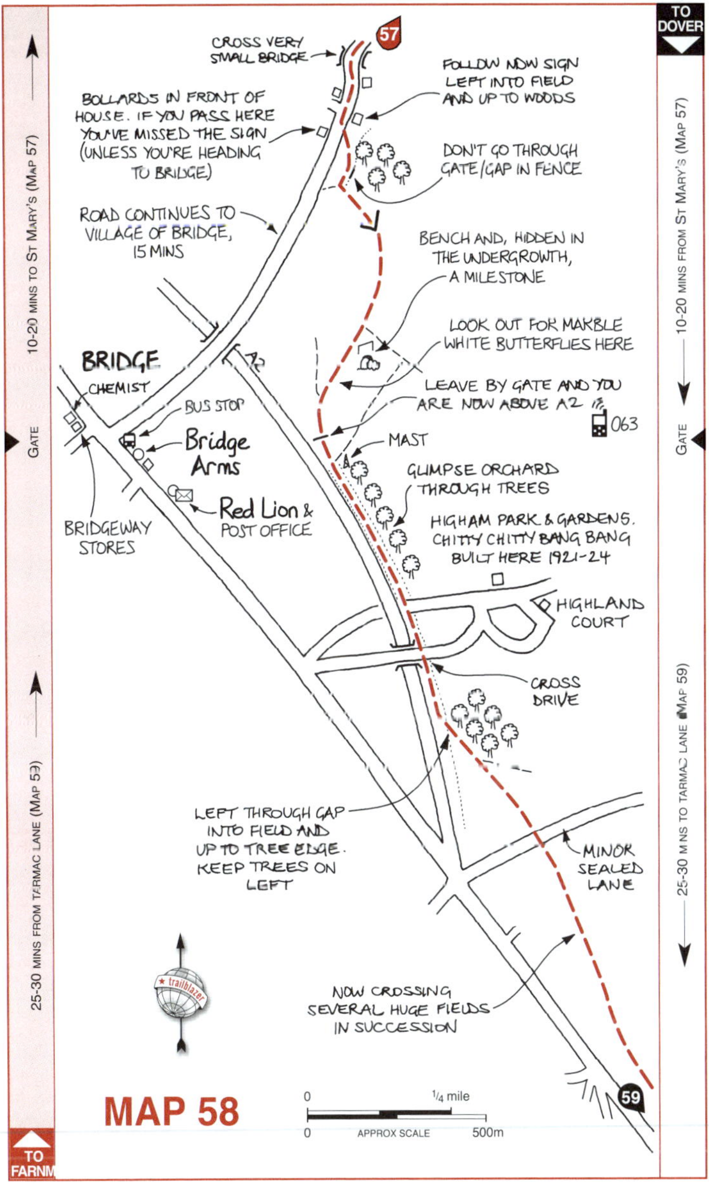
TO DOVER
10-20 MINS TO ST MARY'S (MAP 57)
10-20 MINS FROM ST MARY'S (MAP 57)
GATE
GATE
25-30 MINS FROM TARMAC LANE (MAP 53)
25-30 MINS TO TARMAC LANE (MAP 59)
57
CROSS VERY SMALL BRIDGE
FOLLOW NOW SIGN LEFT INTO FIELD AND UP TO WOODS
BOLLARDS IN FRONT OF HOUSE. IF YOU PASS HERE YOU'VE MISSED THE SIGN (UNLESS YOU'RE HEADING TO BRIDGE)
DON'T GO THROUGH GATE/GAP IN FENCE
ROAD CONTINUES TO VILLAGE OF BRIDGE, 15 MINS
BENCH AND, HIDDEN IN THE UNDERGROWTH, A MILESTONE
LOOK OUT FOR MARBLE WHITE BUTTERFLIES HERE
BRIDGE
CHEMIST
A2
LEAVE BY GATE AND YOU ARE NOW ABOVE A2
063
BUS STOP
Bridge Arms
MAST
GLIMPSE ORCHARD THROUGH TREES
Red Lion &
POST OFFICE
BRIDGEWAY STORES
HIGHAM PARK & GARDENS. CHITTY CHITTY BANG BANG BUILT HERE 1921-24
HIGHLAND COURT
CROSS DRIVE
LEFT THROUGH GAP INTO FIELD AND UP TO TREE EDGE. KEEP TREES ON LEFT
MINOR SEALED LANE
NOW CROSSING SEVERAL HUGE FIELDS IN SUCCESSION
trailblazer
MAP 58
0
1/4 mile
0
APPROX SCALE
500m
59
TO FARNM

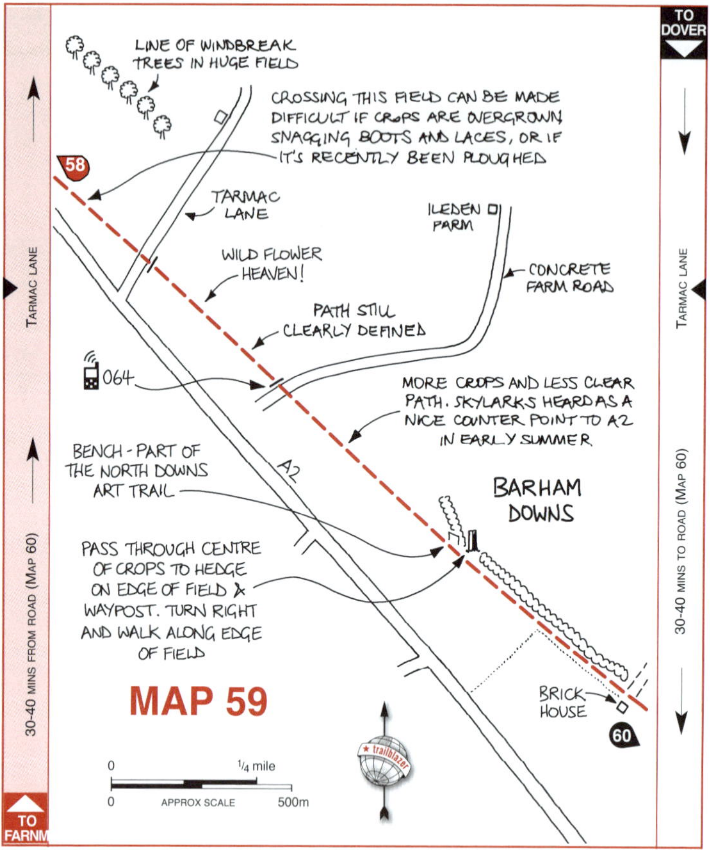

SHEPHERDSWELL [MAP 62, p179]

As the biggest stop between Canterbury and Dover, Shepherdswell is a welcome spot for walkers striving to finish the trail in one day and there are just enough facilities to warrant a brief stop here.

The Co-op **convenience store** (Mon-Sat 6am-10pm, Sun 7am-10pm) has snacks and food for meals on the go, plus an **ATM**.

For food during the day, the heritage East Kent Railway Station, next to the main Shepherds Well station (see p180), has ***Colonel's Café*** (☎ 01304-832042, 💻 eastkentrailway.co.uk/colonels-cafe; Tue-Sun 9am-4pm) where you can enjoy a jacket potato while watching the heritage trains chug by. If you're happy to forego the full café experience in order to save yourself that tiring schlep down to Colonel's then, wonderfully, ***Fry's Farm Shop*** (💻 frysfarmshop.co.uk, **fb**) Tue-Sat 9am-5pm, Sun 10am-2pm) has recently opened right on the trail just as you leave the village, below the church.

[*cont'd on p180*]

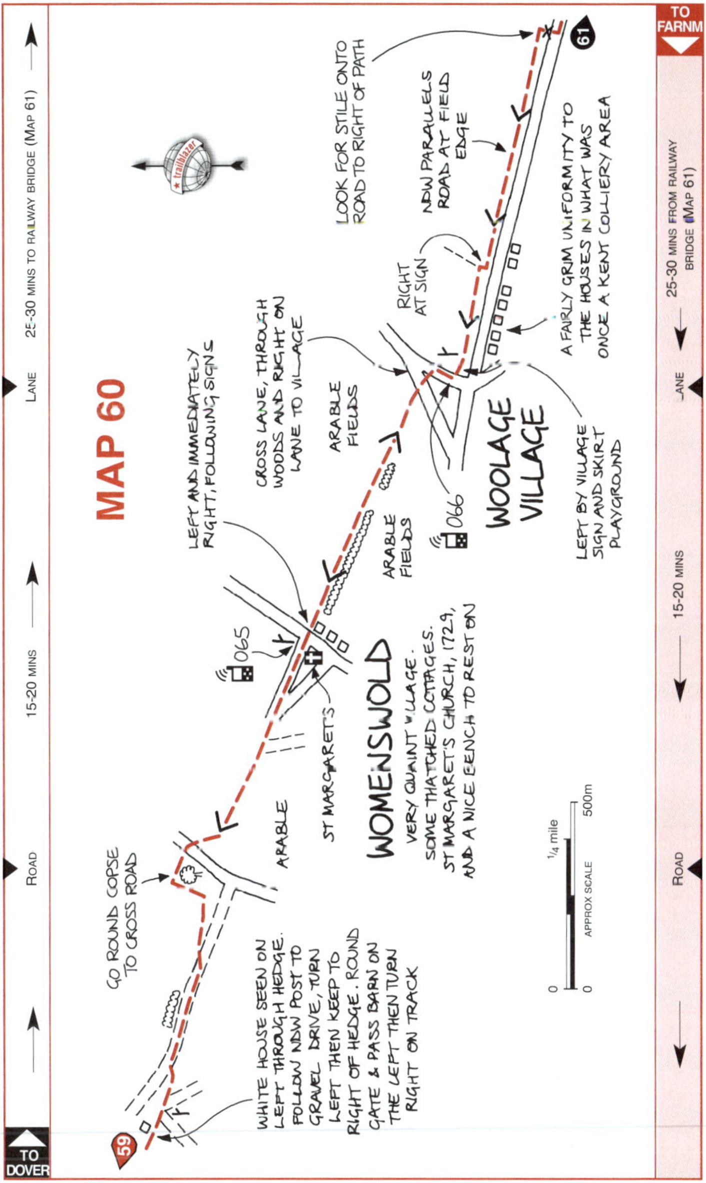
MAP 60
25-30 MINS TO RAILWAY BRIDGE (MAP 61)
ROAD
15-20 MINS
LANE
TO DOVER
TO FARNM
59
61
trailblazer
WHITE HOUSE SEEN ON LEFT THROUGH HEDGE. FOLLOW NDW POST TO GRAVEL DRIVE, TURN LEFT THEN KEEP TO RIGHT OF HEDGE. ROUND GATE & PASS BARN ON THE LEFT THEN TURN RIGHT ON TRACK
GO ROUND COPSE TO CROSS ROAD
ARABLE
ST MARGARET'S
WOMENSWOLD
VERY QUAINT VILLAGE. SOME THATCHED COTTAGES. ST MARGARET'S CHURCH, 1729, AND A NICE BENCH TO REST ON
065
LEFT AND IMMEDIATELY RIGHT, FOLLOWING SIGNS
ARABLE FIELDS
CROSS LANE, THROUGH WOODS AND RIGHT ON LANE TO VILLAGE
ARABLE FIELDS
066
WOOLAGE VILLAGE
LEFT BY VILLAGE SIGN AND SKIRT PLAYGROUND
RIGHT AT SIGN
A FAIRLY GRIM UNIFORMITY TO THE HOUSES IN WHAT WAS ONCE A KENT COLLIERY AREA
NDW PARALLELS ROAD AT FIELD EDGE
LOOK FOR STILE ONTO ROAD TO RIGHT OF PATH
APPROX SCALE
0 1/4 mile
0 500m
ROAD
15-20 MINS
LANE
25-30 MINS FROM RAILWAY BRIDGE (MAP 61)

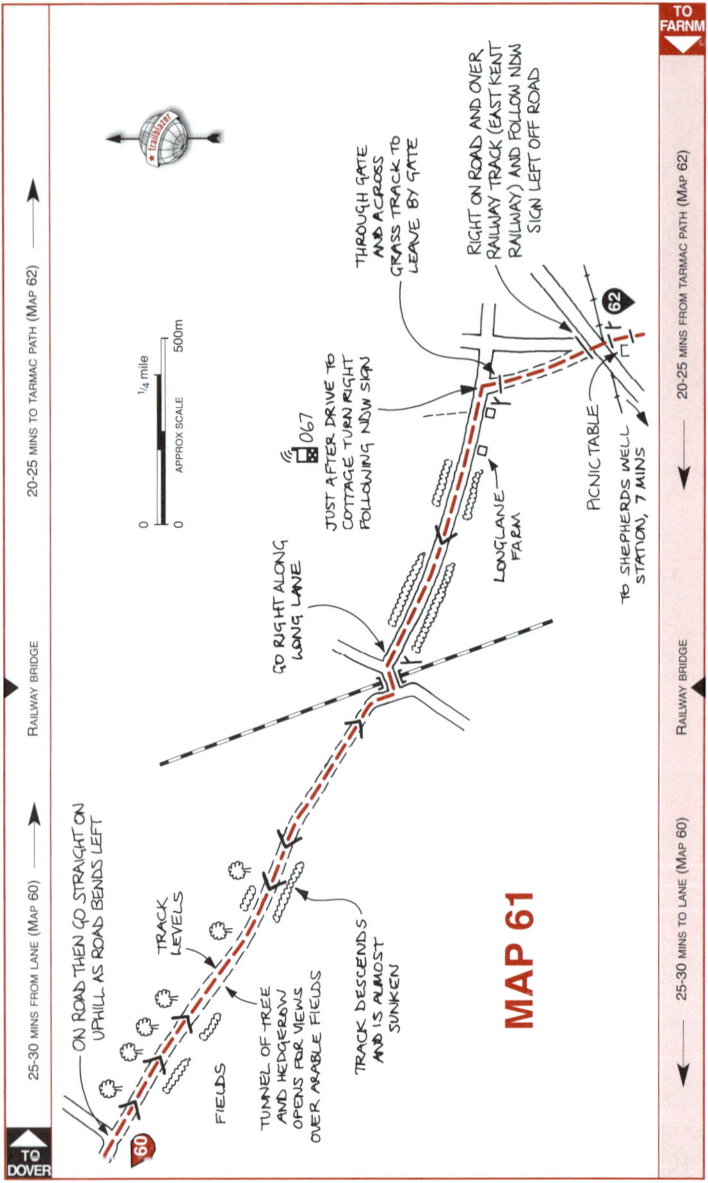
TO DOVER
25-30 MINS FROM LANE (MAP 60)
RAILWAY BRIDGE
20-25 MINS TO TARMAC PATH (MAP 62)
60
ON ROAD THEN GO STRAIGHT ON UPHILL AS ROAD BENDS LEFT
TRACK LEVELS
FIELDS
TUNNEL OF TREE AND HEDGEROW OPENS FOR VIEWS OVER ARABLE FIELDS
TRACK DESCENDS AND IS ALMOST SUNKEN
MAP 61
GO RIGHT ALONG LONG LANE
0 1/4 mile
0 APPROX SCALE 500m
067
JUST AFTER DRIVE TO COTTAGE TURN RIGHT FOLLOWING NDW SIGN
LONGLANE FARM
THROUGH GATE AND ACROSS GRASS TRACK TO LEAVE BY GATE
RIGHT ON ROAD AND OVER RAILWAY TRACK (EAST KENT RAILWAY) AND FOLLOW NDW SIGN LEFT OFF ROAD
PICNIC TABLE
TO SHEPHERDS WELL STATION, 7 MINS
62
TO FARNM
20-25 MINS FROM TARMAC PATH (MAP 62)
RAILWAY BRIDGE
25-30 MINS TO LANE (MAP 60)

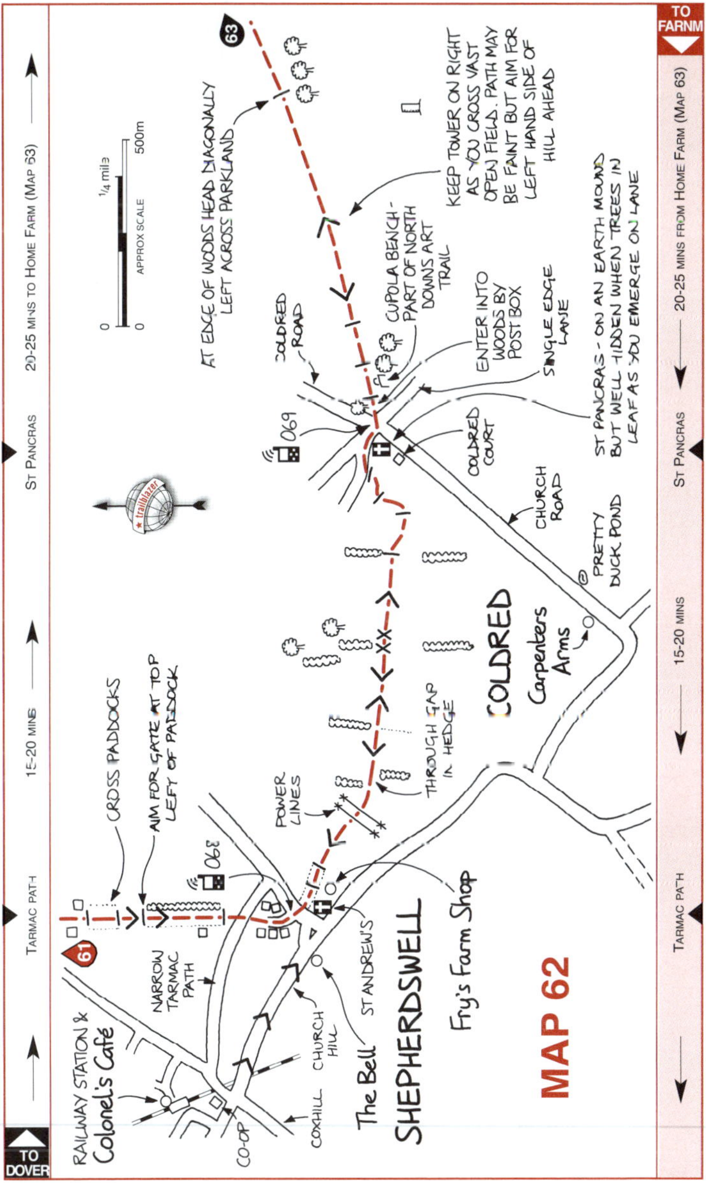

TO DOVER
TARMAC PATH
15-20 MINS
ST PANCRAS
20-25 MINS TO HOME FARM (MAP 63)
APPROX SCALE
0
1/4 mile
0
500m
trailblazer
RAILWAY STATION &
Colonel's Cafe
CO-OP
COXHILL
CHURCH HILL
NARROW TARMAC PATH
61
CROSS PADDOCKS
AIM FOR GATE AT TOP LEFT OF PADDOCK
068
POWER LINES
The Bell
SHEPHERDSWELL
ST ANDREW'S
Fry's Farm Shop
MAP 62
THROUGH GAP IN HEDGE
COLDRED
Carpenters Arms
PRETTY DUCK POND
CHURCH ROAD
COLDRED COURT
069
COLDRED ROAD
CUPOLA BENCH - PART OF NORTH DOWNS ART TRAIL
ENTER INTO WOODS BY POST BOX
SINGLE EDGE LANE
ST PANCRAS - ON AN EARTH MOUND BUT WELL HIDDEN WHEN TREES IN LEAF AS YOU EMERGE ON LANE
AT EDGE OF WOODS HEAD DIAGONALLY LEFT ACROSS PARKLAND
KEEP TOWER ON RIGHT AS YOU CROSS VAST OPEN FIELD. PATH MAY BE FAINT BUT AIM FOR LEFT HAND SIDE OF HILL AHEAD
63
TO FARNM
20-25 MINS FROM HOME FARM (MAP 63)
ST PANCRAS
15-20 MINS
TARMAC PATH

[**Shepherdswell** *cont'd from p176*] Fry's Farm Shop's target audience is more locals than hikers, but they do hot and cold drinks and snacks and have a couple of tables outside where you can sit and rest your wearying bones; given its location, this could become a major stopping post for hikers in years to come. The only pub remaining in the village is ***The Bell*** (☎ 01304-830661; bar Tue-Sun from 2pm). It doesn't do food though fish and chips are available from a mobile van on Fridays (5-6.30pm).

Note that the **railway station** is called Shepherds Well – ie two words – so bear that in mind if you are struggling to find mention of it online; it is a stop on Southeastern Railway's London Victoria to Dover Priory service (see box pp42-3). To reach it, stay on the road where it crosses the railway line (Map 61).

NORTHERN ROUTE: SHEPHERDSWELL TO DOVER [MAPS 62-66]

This last **8.6-mile/13.8km (2½hrs to 3¼hrs)** section is easy walking through park landscape and pockets of woodland with no villages en route until, before you know it, the trail descends the Roman road into Dover. Not especially thrilling, these last few miles of the North Downs Way do tend to 'dribble on' a bit but there are a couple of highlights to make the walk worthwhile, including a crossing of attractive Waldershare Park and, at its end, a lovely overgrown graveyard by an abandoned church. Glimpsing the flag flying proudly above Dover Castle for the first time is always a bit of a thrill too, as well as a sure sign that you are approaching one of the country's most historic ports – and the finale of your North Downs Way adventure.

Beginning at Shepherdswell, the trail weaves its way through undulating fields to **Coldred** (Map 62) where it's easy to miss the Church of St Pancras. Nearby, the ***Carpenters Arms*** (bar Tue-Sat from 5pm, Sun 11am-5pm) across the village green – complete with 'slow ducks crossing' sign – is a true local pub (drinks only, no food), but worth a quick look at least.

From **Waldershare Park** (Map 63) the trail climbs through **Ashley** (Map 64) to rise again to the A2 beyond **Pineham** (Map 65). A little detour ensures a safe crossing of the A2 before you begin your descent along the Roman road to **Dover**.

There'll probably be no marker, signboard, klaxon or bunting to greet your arrival, and the good citizens of Dover will doubtless be milling about the Market Square (formerly the Way's official end) shopping, mooching and completely unaware of your achievement. But don't be disappointed or downcast: just put your head down and plough on through the crowds of dawdlers, dotards and drunks, down King St and Gaol Lane (which runs past the tourist office), through the underpass to emerge at the seafront, where you'll find a metal finishing line in the pavement to mark the **official end of the North Downs Way**.

> '[Dover is] *like other sea-port towns; but really much more clean, and with less blackguard people in it than I ever observed in any sea-port before. It is a most picturesque place, to be sure*'
>
> **William Cobbett**, writing in 1823 in ***Rural Rides***

Nearby is a monument to those who've swum the channel, and a bench where you can sit surrounded by three local icons – James Bond creator Ian Fleming, who had a house further down the coast, WWII forces' sweetheart and singer, Dame Vera Lynn, and 2012 Olympic torchbearer Jamie Clark – each rendered in rusting steel. It's as good a spot as any to sit awhile and contemplate your achievement. After all, it's no small feat to have walked over 131 miles across the south-eastern corner of England – and you should feel mighty proud that you've done so.

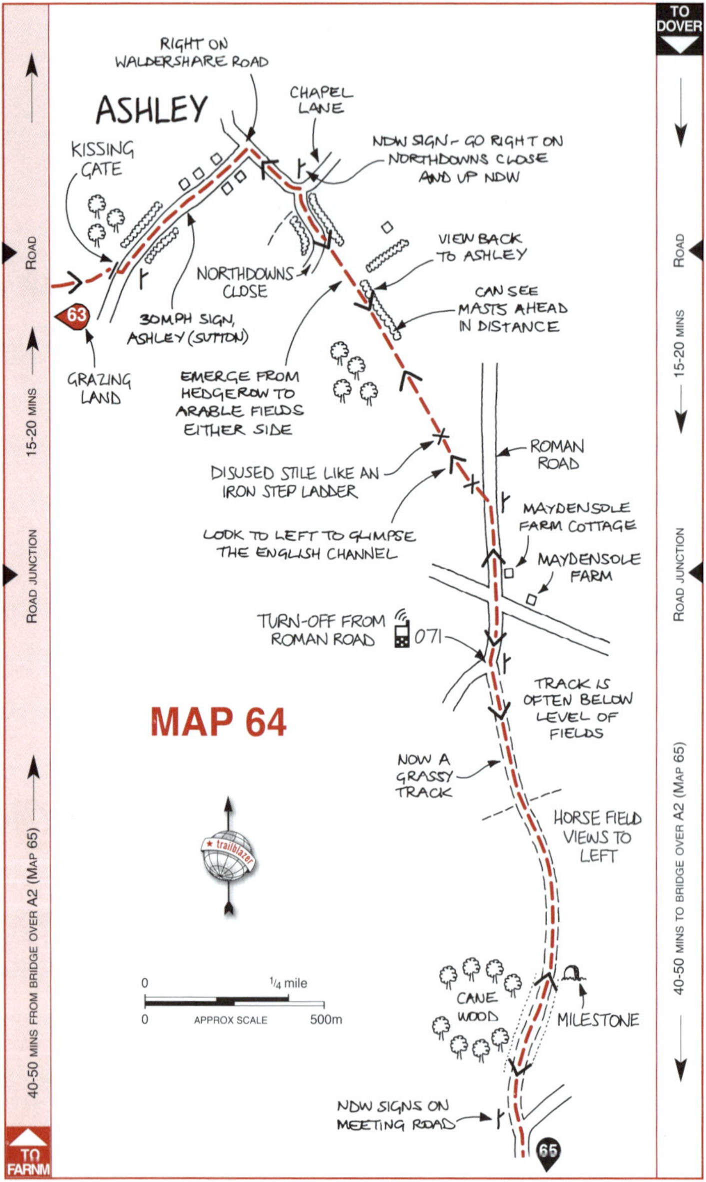

TO DOVER
ASHLEY
RIGHT ON WALDERSHARE ROAD
CHAPEL LANE
KISSING GATE
NDW SIGN – GO RIGHT ON NORTHDOWNS CLOSE AND UP NDW
VIEW BACK TO ASHLEY
NORTHDOWNS CLOSE
CAN SEE MASTS AHEAD IN DISTANCE
30MPH SIGN, ASHLEY (SUTTON)
63
GRAZING LAND
EMERGE FROM HEDGEROW TO ARABLE FIELDS EITHER SIDE
ROMAN ROAD
DISUSED STILE LIKE AN IRON STEP LADDER
MAYDENSOLE FARM COTTAGE
LOOK TO LEFT TO GLIMPSE THE ENGLISH CHANNEL
MAYDENSOLE FARM
TURN-OFF FROM ROMAN ROAD
071
TRACK IS OFTEN BELOW LEVEL OF FIELDS
MAP 64
NOW A GRASSY TRACK
HORSE FIELD VIEWS TO LEFT
trailblazer
0
1/4 mile
0
APPROX SCALE
500m
CANE WOOD
MILESTONE
NDW SIGNS ON MEETING ROAD
65
ROAD
15-20 MINS
ROAD JUNCTION
40-50 MINS FROM BRIDGE OVER A2 (MAP 65)
40-50 MINS TO BRIDGE OVER A2 (MAP 65)
TO FARNM

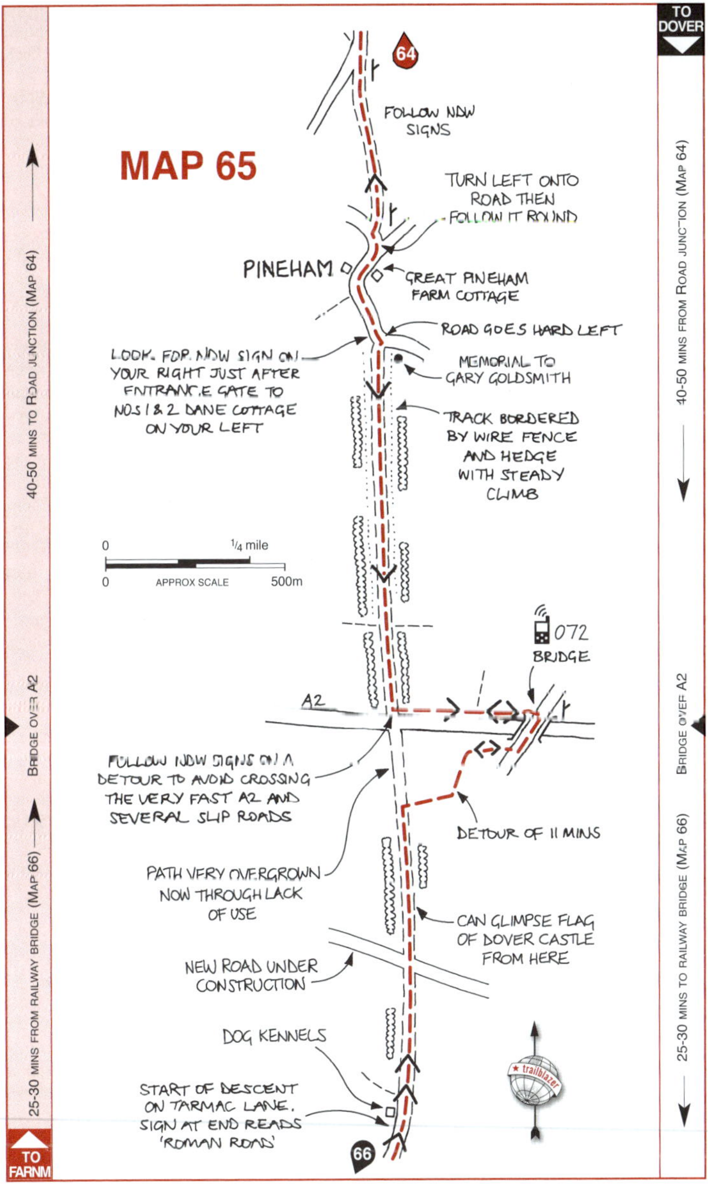
MAP 65
TO DOVER
TO FARNM
64
66
FOLLOW NDW SIGNS
TURN LEFT ONTO ROAD THEN FOLLOW IT ROUND
PINEHAM
GREAT PINEHAM FARM COTTAGE
ROAD GOES HARD LEFT
LOOK FOR NDW SIGN ON YOUR RIGHT JUST AFTER ENTRANCE GATE TO NOS 1 & 2 DANE COTTAGE ON YOUR LEFT
MEMORIAL TO GARY GOLDSMITH
TRACK BORDERED BY WIRE FENCE AND HEDGE WITH STEADY CLIMB
0 1/4 mile
0 APPROX SCALE 500m
072
BRIDGE
A2
FOLLOW NDW SIGNS ON A DETOUR TO AVOID CROSSING THE VERY FAST A2 AND SEVERAL SLIP ROADS
DETOUR OF 11 MINS
PATH VERY OVERGROWN NOW THROUGH LACK OF USE
CAN GLIMPSE FLAG OF DOVER CASTLE FROM HERE
NEW ROAD UNDER CONSTRUCTION
DOG KENNELS
START OF DESCENT ON TARMAC LANE. SIGN AT END READS 'ROMAN ROAD'
trailblazer
40-50 MINS TO ROAD JUNCTION (MAP 64)
BRIDGE OVER A2
25-30 MINS FROM RAILWAY BRIDGE (MAP 66)
40-50 MINS FROM ROAD JUNCTION (MAP 64)
BRIDGE OVER A2
25-30 MINS TO RAILWAY BRIDGE (MAP 66)

DOVER [MAP 66]

Dover struggles as a destination. People either pass through on the way to the Continent or use it as a gateway to somewhere else in England. As with any busy port town it has its fair share of life's flotsam and jetsam and after the cultural high point of Canterbury it's a disappointment. There's an impressive castle, a museum, a fine Roman house and a view of the White Cliffs but little else to keep you here long.

What to see and do

Dover Museum (💻 dovermuseum.co.uk; free; same phone and opening hours as the TIC, see Services), on Market Square in the tourist information centre, has extensive exhibits on the town's history since 1066 as well as the Bronze Age Boat Gallery, where you can see the remains of the world's oldest seagoing vessel, dating back to 1500BC.

Dover Castle (☎ 01304-211067, 💻 english-heritage.org; Apr-Sep 10am-6pm, Oct 10am-5pm, Nov & Mar Sat & Sun only 10am-4pm; £23.60) 'guardian of the gateway to England' is strategically placed on the White Cliffs of Dover. It's a prime site for English Heritage and the tours of the secret tunnels used in the Napoleonic Wars and WWII are fascinating.

The **Roman Painted House** (💻 karu .org.uk/roman_painted_house) was discovered in 1970 and is reckoned to be one of the best-preserved Roman buildings in England, largely because it was buried to make way for a new building in AD270. Over 400 sq metres of painted plaster survive. It was closed for repairs at the time of writing, but is due to reopen in Spring 2025. Phone ☎ 01304-203279 to check before visiting.

Finally, a good view of the **White Cliffs of Dover** is free from the Prince of Wales pier by the Hoverport.

'Neither Dover nor its Castle has anything of note to be said of them… and has it self an ill repaired, dangerous, and good for little harbour and peir, very chargeable and little worth.'

Daniel Defoe, writing in 1724 in ***A Tour thro' the Whole Island of Great Britain*** [note: the spelling 'mistakes' are all Defoe's!]

Services

On Market Square is the **tourist information centre** (TIC; ☎ 01304-201066, 💻 whitecliffscountry.org.uk; Mon-Sat 9.30am-5pm, Easter-Sep also Sun 10am-3pm) and some **ATMs,** conveniently located in the heart of town and right on the trail.

Before you reach the square, Boots **pharmacy** (Mon-Sat 9am-5.30pm, Sun 10am-4pm) is in Biggin St with the **post office** opposite (Mon-Tue 8am-8pm, Wed & Fri from 8.30am, Thur & Sat 8am-2pm), and a little further down is a branch of the **boot repairer** Timpson (Mon-Sat 9am-5.30pm). There's an **M&S food hall** (Mon-Sat 8am-9pm,-Sun 10am-4pm) on the southern side of St James Retail Park, with a branch of the **outdoor/hiking shop** Trespass (Mon-Sat 9am-6pm, Sun 10am-4pm) virtually next door.

Transport

Trains operated by Southeastern Railway (see box pp42-3) go from Dover Priory to London Victoria, Charing Cross and St Pancras. National Express **coach** service NX007 (see p40) operates to London via Canterbury from Pencester Rd bus station.

Stagecoach's **bus** service No 15 (to Canterbury) calls at Pencester Rd; see pp44-7. There is also a No 91 Stagecoach service to Folkestone.

Where to stay

Campers will find the closest pitch is over three miles away at ***Hawthorn Farm*** (☎ 01304-852658, 💻 keatfarm.co.uk/park/hawthorn-farm; Mar-Nov; 🐕), situated at Martin Mill, off the A258. To get there it's best to take the train to Martin Mill station (8 mins; 1-2/hr) and walk about 400m from there. Now part of the Keat Farm network of campsites, a pitch for a one-/two-man tent for walkers costs from £22.

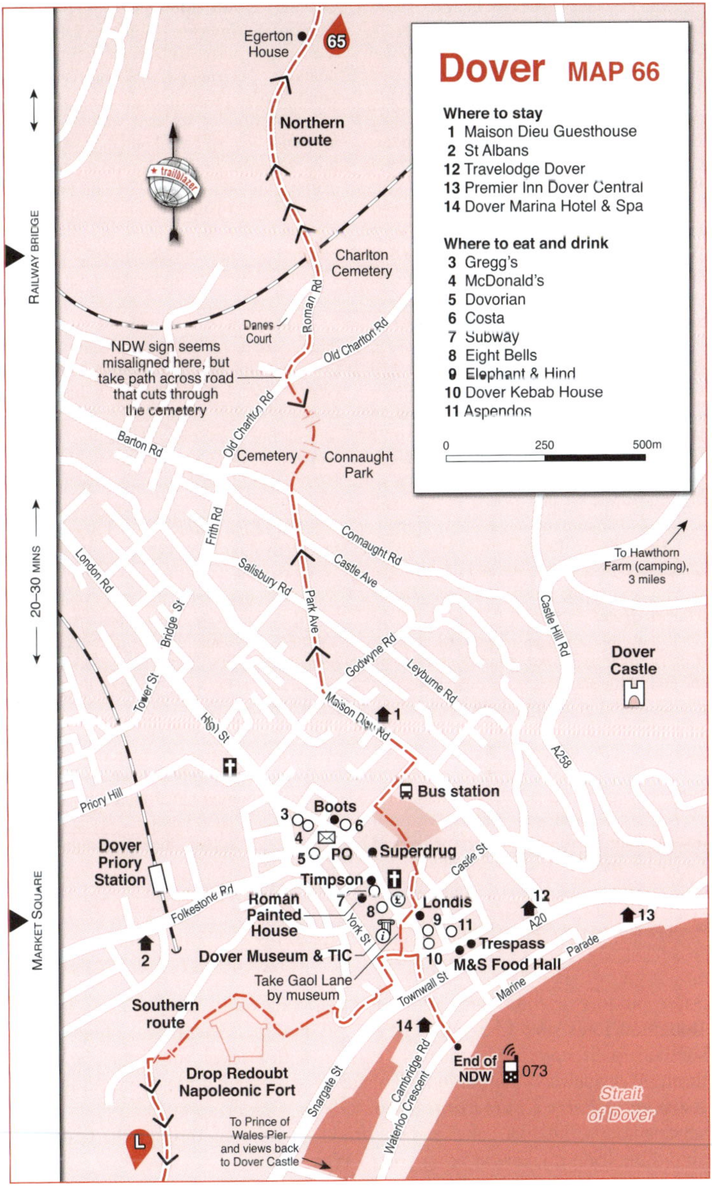
Dover MAP 66
Where to stay
1 Maison Dieu Guesthouse
2 St Albans
12 Travelodge Dover
13 Premier Inn Dover Central
14 Dover Marina Hotel & Spa
Where to eat and drink
3 Gregg's
4 McDonald's
5 Dovorian
6 Costa
7 Subway
8 Eight Bells
9 Elephant & Hind
10 Dover Kebab House
11 Aspendos
0
250
500m
Railway Bridge
20–30 mins
Market Square
Egerton House
65
Northern route
Charlton Cemetery
Roman Rd
Danes Court
Old Charlton Rd
NDW sign seems misaligned here, but take path across road that cuts through the cemetery
Barton Rd
Old Charlton Rd
Cemetery
Connaught Park
Frith Rd
Connaught Rd
Castle Ave
To Hawthorn Farm (camping), 3 miles
London Rd
Salisbury Rd
Park Ave
Castle Hill Rd
Bridge St
Godwyne Rd
Leyburne Rd
Dover Castle
Tower St
Maison Dieu Rd
High St
A258
Bus station
Priory Hill
Boots
Superdrug
PO
Dover Priory Station
Castle St
Timpson
Folkestone Rd
Roman Painted House
Londis
York St
Trespass
A20
Dover Museum & TIC
M&S Food Hall
Parade
Take Gaol Lane by museum
Townwall St
Marine
Southern route
Drop Redoubt Napoleonic Fort
End of NDW
073
Snargate St
Cambridge Rd
Waterloo Crescent
Strait of Dover
To Prince of Wales Pier and views back to Dover Castle
L
Route Guide and Maps

In Dover itself, the best budget options in town are the branches of ***Travelodge*** (☎ 08719 846532, 🖳 travelodge.co.uk; 108 en suite rooms; ☕; 🐕) on St James St and ***Premier Inn Dover Central*** (☎ 0333 777 4649, 🖳 premierinn.com; 126 en suite rooms; ☕) on Marine Parade. Both advertise rooms starting at £35, and the Premier Inn has sea views from most rooms.

Walking into town on the trail, after turning left into Maison Dieu Rd, there is the walker-friendly ***Maison Dieu Guesthouse*** (☎ 01304-204033, 🖳 maisondieu.co.uk; 1S/2D/1T/2D, T or Tr, all en suite or with private facilities; Mar-Dec) charges £26-38pp (sgl from £45, sgl occ room rate) for room only. Breakfast is £10 extra.

St Albans Guest House (book via 🖳 booking.com; 2S/5D/2T, all en suite) at 71 Folkestone Rd is closest to the railway station. Room rates are £38-51.50pp (sgl £56-76). Breakfast is only served in the main season and costs extra.

Smartest of the lot, however – and a great place to celebrate the end of your hike if you're feeling flush – is the ***Dover Marina Hotel & Spa*** (☎ 01304-20633, 🖳 dovermarinahotel.co.uk; 4S/64D/15T/15D, T or Tr, all en suite; ☕; Mar-Dec), right by the end of the trail. Part of the Best Western chain, rates start at around £80 for a single, £50pp for a double or twin, though both rates are highly variable.

Where to eat and drink

Dover is not a culinary centre. The town does have its fair share of representatives of the international and national chains, including ***Costa*** (Mon-Sat 8am-6pm, Sun 9am-5pm), ***Subway*** (Mon-Sat 7am-8pm, Sun 8am-7pm), ***McDonald's*** (open 24 hours) and ***Greggs*** (Mon-Sat 6am-7pm, Sun 8.30am-3.30pm).

For simple no-frills cafeteria-style food supplied by a local outlet, try the spotless ***Dovorian*** (**fb**; Mon-Sat 8.30am-3.30pm) on Worthington St. The Formica-topped tables fill up fast at lunch-time when the blue-rinse brigade descend for large portions of their breakfast wrap (£4.50). They also run a chippy (Mon-Sat 11am-3pm) where cod costs £8.30.

There are a few **pubs**. For evening dining, you can't get a more central venue than the 18th century ***Elephant & Hind*** (☎ 01304-215654, 🖳 elephantandhind.com; food daily from 11am) on Market Square, serving home-cooked pub classics such as burgers (from £12.99) and pizza (from £9.99) using locally sourced ingredients where possible.

The Eight Bells (☎ 01304-205030; food daily 8am-11pm) at 19 Cannon St, is a Wetherspoon's with good-value food served throughout the day and evening.

For finer fare, ***Aspendos*** (☎ 01304-268647, 🖳 aspendosdover.co.uk; daily noon-10pm) is a highly regarded Turkish restaurant at 12 King St (*mezze* from £5, lamb shish kebab from £13) with a takeaway and delivery service.

If only a late-night **takeaway** will hit the spot, ***Dover Kebab House*** (☎ 01304-784803, 🖳 dover-kebab-house.com; Mon, Wed & Thur-Sat 4-11pm, Fri & Sat to 2am, Tue closed) is the most convenient for Market Square.

SOUTHERN ROUTE: BOUGHTON LEES TO ETCHINGHILL [MAP 49, p157 & MAPS A-G]

After bidding a fond farewell to the northern route shortly after leaving Boughton Lees, the **13.3 mile/21.5km (4½hrs to 5½hrs) first stage** of the southern path starts off mundanely enough with a level, unspectacular tramp through agricultural fields, though there is a pleasant little **farm shop** with **tearoom** at ***Perry Court Farm*** (Map A; 🖳 perrycourt.farm; daily 8am-6pm), serving soups, quiches, cakes and hot drinks. Continuing through the fields and across the train tracks will bring you to **Wye**.

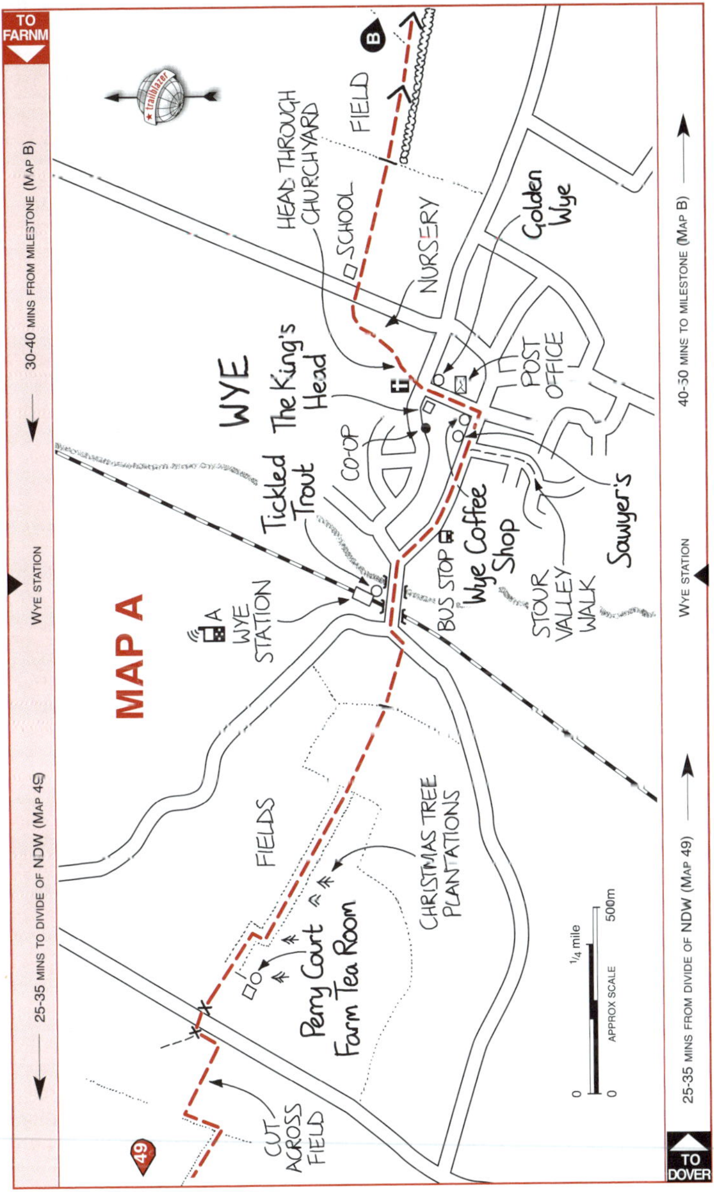
TO FARNM
MAP A
30-40 MINS FROM MILESTONE (MAP B)
WYE STATION
25-35 MINS TO DIVIDE OF NDW (MAP 49)
40-30 MINS TO MILESTONE (MAP B)
WYE STATION
25-35 MINS FROM DIVIDE OF NDW (MAP 49)
TO DOVER
B
49
WYE
HEAD THROUGH CHURCHYARD
FIELD
SCHOOL
NURSERY
Golden Wye
POST OFFICE
The King's Head
CO-OP
Tickled Trout
Wye Coffee Shop
BUS STOP
Sawyer's
STOUR VALLEY WALK
A WYE STATION
FIELDS
CHRISTMAS TREE PLANTATIONS
Perry Court Farm Tea Room
CUT ACROSS FIELD
0
¼ mile
0
500m
APPROX SCALE

❑ THE CHALLENGES OF THE SOUTHERN ROUTE

Perhaps one reason why this southern route tends to be less popular is owing to the lack of facilities en route. Apart from some accommodation near the start (but off the path) at **Brabourne** (see p190), there is only one B&B that's convenient for the route – at **Etchinghill** (see p194), about 13 miles from Boughton Lees.

True, you could drop the 2 miles from Etchinghill into **Folkestone**. There is a bus service (see pp44-7), but if you choose to walk, bear in mind that it is a steep 2-mile descent from the trail; plus, of course, you then have an equally steep *ascent* back to the trail again the next morning. Another option is to drop down off the trail at **Postling** (see p193), about 11¼ miles into the trail from Boughton Lees, to catch a bus.

If none of those options appeal then your only choice is to walk the entire section from Boughton Lees to Dover (24.3 miles/39.1km) in one day – which is possible, though an early start and a high level of fitness are essential.

Food, thankfully, is in more plentiful supply, with a farm shop just a few minutes into the walk, plenty of options in Wye (including a supermarket, for those who want to construct a picnic), and a few pubs and cafés spaced along the trail leading into Dover.

WYE [MAP A, p187]

Wye is a lovely and fairly large village that's home to some useful services and places to eat, all within a few metres of the trail. There is a **post office** (Mon-Fri 9am-1pm & 2-4.30pm, Sat 9am-12.30pm) and a Co-op **supermarket** (daily 7am-10pm).

The village has a wonderful **café**, ***Wye Coffee Shop*** (☎ 01233-812452, 💻 wyecoffee.co.uk; Mon 8.30am-3pm, Tue-Fri 8.30am-4pm, Sat 9am-4pm, Sun 10am-3pm, kitchen closes 1hr earlier; 🐕). ***Wye Wholefoods*** (💻 wyewholefoods.co.uk; Wed-Fri 8.30am-2pm, Sat to 12.30pm) is a shop that also sells homemade soup, rolls and cakes. There is also a **Chinese restaurant and takeaway** (***Golden Wye***: ☎ 01233-811871; Sun-Thur noon-1.30pm & 5-10pm, Fri & Sat to 10.30pm).

The trail also takes you past the front door of a decent pub, the beautifully situated ***Tickled Trout*** (☎ 01233-812227, 💻 thetickledtrout.co.uk; food served summer daily noon-2.30pm & 5-7.45pm, Sat noon-8pm, Sun noon-5pm; winter hours vary; 🐕) with a varied menu including chicken lemon linguine (£21) as well as familiar pub classics. Down the road, next to the café, bohemian micro-pub ***Sawyers*** (☎ 01233-812452, 💻 sawyersbar.co.uk; Wed & Thur 6-10pm, Fri 5-11pm, Sat 2-11pm, Sun 5-8pm) doesn't serve food but packs in the punters nonetheless by focusing on local ales, beers, ciders and wines.

On Church St, **The King's Head** was closed at the time of writing but was recently bought by Contemporary Pubs with plans to reopen in 2025.

Wye **railway station** is a stop on the London Charing Cross to Ramsgate service operated by Southeastern Railway; see box pp42-3. Stagecoach's No 14 **bus** service (see pp44-7) from Ashford calls here.

It's after Wye that the scenery truly grows more majestic, reaching fairly spectacular heights at **Wye Crown** (Map B), a crown etched into the chalk on the hills overlooking the village, which was carved into the ground by local schoolchildren in 1902 to celebrate the accession of Edward VII to the throne. Further delights await just a few minutes further along at the **Devil's Kneading Trough**, a sheer-sided valley and part of Wye National Nature Reserve, which is home to no fewer than 21 different species of orchid.

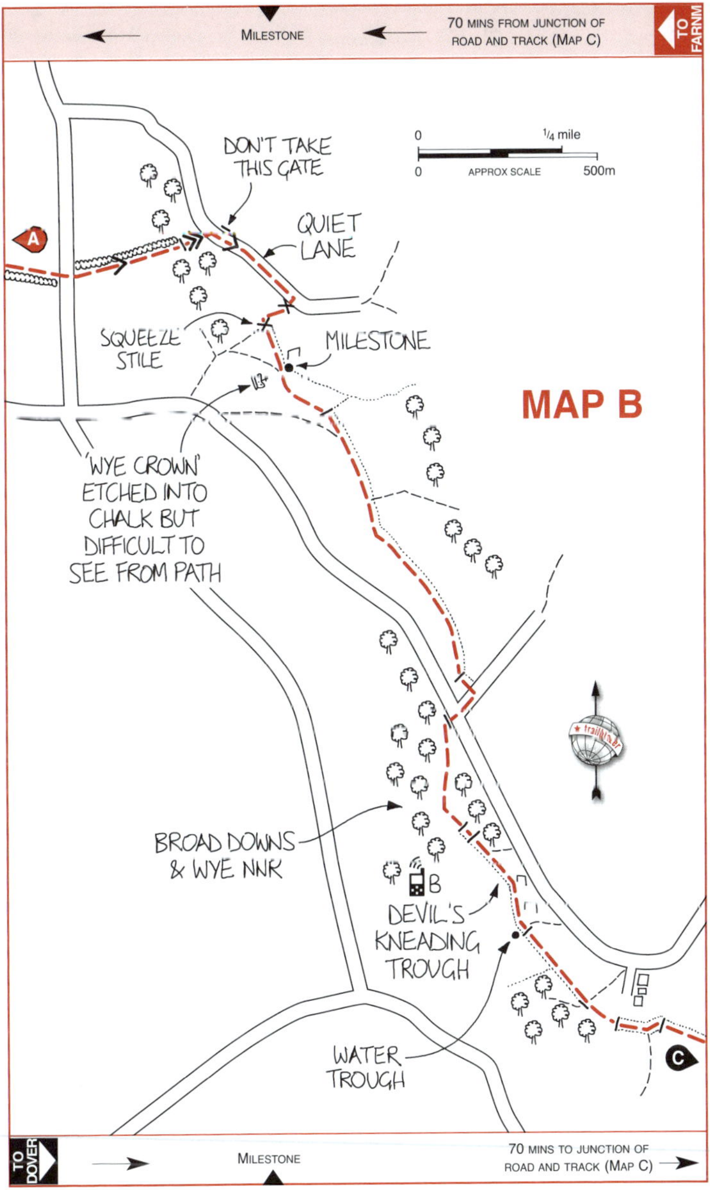
MILESTONE
70 MINS FROM JUNCTION OF ROAD AND TRACK (MAP C)
TO FARNM
0 1/4 mile
0 APPROX SCALE 500m
DON'T TAKE THIS GATE
QUIET LANE
A
SQUEEZE STILE
MILESTONE
MAP B
'WYE CROWN' ETCHED INTO CHALK BUT DIFFICULT TO SEE FROM PATH
BROAD DOWNS & WYE NNR
B
DEVIL'S KNEADING TROUGH
WATER TROUGH
C
TO DOVER
MILESTONE
70 MINS TO JUNCTION OF ROAD AND TRACK (MAP C)

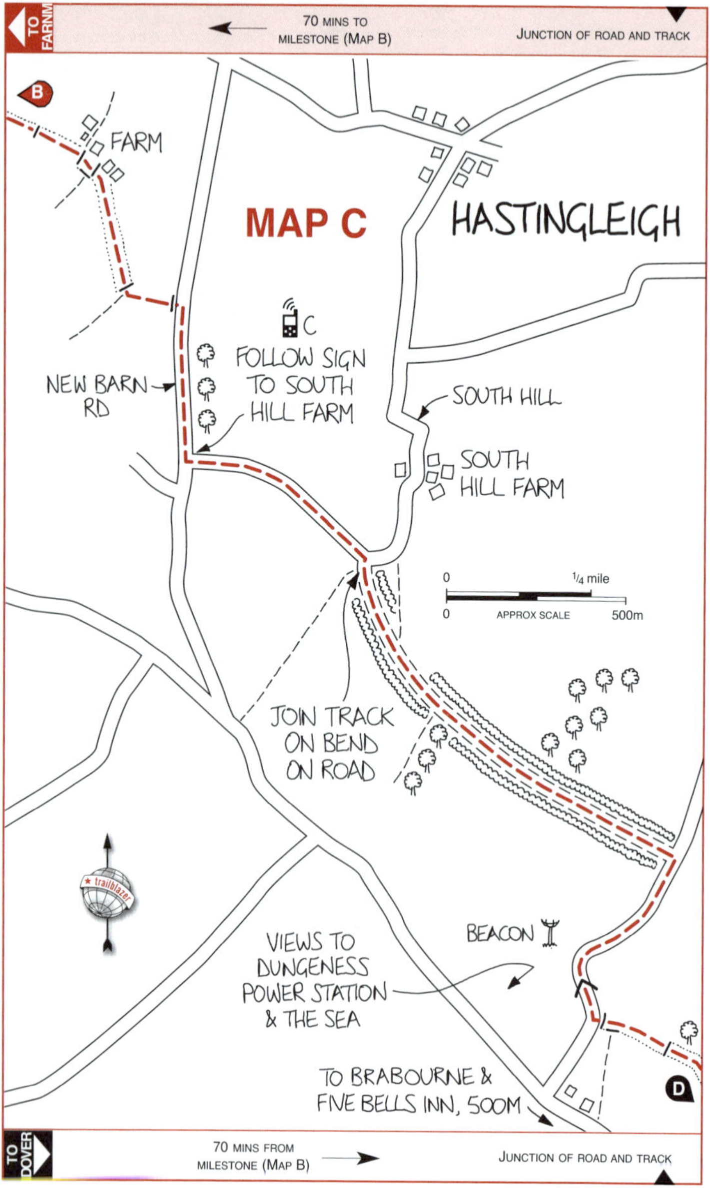

TO FARNM
70 MINS TO MILESTONE (MAP B)
JUNCTION OF ROAD AND TRACK
B
FARM
MAP C
HASTINGLEIGH
C
FOLLOW SIGN TO SOUTH HILL FARM
NEW BARN RD
SOUTH HILL
SOUTH HILL FARM
0
1/4 mile
0
APPROX SCALE
500m
JOIN TRACK ON BEND ON ROAD
trailblazer
BEACON
VIEWS TO DUNGENESS POWER STATION & THE SEA
TO BRABOURNE & FIVE BELLS INN, 500M
D
TO DOVER
70 MINS FROM MILESTONE (MAP B)
JUNCTION OF ROAD AND TRACK

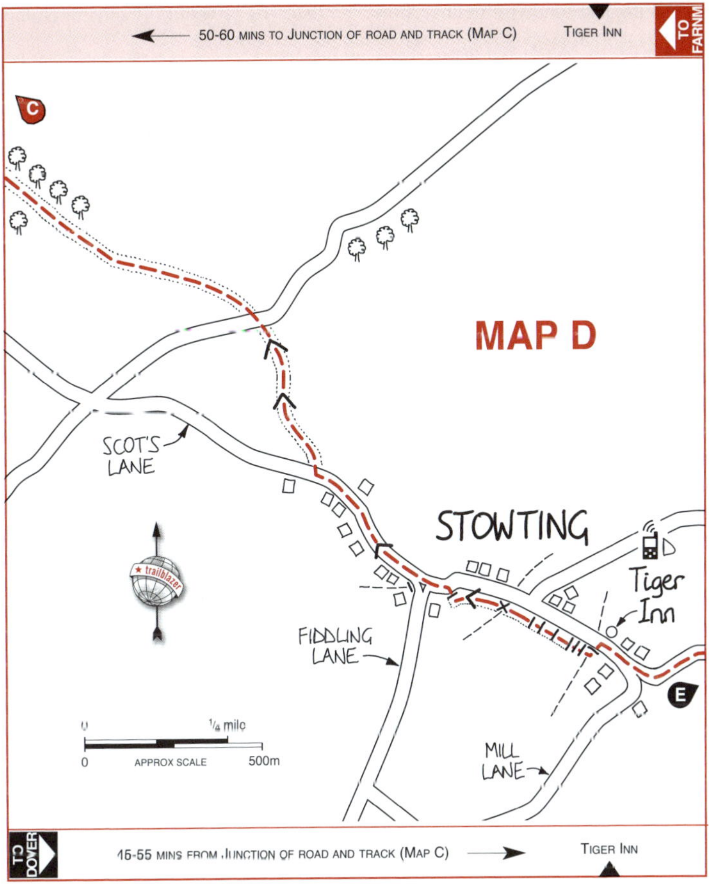

A lengthy stretch of roadside rambling follows, leavened in part by your first views of the **English Channel** (Map C) and, in the distance to your right, the thin spit of land that is Dungeness, with the nuclear-power plant on its tail. Off the path to the south in **Brabourne** there is a pub with rooms.

BRABOURNE **[off MAP C]**

For **accommodation**, about a kilometre off the path are the four luxury suites at the 16th-century ***Five Bells Inn*** (☎ 01303-813334, 💻 fivebellsbrabourne.co.uk; 4D en suite; ☕; 🐕; from £90pp in high season, sgl occ full room rate). They also serve **food** every day (breakfast Mon-Sat 9-11am; Mon-Sat noon-3pm, Sun noon-5pm; evening Mon-Thur 5-9pm, Fri & Sat to 9.30pm), with smart mains from £19, including ribeye steak (from £36.50).

If it's just food you're after, however, then you're better off staying on the path as it soon takes you on down to the pub at **Stowting**.

STOWTING **[MAP D, p191]**

Usefully right on the trail, the secluded ***Tiger Inn*** (☎ 01303-862130, 🖳 tigerinn.co.uk; food Mon-Fri noon-2.30pm & 6-9pm, Sat noon-3pm & 6-9pm, Sun noon-5pm) has lunchtime sandwiches from £10-13.

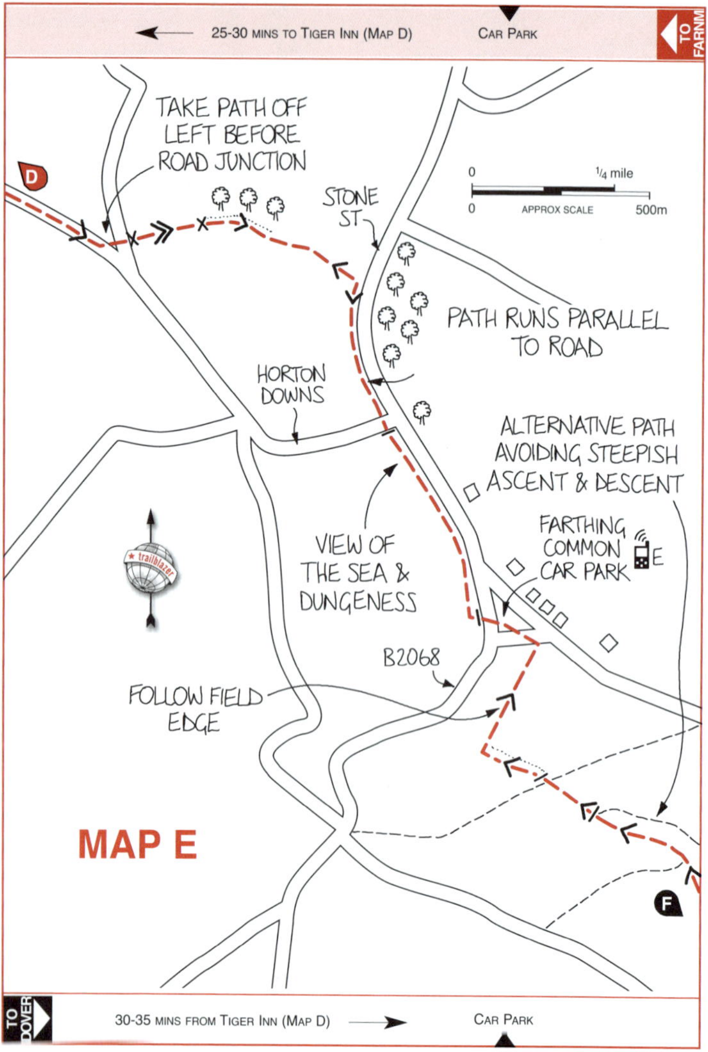

You've got a lot of hard walking to do before you reach the shoreline, however, as the trail meanders through more farmland. Do pause awhile, however, as some of the views are lovely, particularly from the bench, **Heather's Resting Place**, overlooking **Postling** (Map F).

This is also where those who have decided to stay in **Canterbury** (see p166-72) must leave the trail to catch the **No 18 bus** which runs about five times a day (except Sunday; 50 mins), returning via the same bus the next day. The bus leaves from the junction of Sandling Rd and Cuckoo Lane, about three-quarters of a mile from the trail itself.

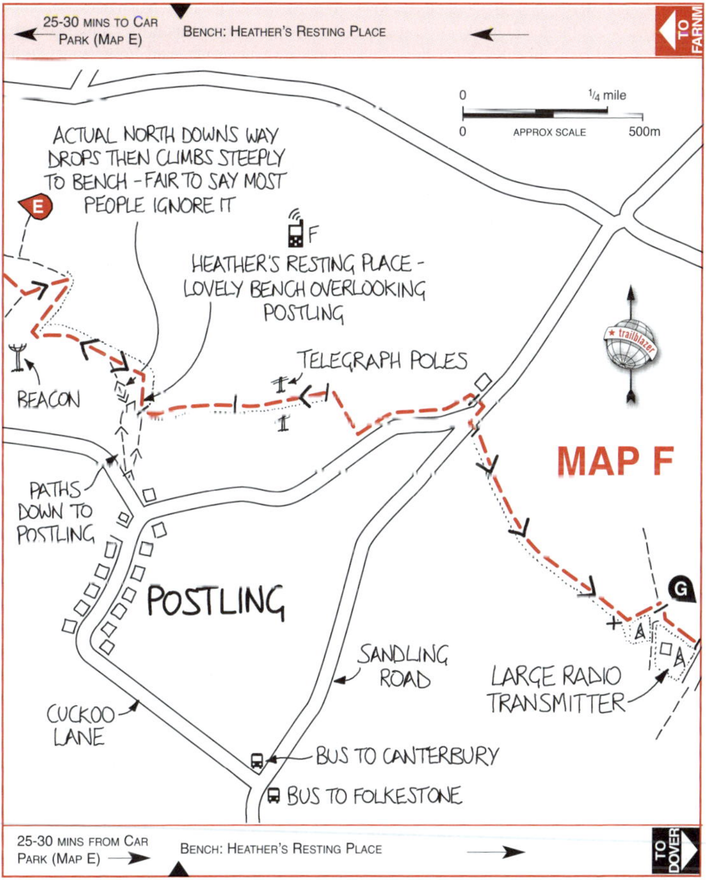

Just over 13 miles into the southern route, it passes, to the north of the trail, the small cluster of houses known as **Etchinghill** (Map G) where you can stay, eat or catch a bus to Folkestone.

ETCHINGHILL [MAP G]

The interest for walkers actually lies to the south of the village, for it's here you'll find ***Beachborough Park*** (☎ 07496 428613, 🖳 beachboroughpark.org.uk; 4D/1T en suite; 🐕), where the rooms are housed in a converted barn looking out on a garden courtyard. For those wanting to divide this trail into two equal parts you won't find a better place. Although it's on a busy road the helpful owners are happy to pick up walkers from the trail (and drop them off the next morning) for free. Room rates are around the £45-50pp mark (sgl occ full room rate). Though the only food they do is a continental breakfast in the morning for guests, their local, ***The Gatekeeper Inn*** (☎ 01303-864345, 🖳 gatekeeperinn.co.uk), serves evening meals (Mon-Sat 11am-8.45pm, Sun noon-6pm) with mains for £14-20; or you can always order a take out from one of the many eateries in Folkestone.

Stagecoach's **bus** no 17 runs regularly between Canterbury and Folkestone, stopping by the Gatekeeper Inn.

SOUTHERN ROUTE: ETCHINGHILL TO DOVER [MAPS G-L & MAP 66, p185]

From Etchinghill this **11-mile/17.6km final stage (4¼hrs to 5hrs)** begins with a climb up to the Folkestone Downs, an SSSI, and on around the outskirts of **Folkestone** itself, with the cacophony of the Eurotunnel train terminus immediately beneath you. Folkestone can be reached from the trail via a footpath, though it's a steep 2-mile downhill trudge, which means of course an equally steep 2-mile *uphill* trudge to return to the North Downs Way.

If it's just a bite to eat that you're after, we recommend instead keeping to the trail round the unusual cliff-edge mound hiding the remnants of **Folkestone Castle** (believed to be Norman in origin, dating from approximately the 12th century), known locally, if inaccurately, as **Caesar's Camp** (Map H) and on past its neighbour, the rutted, conical hill of **Sugar Loaf** (Map I) next door (thought to have once been a pagan religious centre around 4000 years ago), towards **Capel-le-Ferne**.

CAPEL-LE-FERNE [MAP I, p197]

There are several options for sustenance strung out along the path here.

The ***Valiant Sailor*** (☎ 07707 836089, 🖳 thevaliantsailor.co.uk; food Wed-Sun noon-2.30pm & 4.30-8pm) marks the point where the path reaches the sea (or rather, the cliff tops above the sea), a point that you can celebrate with one of their 'posh fish butties & chips' (£9).

Alternatively, carry on for another 15 minutes or so to the **Battle of Britain Memorial** (🖳 battleofbritainmemorial.org; Mar-Sep 10am-5pm, Oct-Feb to 4pm), a great place to rest, peruse the exhibits (most of which are free) and take advantage of their good value ***Cockpit Café*** (10am-4.30pm). The café serves sandwiches and paninis but limited hot food, so for a more satisfying fill-up, continue for a further 15 minutes along the coast to the dog-friendly ***Cliff Top Café*** (☎ 01303-901687; Tue-Sun 10am-4pm; 🐕) serving a fair range of breakfasts, doorstop sandwiches, burgers and hot dogs.

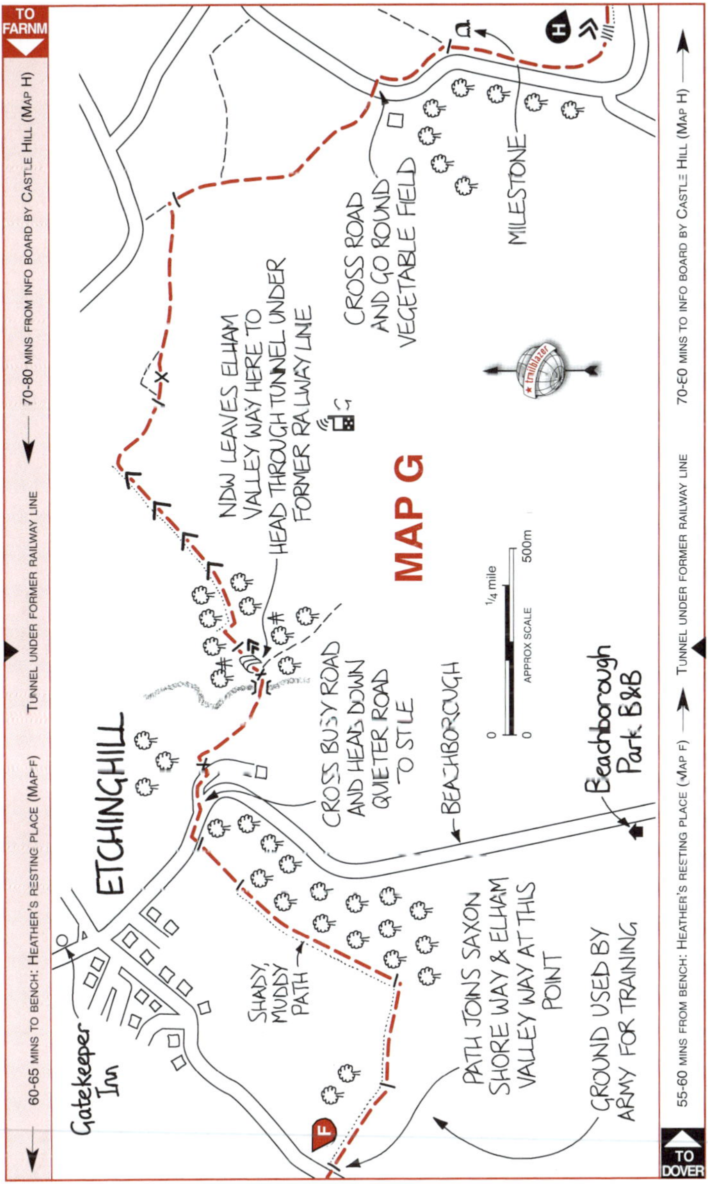
TO FARNM
60-65 MINS TO BENCH: HEATHER'S RESTING PLACE (MAP F)
TUNNEL UNDER FORMER RAILWAY LINE
70-80 MINS FROM INFO BOARD BY CASTLE HILL (MAP H)
Gatekeeper Inn
ETCHINGHILL
SHADY, MUDDY PATH
PATH JOINS SAXON SHORE WAY & ELHAM VALLEY WAY AT THIS POINT
GROUND USED BY ARMY FOR TRAINING
CROSS BUSY ROAD AND HEAD DOWN QUIETER ROAD TO STILE
BEACHBOROUGH
Beachborough Park B&B
0
0
APPROX SCALE
1/4 mile
500m
MAP G
NDW LEAVES ELHAM VALLEY WAY HERE TO HEAD THROUGH TUNNEL UNDER FORMER RAILWAY LINE
trailblazer
CROSS ROAD AND GO ROUND VEGETABLE FIELD
MILESTONE
F
H
55-60 MINS FROM BENCH: HEATHER'S RESTING PLACE (MAP F)
TUNNEL UNDER FORMER RAILWAY LINE
70-80 MINS TO INFO BOARD BY CASTLE HILL (MAP H)
TO DOVER

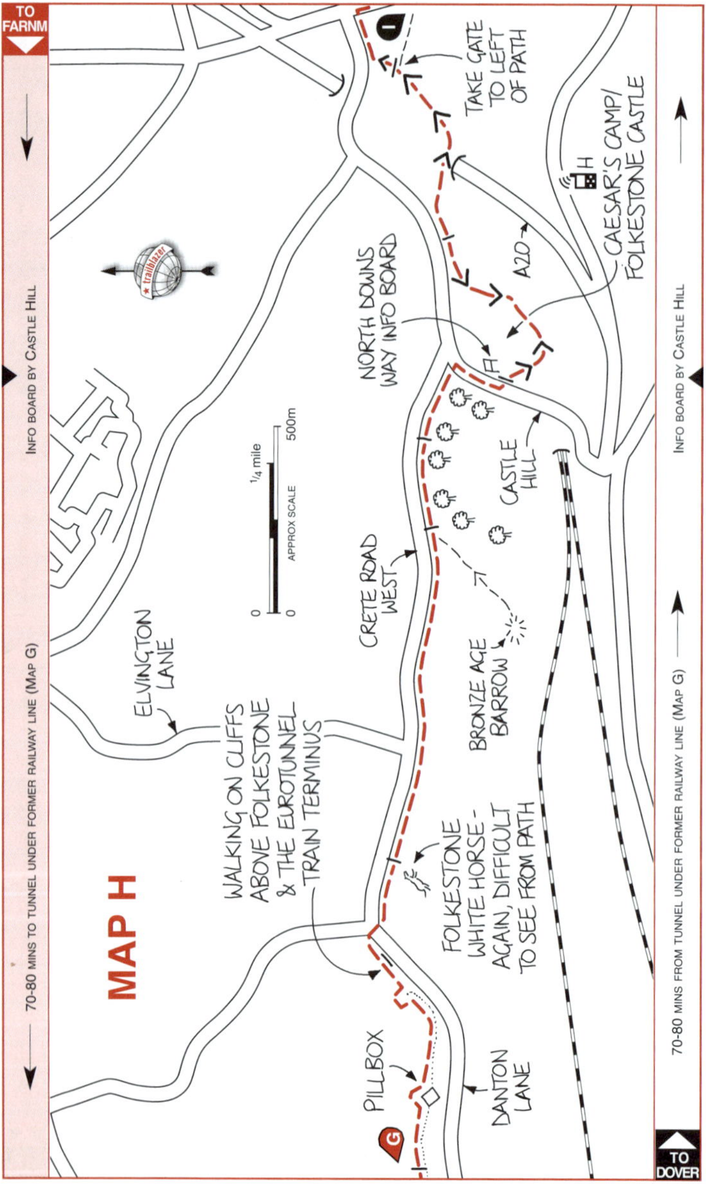
MAP H
TO FARNM
TO DOVER
70-80 MINS TO TUNNEL UNDER FORMER RAILWAY LINE (MAP G)
70-80 MINS FROM TUNNEL UNDER FORMER RAILWAY LINE (MAP G)
INFO BOARD BY CASTLE HILL
INFO BOARD BY CASTLE HILL
trailblazer
APPROX SCALE
0
1/4 mile
0
500m
PILLBOX
DANTON LANE
WALKING ON CLIFFS ABOVE FOLKESTONE & THE EUROTUNNEL TRAIN TERMINUS
ELVINGTON LANE
FOLKESTONE WHITE HORSE - AGAIN, DIFFICULT TO SEE FROM PATH
CRETE ROAD WEST
BRONZE AGE BARROW
CASTLE HILL
NORTH DOWNS WAY INFO BOARD
A20
CAESAR'S CAMP/ FOLKESTONE CASTLE
TAKE GATE TO LEFT OF PATH
G
I

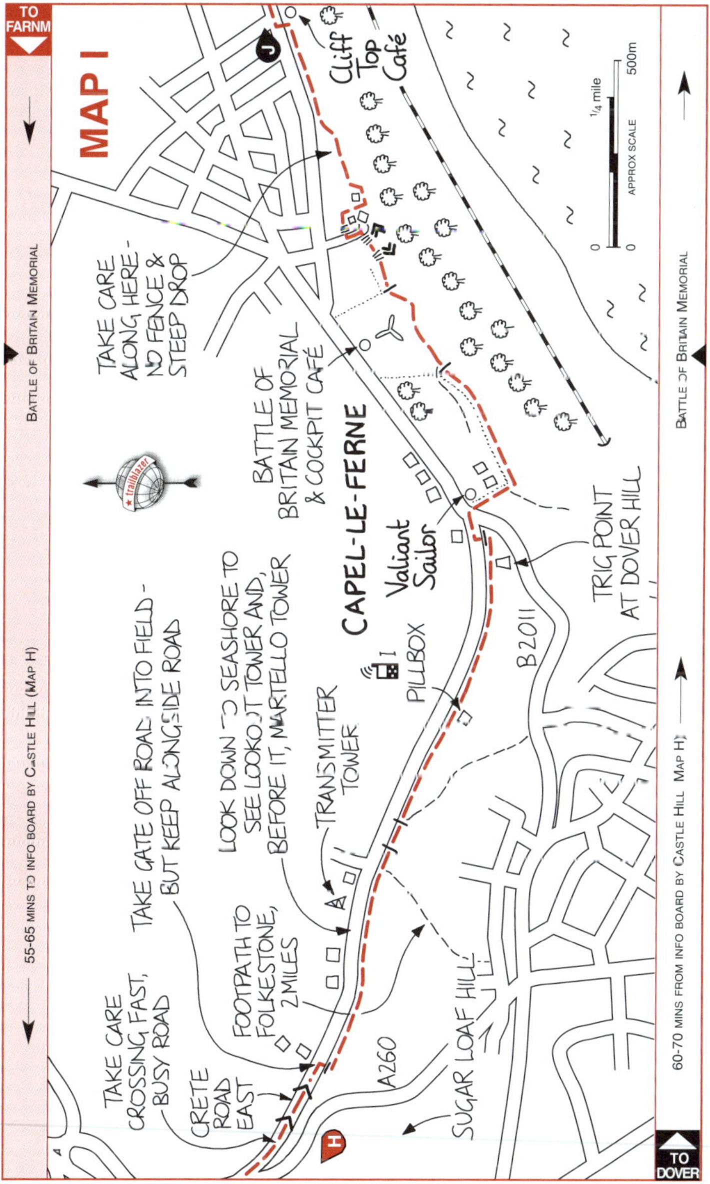
MAP I
TO FARNM
BATTLE OF BRITAIN MEMORIAL
55-65 MINS TO INFO BOARD BY CASTLE HILL (MAP H)
J
Cliff Top Café
TAKE CARE ALONG HERE - NO FENCE & STEEP DROP
BATTLE OF BRITAIN MEMORIAL & COCKPIT CAFÉ
CAPEL-LE-FERNE
Valiant Sailor
TRIG POINT AT DOVER HILL
B2011
PILLBOX
TRANSMITTER TOWER
LOOK DOWN TO SEASHORE TO SEE LOOKOUT TOWER AND, BEFORE IT, MARTELLO TOWER
TAKE GATE OFF ROAD INTO FIELD - BUT KEEP ALONGSIDE ROAD
FOOTPATH TO FOLKESTONE, 2 MILES
TAKE CARE CROSSING FAST, BUSY ROAD
CRETE ROAD EAST
A260
SUGAR LOAF HILL
H
0
1/4 mile
0
500m
APPROX SCALE
BATTLE OF BRITAIN MEMORIAL
60-70 MINS FROM INFO BOARD BY CASTLE HILL (MAP H)
TO DOVER

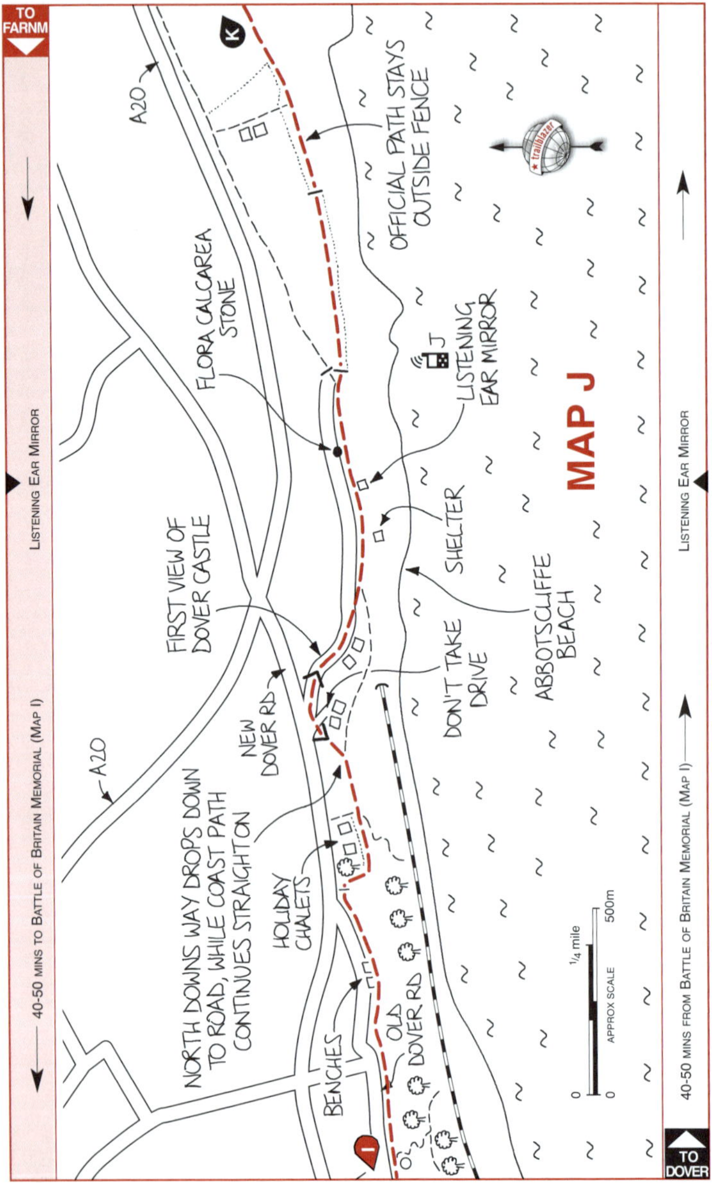
TO FARNM
40-50 MINS TO BATTLE OF BRITAIN MEMORIAL (MAP I)
LISTENING EAR MIRROR
A20
A20
NORTH DOWNS WAY DROPS DOWN TO ROAD, WHILE COAST PATH CONTINUES STRAIGHTON
NEW DOVER RD
FIRST VIEW OF DOVER CASTLE
FLORA CALCAREA STONE
BENCHES
HOLIDAY CHALETS
OLD DOVER RD
DON'T TAKE DRIVE
SHELTER
LISTENING EAR MIRROR
J
OFFICIAL PATH STAYS OUTSIDE FENCE
K
I
ABBOTSCLIFFE BEACH
MAP J
trailblazer
1/4 mile
500m
APPROX SCALE
0
0
40-50 MINS FROM BATTLE OF BRITAIN MEMORIAL (MAP I)
LISTENING EAR MIRROR
TO DOVER

The clifftop walking begins in earnest now as, accompanied for most of its length by its fellow national trail, the England Coast Path, the North Downs Way soars above the Channel atop the famed **White Cliffs of Dover**.

After several exhilarating miles of this the path finally drops, heads inland and crosses the A20 via an underpass to negotiate the outskirts of Dover. What initially seems like an uninteresting route soon proves to be anything but as the trail leads you via the **foundations of a small medieval chapel** (Map L) built,

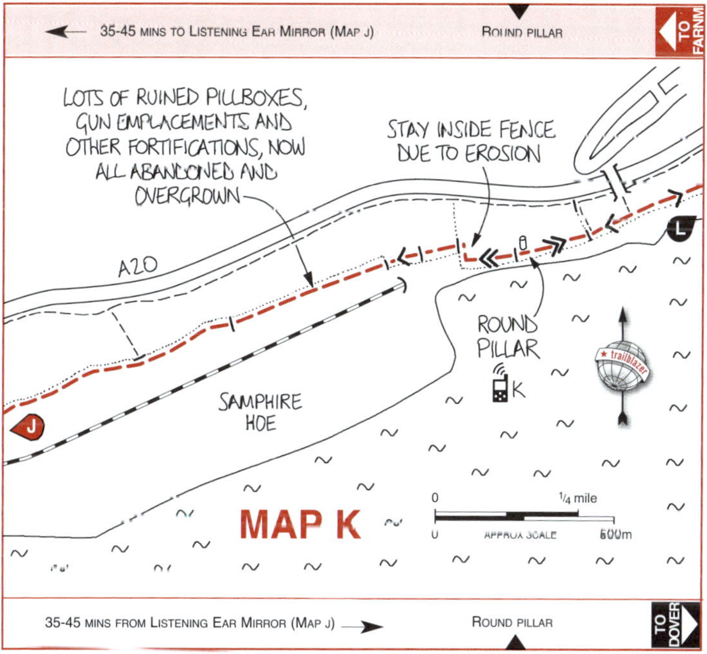

❑ CLIFFS HAVE EARS ...

As you join the England Coast Path, look to your right and if the day is clear you should be able to discern the chalky undulations of the French coast across the Channel. It perhaps comes as little surprise, therefore, to find these last few miles dotted with various pillboxes, gun emplacements and other fortifications. Most striking of all, perhaps, is the '**Listening Ear Mirror**' (Map J; also known as Abbot's Cliff sound mirror), a large square concrete construction, concave on one side, that was built between the wars to act as an early warning system: the shape of the mirror allowing those who stand beneath it to detect the noise of approaching enemy planes from afar. Though several are still standing, they never actually saw active service – radar was brought in soon after and proved a much more reliable and precise system.

possibly, by the Knights Templar, as well as two huge Napoleonic Forts, the second of which, the **Drop Redoubt**, is mightily impressive, particularly when viewed from the trail which passes above it. From here it's a mere tumble down the hill to **Dover** town centre (see pp184-6), from where you can turn left to the main square and the tourist office; or right towards the seafront and the **official end of the North Downs Way**.

It's a lovely ending, to a lovely, lovely walk.

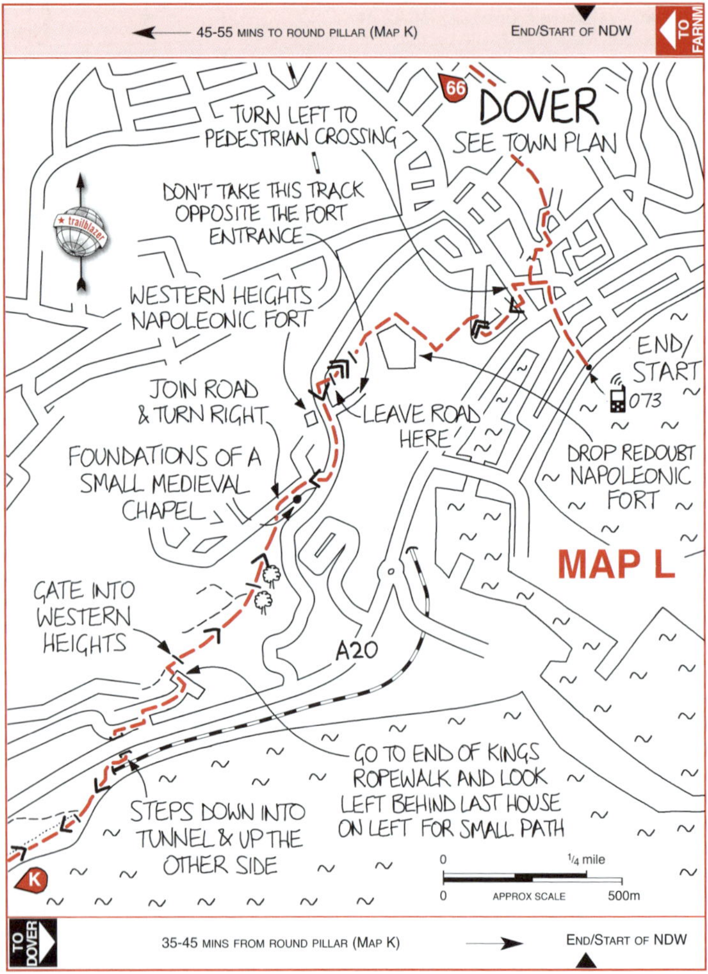

APPENDIX A: GPS & WHAT3WORDS WAYPOINTS

Each waypoint below was taken on the route at the reference number marked on the maps in the route guide. **GPS coordinates** and **what3words references** that correspond to these waypoints are listed here and may be particularly useful in an emergency (see p52). Gpx files for waypoints can be downloaded from 🖳 trailblazer-guides.com.

WAYPOINT & GRID REFERENCE	DESCRIPTION	WHAT3WORDS REFERENCE
001 N51° 12.771' W0° 47.621'	Western end of NDW	///magpie.squaring.comic
002 N51° 13.007' W0° 44.421'	Bridge off road	///cone.washed.frog
003 N51° 13.236' W0° 42.944'	Turn-off to Seale	///tamed.noses.puppy
004 N51° 13.318' W0° 40.087'	The Good Intent at Puttenham	///blazed.eggshell.roadblock
005 N51° 13.218' W0° 37.856'	Junction near Watts Gallery	///greyhound.crowds.duet
006 N51° 13.503' W0° 34.603'	Turn-off after bridge to Guildford	///myself.stow.traded
007 N51° 13.490' W0° 31.779'	St Martha's Church	///zones.upset.frogs
008 N51° 13.894' W0° 30.491'	Path to Countryside Centre, Newlands Cnr	///atom.earth.closer
009 N51° 13.833' W0° 27.918'	Hollister Cottage	///pits.nights.flats
010 N51° 13.757' W0° 27.547'	Turn-off to Shere	///hats.tribe.length
011 N51° 13.963' W0° 26.479'	First large concrete bowl	///parks.landed.edgy
012 N51° 13.991' W0° 23.744'	Turn-off to the right off path	///cares.tools.nearly
013 N51° 14.466' W0° 21.789'	Junction in Ranmore Common	///punch.civic.luxury
014 N51° 15.180' W0° 19.372'	Underpass under A24	///rice.salon.mouth
015 N51° 15.385' W0° 15.707'	Path leaves road north of Betchworth Stn	///admits.stews.losses
016 N51° 15.394' W0° 12.988'	Water tower	///lame.guises.gets
017 N51° 15.362' W0° 11.535'	Car park and snack bar	///fresh.basin.food
018 N51° 15.617' W0° 10.745'	Stonehenge-like slabs	///visit.joins.courier
019 N51° 15.902' W0° 09.185'	Quality St, Merstham	///cheat.harsh.hook
020 N51° 16.058' W0° 06.050'	Whitehill Tower	///sizes.estate.pounds
021 N51° 15.658' W0° 05.061'	Finger post, Gravelly Hill	///props.race.cried
022 N51° 15.935' W0° 03.312'	Entrance to Marden Park & Church Woods	///error.pepper.cheese
023 N51° 16.236' W0° 00.980'	Chalk Pit Lane to Oxted	///pack.upon.purely
024 N51° 17.098' E0° 01.477'	Mole End	///crops.such.clear
025 N51° 17.050' E0° 03.886'	A233	///maple.basis.deputy
026 N51° 17.539' E0° 05.003'	Gate by telegraph pole	///lazy.ruled.rents
027 N51° 18.111' E0° 06.054'	Stile after Melrose	///lonely.wheels.riches
028 N51° 18.702' E0° 07.697'	Turn-off to Knockholt Pound	///slate.lodge.bonus
029 N51° 18.785' E0° 11.273'	Otford Heritage Centre	///jeeps.metals.crop
030 N51° 18.761' E0° 13.844'	Turn-off to Kemsing	///jukebox.unit.quiet
031 N51° 18.932' E0° 15.618'	Milestone	///cure.bottle.couches
032 N51° 18.661' E0° 18.715'	Path behind some public bins	///filled.loose.family
033 N51° 18.847' E0° 19.793'	Hognore Farmhouse	///full.stuck.drops

WAYPOINT & GRID REFERENCE	DESCRIPTION	WHAT3WORDS REFERENCE
034 N51° 19.491' E0° 20.327'	Turn-off for Trosley Country Park	///will.appear.linen
035 N51° 19.803' E0° 23.369'	Turn-off to Ryarsh	///remit.happen.lush
036 N51° 20.710' E0° 23.775'	Fork right over barrier	///diary.smiled.mash
037 N51° 21.175' E0° 24.084'	Signpost to Sole Street Station	///income.lasted.bats
038 N51° 22.727' E0° 26.861'	Bridge over railway	///alive.gifts.ship
039 N51° 22.861' E0° 28.140'	Speed memorial on A228	///fields.behind.taken
040 N51° 21.958' E0° 29.249'	Nashenden Farm	///mice.thick.tops
041 N51° 20.251' E0° 29.213'	Robin Hood pub	///gifted.parent.mouse
042 N51° 19.192' E0° 30.184'	Kit's Coty	///smoker.eliminate.debut
043 N51° 18.895' E0° 30.892'	White Horse Stone	///edgy.downsize.royally
044 N51° 18.854' E0° 31.786'	Into woods after power lines	///paramedic.reprints.pile
045 N51° 17.639' E0° 35.460'	Thurnham Castle	///summit.backhand.steadier
046 N51° 16.971' E0° 37.912'	Turn-off to viewpoint	///matchbox.synthetic.confused
047 N51° 16.092' E0° 38.611'	Join road in Hollingbourne	///loss.exile.verb
048 N51° 14.946' E0° 41.564'	Pilgrim's bench	///strutting.evidently.expansion
049 N51° 14.647' E0° 43.249'	Lenham turn-off	///impresses.apricot.additives
050 N51° 14.213' E0° 45.057'	Sign to Highbourne Park	///brew.deranged.upholds
051 N51° 12.901' E0° 48.003'	Charing turn-off	///isolating.cooks.pads
052 N51° 12.722' E0° 48.448'	Lonebarn Farm	///scrubber.ejects.chambers
053 N51° 11.796' E0° 50.950'	Dunn Street Farm Camping	///continues.relay.alarming
054 N51° 11.472' E0° 54.121'	North Downs Way divides ...	///skylights.dabbled.hungry

Northern route to Dover via Canterbury

055 N51° 11.773' E0° 54.566'	All Saints Church	///blogs.player.traps
056 N51° 13.272' E0° 55.942'	NDW milestone	///curbed.hoops.jolt
057 N51° 14.682' E0° 57.755'	St Mary's, Chilham	///chopper.language.vies
058 N51° 15.826' E0° 59.862'	Under railway	///shapeless.expansion.curry
059 N51° 15.975' E1° 00.681'	Road junction by Hatch Farm	///unloading.kilts.released
060 N51° 16.874' E1° 03.821'	Take underpass to London Rd	///statue.bottle.maps
061 N51° 16.743' E1° 04.858'	Canterbury Cathedral	///fuels.fears.strike
062 N51° 15.357' E1° 08.076'	Roundabout at Patrixbourne	///hills.deeds.bedding
063 N51° 14.689' E1° 08.097'	Gate above A2	///printing.promises.dives
064 N51° 13.411' E1° 09.402'	Gate by drive to Ileden Farm	///vehicle.hopefully.parent
065 N51° 12.675' E1° 11.312'	Signpost in Womenswold	///handyman.hitters.overtones
066 N51° 12.439' E1° 11.859'	Woolage Village	///takers.refutes.dorms
067 N51° 11.696' E1° 14.091'	Turn-off by pebbledash cottage	///pixies.sheds.dares
068 N51° 11.105' E1° 14.162'	Cross road in Shepherdswell	///loosens.hospitals.unpainted

WAYPOINT & GRID REFERENCE	DESCRIPTION	WHAT3WORDS REFERENCE
069 N51° 10.943' E1° 15.247'	Coldred Road	///sums.clip.stiffly
070 N51° 11.253' E1° 17.108'	Gate into overgrown churchyard	///teachers.leave.cheerily
071 N51° 10.779' E1° 18.594'	Turn-off from Roman road	///sizes.eradicate.spaceship
072 N51° 09.046' E1° 19.169'	Bridge over A2	///only.learns.stump
073 N51° 07.333' E1° 18.916'	Eastern end of the NDW	///adapt.unscrew.judges

Southern route to Dover via Etchinghill and the coast

A	N51° 11.094' E0° 55.744'	Wye Station	///vowel.grouping.prepares
B	N51° 10.165' E0° 58.325'	Devil's Kneading Trough	///fingertip.endings.drainage
C	N51° 09.442' E0° 59.212'	Sign for South Hill Farm	///frame.slides.adjusting
D	N51° 07.955' E1° 01.751'	Tiger Inn, Stowting	///teach.arose.spark
E	N51° 07.345' E1° 03.079'	Car park	///detained.streamers.rated
F	N51° 06.785' E1° 03.870'	Heather's resting place	///dolphin.overlook.vibrating
G	N51° 06.583' E1° 06.278'	Tunnel under former railway	///stung.rental.lateral
H	N51° 05.867' E1° 09.632'	Caesar's Camp/Castle Hill	///loaders.vessel.elbowing
I	N51° 05.815' E1° 11.474'	Pillbox	///sediment.skidding.ambushed
J	N51° 06.103' E1° 14.618'	Listening ear mirror	///sprinting.bashed.trader
K	N51° 06.544' E1° 17.049'	Round pillar	///layered.pheasants.thatched
073	N51° 07.333' E1° 18.916'	Eastern end of the NDW	///adapt.unscrew.judges

APPENDIX B: TAKING A DOG

WALKING THE WAY WITH A DOG

Many are the rewards that await those prepared to make the extra effort required to bring their best friend along the trail. But you shouldn't underestimate the amount of work involved. Indeed, just about every decision you make will be influenced by the fact that you've got a dog: how you plan to travel to the start of the trail, where you'll stay, how far you'll walk each day, where you'll rest and where you're going to eat in the evening etc.

If you're sure your dog can cope with (and will *enjoy*) walking 10 miles or more a day for several days in a row, you need to start preparing accordingly. Extra thought needs to go into your itinerary. The best starting point is to study the Town & village facilities table on pp28-31 (and the advice below), and plan where to stop and where to buy food.

Looking after your dog

To begin with, you need to make sure that your dog is fully **inoculated** against the usual doggy illnesses, and also up to date with regard to **worm pills** (eg Drontal) and **flea preventatives** such as Frontline – they are, after all, following in the pawprints of many a dog before them, some of whom may well have left fleas or other parasites on the trail that now lie in wait for their next meal to arrive. **Pet insurance** is also a very good idea; if you've already got insurance, do check that it will cover a trip such as this. On the subject of your dog's health, perhaps the most important implement you should take is a **tick**

remover, available from vets. Although fiddly, this will help you to remove the tick safely (ie without leaving its head behind buried under the dog's skin). Being in unfamiliar territory also makes it more likely that you and your dog could become separated. All dogs must now be **microchipped** but make sure your dog also has a **tag with your contact details on it** (a mobile phone number would be best if you are carrying one with you).

When to keep your dog on a lead

• **On cliff tops** It's a sad fact that, every year, a few dogs lose their lives falling over the edge of the cliffs. It usually occurs when they are chasing rabbits (which know where the cliff-edge is and are able, unlike your poor pooch, to stop in time). This point is particularly relevant if you opt for the Southern Route (pp186-200) which culminates in a lengthy stretch of cliff-top rambling before Dover.

• **When crossing farmland**, particularly in the lambing season (March to May) when your dog can scare the sheep, causing them to lose their young. Farmers are allowed by law to shoot at and kill any dogs that they consider are worrying their sheep. During lambing, most farmers would prefer it if you didn't take your dog at all. The exception is if your dog is being attacked by cows. Some years ago there were three deaths in the UK caused by walkers being trampled as they tried to rescue their dogs from the attentions of cattle. The advice in this instance is to let go of the lead, head speedily to a position of safety (usually the other side of the field gate or stile) and call your dog to you.

• **On National Trust land**, where it is compulsory to keep your dog on a lead.

• **Around ground-nesting birds** It's important to keep your dog under control when crossing an area where certain species of birds nest on the ground. Most dogs love foraging around in the woods but make sure you have permission to do so; some woods are used as 'nurseries' for game birds and dogs are only allowed through them if they are on a lead.

What to take

You've probably already got a good idea of what to bring to keep your dog alive and happy, but the following is a checklist:

I always leave an exterior pocket of my rucksack empty so I can put used poo bags in there (to deposit at the first bin encountered). I always like to keep all the dog's kit together and separate from the other luggage (usually inside a plastic bag inside my rucksack). I have also seen several dogs sporting their own 'doggy rucksack', so they can carry their own food, water, poo etc – which certainly reduces the burden on their owner.

• **Food/water** Remember to bring treats as well as regular food to keep up the mutt's morale. That said, if your dog is anything like mine the chances are they'll spend most of the walk dining on rabbit droppings and sheep poo anyway.

• **Food/water bowl** Foldable cloth bowls are light and take up little room in the rucksack. You can get also get a water-bottle-and-bowl combination, where the bottle folds into a 'trough' from which the dog can drink.

• **Bedding** A simple blanket may suffice, or you can opt for something more elaborate if you aren't carrying your own luggage.

• **A favourite toy** Helps prevent your dog from pining for the entire walk.

• **Lead and collar** An extendable lead is probably preferable for this sort of trip. Make sure both lead and collar are in good condition – you don't want either to snap on the trail, or you may end up carrying your dog through sheep fields until a replacement can be found.

• **Corkscrew stake** Available from camping or pet shops, to keep your dog secure in one place while you set up camp/doze.

• **Medication** If required.

• **Tick remover** See above.

• **Poo bags** Essential.

• **Hygiene wipes** For cleaning your dog after it's rolled in stuff.

• **Raingear** It can rain!

• **Old towels** For drying your dog.

Cleaning up after your dog

It is extremely important that dog owners behave in a responsible way when walking the path. Dog excrement should be cleaned up. In towns, villages and fields where animals graze or which will be cut for silage, hay etc, you need to pick up and bag the excrement.

Staying (and eating) with your dog

In this guide we have used the symbol 🐕 to denote where a place welcomes dogs. However, this always needs to be arranged in advance and some places may charge extra. Many B&B-style places have only one or two rooms suitable for people with dogs; hostels (both YHA and independent) do not permit them unless they are an assistance (guide) dog; smaller campsites tend to accept them, but some of the larger holiday parks do not – however, in either case it is likely the dog will have to be on a lead. Before you turn up always double check whether the place you would like to stay accepts dogs and whether there is space for them. When it comes to eating, some cafés accept dogs and most landlords allow dogs in at least a section of their pubs, though few restaurants do. Make sure you always ask first and ensure your dog is on a lead and secured to your table or a radiator so it doesn't run around.

Henry Stedman

INDEX

Page references in **bold red** type refer to maps

TRAILBLAZER TITLE LIST

Adventure Cycle-Touring Handbook
Adventure Motorcycling Handbook
Australia by Rail
Cleveland Way (British Walking Guide)
Coast to Coast (British Walking Guide)
Cornwall Coast Path (British Walking Guide)
Cotswold Way (British Walking Guide)
The Cyclist's Anthology

Dales Way (British Walking Guide)
Dorset & Sth Devon Coast Path (British Walking Gde)
Exmoor & Nth Devon Coast Path (British Walking Gde)
Glyndŵr's Way (British Walking Guide)
Great Glen Way (British Walking Guide)
Hadrian's Wall Path (British Walking Guide)
Himalaya by Bike – a route and planning guide
Iceland Hiking – with Reykjavik City Guide

Inca Trail, Cusco & Machu Picchu
Japan by Rail
Kilimanjaro – the trekking guide (includes Mt Meru)
London Loop (British Walking Guide)
London to Walsingham Camino
Madeira Walks – 37 selected day walks
Moroccan Atlas – The Trekking Guide
Morocco Overland (4x4/motorcycle/mountainbike)
Nepal Trekking & The Great Himalaya Trail

Norfolk Coast Path & Peddars Way (British Walking Gde)
North Downs Way (British Walking Guide)
Offa's Dyke Path (British Walking Guide)
Overlanders' Handbook – worldwide driving guide
Pembrokeshire Coast Path (British Walking Guide)
Pennine Way (British Walking Guide)
Peru's Cordilleras Blanca & Huayhuash – Hiking/Biking
Pilgrim Pathways: 1-2 day walks on Britain's sacred ways
The Railway Anthology

The Ridgeway (British Walking Guide)
Scottish Highlands – Hillwalking Guide
The Silk Roads – a route and planning guide
Sinai – the trekking guide
South Downs Way (British Walking Guide)
Thames Path (British Walking Guide)
Tour du Mont Blanc
Trans-Canada Rail Guide
Trans-Siberian Handbook

Trekking in the Everest Region
The Walker's Anthology
The Walker's Anthology – further tales
West Highland Way (British Walking Guide)

For more information about Trailblazer and our expanding range of guides, for guidebook updates or for credit card mail order sales visit our website:

trailblazer-guides.com

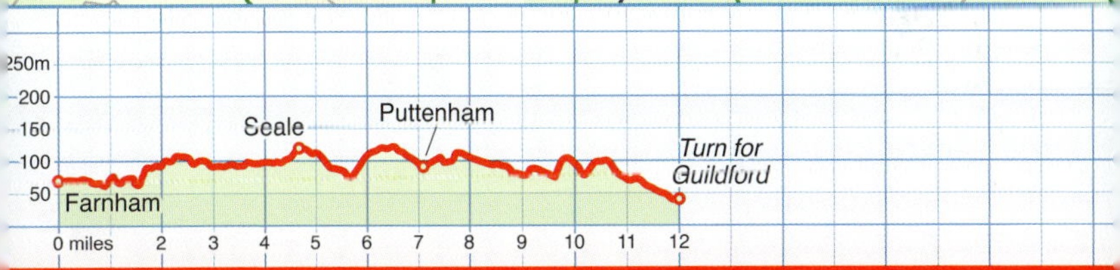

Maps 1-6
Farnham to Guildford

12 miles/19.3km – 3¾hrs-5hrs

NOTE: Add 20-30% to these times to allow for stops

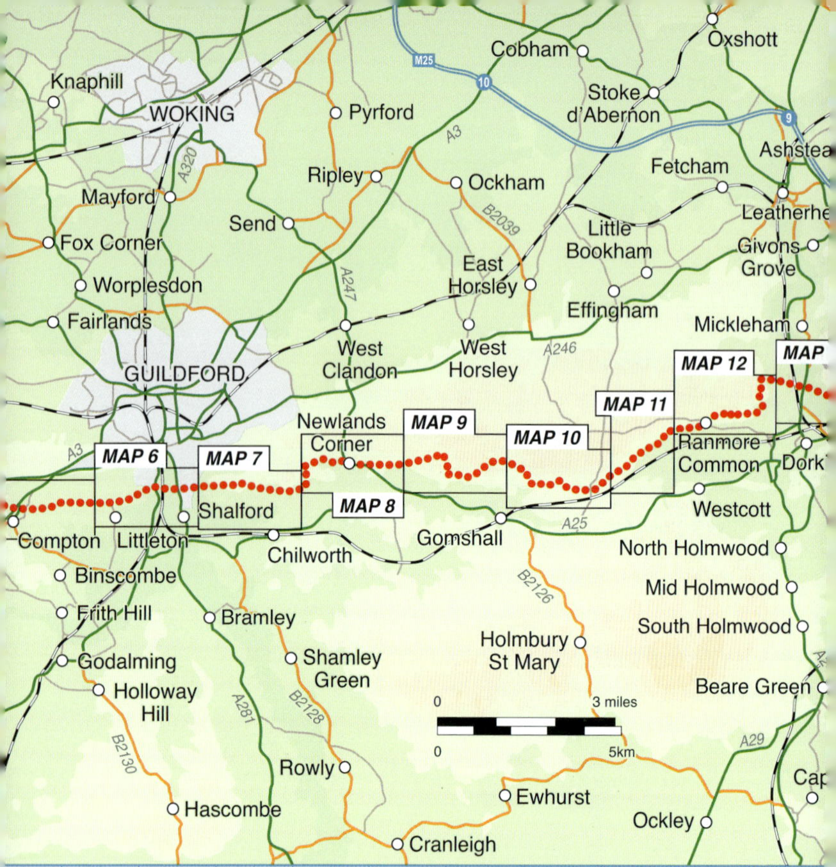

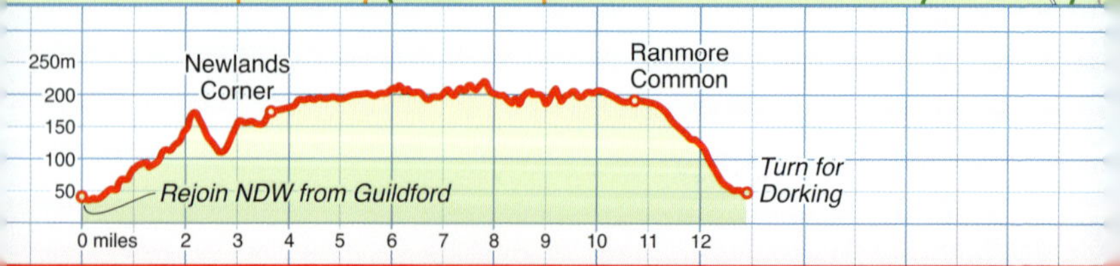

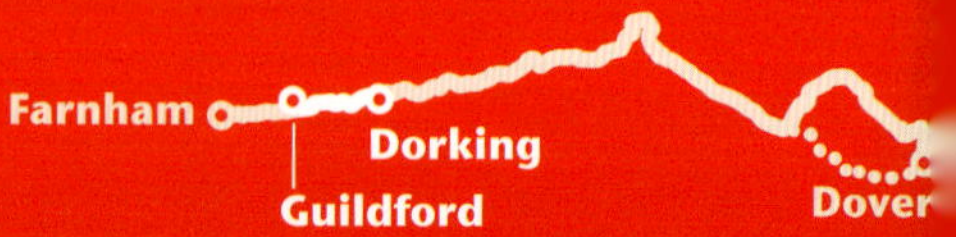

Maps 6-13
Guildford to Dorking

12.9 miles/20.7km – 4¼hrs-5¼hrs

NOTE: Add 20-30% to these times to allow for stops

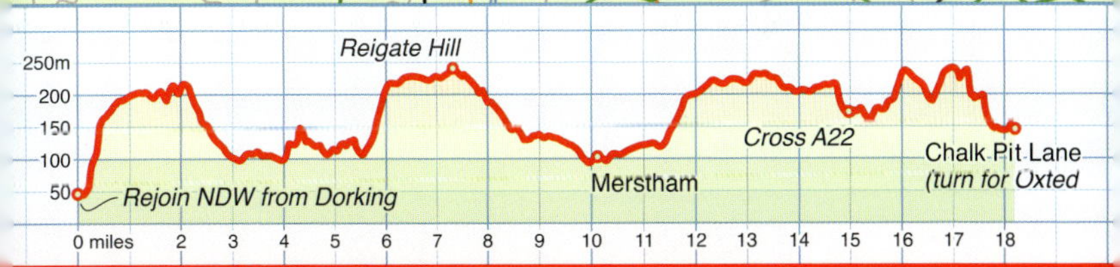

Maps 13-21
Dorking to Oxted

18.2 miles/29.4km – 4¾hrs-6¾hrs

NOTE: Add 20-30% to these times to allow for stops

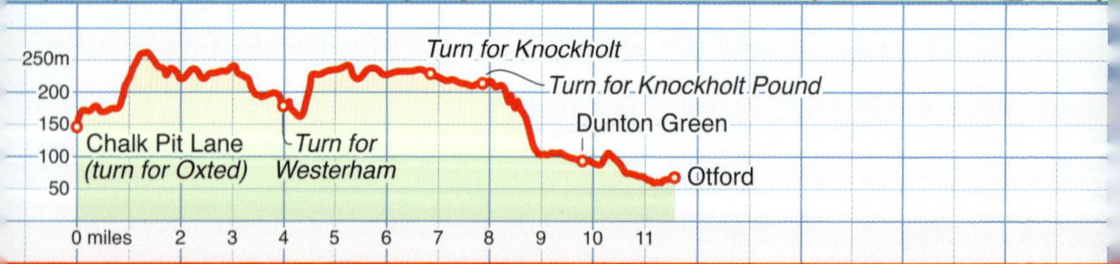

Maps 21-26

Oxted (Chalk Pit Lane) to Otford

11.6 miles/18.6km – 3¾hrs-5¼hrs

NOTE: Add 20-30% to these times to allow for stops

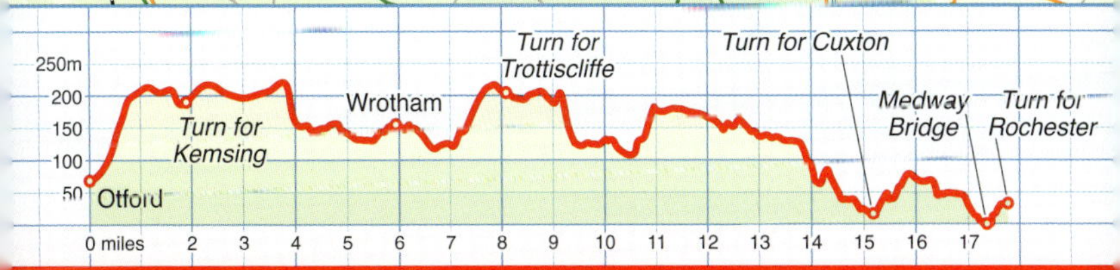

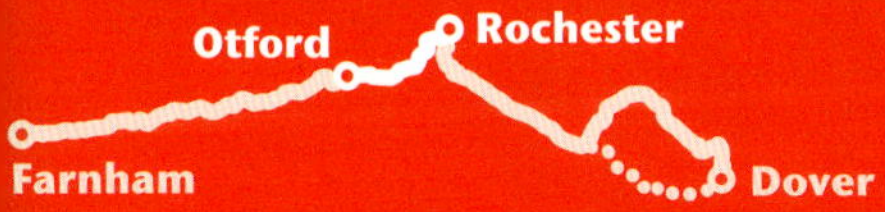

Maps 26-36

Otford to Rochester

17.8 miles/28.6km – 5¼hrs-6¾hrs

NOTE: Add 20-30% to these times to allow for stops

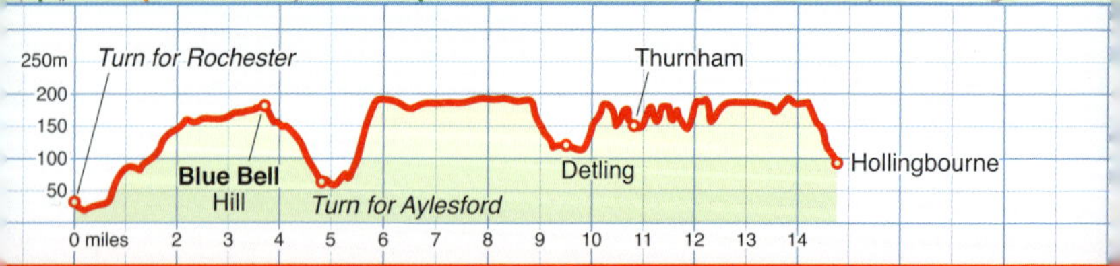

Maps 36-42

Rochester to Hollingbourne

14.8 miles/23.8km – 4½hrs-6hrs

NOTE: Add 20-30% to these times to allow for stops

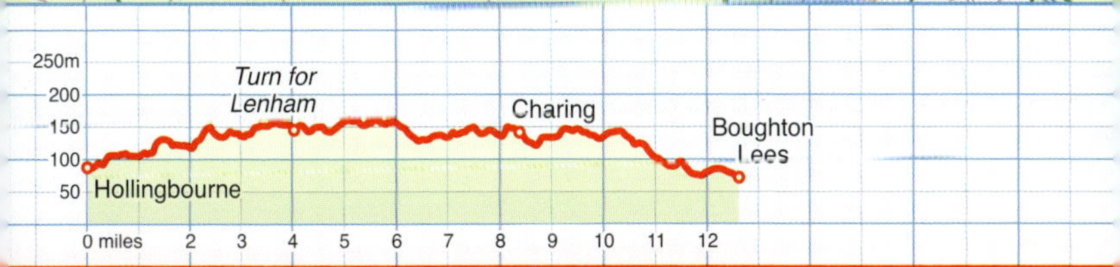

Maps 42-49

Hollingbourne to Boughton Lees

12.6 miles/20.3km – 3½hrs-5¼hrs

NOTE: Add 20-30% to these times to allow for stops

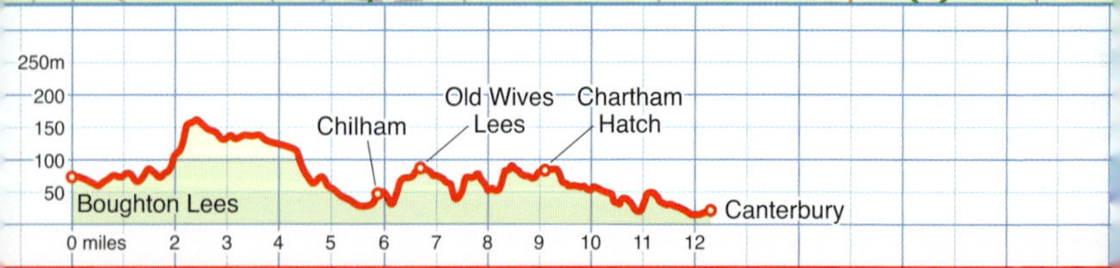

Maps 49-52, Boughton Lees to Chilham

5.9 miles/9.5km – 1¾hrs-2½hrs

Maps 52-56

Chilham to Canterbury

6.4 miles/10.3km – 2¼hrs-3hrs

Northern Route

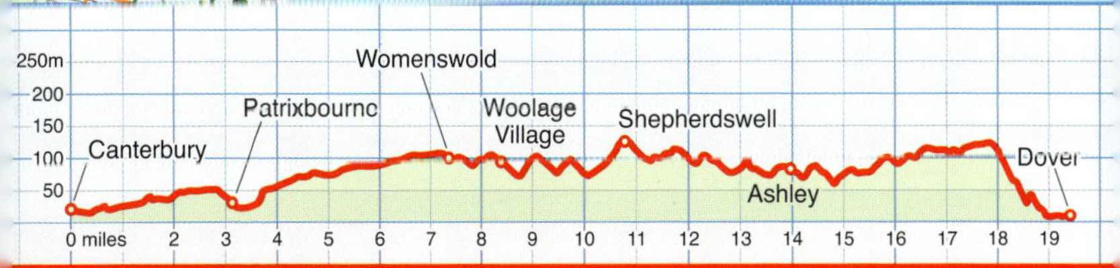

Maps 56-62, Canterbury to Shepherdswell

10.8 miles/17.4km – 2¾hrs -3½hrs

Maps 62-66

Shepherdswell to Dover

8.6 miles/13.8km – 2½hrs-3¼hrs

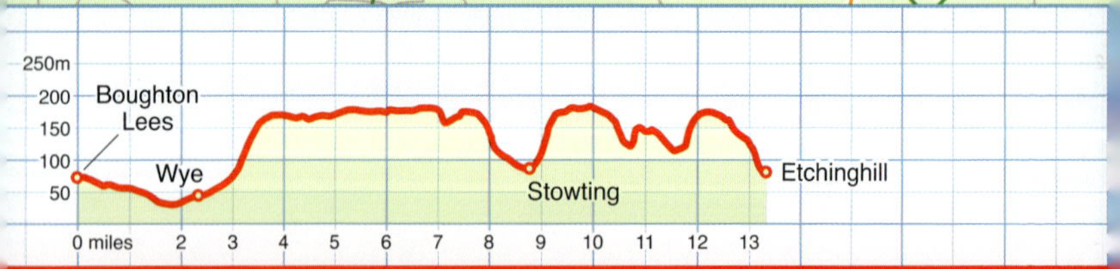

Maps A-G

Boughton Lees to Etchinghill

13.3 miles/21.5km – 4½hrs-5½hrs

NOTE: Add 20-30% to these times to allow for stops

Southern Route

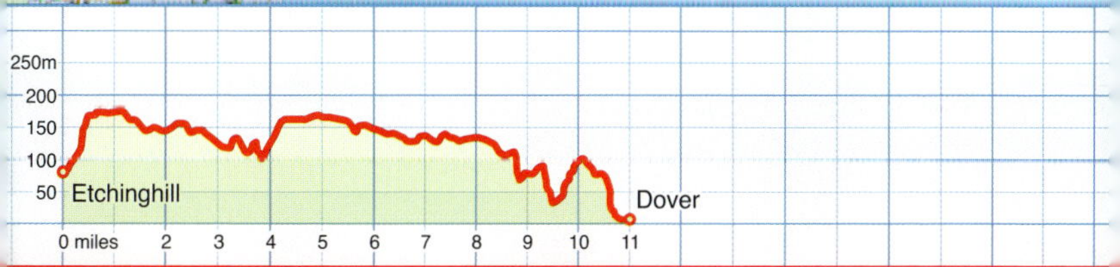

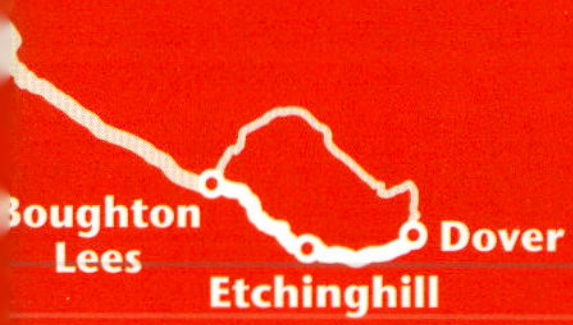

Maps G-L

Etchinghill to Dover

11 miles/17.6km – 4¼hrs-5hrs

NOTE: Add 20-30% to these times to allow for stops

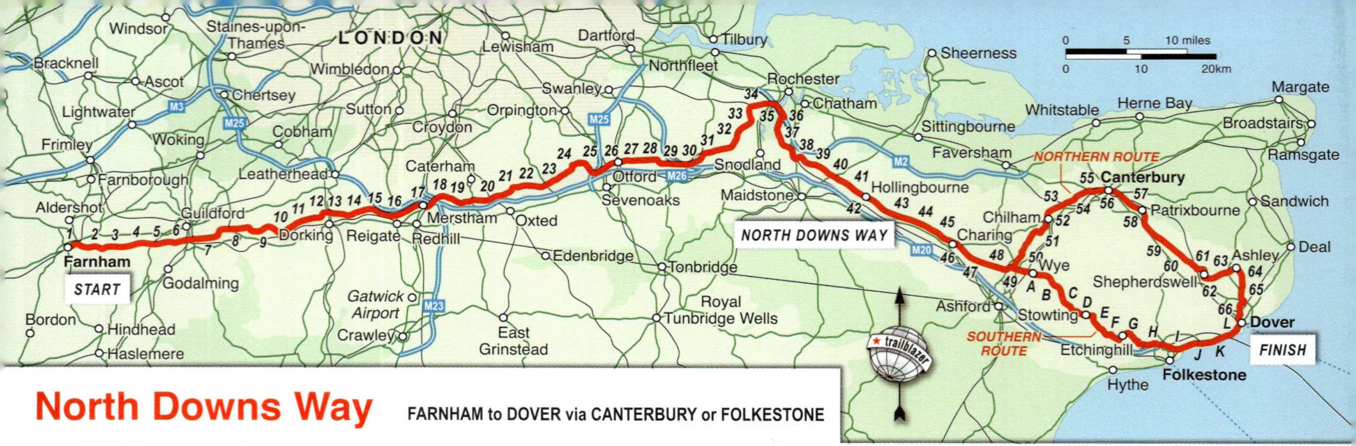

North Downs Way

FARNHAM to DOVER via CANTERBURY or FOLKESTONE

MAP KEY Map 1 – p69 Farnham
Map 2 – p70 Furze Hill
Map 3 – p71 Seale
Map 4 – p73 Puttenham
Map 5 – p74 Compton
Map 6 – p75 Shalford
Map 7 – p81Chilworth
Map 8 – p83 Newlands Corner
Map 9 – p85 Shere
Map 10 – p87 Hackhurst Downs
Map 11 – p88 Pickett's Hole
Map 12 – p89 Ranmore Common
Map 13 – p91 Box Hill
Map 14 – p95 Box Hill Village
Map 15 – p97 Bucklands Hills
Map 16 – p99 Reigate Hill
Map 17 – p102 Merstham
Map 18 – p103 Quarry Hangers NR
Map 19 – p104 Caterham Viewpoint
Map 20 – p105 Tandridge Hill
Map 21 – p107 Chalk Pit Lane
Map 22 – p111 Church Hill
Map 23 – p112 Betsoms Hill
Map 24 – p115 Knockholt
Map 25 – p116 Chevening
Map 26 – p117 Otford & Dunton Green
Map 27 – p121 Kemsing
Map 28 – p122 Cotman's Ash
Map 29 – p123 Wrotham
Map 30 – p124 Hognore Wood
Map 31 – p125 Trosley Country Park
Map 32 – p127 Holly Hill
Map 33 – p128 Wingate Wood
Map 34 – p129 Cuxton
Map 35 – p131 River Medway
Map 36 – p133 S of Mutton Wood
Map 37 – p137 Robin Hood pub
Map 38 – p139 Blue Bell Hill
Map 39 – p141 Harp Farm
Map 40 – p143 Thurnham
Map 41 – p144 Coldblow Farm
Map 42 – p145 Hollingbourne
Map 43 – p147 Mile Hill
Map 44 – p149 Lenham
Map 45 – p151 Cobham Farm
Map 46 – p152 Charing
Map 47 – p153 Beacon Hill Quarry
Map 48 – p155 Westwell
Map 49 – p157 Boughton Lees
Map 50 – p158 Soakham Downs
Map 51 – p159 Godmersham Park
Map 52 – p161 Chilham
Map 53 – p163 Old Wives Lees
Map 54 – p164 Chartham Hatch
Map 55 – p165 Canterbury (outskirts)
Map 56 – pp168-9 Canterbury centre
Map 57 – p173 Patrixbourne
Map 58 – p175 Bridge
Map 59 – p176 Barham Downs
Map 60 – p177 Womenswold
Map 61 – p178 Longlane Farm
Map 62 – p179 Shepherdswell
Map 63 – p181 Waldershare Park
Map 64 – p182 Ashley
Map 65 – p183 Dover (outskirts)
Map 66 – p185 Dover centre
Map A – p187 Wye
Map B – p189 Wye Crown
Map C – p190 Beacon
Map D – p191 Stowting
Map E – p192 Car park
Map F – p193 Postling
Map G – p195 Etchinghill
Map H – p196 Cliffs above Folkestone
Map I – p197 Battle of Britain memorial
Map J – p198 Listening ear mirror
Map K – p199 Round pillar
Map L – p200 Dover centre

Libres par la grâce de Dieu

Sous la direction d'Anne Burghardt

EVANGELISCHE VERLAGSANSTALT
Leipzig

Informations bibliographiques publiées par la Bibliothèque nationale d'Allemagne

La présente publication est inscrite au catalogue de la Bibliothèque nationale d'Allemagne sous l'intitulé Deutsche Nationalbibliografie ; les données bibliographiques détaillées sont disponibles sur internet à l'adresse dnd.dnd.de

Imprimé en Allemagne

Cet exemplaire a été imprimé sur du papier certifié FSC.

Assistance rédactionnelle : Département de théologie et de témoignage public
Mise en page : Département de théologie et de témoignage public
Conception : Bureau des services de communication de la FLM

Impression et reliure : druckhaus köthen GmbH & Co. KG

Publié par Evangelische Verlangsanstalt GmbH, Leipzig, Allemagne, sous les auspices de
La Fédération luthérienne mondiale
150, route de Ferney, BP 2100
CH-1211 Genève 2, Suisse

Éditions parallèles en anglais, allemand et espagnol

ISBN 978-3-374-04300-2